D1207016

BREHONS, SERJEANTS AND ATTORNEYS

IN THIS SERIES

Brehons, Serjeants and Attorneys:
Studies in the History of the
Irish Legal Profession (1990)

Colum Kenny, *King's Inns and*
the Kingdom of Ireland : The Irish
'Inn of Court', 1541-1800
(forthcoming)

ALSO AVAILABLE

The Irish Legal History Society (1989)

Brehons, Serjeants and Attorneys

Studies in the History of the Irish Legal Profession

DAIRE HOGAN AND W.N. OSBOROUGH,
EDITORS

IRISH ACADEMIC PRESS
in association with
THE IRISH LEGAL HISTORY SOCIETY

Typeset by Seton Music Graphics Ltd, Bantry, Co. Cork
for Irish Academic Press,
Kill Lane, Blackrock, Co. Dublin.

© Individual contributors 1990, 1991

First edition 1990
Second impression 1991

A catalogue record for this book
is available from the British Library.

ISBN 0-7165-2466-X

Printed by
Colour Books Ltd, Dublin

Preface

THE IRISH LEGAL HISTORY SOCIETY was established three years ago to encourage the study and advance the knowledge of the history of Irish law, and the Council of the Society decided at the time that the theme of its first annual volume should be the history of the profession. In recent years, a great deal of scholarly interest has been shown in the history of the professions, and perhaps above all in that of the legal profession. Historians and lawyers working in Ireland have participated in this development, and it seemed most appropriate to the Council that this interest should be made to serve as the focus for a collection of essays. If—to stress a more pragmatic point—the particular decision as to the inaugural publication of the Society might, in addition, help to advance the study of Ireland's legal history and thus promote the objects of the Society itself—so the line of thinking proceeded—so much the better.

Reflecting the longevity of the Irish legal tradition, *Brehons, serjeants and attorneys* seeks to cover a considerable chronological span, a period that stretches no less than from the sixth century AD to the nineteenth. Whilst the ten contributors, we venture to think, offer insight into a wide range of issues connected with the presence and involvement of lawyers in Irish life over so many centuries, there is neither uniformity of approach nor comprehensiveness of treatment. It would have been wrong to insist on the former and premature to aspire to the latter. In the circumstances, a sketch of the entire collection of essays will not, we think, be found out of place.

Liam Breatnach opens with a survey of the lawyers in pre-Norman Ireland—who they were and what they did. So far as the group of practising lawyers is concerned, he is able to demonstrate, through reliance on previously unedited passages from the early Irish law-texts, that both judges and advocates could be, and were, differentiated according to the precise function each discharged. In a complementary essay, devoted to the brehons of later medieval Ireland, Katharine Simms explains the background against which the great secular learned dynasties of the Gaelic Ireland of the period were set to emerge. The impact of the canon law of the church and of a new arrival on the scene—the common law—is also critically assessed.

A greater quantity of evidence makes it somewhat easier to relate the evolution of the professional groups linked to legal practice within the common law tradition. Paul Brand nevertheless breaks much fresh ground with his exhaustive survey of serjeants and attorneys in the medieval Irish lordship for the period 1250-1350. A.R. Hart resumes coverage of the history of these groups in a contribution which concentrates on the king's and queen's serjeants of the Tudor era.

Both authors point out—Brand directly, Hart more obliquely—that, while developments in Ireland were generally modelled on earlier English precedent, significant variations could and did occur. This is one of the topics too that is explored in W.N. Osborough's presentation of the rules that governed admission into the 'lower branch' and that remained in place until the mid-Victorian era.

C.E.B. Brett's cameo portraits of two eighteenth-century Ulster attorneys furnish much human interest, and underscore the need for prosopographical exercises of this kind for other parts of the country and for other periods.

Whilst eighteenth-century attorneys like Matthew and Jack Brett performed a number of mundane legal and business tasks in circumstances not conspicuously controversial, in the larger world the Irish legal profession was not untouched by major political events—shifts in governmental policy, constitutional change itself. T.P. Power's essay tackles one vexed eighteenth-century question—the role of the penal laws in inducing catholic lawyers to conform to the established anglican church and the practical consequences of such conformity. Jacqueline Hill explores a no less sensitive issue in her description of the attitude displayed by a group of talented Irish protestant lawyers to major political and constitutional change of which, in the 1820s and beyond, catholic emancipation was rightly perceived as the inevitable precursor. Judicial patronage also connects with the world of politics, if in a somewhat different fashion. The essay by Daire Hogan sets out the extraordinary sequence of events over the course of nine months in 1866 and 1867 associated with filling vacancies in two top positions—the offices of chief justice in queen's bench and lord chancellor.

It is implicit in many of the contributions that very much more remains to be found out about the history of lawyers in Ireland. Colum Kenny's survey of the records of King's Inns, the sole Irish inn of court prior to the 1920s, draws attention to one major archival repository that future researchers will ignore at their peril. A second offering from W.N. Osborough suggests that literary sources should not be neglected either by those seeking a more rounded picture of the Irish legal profession.

We are pleased to have had the opportunity of editing this collection of essays on so many aspects of the history of the legal profession in Ireland. We are keenly aware, as are all who work in this field of law and history, that much more remains to be done both on a survey level and in more specialised studies to investigate the history of Irish lawyers. We hope and expect that the publication of this volume, and the establishment of The Irish Legal History Society, will give encouragement to that work.

DAIRE HOGAN
W.N. OSBOROUGH

October 1990

Contents

Contributors

LIAM BREATNACH is a lecturer in the School of Irish, Trinity College, Dublin and co-editor since 1988 of *Ériu*. Dr Breatnach has published *Uraicecht na Ríar: the poetic grades in early Irish law* (1987) in the Dublin Institute for Advanced Studies Early Irish Law Series and acted as one of the joint editors of *Sages, saints and storytellers: Celtic studies in honour of Professor James Carney* (1989).

PAUL BRAND is engaged in full-time research in legal history, being previously an assistant keeper in the Public Record Office, London, and a lecturer in the Faculty of Law of University College, Dublin. Dr Brand has published various articles on English and Irish legal history and is currently writing a book on the origins of the English legal profession and editing several volumes of early law reports for the Selden Society. Dr Brand is also the assistant editor of the *Irish Jurist*.

KATHARINE SIMMS is a lecturer in medieval history, Trinity College, Dublin. Dr Simms' research has concentrated on Gaelic society in the later middle ages and the use of medieval Irish literature, in particular bardic poetry, as a historical source. She has published *From kings to warlords* (1987), an account of Gaelic political culture in the later middle ages.

A.R. HART was called to the bar of Northern Ireland in 1969, and became a QC in 1983. He was made a county court judge in 1985 and acted as recorder of Londonderry, 1985–1990. He has served on committees concerned with legal education in Northern Ireland and on the Standing Advisory Commission on Human Rights. Judge Hart was consultant editor to *Valentine on criminal procedure in Northern Ireland* (1989). He is preparing a longer study on the serjeants in Ireland.

W.N. OSBOROUGH is professor of laws at Trinity College, Dublin. The author of various articles on modern Irish law and on Irish legal history, Professor Osborough has also published *Borstal in Ireland 1906–74* (1975) and edited *The Irish Legal History Society: inaugural addresses* (1989). He is currently preparing a study of the Irish ecclesiastical courts. Professor Osborough is editor of the *Irish Jurist*.

T.P. POWER is currently teaching in the Department of History, University of New Brunswick, in Canada. He jointly edited *Endurance and emergence : catholics in Ireland in the eighteenth century* (1990). Dr

Power is preparing for publication a book based on his Trinity College, Dublin dissertation, 'Land, politics and society in eighteenth-century Tipperary'.

C.E.B. BRETT is senior partner in the firm of L'Estrange & Brett, solicitors, Belfast. He has served as chairman, Ulster Architectural Heritage Society; Northern Ireland Housing Executive; and International Fund for Ireland. He was knighted in 1990. Sir Charles Brett has published *Buildings of Belfast* (1967, revised ed. 1985); *Court houses and market houses of the province of Ulster* (1973); *Long shadows cast before* (1978); *Housing a divided community* (1986).

JACQUELINE HILL is a lecturer in modern history at St Patrick's College, Maynooth. The author of a number of articles on eighteenth and nineteenth-century Irish history, Dr Hill is currently completing a book on politics in Dublin, 1660–1840.

DAIRE HOGAN is a partner in the firm of McCann FitzGerald, solicitors, Dublin. He is the author of *The legal profession in Ireland, 1789–1922* (1986) and *The honorable society of King's Inns* (1987). Mr Hogan is currently researching aspects of the history of the judiciary in nineteenth-century Ireland.

COLUM KENNY was called to the Irish bar in 1974 and worked in television current affairs for RTE before becoming a lecturer in communications at Dublin City University. He has produced a variety of articles, interviews and programmes in the national and international media about broadcasting in Ireland as well as a number of papers on Irish legal history. Dr Kenny is currently preparing for publication a book based on his Trinity College, Dublin, dissertation, 'A history of King's Inns, Dublin, to 1800'.

Abbreviations

AC	*Annála Connacht (1224–1544)*, ed. A.M. Freeman. Dublin, 1944
AFM	*Annals of the kingdom of Ireland by the Four Masters*, ed. J. O'Donovan. 7 vols. Dublin, 1851
AI	*Annals of Innisfallen*, ed. S. MacAirt. Dublin, 1951
ALC	*The Annals of Loch Cé*, ed. W.M. Hennessy. 2 vols. London, 1871
AU	*Annals of Ulster*, ed. W.M. Hennessy and B. MacCarthy. 4 vols. Dublin, 1887–1901
Abh Preuss Akad Wiss	*Abhandlungen der Preussischen Akademie der Wissenschaften*
Alen's reg.	*Calendar of Archbishop Alen's register c. 1172–1534*, ed. Charles McNeill. Dublin, 1950
Anal Hib	*Analecta Hibernica*
Anc. laws Ire.	*Ancient laws and institutes of Ireland.* 6 vols. Dublin, 1865–1901.
Anc. rec. Dublin	*Calendar of ancient records of Dublin, in the possession of the municipal corporation*, ed. Sir J.T. Gilbert and Lady Gilbert. 19 vols. Dublin, 1889–1944
Ann. Clon.	*The Annals of Clonmacnoise*, ed. D. Murphy. Dublin, 1896
Ann. Tig.	The 'Annals of Tigernach', ed. W. Stokes, in *Rev Celt*, xvi–xviii (1895–7)
Archiv Hib	*Archivium Hibernicum*
BL	British Library
Ball, *Judges*	F.E. Ball, *The judges in Ireland 1221–1921.* 2 vols. London, 1926
Blackburne, *Life*	E. Blackburne, *Life of Francis Blackburne.* London, 1874

Blake, *Disraeli*	Robert Blake, *Disraeli*. London, 1966
Boulter, *Letters*	*Letters written by his excellency Hugh Boulter, D.D., lord primate of all Ireland.* 2 vols. Dublin, 1770
Brooks, *Pettyfoggers and vipers*	C.W. Brooks, *Pettyfoggers and vipers of the Commonwealth: the 'lower' branch of the legal profession in early modern England.* Cambridge, 1986
CIH	D.A. Binchy, *Corpus Iuris Hibernici.* 6 vols. Dublin, 1978
CP	Common pleas
Cal. Carew MSS	*Calendar of the Carew manuscripts preserved in the archiepiscopal library at Lambeth.* 6 vols. London, 1867–73
Cal. Ch. Ch. Deeds	*Calendar to Christ Church Deeds*, ed. M.J. McEnery, in *P.R.I. rep. D.K.* 20, 23, 24 (1888, 1891, 1892)
Cal. close rolls	*Calendar of the close rolls*
Cal. doc. Ire.	*Calendar of documents relating to Ireland.* 5 vols. London 1875–86
Cal. justic. rolls, Ire.	*Calendar of the justiciary rolls, Ireland*
Cal. pat. rolls	*Calendar of the patent rolls*
Cal. S. P. Ire.	*Calendar of the state papers relating to Ireland*
Chartul. St Mary's, Dublin	*Chartularies of St Mary's Abbey, Dublin . . .*, ed. J.T. Gilbert. 2 vols. London, 1884–6
Cl & Fin	Charles Clark and William Finnelly, *Reports of cases heard in the house of lords, on appeals and writs of error.* 12 vols. London, 1835–47
Commons' jn. Ire.	*Journals of the house of commons of the kingdom of Ireland*
Crawf & Dix	George Crawford and E.S. Dix, *Abridged notes of cases argued and determined in the several courts of law and equity in Ireland, 1837–8, with some decisions at nisi prius and on the circuits.* Dublin, 1839
D.	Justinian's *Digest*
DHR	*Dublin Historical Record*
DNB	*Dictionary of national biography*

Dowdall deeds	*Dowdall deeds*, ed. Charles McNeill and A.J. Otway-Ruthven. Dublin, 1960
Dr & Walsh	W.B. Drury and F.W. Walsh *Reports of cases argued and determined in the high court of chancery, during the time of Lord Chancellor Plunket.* 2 vols. Dublin, 1839–42
Duhigg, *History of King's Inns*	Bartholomew Duhigg, *History of the King's Inns.* Dublin, 1806
E	Exchequer
EHR	*English Historical Review*
Ellis, *Tudor Ireland*	S.G. Ellis, *Tudor Ireland: crown, community and the conflict of cultures 1470–1603.* London, 1985
Eng Rep	*The English Reports.* 178 vols. Edinburgh and London, 1900–32
Facs. nat. MSS Ire.	*Facsimiles of the national manuscripts of Ireland,* ed. J.T. Gilbert. 4 vols. Dublin, 1874–84
Fiants, Ire.	Calendar to fiants, reigns Henry VIII – Eliz, in *P.R.I. rep. D.K.* 7–22 (1875–90)
FitzGerald, *Memories of an author*	Percy FitzGerald, *Memories of an author.* London, 1895
GO	Genealogical Office, Dublin
Galway Arch Soc Jn	*Journal of the Galway Archaeological Society*
Glascock	Walter Glascock, *Miscellaneous reports of cases argued and determined in the courts of king's bench, common pleas, and exchequer, in Ireland, 1831–32.* Dublin, 1832
H.M.C. rep.	Historical Manuscripts Commission report
Hand, *Eng. law in Ire.*	G.J. Hand, *English law in Ireland, 1290–1324.* Cambridge, 1967
Hayes	Edmund Hayes, *Reports of cases argued and determined in the court of exchequer in Ireland.* Dublin, 1837
Hist. & mun. doc. Ire.	*Historic and municipal documents of Ireland, 1172–1320,* ed. J.T. Gilbert. London, 1870
Hogan	William Hogan, *Reports of cases argued and determined in the rolls court in Ireland, during the time of the rt hon. Sir William McMahon, bart., master of the rolls.* 2 vols. Dublin, 1828–38

Hogan, *Legal profession in Ireland*	Daire Hogan, *The legal profession in Ireland 1789–1922.* Dublin, 1986
Hoppen, *Elections . . . in Ireland*	K. Theodore Hoppen, *Elections, politics and society in Ireland 1832–85.* Oxford, 1984
Hughes, *Patentee officers*	*Patentee officers in Ireland, 1173–1826,* ed. J.L.J. Hughes. Dublin, 1960
ICLR	Irish Common Law Reports
IER	*Irish Ecclesiastical Record*
IHS	*Irish Historical Studies*
Inst	Justinian's *Institutes*
Ir Ch R	Irish Chancery Reports
Ir Eq R	Irish Equity Reports
Ir Georgian Soc Bull	*Irish Georgian Society Bulletin*
Ir Jur	*Irish Jurist*
Ir L R	Irish Law Reports
JP	Justice of the peace
KB	King's bench
Kelly, *Guide*	Fergus Kelly, *A guide to early Irish law.* Dublin, 1988
King' Inns admission papers	*King's Inns admission papers, 1607–1867,* ed. Edward Keane, P.B. Phair and T.U. Sadleir. Dublin, 1982
JSSISI	*Journal of the Statistical and Social Inquiry Society of Ireland*
Jones	Thomas Jones, *Reports of cases argued and determined in the court of exchequer in Ireland.* 2 vols. Dublin, 1838–47
L . & P. Hen. VIII	*Letters and papers, foreign and domestic, Henry VIII.* 21 vols. London, 1862–1932
LQR	*Law Quarterly Review*
Law Rec	Law Recorder
Law Rec ns	Law Recorder, new series

Lefroy, *Report*	Thomas Lefroy, *Report of the speech delivered . . . at the second general meeting of the Brunswick constitutional club of Ireland.* Dublin, 1829
Liber. mun. pub. Hib.	Rowley Lascelles, *Liber munerum publicorum Hiberniae.* 2 vols. London, 1852
Lloyd & Goold temp. Sugden	B.C. Lloyd and Francis Goold, *Reports of cases argued and determined in the high court of chancery in Ireland, during the time of Lord Chancellor Sugden.* London and Dublin, 1836
Lodge, *Peerage Ire.*	John Lodge, *The peerage of Ireland*, rev. ed. 7 vols. Dublin, 1789
Long & Town	Robert Longfield and J.F. Townsend, *Reports of cases argued and determined in the court of exchequer in Ireland, 1841–42.* Dublin, 1843
Malcomson, *John Foster*	A.P.W. Malcomson, *John Foster: the politics of the Anglo-Irish ascendancy.* Oxford, 1978
Molloy	Philip Molloy, *Reports of cases argued and determined in the high court of chancery in Ireland, during the time of Lord Chancellor Hart.* 3 vols. Dublin and London, 1832–33
Moore & Lowry	R.S. Moore and T.K. Lowry, *A collection of the general rules and orders of the courts of queen's bench, common pleas and exchequer of pleas in Ireland.* Dublin, 1842
NILQ	*Northern Ireland Legal Quarterly*
NLI	National Library of Ireland
O'C. *Corr.*	*The correspondence of Daniel O'Connell*, ed. M.R. O'Connell. 8 vols. Dublin, 1972–80
Ormond deeds	*Calendar of Ormond deeds*, ed. Edmund Curtis. 6 vols. Dublin, 1932–43
P.R.I. rep. D.K.	*Report of the deputy keeper of the public records in Ireland*
PRO	Public Record Office, London
PROI	Public Record Office, Ireland (= National Archives)
PRONI	Public Record Office of Northern Ireland
R Hist Soc Trans	*Transactions of the Royal Historical Society*
RA	Royal Archives

RC	Record Commission
RIA	Royal Irish Academy
RIA Proc	*Proceedings of the Royal Irish Academy*
RM	Resident magistrate
RSAI Jn	*Journal of the Royal Society of Antiquaries of Ireland*
Rec. comm. Ire. rep.	*Reports of the commissioners appointed by his majesty to execute the measures recommended in an address of the house of commons respecting the public records of Ireland.* 3 vols. London, 1815–25.
Red Bk Ormond	*The Red Book of Ormond,* ed. N.B. White. Dublin, 1932.
Reg. Kilmainham	*Registrum de Kilmainham, 1326–50,* ed. Charles McNeill. Dublin, 1932.
Reg. St John, Dublin	*Register of the hospital of S. John the Baptist without the Newgate, Dublin,* ed. E. St John Brooks. Dublin, 1936.
Report, M.C. (I)	*First report of the commissioners appointed to inquire into the municipal corporations in Ireland.* H.C. 1835, xxvii, xxviii.
Rev Celt	*Revue Celtique*
Richardson & Sayles, *Admin. Ire.*	H.G. Richardson and G.O. Sayles, *The administration of Ireland, 1172–1377.* Dublin, 1963.
Richardson & Sayles, *Ir. parl. in middle ages*	H.G. Richardson and G.O. Sayles, *The Irish parliament in the middle ages.* Philadelphia, 1952.
Ridg PC	William Ridgeway, *Reports of cases upon appeals and writs of error in the high court of parliament in Ireland, since the restoration of the appellate jurisdiction.* 3 vols. Dublin, 1795–8.
Rolls	E. O'Byrne, *The convert rolls.* Dublin, 1981.
Rot. pat. Hib.	*Rotulorum patentium et clausorum cancellariae Hiberniae calendarium.* Dublin, 1828.
S.P. Hen. VIII	*State papers, Henry VIII.* 11 vols. London, 1830–52
S.P. Ire.	State papers, Ireland
Saurin, *Speech*	William Saurin, *Speech. . . delivered at the Rotunda in the city of Dublin, on . . . the 19th February, 1829: being the second general meeting of the Brunswick constitutional club of Ireland.* Dublin, 1829.

Sayles, *Affairs of Ire.*	*Documents on the affairs of Ireland,* ed. G.O. Sayles. Dublin, 1979
Sch & Lef	John Schoales and Thomas Lefroy, *Reports of cases argued and determined in the high court of chancery, in Ireland, during the time of Lord Redesdale.* 2 vols. Dublin and London, 1806–10
Smythe	Hamilton Smythe, *Reports of cases argued and determined in the courts of common pleas and exchequer chamber in Ireland.* Dublin, 1840
Stat. realm	*The statutes of the realm* [of England and Great Britain], to 1713. 9 vols. in 10 + 2 index vols. London, 1810–28
Stud Hib	*Studia Hibernica*
TCD	Trinity College Dublin
ZCP	*Zeitschrift für celtische Philologie*

Lawyers in early Ireland

LIAM BREATNACH

BY FAR THE MOST IMPORTANT source of knowledge about the pre-Norman Irish lawyers are the Early Irish law-texts,[1] although information from these can be supplemented by information from the annals and other texts. The greater part of the law-texts is of course concerned with the law itself rather than the lawyers, and thus serves mostly to give us an insight into the minds of the academic lawyers. There are, however, two varieties of legal text which are closely concerned with practising lawyers, namely, texts on legal procedure,[2] and status-texts.[3] The latter form a very important group amongst the early Irish law-texts, and deal with the various classes and grades of person in society, for example, kings, nobles, churchmen, craftsmen, etc. The subject matter of these texts, which might well be regarded as the earliest socio-logical textbooks of Western Europe, is relevant to the law in that the legal standing of any person (for example, the value of one's oath, the amount one might enter into a contract for, etc.) was determined by one's position in society, and the measurement used for this was *lóg n-enech* (honour-price), which varied greatly. Thus the king of a petty kingdom (*rí túaithe*) had an honour-price of 42 *séts* (= 21 cows), the ordinary self-sufficient farmer (*bóaire*) one of 5 *séts*, the chief poet (*ollam filed*) also had 42 *séts*, whereas the lowest grade of poet (*fochloc*) had 1½ *séts*. The status of the lawyers in early Irish society is a matter of some interest, and, as we will see, this is something which the texts give us information on.

1. D.A. Binchy, *Corpus Iuris Hibernici* (Dublin, 1978)—hereafter *CIH*—consists of a diplomatic edition of the vernacular Irish law-texts. The best general work on the laws is Fergus Kelly, *A guide to early Irish law* (Dublin, 1988). For editions of individual texts see the latter, pp. 264-83.

2. E.g. R. Thurneysen, 'Cóic Conara Fugill: Die fünf Wege zum Urteil', *Abh Preuss Akad Wiss*, Phil-Hist Kl, Jahrg. 1925, Nr. 7; Fergus Kelly, 'An Old-Irish text on court procedure', *Peritia*, v(1986), 74.

3. E.g. *Críth Gablach, Uraicecht Becc, Míadslechta*, etc.; see F. Kelly, *Guide*, p. 267.

In this essay I propose first to look at the academic lawyers and their work, and then go on to the practising lawyers, both judges and advocates, which will involve examining some previously unedited texts.

Some remarks on the date of the law-texts will be appropriate at this point. The vast majority of Irish law-texts survive only in manuscript copies dating from the fourteenth to the seventeenth centuries; the earliest surviving manuscript containing legal material is Rawlinson B 502, written in the 1120s.[4] The date of the manuscript is not of course the same as the date of composition of a particular text; on the basis of linguistic and historical criteria one can determine in varying degrees of precision the period to which a text belongs; in some cases this period is as narrow as a few years, while in others it is as broad as a century or two. We can thus build up a picture of a continuous legal tradition from the Old Irish period (*c.*600–900), through the Middle Irish period (*c.*900–1200), to the Classical Modern Irish period (*c.*1200–1650). The end of this tradition coincides with the demise of the Gaelic aristocracy and the social system which supported it.

Towards the beginning of the written tradition belong four important texts, the first three in Old Irish, and the fourth in Latin; *Bretha Nemed Toísech*, written in Munster in the second quarter of the eighth century,[5] the *Senchas Már*, probably written towards the beginning of the eighth century,[6] *Cáin Fuithirbe*, another Munster text, completed some time between 678 and 683,[7] and the *Collectio Canonum Hibernensis*, which belongs to the early eighth century.[8] The *Collectio Canonum Hibernensis* consists mostly of citations from Scripture, early church Fathers, and

4. This manuscript is preserved in the Bodleian Library in Oxford; that it was written at Glendalough is argued by Pádraig Ó Riain, 'The Book of Glendalough or Rawlinson B 502', *Éigse*, xviii (1980-1), 161.

5. See Liam Breatnach, 'Canon law and secular law in early Ireland: the significance of *Bretha Nemed*', *Peritia*, iii (1984), 439. The text is in *CIH* 2211-2232; my edition of the first part has appeared in *Ériu*, xl (1989), 1.

6. It is in fact a compilation of individual texts on various legal topics. See R. Thurneysen, 'Aus dem irischen Recht IV: 6. Zu den bisherigen Ausgaben der irischen Rechtstexte: I. Ancient Laws of Ireland und Senchas Már', *ZCP*, xvi (1926), 167; idem, 'Aus dem irischen Recht V: 8. Zum ursprünglichen Umfang des Senchas Már', *ZCP*, xviii (1930), 356.

7. See Liam Breatnach, 'The ecclesiastical element in the Old-Irish legal tract *Cáin Fhuithirbe*', *Peritia*, v (1986), 36.

8. Herrmann Wasserschleben (ed.), *Die irische Kanonensammlung* (2nd ed., Leipzig, 1885). For the authorship and date see James F. Kenney, *Sources for the early history of Ireland: ecclesiastical* (New York, 1929), pp. 247-50.

synods, both Irish and foreign, but it also contains secular regulations which are paralleled in the vernacular law-texts. Similarly many of the vernacular law-texts are concerned with ecclesiastical matters, and I have recently shown that some passages in these are in fact translations of sections of the *Collectio Canonum Hibernensis*.[9] There are furthermore some instances, admittedly not very many, of a mixture of Latin and Irish in a single text.[10] It should be noted, however, that the vast majority of the texts of all periods are written in Irish. The earliest datable text of the four mentioned above is *Cáin Fuithirbe*; there are, of course, other, shorter, texts which belong among the oldest stratum of Irish law-texts, but no text is earlier than the seventh century.

The early law-texts are composed in two forms, prose and verse: some are composed mostly or entirely in prose,[11] others mostly or entirely in verse,[12] while in others we find roughly the same amount of prose and verse.[13] I have recently shown that a particular verse-type, based on alliteration and stress-count, which had been believed to be much more archaic than the prose texts is in fact nothing of the sort.[14] The verse passages do, however, call to mind the poets. Already in the early law-texts we find references to, or citations from, other law-texts, which show that they are the work of literate scholars, rather than transcriptions of oral doctrine.[15] The academic lawyers do not confine themselves to other law-texts, but in order to explicate various legal principles they press into service tales and sagas, which were normally the preserve of the poets.[16]

Who then were the scholars who wrote the early Irish law-texts? One class of person involved in their composition was the *fili* (poet), whose competence in the law is explicitly required by the Old Irish status-text *Uraicecht na Ríar*, when it lists the

9. See the article referred to in note 5, and Donnchadh Ó Corráin, Liam Breatnach, Aidan Breen, 'The laws of the Irish', *Peritia*, iii (1984), 382 at 417-20.

10. E.g. *CIH* 1192.

11. E.g. *Uraicecht Becc* (*CIH* 1590-1618, etc.); see Kelly, *Guide*, p.267.

12. E.g. *Bretha Nemed Toísech*; see note 5.

13. E.g. D.A. Binchy (ed.), 'Bretha Déin Chécht', *Ériu*, xx (1966), 1.

14. See the article referred to in note 5.

15. E.g. in *Bretha Nemed Toísech*, *CIH* 2211.25 citing from *Antéchtae mBreth*, and *CIH* 2213.29-30 referring to *Críth Gablach*.

16. E.g. the story of 'Finn and the man in the tree', *CIH* 879.23–880.14, ed. Kuno Meyer, *Rev Celt*, xxv (1904), 344 (see also *ZCP*, xxx (1967), 17), and 'The saga of Fergus mac Léti', *CIH* 882.4–883.22, ed. D.A. Binchy, *Ériu*, xvi (1952), 33; both of these are found among the Old Irish glosses on the *Senchas Már*.

qualifications of the *ollam filed* (master poet), the highest grade of *fili*, as *secht cóecait drécht lais . . . is éola i cach coimgniu, 7 is éola i mbrithemnacht fénechais* (he has three hundred and fifty compositions/tales . . . he is knowledgeable in all historical science, and he is knowledgeable in the jurisprudence of Irish law).[17] The word *fili* (plural *filid*) is usually translated 'poet', but it is clear that the *fili* was much more than a versifier—he was a learned academic who had undergone a rigorous education in all branches of secular knowledge; furthermore, he wrote in prose as well as verse.[18] The *fili* as *fili* was mainly concerned with secular learning, but that is not to say that he was isolated from ecclesiastical learning; quite the opposite, for in very many cases of identifiable *filid* in the early period we find that they are either clerics as well as *filid* or at least have close connections with monasteries. Three instances will suffice: Colmán mac Lénéni (d. 604), who began his career as a *fili*, entered the church in later life, and founded the monastery of Clúain Úama (Cloyne, Co. Cork),[19] Máel Muru Othna (d. 887), whose epithet *Othna* 'of Fahan' (Co. Donegal) shows that, if not a cleric, he was at least attached to the monastery there,[20] and Fland Mainistrech (d. 1056), the *fer léiginn* (man of Latin learning) of the monastery of Monasterboice, who wrote extensively on secular subjects, as a *fili*.[21] The majority of the early law-texts are anonymous; two of the rare cases, however, where we have names of authors are revealing in this context. Both of these texts have already been mentioned above. The first is *Cáin Fuithirbe*, the prologue to which names those involved in the commissioning and drafting of the text, namely, Cummíne, Díblíne, Banbán, all clerics, and Amairgen, a *fili*.[22] It also names secular and ecclesiastical rulers who adopted and promulgated the laws contained in this text.[23] The second is *Bretha Nemed Toísech*, the authorship of which is ascribed to three kinsmen,

---

17. Liam Breatnach, *Uraicecht na Ríar: the poetic grades in early Irish law* (Dublin, 1987), p. 102, §2.

18. See the work referred to in the preceding note, especially pp. 98-100.

19. See R. Thurneysen, 'Colmán mac Lénéni und Senchán Torpéist', *ZCP*, xix (1932), 193.

20. See James Carney, 'The dating of Early Irish verse texts, 500-1100', *Éigse*, xix (1982-3), 177 at 178, 187.

21. See Eoin MacNeill, 'Poems by Flann Mainistrech on the dynasties of Ailech, Mide and Brega', *Archiv Hib*, ii (1913), 37.

22. *Peritia*, v (1986), 46-7.

23. *Peritia*, v (1986), 42-6.

collectively known as the Ui Búirecháin, that is, Forannán, a bishop, Máel Tuili, a *fili*, and Báethgalach, a judge.[24]

All of this shows that the early Irish law-texts were written in a context of cooperation and mutual influence between ecclesiastics and lay academics, which also included the involvement of practising members of the legal profession. That this applies also to the anonymous texts can be seen both from their content, and from certain general statements about the nature of early Irish law, which we are fortunate to have, so to say, from the horse's mouth. Thus, for example, the discussion of the sources of Irish law with which the *Senchas Már* begins: *Senchas fer nÉrenn, cid conid roíter? Comchuimne da sen, tindnacul clúaise di araili, díchetal filed, tórmach ó recht litre, nertad fri recht n-aicnid* (What has preserved the tradition of the men of Ireland? The joint memory of the ancients, transmission from ear to ear, the chanting of poets, its being augmented by the law of Scripture, its being founded on the law of nature),[25] or the following statement in the prologue to *Cáin Fuithirbe* concerning the content of the main body of the text, but which may be taken to refer to early Irish law in general: *ro dílsiged la dub in díchubus* (That which is contrary to (Christian) conscience has been made forfeit by ink).[26]

Again, what little we can determine of the place of writing of the legal texts is consistent with what has been said above. In some cases we can do no more than assign a text to a particular province, for example, *Bretha Nemed Toísech* to Munster.[27] The following passages on law-schools, from *The Triads of Ireland*,[28] however, are much more specific: *Féinechas Hérenn Clúain Húama* (The Jurisprudence of Ireland—Cloyne) (§12), *Bérla Féine Hérenn Corcach* (The Legal Speech of Ireland—Cork) (§16), *Brethemnas Hérenn Sláine* (The Judgment of Ireland—Slane) (§21). It is surely of significance that these, the only places mentioned in this ninth-century text as being renowned for their law-schools, are all monasteries.[29]

The gradual build-up of a corpus of written law-texts provided a substantial amount of material for study and comment, and

24. See the article referred to in note 5.
25. I have made some minor adaptations to the text of R. Thurneysen, 'Aus dem irischen Recht IV', *ZCP*, xvi (1926), 167 at 175, §1.
26. *Peritia*, v (1986), 43, §15.
27. See the article referred to in note 5,
28. Kuno Meyer (ed.), *The triads of Ireland*, Todd Lecture Series 13 (Dublin, 1906).
29. For the dating see Meyer, op. cit., pp. x-xi.

already in the Old Irish period we have a significant body of secondary matter in the form of glosses on two of the primary Old Irish texts, namely, the *Senchas Már* (*CIH* 874.35–924.31)[30] and *Cáin Fuithirbe* (*CIH* 766.36–777.5; 1553.26–1555.40).[31] The method employed in these glosses is usually to attach scholarly comment to a short citation, often consisting of no more than one or two words, from the original text; sometimes, however, the text being commented on occasions the citation of a complete text from elsewhere, either another law-text, or even a saga. Such works were clearly intended to be used with a complete copy of the text to hand, the citations serving simply to refer the reader to the particular part of the text to which the comment refers. In the Middle Irish period, and later, the method of glossing changes to one where a complete copy of the original text appears with glosses and commentary written between the lines, and in the margins. It should also be noted that the later the date the greater is the volume of commentary, a feature no doubt in part due to the widening gap between the contemporary form of the language and that of the original.[32]

The glosses and commentaries are mainly of four kinds: (i) clarification of the plain sense of the original text, either by re-wording, or by illustrating the relevant legal point with an example; (ii) citation of parallel passages from other texts; (iii) treatment of a statement in the original text in a far more detailed way by giving all imaginable attendant circumstances and showing how they affect the basic legal principle—this kind of extended gloss is usually referred to as 'commentary'; (iv) etymological glosses which explain words by means of sentences or phrases consisting

---

30. These glosses have been dated to the eighth century by Thurneysen, 'Irisches Recht', *Abh Preuss Akad Wiss*, Phil-Hist Kl, Jahrg. 1931, Nr. 2, 60, and to the ninth by Binchy, *Celtica*, x (1973), 72.

31. See *Peritia*, v (1986), 36-7.

32. Glossing is, of course, not unique to Irish law-texts. In David M. Walker, *The Oxford companion to law* (Oxford, 1980), s.v. gloss, we find the following: 'Textual interpretation by marginal or interlinear note, the basic method of the jurists who revived the study of Roman law at Bologna, and then of the canonists after Gratian's *Decretum* and the beginning of papal decretal legislation. It was a long established traditional method in the study of classical literature, and also of Biblical texts. The Bolognese jurists were, however, the first to apply the method to legal texts...'. The dating here is far too late; for the glossing of Roman law-texts from an early period see Max Conrat, *Geschichte der Quellen und Literatur des römischen Rechts im früheren Mittelalter* I. Band [all published] (Leipzig, 1891), p. 108 ff. I am indebted to Professor Donnchadh Ó Corráin for this reference.

of words which both bear a phonetic similarity to the individual syllables of the words to be explained, and which are semantically relevant to the explanation.[33]

One of the last developments in this scholarly tradition was the type of text which consists of citations from various texts arranged under a particular heading, and which provided a convenient handbook of the principles of Irish law.[34]

We may now proceed to look at something of what the texts of the Old Irish period can tell us about the practising lawyers, beginning with the judge. The Old Irish status-text *Uraicecht Becc* distinguishes the following types of judge, which I list in ascending order, according to their honour-prices: (i) *brithem bes túalaing fuigell frisin n-áes dána* (a judge who is capable of giving judgment in matters relating to craftsmen), who has an honour-price of 7 *séts* (§43); (ii) *brithem bélrai Féne ocus filedachtae* (a judge both in matters concerning the laity and the poets), who has an honour-price of 10 *séts* (§44); (iii) *brithem* (a judge), who has an honour-price of 15 *séts* (§37); (iv) *brithem téora mbreth* (a judge of three judgments, namely, in matters concerning the laity, the poets, and the church), who has an honour-price of 20 *séts* (§38).[35] The information given here is of particular value in that it enables us to see how high their status in society was, as these honour-prices correspond respectively to those of the first four grades of nobles as given earlier on in the same text (§§11–14), namely, *aire désa, aire échta, aire tuise*, and *aire ard*. This text is concerned with judges within the *túath*, the petty kingdom, the smallest political unit in early Ireland; there were, however, judges of even higher status, as can be seen from the following previously unedited passage, which is concerned with the privileges of the judge.[36]

33. On mediaeval etymology see Rolf Baumgarten, 'A Hiberno-Isidorian etymology', *Peritia*, ii (1983), 225.

34. See Máirín Ní Dhonnchadha, 'An address to a student of law', Donnchadh Ó Corráin, Liam Breatnach, Kim McCone (ed.), *Sages, saints and storytellers: Celtic studies in honour of Professor James Carney* (Maynooth, 1989), p. 159 at pp. 161-2.

35. For the Irish text see note 11. I follow the paragraph numbers of the translation by Eoin MacNeill, 'Ancient Irish law: the law of status or franchise', *RIA Proc*, xxxvi (1923), sect. c, 265 at 272-81.

36. *CIH* 1268.35—1269.20. My punctuation differs from that in *CIH*; also I expand abbreviations, omit the glosses, supply length-marks, and add some letters in square brackets. I would date this passage on linguistic grounds to the ninth century.

A folad o túaith nodo saora: a bíatha cethruir, .i. a fer mancuine ⁊ a dias fogluma do torba túaithe ⁊ hé fadesin.Et ní bí a mías cen féoil ara-gella im, ara-gealla as maith *acht* ná roib cleith ná díchell and; dia roib dligid a réir ná téit tar díabal a b[i]id la lóg n-einech fó míad.

Mad fer túaithe b[i]id i cétud fri ríg *nó* tuíseach oca mbé; diam clérech b[i]id i cétu fri aircindech n-úasal. Dligid toircsin taulche dó ó cách ⁊ étsecht a airberta, a lá n-air, a lá mbúana, a lá n-ime a lá coibdine, suíre athgabála, a faosam *dechmaide*; it é folad brithemon fo-gní rí[g] ⁊ túa[i]th cenmothá ní do-formaig a suíre ar séota ⁊ céile.

Dliged ollum áiriullud /—*aile deac* do derbfiachad / o fir dian fíach fothaigedar / nó dia ndíla tromcinta / ⁊rl—

Suíre ⁊ bíathad cacha brithemon in cach túaith imbi brithem; is innti a cháta ⁊ a suíre

Mad ardmaor las bet iltúatha ⁊ ilmuire a cháta ⁊ a toichned ⁊ a sárugud fo cátaid a ríg oca mbí i coimríadh.

His considerations from the kingdom which ennobles [that is, appoints] him: he is to be given refection as one of four, that is, his servant and his two students [whom he instructs] for the benefit of the kingdom, and he himself. And his dish is not without meat, for which butter is a substitute, for which full milk is a substitute, provided that there be no deception or remissness there; if there be he is entitled to whatever he stipulates up to twice the value of his food, together with [the payment of] his honour-price in accordance with his status.

If he be a layman he sits with the king or lord who employs him, if a cleric he sits with the noble abbot. He is entitled to [demand] attendance by all at the mound [of judgment], and listening in silence to his exposition of law, his day's ploughing, his day's reaping, his day's fencing, his day's military assistance, immunity from distraint,[37] his ten days' conferring of protection; these are the considerations of a judge who serves king and kingdom, apart from whatever his nobility in the matter of wealth and clients adds.

A chief judge is entitled to earnings—a twelfth as certain fees from a man to whom he awards a payment, or whom he absolves from heavy liabilities, etc.

The noble status and refection of any judge is in whichever kingdom he is a judge in; in it is his status and his nobility.

If he be a superior officer with many kingdoms and many justices under him, his status and the penalty for refusing him food, and that for dishonouring him is in accordance with the status of his king who appoints him in a position of authority.

37. I take this to refer to vicarious liability, *cin inbleogain*, for which see D.A. Binchy, 'Distraint in Irish law', *Celtica*, x (1973), 22 at 32-3. Freedom from vicarious liability was a privilege of other persons who performed a public function in the kingdom, for example, the poet (*CIH* 954.5) and the smith (*CIH* 1593.18f. (*Uraicecht Becc*)).

This passage tells us that the judge was an official appointed either by church or state. It lists the various entitlements of his office, including the provision of refection for himself and his retinue, and labour services due; these are in addition to any advantages accruing to him from his own property and clients. Furthermore, it specifies the fee he is entitled to receive for hearing a case (from the successful party), and concludes with a statement on the greater status of a judge appointed by a king of higher rank than the king of a single petty kingdom (for example, king of a province).

These entitlements imply of course their corresponding duties, with which the next passage I wish to cite is mostly concerned.[38]

Ceasc, caide ord breitheman do túaith nodo mbíatha? Do-gní a trí cach lae acht a ndomnach. Cadiat? .i. breath ⁊ astad airberta ⁊ airbert aoí iarna hastad. Ní tíaghuit a n-áirem dó bretha im thuinidhe tíre ⁊ im chórus comaithcesa ⁊ im córus n-athgabála ⁊ im córus fine, ar is focuru breithe ind sin beiris cen fochruic. Ní dlegar fochruic na hurcor díb acht díanbretha umpa di maigin. Is di foltaib breitheman dia túaith combeart dá crích, airbert fri flaith, fri senad, fri aes cerda, coná toirceat a túaith i n-indlighe; treiniugud dáil ⁊ turbaid ⁊ breatha im tuinidhe tíre gan áirium.

Ceist, caite cia breth[em] cosin iubreithe [*leg.* inbreithe] eitergleoug [*leg.* etergléod] cach cesta? Ní *hansae*, co breithemain na ceannaithe i turgaib in cest má beth inde, ⁊ mana bé, téit i réir n-aigneda is gaíthe isin crích co triur ara-bídh a túaith; tíagat a comrér chuice.

Inad in ollaman ag dáil urdligid a n-airecht cáid, i medón ardaireachta, i fíadnaise airdrígh, airm nó áit ina cluinither caisi cáich. Dligid sin somaíne—lógh a deghdána, re taobh a fírdligid—cíall conn cuibsech cuirethar ar gleo[d] dligid do cách.

What is the duty of a judge to the kingdom which feeds him? He does three things every day except on Sunday. What are they? Judging, and determining [the correct method of] procedure, and proceeding with the case after it has been determined. Judgments concerning ownership of land, and concerning the regulations of neighbourhood law, and of distraint, and of the kin are not taken into account for him, for those are minor matters (?) of judgment which he adjudges without a fee. One is not entitled to a fee for them nor to postpone them; rather they are to be swiftly judged on the spot. Among the duties of a judge to his kingdom are joint adjudication of [matters which involve] two territories, expounding law with a lord, with a synod, with men of art, lest they act illegally towards their kingdom; tripartition,[39] [fixing grounds for] delay

---

38. *CIH* 1932.1–17. My punctuation differs from that in *CIH*; also I expand abbreviations, supply length-marks, and add some letters in square brackets. This passage can also be dated to the ninth century on linguistic grounds.

and exemption, and giving judgments concerning ownership of land are
not taken into account.

Who is the judge to whom it is proper to bring any problem for
decision? It is not difficult, to the judge of the territory in which the
problem arises, if there be one there, and if not, it goes for decision to
the most skilled advocate in he kingdom together with the three people
who are at the head of the kingdom;[40] they pass a decision on it together.

The place of the chief dispensing entitlements is in a noble assembly,
[or] in the middle of a superior assembly, in the presence of a high-king,
where he hears the cases of all. He is entitled to benefits—the fee for his
goodly profession, together with his true entitlements—he who applies
sense and conscientious intelligence to deciding entitlement for all.

The most important duty attaching to the office, then, is to give
judgment in such matters as disputes over ownership of land, or
disputes between neighbouring landholders or kinsmen, etc., without any entitlement to a fee, and with the requirement that such
cases be settled without delay. This passage is concerned with the
judge of the petty kingdom. Elsewhere we find a statement to the
effect that one of the kinds of case which such a judge is to decide
for no fee is not the concern of the higher grade of judge: *brithim
ard arberta breith* [read *breth*] *fir fiad rig ⁊ tuath.Ni he as fuidlidi im
comaidces crich* (a noble judge who expounds true judgments in
the presence of kings and kingdoms, it is not he to whom cases
concerning relationships between neighbours are to be submit-
ted), *CIH* 573.18. It is reasonable to assume that the other minor
types of dispute listed in the passage above are similarly not the
concern of the latter kind of judge (doubtless the judge of a
provincial king). In other words judges were distinguished not
only by the level of their appointment, but also by the type of case
which would normally come before them.

We can now go on to look at the advocates. The most
important source is the following previously unedited passage,
which is found amongst the Old Irish glosses on the *Senchas Már*,
and is at least as early as the ninth century.[41]

39. I.e. threefold division of land between the lord, the kin, and the church, for
    which see the notes on §21 of my 'The first third of *Bretha Nemed Toísech*',
    Ériu, xl (1989), 1.

40. I.e. king, bishop, and chief poet, as specified in a similar passage in *Bretha
    Nemed Toísech*, *CIH* 2225.7-9.

41. *CIH* 896.19-41. D.A. Binchy makes reference to this passage in his '*Féchem,
    fethem, aigne*', *Celtica*, xi (1976), 18 at 26–7. My punctuation, etc. differs
    from *CIH* as in the preceding passage. For *nairidi* in *CIH* 896.28 the
    manuscript has *airidi*, and for *immm*, *CIH* 896.34 I read *immin*. For the
    dating see note 30.

Cis lir aigni? Ní *hansae*, a trí: glasaigni ⁊ aigni airechta ⁊ aigni fris-n-innle brith.

Cid a nglasaigne? Ní *hansae*, fer benus for éolus conách n-élai a lles coruici airecht. Naidm n-airechta lais etar aitire ⁊ imitechta ⁊ fóeth imitechta. Naidm fri téchta .i. naidm comraicc má as-laíther in fiach. Cach naidm cona foasndís.

Coic séoit a llóg óad in sen do fer bélrai las ndéne. Trian cach lesa do[n]d aigne má[d] tobach, lethtrian ar frithbert, ⁊ ní acair acht ó bóairechuib aithech ⁊ bachlach—is é glasaighni in sin.

Aighni airechta im*murgu*, fer són ru-huca a les do airecht ⁊ dod-n-acair indi. In-fíadar dó in les; ta-n-acair íarum ón tráth co 'raile, ná tintai fora tacra in cétna co tici astad airbertai. Ní airidi im*murgu* cin astad n-airberta, cin athchomairc do brethemain mád ar bélaib brithi. Aignis lais uile ⁊ nascairecht ⁊ berrad ⁊ comaidhches ⁊ cáin lánomhnai ⁊ maccslechtai.

Ocus deich *séoit* úad do fer bélrai lais ndéni ⁊ a recht. *Ocus* trian cach besa [*leg*. lesa] dó cadesin má[d] tobach, lethtrian ar airbert. Do-gníd-side lesa aithech ⁊ bachlach ⁊ airech co ruici tuísech túaithi—is é aigne airechta in sin.

Aigne fris-n-innle breith, fer són taurrig tacrai fri bruinne breithi. As-beir fris aigne ad-gair: 'Aigni dom-air-so co rraib do lethi lim indíu immin les-[s]a'. Taurrig-sidi tacra di*diu* ⁊ ad-suidhi cin athcomarc do breithemain ⁊ berair breth fair. Is é fer in sin berus letrian ar oirtaccra. Bélrai Féni lais uile acht tulbretha ⁊ ainches mbreithe.

.X. u.s. déc [*leg*. Cóic séoit deac] húaid do fiur forid-cain ⁊ a gairi ⁊ a recht. Trian cach lesa dó cachdesin [*leg*. cadesin] ⁊ is é in fer-sa a[d]-gair ó tosach [*leg*. thoísech] túaithi ⁊ ó breithemain ⁊ ó ríg, acht gníma rachtairi, ⁊ ní beir baa ó breithemain acht a folta. A les ría cach les; trian dó ó cách ó n-acair olcena, a lethtrian ar frithbert. Is becc nach úais in fer-so ar aith*gabáil* fo bíth combi [*leg*. con-mbí] dochur dó.

How many [types of] advocate are there? It is not difficult, three: a 'fettering advocate', and a 'court advocate', and an 'advocate whom judgment encounters'.

What is the [meaning of the word] 'fettering advocate'?[42] It is not difficult, a man who locks in expertise so that his case does not depart from him to a court. He is competent in enforcing [on behalf] of a court, including [taking] hostage-sureties, and driving off [distrained cattle], and swearing the driving off [was carried out lawfully].[43] Enforcing in

---

42. Binchy, *Celtica*, xi (1976), 26 takes *glasaigne* to mean '"fresh" or "raw" *a*. (cf. "green" in colloquial English)'. It is clear from the text, however, that the first element in the compound is not the adjective *glas*, but rather the noun *glas* 'shackle, fetter' etc., referring to his function as enforcer.

43. I take the rarely attested word *fóeth* to be a compound of *fo* + *óeth* 'oath'. For *fóeth*, and *foaisndís* below, cf.: '. . . the average man must enlist the service of a professional jurist who will be able to assure the arbitration tribunal, should any dispute arise, that the seizure was made in accordance with the rules', D.A. Binchy, 'Distraint in Irish law', *Celtica*, x (1973), 22 at 32.

accordance with legality, that is, enforcing by means of combat if one absconds from [paying] the debt. Every enforcing with its accompanying declaration [that it was carried out lawfully].

Five *séts* are the payment from that person to the man of law with whom he studies.[44] A third of [the amount at issue in] every case to the advocate if it be levying, a sixth for opposing, and he only pleads on behalf of secular and ecclesiastical *bóaires*—that man is the 'fettering advocate'.

The 'court advocate', on the other hand, that is a man who can take his case to a court and who pleads it there. The case is related to him; he pleads it then by the same time next day, and does not return to the same pleading until [the correct method of] procedure has been determined. There is, moreover, no acceptance [of a case] without determining [the correct method of] procedure, without consulting with a judge, if it be immediately before judgment. He is competent in all of advocacy, and enforcing, and abridgement, and neighbourhood law, and the law of marital union, and the law relating to sons.

And ten *séts* from him to the man of law with whom he studies, and his entitlement. And a third of [the amount at issue in] every case to him himself if it be levying; a sixth for acting in court. He acts for secular and ecclesiastical commoners, and nobles up to the leader of a *túath*—that man is the court advocate.

An 'advocate whom judgment encounters', that is a man who takes a pleading over at the brink of judgment.[45] The advocate who pleads says to him: 'Advocate come to me so that you may be beside me today for this case'. He takes pleading over then, and fixes it without consulting with a judge, and judgment is given on it. That is the man who gets a sixth for preliminary pleading. He is competent in all of law except for immediate judgments and perplexity of judgment.

Fifteen *séts* from him to the man who teaches him, and dutifulness towards him, and his authority [over the student]. A third of [the amount at issue in] every case to him himself, and it is this man who pleads a case on behalf of the leader of a *túath* and a judge and a king, except for [matters which pertain to] the functions of a steward, and he takes nothing from a judge except his expenses. His case takes precedence over every other case; a third to him from those on behalf of whom he pleads otherwise, a sixth for opposing. This man is nearly of too high a status to be distrained, for he will overcome [anything which is] a disadvantage to him.[46]

Thus we see that at least as early as the ninth century there was in place a well developed class of advocates who pleaded before

44. Lit. 'does [it, viz. law]'.

45. The two instances of *taurrig* in this passage are the only examples known to me of finite forms of this verb, the verbal noun of which, *taurráin*, is fairly well attested.

46 Cf. note 37.

the court on behalf of all classes of person from commoner up to king. In the above passage the honour-prices of the various grades of advocate are given in an indirect way, expressed in terms of the fee paid by the student to the teacher on completion of his studies, which was equivalent to the honour-price of the grade the student attained.[47] The honour-prices of the two highest grades correspond to those of two of the grades of judge and of noble (see above), whereas that of the *glasaigne* is lower than that of the lowest grade of judge and corresponds to that of the normal commoner of early Irish law, the *bóaire* (self-sufficient farmer). They are distinguished according to their functions, their competence in the law, and the class of person they act for. The fee for acting for the defendant is specified as one sixth for the *glasaigne* and the *aigne fris-n-indlea breth*, and this no doubt also applies to the *aigne airechta*. On the other hand, the fee for *tobach* (levying), that is, successfully prosecuting on behalf of one's client, is even more substantial, one third for all three, except when the *aigne airechta* and the *aigne fris-n-indlea breth* act together; in that case they take a sixth each.[48]

The practising lawyers, then, both judges and advocates, are distinguished not only according to their competence in the law, but also according to the societal and political divisions of early Christian Ireland. Judges were appointed either by church or lay authorities, and advocates acted for both laymen and ecclesiastics.[49] Advocates were distinguished according to the status of the persons they acted for, while judges were distinguished according to the political importance of the king or monastery which appointed them.

In this essay I have attempted to give some account of the lawyers of early Christian Ireland, which could not have been done without taking into account previously unedited texts. Much work remains to be done at the basic level of providing editions, with translations and annotations, of the Irish law-texts, and as this work progresses so will it be possible to present a fuller picture of the early Irish lawyers than that which is presented here.

---

47. Cf. *CIH* 504.3 (= 1949.2; 1613.34, 2278.13, 2330.16), 1838.10 (= 2006.16).

48. Binchy, *Celtica*, xi (1976), 26-7, takes it that they must always act together, but the text does not bear this interpretation.

49. For ecclesiastical judges see also Donnchadh Ó Corráin, Liam Breatnach, Aidan Breen, 'The laws of the Irish', *Peritia*, iii (1984), 382 at 386-7 n.3.

The early history of the legal profession of the lordship of Ireland, 1250-1350

PAUL BRAND

I

IN 1295 A COMPLAINANT alleged misconduct on the part of William de Morton, a clerk of the Dublin Bench.[1] William was responsible for making enrolments on the Bench plea-roll, the official record of litigation in the court. The complainant had brought litigation there to recover certain lands. His opponent had asked for an adjournment to give various other interested persons an opportunity to join in the litigation. The opponent had made an error in giving the names of those whom he wanted to be summoned, potentially a fatal mistake in litigation of this kind. The enrolment had, however, silently corrected his mistake and given the names in their correct form, thereby depriving the complainant of his chance to profit from his opponent's error. As enrolling clerk, William was responsible. William had no difficulty in clearing himself. He had, he said, simply enrolled the names as he had found them written on the dorse of the appropriate writ; and that endorsement had been the work of a different and more senior clerk, Nicholas of Berkeley, keeper of rolls and writs in the Bench. Nicholas accepted responsibility for the endorsement and did not deny that the endorsement itself had been altered. But, he said, he had not acted fraudulently or in return for a bribe. He had made the alteration by the direction of the justices of the court. To establish this and to clear himself of any misconduct he asked to be 'tried' by the verdict of those best in a position to know the truth of the matter: the serjeants (*narratores*) and attorneys who had then been present in the Bench.

1. *Cal. justic. rolls, Ire., 1295–1303*, pp. 5–6. For reasons that are unclear the complainant's name is not given in this entry and he is represented simply by the initial B.

It has long been known that 'serjeants' and 'attorneys' were the two main groups of professional lawyers active in the Westminster Bench at the end of the thirteenth century.[2] The main function of the serjeants was to speak in court on behalf of their clients when litigation came on for a hearing and in 1300 they were the much smaller (and the more select) of the two groups, numbering no more than about thirty individuals. The primary function of the professional attorneys active in the court was simply to put in an appearance at the court on behalf of their clients on each day appointed for a hearing; but by 1300 they had also become responsible for ensuring that the court took the necessary steps to ensure the appearance of their client's opponent and perhaps for engaging and briefing serjeants on behalf of those clients. In 1300 there were over two hundred professional attorneys practising in the Westminster Bench. This case suggests that by 1300 two similar groups of professional lawyers were also to be found in the Dublin counterpart of the Westminster Bench; and other evidence indicates that by the same date professional lawyers were also to be found in various other courts in the English lordship of Ireland (as they were also to be found in various other courts in England). In this essay I want to examine the evidence for the existence and functioning of these two types of professional lawyer not just in the Dublin Bench but also in the other law courts of the English lordship of Ireland during the half century or so preceding this case (which will take us back to the earliest evidence for the existence of professional lawyers in the lordship) and also during the half century or so after it (to *c*.1350).

II

The Westminster Bench seems to have been the centre of the English legal profession and to have contained the largest number of professional lawyers. The same was possibly also true of its Dublin counterpart, though deficiencies in the surviving evidence make it impossible to be certain about this. The Dublin Bench is, however, certainly the best documented of the courts of the lordship of Ireland and thus it is with its lawyers that we will start.

2. A detailed discussion of the English legal profession, its functions and organisation at the end of the thirteenth century will be found in my forthcoming book, *The origins of the English legal profession*. Wherever in the following discussion reference is made to the English legal profession the material is drawn from this much fuller study and so no supporting references will be given.

It is unfortunately the case that we possess virtually no direct evidence as to the functions performed by the serjeants of the Dublin Bench. However, it seems reasonable to suppose that these were much the same functions as those performed by their Westminster counterparts since litigation seems to have been conducted along the same general lines in both courts; and thus we can probably get a reasonably accurate picture of the functions of the Dublin serjeants from the unofficial Norman French reports of litigation heard in the Westminster Bench which survive from *c.*1270 onwards and are generally known as the Year Book reports. These show that hearings in the Bench normally commenced with a serjeant acting for the plaintiff making a formal count, expounding the plaintiff's claim or complaint, and with a serjeant acting for the defendant making a formal defence, a blank denial of everything contained in the plaintiff's count, before going on to make a more specific defence. They also indicate that it was at this point in the proceedings that the real skills of the serjeants on both sides came into play. The plaintiff's serjeant might respond that the defence advanced was not a valid one in law or answer by alleging other, additional facts which showed that the plaintiff's claim was nonetheless a good one. The defendant's serjeant would then have to answer the argument or reply to the allegation or might (since the pleading was normally only tentative and exploratory) abandon his first line of defence altogether and advance another one instead. Eventually, though generally only after a prolonged series of arguments between the serjeants for the two litigants, in which the justices of the court would also take an active part, the parties would reach an 'issue'. This was either an issue of law, a point of law which was to be decided by the justices after further consideration, or (more commonly) an issue of fact. The latter would be decided on the basis of a verdict by a jury as to whether or not certain facts alleged in the course of pleading by one of the serjeants and material to his client's claim or defence were true. A decision on either type of issue would then lead to judgment being given in favour of one of the parties. The skill of the serjeant lay in his ability to argue convincingly and in knowing when to continue or abandon a particular line of defence or of attack.

The Year Book reports make it clear that it was common practice in the Westminster Bench for litigants to have at least two serjeants to act and speak on their behalf. There is some evidence to suggest that this may also have been common practice in the Dublin Bench. From the Record Commission calendars of Bench plea-rolls formerly in the Public Record Office in Dublin but now destroyed it is known that between 1299 and 1317 those rolls sometimes recorded in detail the assignment by successful litigants of part or all of the damages which they had recovered.[3] When such assignments were made the clerks of the Bench commonly got a share, as did other officials associated with the court such as its marshal and usher. The most likely explanation is that the assignment was made in lieu of fees owed by the successful litigant. Serjeants also often commonly got a share of such damages: sometimes specifically as serjeants, more often simply by name. On occasion only one serjeant is assigned a share, but more commonly we find two, three, four or even five serjeants sharing a lump sum or being given individual shares.[4] The assignment of damages to the serjeants must normally have been a reward for their services. In these cases at least, therefore, there must be a strong presumption that the litigant had employed the services of a group of serjeants rather than just one; and there seems no reason to doubt that this was common practice in other cases as well.

The serjeant spoke on behalf of his client without any kind of prior formal authorisation from his client. At Westminster we know that it was possible for the litigant or the litigant's representative to disown what a serjeant had said after he had said it (the technical term for this was 'disavowing' him), although the normal expectation was that a serjeant would not be disowned in this way. Disavowal is also something specifically mentioned in the custumal of the city of Dublin which apparently belongs to this period, though only in connection with litigation in the city court.[5] This suggests that disavowal must also have been a possibility in the Dublin Bench although it is not specifically mentioned in any of the surviving evidence relating to the court from this period.

There must normally always have been some kind of prior contact between serjeant and litigant before the serjeant stood up

---

3. The first such assignment is recorded in the calendar of a plea-roll for Easter term 1299: PROI RC 7/6, p. 11; the latest in the calendar of a plea-roll for Hilary term 1317: RC 8/11, p. 175.

4. For an example of the assignment of damages to a single serjeant see PROI RC 8/2, p. 174; of individual assignments to two serjeants: RC 7/10, p. 103; of joint assignment to two serjeants: RC 8/2, p. 155; of individual assignments to three serjeants: RC 7/9, p. 299; of joint assignment to three serjeants: RC 7/9, pp. 275–6; of joint assignment to four serjeants: RC 8/5, p. 76; of individual assignments to five serjeants: RC 7/10, pp. 112–13; of joint assignment to five serjeants: RC 7/13/3, p. 76.

5. *Hist. & mun. doc. Ire.*, p. 257.

in court. The serjeant needed to have been properly instructed as to the main facts concerning the litigation in question and perhaps also about the strengths and weaknesses of his client's case. But even before that could take place the client needed to have secured the serjeant's agreement to act on his behalf. In the Westminster Bench serjeants seem to have enjoyed total freedom in deciding whether or not they would act for a particular litigant in any particular case. This was qualified only by their obligation to provide 'advice and assistance' to those paying them annual pensions for this purpose. The court would not force them to act for such clients; but if they failed to do so the court would hold the client justified in refusing payment of the pension. A much greater degree of restraint on the individual serjeant's freedom of contract seems to have existed in the Dublin Bench for litigants in this court seem to have been able to go to the court to ask the justices to assign them a serjeant. Four different entries from plea-rolls now lost of various dates between 1312 and 1336 transcribed in the Record Commission calendars show serjeants who had been assigned to litigants by the court asking for their 'salary', their fee for their professional services, to be 'taxed' or set by the court[6] or taking steps to recover a 'salary' which had already been 'taxed' for such services.[7]

Most litigants in the Dublin Bench seem, however, to have been able to obtain the services of a serjeant without invoking the court's assistance in this way. Agreements between serjeants and clients in the Dublin Bench (as in the Westminster Bench) seem to have taken a variety of forms. A serjeant might agree to act for a litigant in one particular piece of litigation only. Such agreements probably lie behind a majority of assignments of damages to serjeants recorded on the plea-rolls. But many litigants made longer-term agreements with their serjeants. Some appear to have been of indefinite duration and were perhaps terminable at the will of either party. We hear of one such agreement (between the serjeant Henry of Beningbrough and the general attorney of Thomas of Moulton) in litigation in 1308. The litigation was brought by Henry to recover arrears of a fee of one mark a year owed him for acting as Thomas of Moulton's serjeant in the Dublin Bench. This agreement was probably not recorded in writing; and this may have been common in agreements of this kind.[8] More commonly the serjeant agreed to serve the client (and

6. For examples see PROI RC 8/6, pp. 406–7, 436 and RC 8/19, pp. 478–80.

7. PROI RC 7/12, p. 380.

8. PROI RC 7/13/3, p. 130.

sometimes the client's heirs) for the remainder of his life. Such agreements were normally (perhaps invariably) recorded in writing and the terms of several of them were subsequently recorded on the plea-rolls of the Bench and of the justiciar's court, either because they were cited in the course of litigation or because one of the parties (perhaps generally the serjeant) had them enrolled soon after they were made as a safeguard against possible loss of or damage to the deed concerned. Fortunately the Record Commission calendars contain full transcripts of several of them. The earliest such deed to be enrolled is one of 1297 between the serjeant William of Bardfield and Robert Mansel, which was enrolled on a Bench plea-roll in 1299.[9] Under its terms Robert agreed to pay William an annuity of twenty shillings a year and to give him each year a robe of the same value, in return for William's 'praiseworthy service' for the remainder of his life ('pro laudabili servicio michi quamdiu vixerit impendendo'). If payments were in arrears it was agreed that William could distrain Robert's manor of 'Moyglas' in Co. Limerick to enforce payment. It is, however, only our knowledge of William's career as a serjeant which makes it clear that the 'praiseworthy service' here referred to must be service to Robert as his serjeant. Also enrolled in the same year was a deed recording an agreement made in 1299 between the same William of Bardfield and Nicholas son of John of Inkbarrow ('Inteberge').[10] This agreement is much more precise and refers rather more directly to the nature of the service which William was expected to provide. Under its terms Nicholas agreed to pay twenty shillings a year to 'his' serjeant William of Bardfield for his 'service, advice and aid in the king's court' ('pro servicio, consilio et auxilio suo in curia regis'). If the twenty shillings was not paid William was to be entitled to distrain Nicholas' manor of 'Rathdrum', Co. Tipperary. The serjeant's obligation was a qualified one: it was 'service, advice and aid in the king's court, *where I find him*' ('ubi eum invenio'). A similar phrase occurs in other such agreements[11] and seems to mean that William is only obliged to act on behalf of Nicholas in whatever royal court (be it Dublin Bench, eyre or justiciar's court) he is working when Nicholas makes a request for his services. If he is then working as a serjeant in the eyre Nicholas cannot require

9. PROI RC 7/6, p. 53.

10. PROI RC 7/6, p. 63.

11. E.g. PROI RC 7/6, p. 45 ('ubi invenitur'); RC 7/10, pp. 528–9 ('ubicumque in curia regis fuerit inventus'); RC 8/17, pp. 513–16 ('ubicumque ipsum Johannem presentem esse contigerit').

him to travel to Dublin to act for him there (nor vice versa). The deed also contains one further qualification: 'saving the service of the king, and his other prior lords before the making of the present deed' ('salvo servicio regis et aliorum primorum dominorum suorum ante confeccionem presencium'). Again similar phrases are found in other such deeds.[12] They seem to mean that if Nicholas becomes involved in litigation with the king or with any of the clients whom William has taken on in return for a similar annuity before the making of this agreement then those clients and the king have a prior claim to William's services. William had been retained as a serjeant by the king since 1297.[13] In other such deeds involving serjeants not in the service of the king no such reservation is made in his favour, though commonly to the reservation in favour of prior clients is added one in favour of the serjeant's own relatives.[14] Later agreements are all with one exception of the same general form but with a number of minor variations in their wording. The exception is an undated agreement enrolled on the plea-rolls of the justiciar's court in 1333 between the otherwise unknown serjeant Adam de la Galeye and William de Launeye.[15] Under its terms William granted Adam an annuity of twenty shillings a year for life, secured on his manor of 'Turvylauneyston' in Co. Dublin. This annuity was simply said to have been granted in return for Adam's service to William and his heirs 'in the office of serjeant' ('in officio narratoris').

Serjeants who made agreements of this sort seem commonly in England to have had to sue for arrears of their annuity or to have had to distrain for it; and behind many such suits and distraints may have lain disputes between serjeant and client as to whether the serjeant had forfeited his right to the annuity by failing to provide the client with the service to which he was entitled. The surviving Record Commission transcripts of the Bench plea-rolls, however, only provide hard evidence of a single such dispute involving a serjeant of the Dublin Bench, and that in the form of a memorandum recording the terms on which it was settled.[16] The

12. E.g. PROI RC 7/6, p. 45 ('salvo servicio aliorum primorum suorum habitorum ante confeccionem presencium'); RC 7/10, pp. 528–9 ('exceptis primis dominis suis'); *Reg. St John, Dublin*, pp. 18–19 ('salvis personis quibus idem Rogerus ante confeccionem presencium exstiterat obligatus per sacramentum').

13. Richardson & Sayles, *Admin. Ire.*, p. 174.

14. E.g. PROI RC 7/10, pp. 528–9 ('exceptis ... consanguinitate et affinitate'); RC 8/18, pp. 202–15 ('exceptis ... proximis affinibus suis et sanguine suo').

15. PROI RC 8/17, pp. 328–9.

16. PROI RC 7/11, pp. 426–7.

dispute was between the serjeant Robert of Dalinghoo and one rather special client of his, Walter of Kenley. By the time the settlement was reached Walter had himself become a justice of the Dublin Bench. The settlement was made in 1306. Walter had granted Robert an annuity of two marks a year for life in return for his services but claimed that Robert had failed in their performance ('occasione servicii ipsius Roberti eidem Waltero minus plene facti'). Robert now renounced the annuity and agreed to make satisfaction to Walter by giving him a palfrey worth £40. Robert also agreed to continue performing his obligations to Walter under their agreement. These obligations are spelled out in some detail. Robert was to act as Walter's serjeant and also to be his adviser ('consiliator') as best he knew how ('in quantum sciverat') in all matters belonging to his 'office' ('in omnibus que ad officium ipsius Roberti pertinent'). This is of particular interest for it seems to indicate that the serjeant was expected not just to plead in court on his client's behalf but also when required to give general legal advice to his clients.

Two cases (of 1299 and 1306) suggest that it may have been possible at this time to obtain the services of a serjeant in the Westminster Bench for a single case for as little as forty pence; and in the mid-fifteenth century it could still be argued that in the absence of any specific agreement in advance to the contrary a fee of forty pence was payable to a serjeant 'as of common right'. Other late thirteenth and early fourteenth-century evidence, however, shows Westminster serjeants being paid much larger sums and it remains unclear how many serjeants were in practice willing at this time to act for so small a sum. The lowest recorded payment to a serjeant of the Dublin Bench is the half mark (or twice forty pence) assigned to three (or perhaps four) serjeants from damages in a case of 1306.[17] The lowest 'salary' awarded to a serjeant whom the court had assigned to a litigant was the one mark adjudged to John of Grantchester for his services in a case of 1312.[18] This is matched by the total of five marks shared between five serjeants from damages awarded in a case of 1308.[19] Twenty shillings,[20] forty shillings[21] and even sixty shillings[22] are the sums

17. PROI RC 7/11, pp. 275–9. There is no direct evidence that the fourth man (Thomas de Balymore) was a serjeant though this seems quite probable.

18. PROI RC 8/6, pp. 406–7.

19. PROI RC 7/13/3, p. 76.

20. E.g. PROI RC 7/9, pp. 275–6; RC 7/10, p. 103; RC 8/11, p. 175.

21. E.g. PROI RC 7/9, p. 299; RC 7/10, pp. 103, 112–13; RC 7/13/2, p. 4.

22. E.g. PROI RC 7/9, p. 299; RC 8/2, p. 174; RC 7/10, pp. 112–13.

more commonly assigned to serjeants for their services from damages. The two lower sums (and in one case, as much as fifty shillings each for two serjeants) are also found as 'salaries' awarded to serjeants in other cases where they were assigned to clients by the court.[23] The highest payment of all for services in a particular case seems to be the ten pounds assigned to Roger of Ashbourne from damages awarded in a case of 1304.[24]

The sums most commonly paid to serjeants of the Westminster Bench by way of retainer were twenty shillings and forty shillings, though retainers of one mark and of two marks are not uncommon. The lowest sum paid to a serjeant of the Dublin Bench as an annuity was twenty shillings.[25] Two marks and forty shillings are also commonly mentioned.[26] The highest annuity known to have been paid to a serjeant of the Dublin Bench (though not specifically for his services as a serjeant) was the five marks and one robe payable to Simon fitzRichard by the archbishop of Armagh which is mentioned in litigation in the justiciar's court in 1318.[27] Some Irish serjeants (like their English counterparts) are known to have accumulated large numbers of annuities. According to a petition of William Bardfield of 1321 his appointment as a royal justice (in 1308) had led to the loss of no less than £32 in fees and robes from such agreements.[28]

The fees which could be charged by individual serjeants for their services must have been affected and were perhaps even largely determined by the amount of competition that existed between those offering their services as serjeants. By the end of the thirteenth century there seems to have existed a regime of restricted competition in the Westminster Bench, which conferred on a small group of professional serjeants the sole right to offer

23. Twenty shillings: PROI RC 8/6, p. 436; forty shillings: PROI RC 7/12, p. 380, RC 8/19, pp. 478–80, *Cal. justic. rolls, Ire., 1305–7*, p. 16 (for service in the justiciar's court); fifty shillings: RC 7/13/2, pp. 9–10 (for services in the Drogheda eyre).

24. PROI RC 7/10, p. 175.

25. For some examples see: *Cal. justic. rolls, Ire., 1305–7*, p. 378; PROI RC 7/4, p. 481; RC 7/6, pp. 53 (plus one robe worth twenty shillings), 63; RC 7/10, p. 539 (plus one robe worth at least twenty shillings); RC 7/11, p. 136; RC 8/11, pp. 395–6 (plus one robe worth twenty shillings); RC 7/13/2, p. 7 (plus one robe worth twenty shillings).

26. For some examples see: (i) for two marks: PROI RC 8/2, pp. 281–2; RC 8/5, pp. 27–8; RC 7/10, pp. 528–9; (ii) for forty shillings: PROI RC 7/6, pp. 14, 45; RC 7/13/2, p. 6; Sayles, *Affairs of Ire.*, p. 53; *Cal. justic. rolls, Ire., 1305–7*, p. 54 (with additional robe worth two marks).

27. PROI RC 7/12, p. 161.

28. Sayles, *Affairs of Ire.*, 103–4.

their services on a regular basis to those with business in the courts. Entry into this group came, in the later fourteenth century, to be controlled by the crown; but this was clearly not the case earlier and then it was probably simply a matter for the court's own justices, perhaps with some advice from the existing serjeants. It is probable that a good knowledge of the law and a mastery of the skills of the serjeant were necessary qualifications for admission to the group; but they may not have been sufficient. It seems possible, even probable, that the size of the group was kept artificially small in the interests of its existing members. A similar situation seems also to have obtained in the Dublin Bench, though the evidence for this is no more than circumstantial. In 1306 and 1333 we find suggestive references to the exercise of the 'office' of serjeant.[29] The existence of a recognised corps of professional serjeants from which individuals could retire (or be expelled) would also explain why and how William of Athy, who was then still alive, could be referred to as being 'late serjeant pleader' in litigation in the justiciar's court in 1305.[30] The most likely context for the liability of a serjeant to be assigned to a litigant by the court is that this was some sort of *quid pro quo* for official 'recognition' of the serjeants and of their monopoly. As early as 1316 we find Nicholas of Snitterby bringing litigation in the Bench by bill specifically as a serjeant, further presumptive evidence of a degree of official recognition of the serjeants by the court, since the privilege of initiating litigation in the Bench by bill was probably restricted to those who were in some sense 'officials' of the court.[31]

How did the would-be professional serjeant set about acquiring the knowledge and technical skill required to enter and succeed in his profession? In England we know that by the 1270s at latest elementary lectures on the common law were being given for students and that by the end of the thirteenth century reports of cases were also being used for teaching purposes (though probably only for the instruction of rather more advanced students). Would-be serjeants were also by then in regular attendance at the court and picked up part of their knowledge both of the serjeant's technical skills and of current law by listening to the arguments of serjeants and justices. Their presence in the court was actively encouraged by the justices; and by the early years of the reign of Edward II there was even a 'crib', a special enclosure set aside for

29. Above, p. 21, notes 15 and 16.

30. *Cal. justic. rolls, Ire., 1305–7*, p. 35.

31. PROI RC 8/11, pp. 827–8.

them, in the court. It is probable that it is to these listeners that we owe the Year Book reports, which were perhaps reports compiled by them for their own instruction and use. By the late 1280s the law students attending the Bench for educational reasons were a sufficiently well-established group to have acquired a distinctive name, 'apprentices of the Bench'.

There is some evidence of men from Ireland going to London for training in the law during this period. In 1287 Robert de St Michael of Ireland was staying at Westminster with the king's permission 'for the purpose of learning in the Bench'. This we learn incidentally from royal letters patent allowing him to be represented by a permanent attorney in Ireland for the whole of the ensuing year.[32] As it happens this is also the earliest specific reference known to a student of the common law. The next (and only other) reference to a law student from Ireland in England prior to 1350 comes from a 1344 inquisition into an affray in the city of London. This mentions two Irish apprentices of the Bench (Richard of Cardiff and John Barry) as involved and as being common malefactors lying in wait at night to rob passers-by of their belts and purses.[33] The two men had an English colleague in their wrongdoing; and it should be added that many other early references to apprentices of the Bench are also to the offences committed by such apprentices.

There is also, however, other evidence to suggest that some instruction in the common law may have been available in Ireland. The early legal treatise known as *Natura Brevium* which survives in a number of different manuscripts seems to be derived from lectures and (as I have noted elsewhere) it (or they) seem to have been 'written or altered with a specifically Irish audience in mind'.[34] This is clear from a passage in the treatise on the action of wardship which is concerned with the problem of claims to the wardship of lands held by socage tenure by lords who are relying on the custom of the lordship of Ireland for their title. It envisages the use of action by bill before the chief justiciar as a way of recov-

32. PRO C 66/106, m. 11: 'Consimiles litteras de attornato habet Robertus de Sancto Michaele in Hibernia qui de licencia regis causa addiscendi in Banco regis apud Westm' moram fecit sub nomine Ade Clythyn clerici per unum annum duraturum, presentibus etc. Teste Edmundo comite Cornub' consanguineo regis apud Westm' xxviij Junii' (calendared in *Cal. pat. rolls, 1281–92*, p. 269). I owe this reference to the kindness of Dr David Higgins.

33. *Calendar of the plea and memoranda rolls of the city of London, 1323–64*, ed. A.H. Thomas (Cambridge, 1926), p. 213.

34. P. Brand, 'Ralph de Hengham and the Irish common law', *Ir Jur*, xix (1984), 107 at n. 6.

ering such a wardship.[35] I have also noted elsewhere that one of the two main manuscript traditions of the pleading manual *Novae Narrationes*, while apparently using precedents drawn from cases heard in the English courts, 'hibernicises' those precedents by the substitution of Irish place–names and personal names for the English originals.[36] The manual clearly played a part in the education of future serjeants. It is conceivable that it only ever circulated in written form; though equally likely that it too derives from lectures. What is important, though, is that the 'hibernicisation' of the treatise indicates that the C manuscript tradition of the manual derives either from lectures given in Ireland or from a manuscript of the manual which was extensively revised with an Irish audience in mind. Nor were the Irish personal names used in the treatise drawn entirely at random. The name most commonly used in the treatise in this manuscript tradition is that of John Plunket;[37] and it can be no coincidence that John Plunket was a prominent serjeant of the Dublin Bench in the early fourteenth century.[38] Other serjeants of the period whose names are used in the treatise are Richard le Blund, John of Cardiff and John Keppok.[39]

35. In Harvard Law Library MS. 162 (at ff. 166r-v) this passage reads: 'Et si cel bref face mencioun de service de chevalier et poet estre qe le tenant ne tient pas ceux tenemenz par service de chevalier mes par altre service auxi com par rente ou siute de court, dount ne seit acordaunt al bref, le deforceour purra transverser le bref e le counte par la resoun de les services de chevalier mes par altres services auxi com par rente etc., e issint abatre son bref a cele foyz solom le dit des asqunes gentz. Et sil velt la garde aver donc covent qil purchase un altre bref qe face nent mencioun de service de chevalier mes dautre service solom la coustume qest usee (in the version in Cambridge University Library MS. Hh. 3. 11 at f. 152v this reads 'solom le custome de Irlaund') et qe le bref die 'si come renablement purra moustrer etc. Et sil ne poet nent aver bref de cele fourme saunz service de chevalier donc covent qil plede par bille devant chef Justice si come il pert e semble a asqune gentz com avunt est dit'.

36. P. Brand, 'Ireland and the literature of the early common law', *Ir Jur*, xvi (1981), at 112.

37. His name appears in the main manuscript tradition of C96 and his wife's name in C55. His name also appears in two manuscripts in place of the initials found in the other manuscripts in C41, C45, C46, C53 and C262. These two manuscripts are probably reproducing faithfully the original text of the C tradition here. All references are to the edition of *Novae Narrationes* edited by E. Shanks and S.F.C. Milsom (Selden Society, vol. 80 (1963)).

38. Below, p.32.

39. Richard le Blund: C 53 (in three manuscripts in place of the anonymous initials of the other MSS.); John of Cardiff: C 26–27 (in a single manuscript and in the distorted form 'Kerdyke'); John Keppok: C 53 (in a single manuscript in place of John Plunket). For Richard le Blund and John of Cardiff see below, pp. 31, 34. John Keppok was a serjeant at law (and royal justice) in Ireland in the second half of the fourteenth century.

III

It is possible to compile a fairly complete list of all serjeants practising in the Westminster Bench from the early 1290s onwards. There are two sources of evidence for the compilation of such a list which fortunately complement each other. One is the plea-roll entries recording the proffer of payments for permission to make final concords, formal agreements made under the court's auspices mainly about land. From mid-October 1293 these normally include a clause noting that the parties to the final concord have the chirograph, the formal document recording their final concord, 'through' (*per*) a certain named individual, 'their' serjeant. The other is the Year Book reports which record serjeants in their more characteristic activity of pleading in court on behalf of their clients and which begin to survive in much larger quantity from this time onwards. Between them these two sources of information indicate that during the sixty-year period from 1290 to 1350 around 150 serjeants practised at some time or other in the court.[40] Unfortunately there are no surviving reports of cases from the Dublin Bench; and the new Westminster enrolment practice associating the making of final concords with particular serjeants does not seem to have been extended to (or been copied by) its Dublin counterpart. From such evidence as does survive it is possible to compile a list of around 35 serjeants who are known or who can reasonably be assumed to have practised in the Dublin Bench during the same sixty-year period.[41] Such a list can have no pretensions to completeness; indeed, there is no way even of knowing what proportion of the total number of serjeants active in the Dublin Bench during this same period they may represent. All that can be said is that given the pattern of survival of the evidence it is possible that it is much closer to being complete in the case of the serjeants practising in the earlier part of this period than in the later.

Some of the serjeants on the list are little more than just names. Of Michael of Sutton ('Sotton'), for example, we know that he is mentioned in passing as a serjeant in a plea-roll entry of 1291. The successful litigant in the case (William Fokeram) is recorded at the end of the entry as acknowledging that he had granted 'his' serjeant ('narrator') Michael one half of the eighty acres at Rathcon, Co. Tipperary which he had recovered through litigation from

40. I have calculated this figure from the material contained in John Baker's *Order of serjeants at law* (Selden Society, supplementary series vol. v (1984)).

41. See below, Appendix.

Walter Uncle.[42] Michael also appears once as an essoiner in the surviving Bench plea-roll of Easter 1290 and is mentioned twice on the rolls of the justiciar's court in 1297, once as the assign of five shillings out of total damages of fifteen shillings, once as enforcing a debt of forty shillings owed to him.[43] Nicholas of Snitterby is described as a serjeant ('serviens narrator') when bringing litigation in the Bench in Michaelmas term 1316 against a man and his wife who had allegedly assaulted him in St Patrick's street by Dublin.[44] From his surname it seems likely that Nicholas was a relative of Thomas of Snitterby, a justice of the Dublin Bench between 1295 and 1307.[45] It is possible that the serjeant is the same man as the Nicholas of Snitterby who served as a baron of the exchequer, justice of the Bench and justice of the justiciar's bench at various dates between 1337 and 1357.[46] He may, however, simply be a namesake and relative of an earlier generation since it was common for the same Christian name to be used by members of a family in successive generations.

It is usually possible, however, to say a little about the man's background, and thus at the very least to distinguish between those serjeants whose immediate origins were English and who only came to Ireland in the course of their careers and those who belonged to English families which had been settled in Ireland for one or more generations. John 'de Ponte' (whose surname should probably be anglicised as 'of Bridgwater') belongs to the first group.[47] John acted as king's serjeant in Ireland from 1292 to 1300 and unlike most king's serjeants seems only to have acted for the king. It may be for this reason that he received a higher fee.[48] John had acted as Edward I's attorney in two cases in the English court of king's bench in 1269 and 1270 before Edward became king.[49] He is then found in the service of Edward's wife

42. PROI RC 7/3, pp. 169–70.

43. BL, Add. Roll 13598, m. 7; *Cal. justic. rolls, Ire., 1295–1303*, pp. 93, 125.

44. PROI RC 8/11, pp. 827–8.

45. Richardson & Sayles, *Admin. Ire.*, pp. 150–2.

46. Richardson & Sayles, *Admin. Ire.*, pp. 109–12, 160, 163, 171.

47. Richardson & Sayles, *Admin. Ire.*, give his surname as 'de Ponz'. For evidence of his property acquisitions in Bridgwater (in Latin simply *Pons*) see *Somerset fines*, ed. E. Green (Somerset Record Society, vol. 6 (1892)), pp. 230, 264.

48. He was paid twenty marks a year when other king's serjeants were paid ten marks a year. For evidence of his activity on the king's behalf in the Irish courts down to 1300 see *Cal. justic. rolls, Ire., 1295–1303*, pp. 29, 102–3, 142–3, 238, 316–7; PRO C 260/18, no. 10, m. 2; PROI RC 7/6, pp. 441–2.

49. PRO KB 26/192, m. 2 and KB 26/197, m. 18.

Eleanor acting as her bailiff in Somerset, as her constable of Leeds castle in Kent and (in 1289) as her under–steward.[50] He seems to have come to Ireland when a promising career in Eleanor's service was ended by her death. Much less is known about the antecedents of John's contemporary, John de Neville, who was also employed by the king as one of his serjeants between 1293 and 1297.[51] It is, however, clear that he also was English by origin. In 1295 he received a protection in respect of property he held in England; and when in 1302 Christ Church priory, Dublin obtained a quitclaim from him of the life interest he possessed in land at Clonturk in Co. Dublin it was dated at York, presumably because he had by then returned to England.[52] William of Bardfield, king's serjeant from 1297 to 1308, whom we have already encountered accumulating annuities for his services as a serjeant to private clients, was of English origin too.[53] William appears to have come from either Great or Little Bardfield in Essex and is to be found acting as an attorney in the Westminster Bench between 1279 and 1284.[54] In 1290 he stood surety for the future chief justice of the Dublin Bench, Simon of Ludgate, when Simon was in trouble in England for obtaining a papal bull whose contents were deemed unacceptable by the king.[55] At some date between 1286 and 1289 William married Katherine, one of two sisters of John of Bayfield. John had been chief clerk to Hamon Hauteyn the senior justice of the exchequer of the Jews between 1273 and 1284 and the marriage brought William property interests in the counties of Norfolk and Middlesex which Katherine had inherited from her brother.[56]

50. *Cal. close rolls, 1279–88*, p. 88; *Cal. close rolls, 1288–96*, p. 113; *Chronica Johannis de Oxenedes*, ed. H. Ellis (Rolls Series, 1859), p. 273.

51. Richardson & Sayles, *Admin. Ire.*, p. 174.

52. *Cal. pat. rolls, 1292–1301*, p. 138; *Calendar to Christ Church deeds* (ed. M.J. McEnery) in *P.R.I.rep.D.K.*, no. 20 (1888), Appendix 7, pp. 36–122, no. 23 (1891), Appendix 3, pp. 75–152 and no. 24 (1892), Appendix 8, pp. 100–94 (continuous enumeration throughout) [hereafter cited as *Cal.Ch.Ch. Deeds*], no. 172. For land acquired by a John de Neville (possibly the Irish serjeant) in Yorkshire in 1300 see *Yorkshire feet of fines, 1300–14*, ed. M. Roper (Yorkshire Archaeological Society, record series, vol. 127 (1965), p. 12, no. 59.

53. Richardson & Sayles, *Admin. Ire.*, p. 174; above, p. 20.

54. PRO CP 40/28, m. 80; /29, mm. 81, 82; /39, mm. 72, 76d; /41, mm. 87, 87d; /42, mm. 154d, 155, 161; /44, m. 91; /51, m. 111d; /52, m. 67d.

55. PRO E 159/63, m. 13d.

56. PRO JUST 1/578, m. 45; CP 40/79, m. 16; JUST 1/544, m. 10; CP 40/109, m. 117.

These English property interests explain why William obtained a protection in England in 1298 and appointed general attorneys to act for him there in 1308, 1311, 1314 and 1318.[57] Henry of Beningbrough, who is to be found acting as a serjeant in the Dublin Bench, the justiciar's court and in eyres during the first decade of the fourteenth century, was also probably of English origin. Beningbrough is close to York; and one John the chaplain of York is mentioned as being one of his executors in 1312 litigation brought to recover the arrears of an annuity owed by one of his clients.[58] Of serjeants active in the second quarter of the fourteenth century only Thomas of Dent (king's serjeant from 1331 to 1334) seems to have been of English birth. Thomas probably came from Dent in Yorkshire. He too appointed general attorneys to act on his behalf in England though only after he had been appointed a justice in Ireland (in 1337, 1344 and 1347).[59] Thomas also seems to have acquired property in Ireland, however, for after his return to England he is to be found (in 1361) appointing general attorneys to act on his behalf in Ireland.[60]

A majority of the Irish serjeants of this period, however, seem to have been of Anglo-Irish origin. Several came from a Dublin bourgeois background. Roger of Ashbourne, active as a serjeant from at least the 1290s up to the time of his death (in 1307/8) for example, had been one of the bailiffs of the city in 1287 and was clearly related to the Roger of Ashbourne who was mayor of Dublin in the 1260s and 1270s (who was probably his father).[61] Roger held significant amounts of property in the city as well as in the county of Dublin. He also acquired property in Co. Kildare and in the suburbs of the city of Cork but later disposed of them.[62] Robert of Bristol, who was active as a serjeant from the late thirteenth century through to the early 1320s (when he was

57. *Cal. pat. rolls, 1292–1301*, p. 358; *Cal. pat. rolls, 1307–13*, pp. 80, 354; *Cal. pat. rolls, 1313–7*, p. 159; *Cal. pat. rolls, 1317–21*, p. 193.

58. PROI RC 8/6, pp. 375–6 (cf. RC 7/10, pp. 528–9).

59. Richardson & Sayles, *Admin. Ire.*, pp. 160, 162, 177; *Cal. pat. rolls, 1334–8*, p. 519; *Cal. pat. rolls, 1343–5*, p. 318; *Cal. pat. rolls, 1345–8*, p. 416.

60. *Cal. pat. rolls, 1361–4*, p. 130.

61. *P.R.I.rep.D.K. 37*, p. 25; *Chartul. St Mary's, Dublin*, vol. I, p. 455 and n.

62. For his property in the city of Dublin see: *Cal. justic. rolls, Ire., 1295–1303*, p. 314; *Reg. St John, Dublin*, no. 34 (pp. 18–9); PROI RC 7/9, pp. 297–8. For his lands in Co. Dublin see: PROI KB 1/1, m. 47; RC 7/10, pp. 78, 281, 340–1; RC 7/11, pp. 464–5, 501; RC 7/13/2, pp. 6–7; RC 7/13/4, p. 50. For his lands in Co. Kildare see: *Cal. justic. rolls, Ire., 1305–7*, pp. 329–30. For his lands in the suburb of Cork see: PROI RC 7/8, pp. 399–400; RC 8/2, pp. 278–9.

appointed a justice of the Bench) was a citizen of Dublin and held property there and in Co. Dublin.[63] He was the son of William of Bristol, another former mayor of the city.[64] John of Grantchester, a serjeant from at least 1312 until his appointment as a baron of the Dublin exchequer in 1326, is probably to be identified with the John son of Ralph of Grantchester who was a citizen of Dublin and who in 1318 was granted an exemption from serving in public offices in the city or county of Dublin against his will.[65] He married Alice, the daughter of Geoffrey of Morton, yet another former mayor of Dublin, and in her right held various properties in the city of Dublin and in Co. Meath.[66] He also acquired further property in the city and lands in Co. Kildare.[67] John seems also, however, to have held lands in England, since in 1330, 1331 and 1334 he appointed attorneys to act for him there and in 1334 obtained an exemption from serving in public offices there against his will.[68] The Philip of Carrick who is mentioned as a serjeant in the justiciar's court in 1305 may also have come from a similar background. A Philip of Carrick, perhaps the same man, is found as bailiff of Dublin in 1297 and is also mentioned in connection with affairs in the city in 1306 and 1307.[69]

An even larger group of serjeants came from the eastern seaboard counties of Ireland, mainly from the area later to be known as the English Pale. Richard le Blund of Arklow was king's serjeant from 1297 to 1322 and acted as a serjeant for others as well during that period.[70] His name indicates that he came from Arklow though there seems to be no other direct evidence to connect him with the town. Richard can be shown to have been a tenant of lands in the city and county of Dublin and in Co. Louth.[71] His

63. *Anc. rec. Dublin*, vol. I, p. 111; PROI RC 7/3, p. 316; RC 7/4, pp. 479–80; RC 8 /11, pp. 269–70.

64. *Cal. justic. rolls, Ire., 1295–1303*, pp. 262–3; PROI RC 7/3, p. 316.

65. PROI RC 7/12, pp. 497–8.

66. *Rot. pat. Hib.*, p. 23b, nos. 105–6; *Cal. pat. rolls, 1321–4*, pp. 330–1; PROI RC 8/10, pp. 791–4; RC 7/12, pp. 434–5; RC 8/17, pp. 516–8.

67. PROI RC 8/15, pp. 64–5; RC 8/19, pp. 563–4; RC 8/11, p. 174; RC 8/17, pp. 316–9, 344–5, 366–9; PRO KB 27/283, m. 155.

68. *Cal. pat. rolls, 1330–4*, pp. 4, 227; *Cal. pat. rolls, 1334–8*, pp. 14, 28.

69. *Cal. justic. rolls, Ire., 1305–7*, pp. 98, 229; *P.R.I.rep.D.K. 38*, pp. 34–5; *Cal. doc. Ire., 1293–1301*, nos. 391 (p. 181) and 408 (pp. 190–1).

70. Richardson & Sayles, *Admin. Ire.*, pp. 174–6; PROI RC 7/6, p. 11; RC 7/8, pp. 151–2; RC 7/9, pp. 266, 275–6, 299; RC 7/10, p. 103; RC 7/11, pp. 275–9; RC 7/13/3, p. 76; RC 8/2, p. 174.

71. *Reg. St John, Dublin*, p. 371; PROI KB 2/7, p. 48; *Ormond deeds, 1172–1350*, nos. 324, 464; PROI RC 8/17, pp. 224–5; *Cal. pat. rolls, 1307–13*, p. 63.

wife seems to have brought him lands in Co. Tipperary and perhaps in Co. Dublin as well.[72] William of Athy was probably active as a serjeant throughout the 1280s and 1290s. By 1305 although still alive he was described as a former serjeant.[73] He is known to have held lands in Co. Kildare close to Athy as well as in Co. Dublin.[74] He was probably a younger son of the John of Athy who may himself have been a serjeant in the 1260s and was the deputy seneschal of the liberty of Kildare in the early 1270s.[75] William of Sully was active as a serjeant during the first decade of the fourteenth century. He is also known to have acquired and held lands in Co. Kildare.[76] In 1296 and 1304 he is to be found seeking lands further west in Co. Limerick, claiming that these had belonged to his grandfather Luke of Sully earlier in the thirteenth century (in the reign of King Henry III).[77] He also appears to have retained some links with the country from which his family had come to Ireland, Wales.[78] The John of Carmarthen who was active as a serjeant in the first and second decades of the fourteenth century seems to have been the eldest son of Adam of Carmarthen who had held lands in the counties of Kilkenny, Dublin and Limerick and property in the city of Dublin.[79] John forfeited all these lands when he adhered to the Bruces in company with Walter and Hugh de Lacy.[80] John Plunket, active as a serjeant from the end of the first decade of the fourteenth century to perhaps the fourth decade of the century, belonged to a

72. PROI CB 1/1, mm. 1d, 6; RC 7/10, p. 410; *Red Bk Ormond,* p. 73; *Registrum Prioratus Omnium Sanctorum juxta Dublin,* ed. R. Butler (Irish Archaeological Society, 1845), p. 125; PROI RC 8/11, pp. 433–4.

73. *Cal. justic. rolls, Ire., 1295–1303,* p. 218; Sayles, *Affairs of Ire.,* p. 53; BL, Add.MS. 4790, f. 141r; PROI RC 7/6, p. 14; *Cal. justic. rolls, Ire., 1305–7,* p. 35.

74. *Cal. justic. rolls, Ire.,1295–1303,* p. 155; *Red Bk Ormond,* p. 16; PROI RC 7/7, pp. 421–2, RC 7/9, pp. 268–9; RC 7/4, pp. 27, 40, 79, 162–4.

75. Below, p. 44 and notes 145–7. For evidence that John's heir was a son named Nicholas see PROI RC 7/3, p. 5; RC 8/1, p. 65; *Cal. doc. Ire., 1254–84,* no. 1862; and for this William being called William son of John of Athy see *Cal. doc. Ire., 1252–84,* no. 1448 and PROI KB 2/5, p. 1.

76. For evidence of William of Sully as a serjeant see *Cal. justic. rolls, Ire., 1305–7,* pp. 16, 69; *Cal. justic. rolls, Ire., 1308–14,* pp. 5–6; PROI RC 7/10, pp. 112–3. For his lands in Co. Kildare see *Cal. justic. rolls, Ire., 1305–7,* p. 151; PROI RC 7/10, pp. 208–9, 362–3, 563–4; RC 7/13/2, pp. 19–20.

77. PROI RC 7/4, pp. 79, 198; RC 7/10, p. 108.

78. *Cal. justic. rolls, Ire., 1305–7,* pp. 768–9.

79. *Cal. justic. rolls, Ire., 1305–7,* pp. 321–3; PROI RC 8/11, p. 175; PRO C 47/10/18, no. 11; *P.R.I.rep.D.K. 42,* p. 19.

80. *Rot. pat. Hib.,* p. 22, no. 33 and p. 24b, no. 126; *P.R.I.rep.D.K. 42,* p. 19.

family which since his grandfather's time had held land in Dublin but which in his father's time had also acquired property in Co. Louth close to Drogheda.[81] His wife Alice brought him further lands in the same county centered on the manor of Beaulieu where they founded a new parish.[82] He also acquired lands in counties Dublin, Meath, Louth and Kildare.[83] Simon fitzRichard seems to have been a serjeant by 1317 and was king's serjeant in Ireland from 1322 to 1331 (before becoming a royal justice).[84] He seems to have come from Co. Louth where he is known to have held and acquired land while a serjeant.[85] He is probably to be identified with the man who had been to Flanders in the company of John fitzThomas in 1298, was sheriff of Co. Roscommon in 1309–10 and in 1317 was sub-escheator in Co. Louth.[86] John Gernoun was king's serjeant from 1327 to 1330 and again from 1334 to 1338.[87] The annuity he was being paid as a serjeant by the seneschal of Christ Church in Dublin in 1343 (at a time when he was chief justice of the Bench) presumably had its origin in an earlier period of service to the priory.[88] The various Irish John Gernouns of the period are difficult to distinguish; there was also at least one contemporary English namesake who appears to have had no connection with Ireland.[89] The John Gernoun who was a serjeant probably belonged to a family who held lands in counties Louth and Meath and himself acquired lands in Co. Louth.[90]

81. P. Brand, 'The formation of a parish: the case of Beaulieu, county Louth' in *Settlement and society in medieval Ireland: studies presented to F.X. Martin*, ed. J. Bradley (Kilkenny, 1988), p. 261 and n. 15.

82. Ibid., p. 265.

83. In Co. Dublin: PROI RC 7/13/3, pp. 107–8; RC 8/15, pp. 179–80. In Co. Meath: RC 8/17, pp. 203–4; RC 8/19, pp. 164, 418; RC 8/20, pp. 6–7. In Co. Louth: RC 7/12, pp. 209–13; *Registrum de Kilmainham: register of chapter acts of the hospital of St John of Jerusalem in Ireland, 1326–1339*, ed. C. McNeill (Irish Manuscripts Commission, 1932), pp. 20–1, 29–30. In Co. Kildare: RC 8/20, pp. 44–8.

84. PROI RC 7/12, pp. 139–41; Richardson & Sayles, *Admin. Ire.*, p. 177.

85. PROI RC 7/12, p. 137; *P.R.I.rep.D.K. 42*, p. 35.

86. *Rot. pat. Hib.*, p. 5, no. 15; *P.R.I.rep.D.K. 39*, p. 27 (and note he was also under consideration as sheriff of Meath in 1313: PROI RC 8/9, p. 6); RC 7/12, pp. 138–9.

87. Richardson & Sayles, *Admin. Ire.*, pp. 176–7.

88. *Account roll of Holy Trinity, Dublin*, pp. 45–6.

89. Robin Frame (in *English lordship in Ireland, 1318–1361* (Oxford, 1982), p. 247) identifies our John with the John Gernun who held property in Essex but cites no evidence to support this improbable identification.

90. *P.R.I.rep.D.K. 39*, pp. 36, 42; *Rot. pat. Hib.*, pp. 75b–76, no. 109; *Dowdall deeds*, no. 125.

His wife Maud was the widow of William of Nottingham who belonged to a prominent Dublin merchant family.[91] John of Cardiff was perhaps already a serjeant in 1317 and was certainly king's serjeant from 1327 to 1330.[92] His father and namesake seems to have held lands in counties Dublin, Meath and Waterford in the reign of Edward I, but the future serjeant spent at least part of his childhood in England to which he was taken by his guardian Guy Cokerel.[93] Hugh Brown was king's serjeant from 1331 to 1346 and is known to have received an annuity as a serjeant from Christ Church priory in Dublin.[94] When he died in 1360 he possessed various lands in Co. Meath, and he probably came from that county.[95]

A minority of serjeants came from more remote areas of the country. Master David le Blund, active as a serjeant in the first decade of the fourteenth century, seems to have held lands in Co. Cork and to have come from this county.[96] His title suggests that he may have possessed a university degree, apparently a unique qualification for a serjeant during this period in either England or Ireland. Richard Locard was active as a serjeant during the same period but by 1313 had been murdered.[97] His property interests lay in counties Cork and Tipperary and it was at Cashel that he was killed.[98] In the late 1280s he had been a clerk in the household of the treasurer Nicholas de Clere and in 1292 served as sheriff of Co. Dublin.[99] In Reginald Macotyr of Co. Tipperary, active as a serjeant in the justiciar's court during the first two decades of the fourteenth century, we even find one serjeant of

91. PROI RC 8/19, pp. 108–15, 487; RC 8/20, pp. 326–330.

92. PROI RC 8/11, p. 175; Richardson & Sayles, *Admin. Ire.*, p. 177.

93. PROI RC 7/4, pp. 39–40; RC 7/11, p. 234; RC 7/13/4, pp. 32–3; RC 8/14, pp. 551–2.

94. Richardson & Sayles, *Admin. Ire.*, p. 176; *Account Roll of Holy Trinity, Dublin*, pp. 46, 93, 103–4, 108–9.

95. *Rot. pat. Hib.*, p. 88, no. 17.

96. For evidence of his career see: PROI RC 7/10, pp. 367–8; RC 7/11, pp. 25–6, 441; RC 7/13/3, p. 76; RC 8/2, pp. 278–9. For evidence of his lands see: PROI RC 7/11, pp. 60–1; RC 8/2, pp. 171, 278–9; RC 8/11, pp. 673–4; CB 1/1, m. 7; *Cal. justic. rolls, Ire., 1305–7*, pp. 367–70, 459.

97. *Cal. justic. rolls, Ire., 1305–7*, pp. 116, 371–2, 393; *Cal. justic. rolls, Ire., 1308–14*, pp. 62, 302–3.

98. PROI RC 7/7, p. 325; RC 7/11, p. 92; *Cal. justic. rolls, Ire., 1308–14*, pp. 108–10, 132–3.

99. *Cal. doc. Ire., 1252–84*, nos. 558, 595, 709, 969, 1148; *P.R.I.rep.D.K.37*, p. 49.

the period who was of native Irish (or more correctly Hiberno-Norse) origin.[100]

The first serjeants of the Westminster Bench to be appointed as justices of the king's courts in England were Richard of Boyland and Alan of Walkingham who were appointed as justices in eyre in 1279. By 1300 such appointments had become common and by 1350 only serjeants were being appointed to the two main royal courts (the Bench and king's bench). A significant number of the serjeants active in the Dublin Bench were likewise appointed as justices of the king's courts in Ireland. When William of Athy and John of Horton were appointed as justices in 1294 it was only for them to act as temporary substitutes for the chief justice of the Bench (Robert Bagod) while he was ill[101] but John of Bridgwater, while still a king's serjeant, was being appointed to hear assizes and deliver gaols all over Ireland and he became a justice of the Bench and sat in various eyres between 1300 and 1306.[102] Subsequently William of Bardfield became a justice of the Bench from 1308 to 1312 and again from 1316 to 1320;[103] Master David le Blund was a justice of the justiciar's court and a justice in eyre from 1308 to 1310 and again in 1317–8 and also an assize justice;[104] Robert of Bristol acted as a justice of the Bench from 1322 to 1324;[105] Richard le Blund of Arklow, who (like John of Bridgwater) heard assizes while still king's serjeant became a justice in eyre and justice of the Bench from 1322 to 1325;[106] John of Grantchester became a baron of the exchequer and then a justice of the Bench and of the justiciar's court between 1326 and 1334;[107] Simon fitzRichard acted as a justice of the Bench from 1331 to 1341;[108] John Gernoun acted as

100. *Cal. justic. rolls, Ire., 1308–14*, pp. 7, 10; PROI KB 1/1, mm. 6, 37, 75, 75d; KB 2/5, pp. 20, 34, 89; KB 2/6, p. 41; KB 2/9, pp. 35, 82, 117; KB 2/10, p. 31; RC 8/5, p. 76.

101. BL, Add. MS 4790, f. 141r.

102. For Bridgwater as an assize and gaol delivery justice see: *Cal. justic. rolls, Ire., 1295–1303*, pp. 9, 15, 19, 55–6, 72, 97, 150, 175, 215, 221–2, 225, 231–2, 236, 244–5, 280–2, 324, 341, 359; PROI RC 7/3, p. 442; RC 7/4, pp. 116–8, 216; RC 7/7, p. 183. For Bridgwater as a Bench and eyre justice see: Richardson & Sayles, *Admin. Ire.*, pp. 142–5, 151, 153 (and for evidence that he may have served earlier as a Bench justice see *Cal. justic. rolls, Ire., 1295–1303*, p. 318).

103. Richardson & Sayles, *Admin. Ire.*, pp. 153, 155.

104. Richardson & Sayles, *Admin. Ire.*, pp. 145, 167–8; PROI RC 8/7, p. 53.

105. Richardson & Sayles, *Admin. Ire.*, p. 155.

106. Richardson & Sayles, *Admin. Ire.*, pp. 147, 155, 157; PROI RC 7/11, p. 298; RC 7/12, pp. 209–13.

107. Richardson & Sayles, *Admin. Ire.*, pp. 107, 156, 169.

a justice of the Bench between 1338 and 1344 and again from 1348 to 1355;[109] Thomas of Dent acted as a justice of the Bench from 1334 to 1336 and again from 1344 to 1358;[110]William Petit was a temporary justice of the justiciar's bench from 1347 to 1348 and again in 1359;[111] and Robert of Preston was a justice of the Bench from 1358 to 1378.[112] The serjeants of the Dublin Bench did not, however, succeed in securing a monopoly of judicial appointments in Ireland. Partly this was because English serjeants were eligible for appointment to the Irish bench and were sometimes appointed to it. Thus Richard of Willoughby and Henry of Hambury, both long-serving serjeants of the Westminster Bench, were appointed chief justice of the Dublin Bench in 1324 and 1325 respectively; and Robert of Scarborough, another Westminster serjeant, was appointed chief justice of the Dublin Bench in 1332 and of the justiciar's court in 1334.[113] More puzzlingly it seems also to have remained possible to appoint men who seem to have had no experience as a serjeant in either country, men such as Thomas of Montpellier, who served as a justice of the Dublin Bench between 1335 and 1341.[114]

Other ties also existed between the serjeants of the Dublin Bench and the Irish judiciary. Nicholas of Snitterby was surely related to the Bench justice Thomas of Snitterby; and beside him we can place the serjeant Robert of Preston, son of Roger of Preston, a justice of the justiciar's court and of the Bench[115] and Roger of Ashbourne, father of the Bench justice, Ellis of Ashbourne.[116] Although it is not now possible to trace the family tree in detail it seems clear that the early fourteenth-century serjeant John Plunket was related to the many members of the family of that name who later became serjeants and justices in Ireland. Nicholas of Edgefield, a serjeant active in the first decade of the fourteenth century, was not directly related to any member of the Irish judiciary but is known to have married the widow of the former Bench justice, Simon of Ludgate.[117]

108. Richardson & Sayles, *Admin. Ire.*, pp. 156, 158, 160.
109. Richardson & Sayles, *Admin. Ire.*, pp. 160, 163.
110. Richardson & Sayles, *Admin. Ire.*, pp. 158, 160, 162.
111. Richardson & Sayles, *Admin. Ire.*, pp. 171 n. 2, 172.
112. Richardson & Sayles, *Admin. Ire.*, pp. 162, 164.
113. Baker, *Order of serjeants at law*, pp. 516, 535, 545.
114. For his career see Frame, *English lordship in Ireland*, pp. 105–6.
115. Ibid., p. 95.
116. PROI KB 1/1, m. 47; RC 7/13/2, pp. 66–7; RC 7/13/4, p. 50.
117. *Cal. justic. rolls, Ire., 1305–7*, pp. 231, 261.

IV

Such information as we possess about the functions performed by attorneys in the Dublin Bench seems congruent with them performing much the same functions as their much better-documented English counterparts. The basic, primary function of the attorney was simply to attend court on the client's behalf; to come forward to the bar of the court when the client's name was called out by one of the criers of the court and show that his client was present through his attorney. If his client was the plaintiff in the case several such appearances in successive terms would normally be necessary before the court's procedures secured the appearance of the defendant and the case could be pleaded. Even after that several more such appearances were commonly required before final judgment was given. If a plaintiff was not present either in person or through his attorney at any of the days appointed by the court for the hearing of his case and failed to make his excuse for absence in proper form, the case would be dismissed and his sureties for pursuing the case would be amerced and he would have to start the case all over again. If his client was the defendant the attorney had fewer appearances to make. He had simply to attend the court as and when the client required him to do so for the pleading of the case. By the later thirteenth century these basic functions had attracted to themselves certain other subsidiary ones. The plaintiff's attorney seems commonly to have seen to the acquisition of the appropriate writ for the initiation of the litigation. He seems also to have become responsible (at the purely procedural stages of litigation) for ensuring that his own appearance and the defendant's absence were recorded on the plea-rolls of the court by one of the court clerks and for ensuring that the appropriate judicial writ authorising the next stage of process against the defendant was issued and delivered to the appropriate local sheriff. At the pleading stage the attorneys on both sides had the ultimate power to avow or disavow what had been said by the serjeants. They may also commonly have engaged those serjeants on behalf of the client and have 'briefed' them on the main facts of the case.

A much greater degree of formality attached to the appointment of an attorney than to the authorisation of a serjeant. All appointments of attorneys were supposed to be recorded on the plea-rolls of the Bench. What was recorded, however, was the purely oral authorisation of the attorney. Litigants did not have to draw up any kind of written document giving the attorney authority to act on their behalf. Originally both litigant and attorney had to

appear before the court during term-time for such an appointment to be made; but it seems probable that by this date the
requirement had been relaxed in Ireland as it is known to have
been in England, where it was possible to appoint an attorney out
of term before a justice of any of the royal courts or even one of
the senior clerks of the Bench in any locality which they visited.

Such appointments must, of course, have been preceded by
agreements between litigant and attorney as to the terms on
which the attorney was willing to act. In the Westminster Bench
these varied very considerably: from agreements to act in one
particular case to longer term agreements to act for a particular
client until further notice or for life. There were also variations as
to the remuneration agreed. Very little evidence survives about
the terms of such agreements in the case of attorneys appointed to
act in the Dublin Bench. A surviving transcript, however, does
give us the terms of one agreement made between the attorney
John le Blound of Gowran, Co. Kilkenny, and the abbot of
Monasteranenagh, which was confirmed by the successor of the
abbot who had made the original agreement in 1317. Under its
terms John received an annuity of twenty shillings for the services
done by him for the abbey in the Dublin Bench. The annuity
presumably also paid for his future service as well.[118]

It clearly remained possible throughout this period for a litigant
in either of the Benches to appoint as his attorney a friend or
relative with no pretensions to any professional expertise. Both
Benches did, however, recognise the existence of the professional
attorney at least to the extent of applying special measures
against him if found guilty of professional misconduct (including
debarring such an attorney from practice in the court). In the
Westminster Bench there appears even to have been an unsuccessful attempt in 1292 to confine regular paid practice as an
attorney in the court to a closed group of around one hundred
and forty members chosen by the justices of the court. No such
measure is known to have been attempted in the Dublin Bench;
and it is probably correct to assume that a regime of wholly free
competition obtained in the court.

It is quite difficult even in England to identify for certain the
professional attorneys who practised in the Bench. There are no
sources comparable to those which make it so easy to identify the
professional serjeants who practised there. A few professional
attorneys can be identified from the litigation brought against
them by dissatisfied clients but most can only be identified by the

118. PROI RC 7/12, pp. 322–3.

laborious process of searching through those sections of the plea-rolls which are devoted to recording the individual appointments of attorneys in particular cases and looking for names which recur with sufficient frequency to suggest that the individuals in question are professionals. The loss of almost all the plea-rolls of the Dublin Bench renders a comparable exercise looking for professional attorneys quite impossible; and we are therefore dependent for the most part on occasional passing references and the comparatively few appointments of attorneys which are recorded in the Record Commission calendars for the identification or possible identification of professional attorneys active in the Dublin Bench. The surviving Bench plea-roll for Easter term 1290 does, however, allow us to identify at least two possibly professional attorneys then practising in the Bench. About Alexander Giffard nothing more seems to be ascertainable.[119] Maurice Honne or Houne, however, can be traced in the calendars being appointed as an attorney down to 1309;[120] and some indication of his possible place of origin is provided by litigation of 1306 between him and Leticia daughter of Andrew Honne/Houne which shows him claiming lands at 'Balyhokyn' in Co. Dublin.[121] Confirmation of his professional status, if not of his professional skill, comes from a case of 1301 in which his negligence as an attorney caused his clients to lose their case.[122] He was committed to gaol for that negligence, a punishment suitable for a professional but not for an amateur. Other professional attorneys who can be identified as such from the surviving evidence include John le Blound of Gowran (whom we have already encountered) who was active as an attorney from 1308 to at least 1318 (and perhaps till his death in 1331).[123] John is known to have sued the abbot of Monasteranenagh and the archbishop of Armagh for arrears of annuities of twenty shillings a year each (and the former was certainly for his services in the Bench).[124] He is also known to have sued two other probable clients for arrears of annuities of

119. BL, Add. Roll 13598, mm. 2, 2d (seven appointments).

120. For his seven appointments as an attorney in Easter term 1290 see ibid. (and for his activity as an essoiner in the same term see ibid., m. 7). For subsequent appointments see PROI RC 7/3, p. 332; RC 7/5, p. 139; RC 7/9, pp. 384–5; RC 7/10, p. 519; RC 7/13/4, p. 71.

121. PROI RC 7/11, p. 466 (though the surname is here transcribed as Howe).

122. PROI RC 7/8, pp. 107–8.

123. PROI CB 1/1, mm. 26, 26d; RC 8/11, pp. 202–216, 442–53, 857–65; RC 7/12, pp. 400–1. For the date of his death see *P.R.I.rep.D.K.44*, p. 54.

124. PROI RC 8/11, pp. 426, 599; RC 7/12, p. 367.

one mark each.[125] John Gothemund, probably from Cashel, is
described as an 'attorney in the (king's) bench at Dublin' after his
murder in 1314. This suggests that he too was a professional
attorney of the court.[126] At least two other possible professional
attorneys of the period seem to have come from Co. Tipperary.
One was Peter 'de Halleton' whose name occurs with some
frequency in the surviving lists of attorneys in the Record
Commission plea-roll calendars between 1317 and 1336.[127] The
second is Roger de Sancta Brigida. He only occurs as an attorney
on the plea-rolls between 1299 and 1305 but was specially
authorised in 1302/3 by Nicholas of Inkbarrow (Inteberge) to
surrender an advowson to the hospital of St John the Baptist in
Dublin and in 1315 sued the archbishop of Cashel for five years
arrears of a forty shilling annuity, which may have been granted
him for his legal services.[128] Roger is known to have held property
at Knockgraffon in Co. Tipperary.[129] Nicholas of Tintagel occurs
as a Bench attorney in 1325, 1332 and 1336.[130] In 1336 he was
seeking land in his own right in Co. Cork, seeking land in
right of his wife (as the dower of a previous husband) in Kildare
town, and also suing for an alleged assault against himself at
Oxmantown.[131] Richard Manning was the king's attorney from
1313 to 1328 but is found acting for others at various dates
between 1305 and 1327.[132] He is known to have held lands in Co.

125. PROI RC 8/15, pp. 130, 144–5.

126. *Cal. justic. rolls, Ire., 1308–14*, p. 313. For evidence linking him with Cashel
    see PROI KB 1/1, m. 34 (=*Reg. St John, Dublin*, pp. 302–3); KB 2/5, p.
    35.

127. PROI RC 8/11, pp. 442–53 passim, 730; RC 8/15, pp. 68–77 passim; RC
    8/19, pp. 168–78 and 370–9 passim; KB 2/9, p. 124. For his connexions
    with Co. Tipperary see PROI RC 8/16, pp. 170–1; RC 8/19, p. 431; RC
    8/20, pp. 282–3.

128. PROI RC 7/6, pp. 2, 60, 575–6; RC 7/7, pp. 132, 273–4; RC 7/8, pp.
    202–3; RC 7/9, pp. 383, 477; RC 7/10, pp. 517–8; *Reg. St John, Dublin*, p.
    309; RC 8/10, p. 318.

129. PROI RC 7/9, pp. 266–7; RC 8/17, pp. 52–3. For his attempts to recover
    land there see RC 7/5, p. 285; RC 7/10, pp. 185, 600–2.

130. PROI RC 8/14, p. 581 et seq.; RC 8/17, pp. 267–304 passim; RC 8/19,
    pp. 370–9 passim; RC 8/20, pp. 53–70 passim.

131. PROI RC 8/20, pp. 149, 153–4, 347–8.

132. Richardson & Sayles, *Admin. Ire.*, pp. 174, 176; *Rot. pat. Hib.*, pp. 16, no.
    34, 18b, no. 143; *Cal. justic. rolls, Ire., 1305–7*, pp. 291–2; PROI RC 7/10,
    pp. 397, 519, 630; RC 7/11, pp. 102, 378, 380–1, 524, 563; RC 7/12,
    pp.185, 400–1; RC 7/13/4, pp. 71–2; RC 8/1, pp. 177–8, 202–16, 442–53,
    857–65; RC 8/5, pp. 76–7; RC 8/15, pp. 5, 68–77; KB 2/11, pp. 2–3.

Kildare.[133] No more than names are the Martin le Reve who is commonly found as a Bench attorney between 1316 and 1336[134] and William of Woodworth who acted as the king's attorney from 1328 to 1334 but who had also previously acted for (and been rewarded by) the prior of the Hospitallers.[135]

V

Professional serjeants are also to be found at work in the court of the justiciar in Ireland. The surviving evidence, however, suggests that the court did not possess its own separate corps of serjeants. The same group of men appear to have practised indifferently in this court and in the Dublin Bench. In this feature the Irish legal profession again resembles its English counterpart. In England by 1300, if not before, the same group of serjeants seem to have acted both in the Bench and in king's bench. Combining practice in the two courts was, of course, quite easy when both were holding sessions in Dublin; but the justiciar's court often held its sessions elsewhere and we do not know how individual serjeants then decided which court to attend. There is a similar problem with the two courts in England. Professional serjeants may have enjoyed a qualified monopoly in the justiciar's court similar to that which they enjoyed in the Bench. On one occasion at least (in 1305) two of them (Henry of Beningbrough and William of Sully) were assigned by the court to the service of a litigant (the communities of the city of Drogheda) and it has already been suggested that this practice may be associated with such a monopoly.[136] It is possible that there were also professional attorneys practising in the court; but there seems to be no definite evidence to either prove or disprove this.

The king's serjeants acted for him in the eyre as well as in the Bench (and sometimes in other courts as well). In 1292–3 John of Bridgwater was paid for prosecuting and defending pleas and business on the king's behalf 'before the justices of the Bench, the

---

133. PROI RC 7/10, p. 318; RC 8/10, p. 299; RC 8/11, pp. 185–7.

134. See passim: PROI RC 8/11, pp. 202–16, 240–2, 442–53, 857–65; RC 8/14, p. 581 et seq.; RC 8/15, p. 200 et seq.; RC 8/17, pp. 267–304; RC 8/19, pp.168–78, 370–9; RC 8/20, pp. 53–70.

135. Richardson & Sayles, *Admin. Ire.*, p. 176; *Reg. Kilmainham*, pp. 2–3, 11–2; *Cal. justic. rolls, Ire., 1305–7*, p. 50; *Cal. justic. rolls, Ire., 1308–14*, p. 47; PROI RC 7/10, pp. 517, 631; RC 7/11, p. 337; RC 8/4, p. 7.

136. *Cal. justic. rolls, Ire., 1305–7*, p. 16.

justices in eyre and the barons of the exchequer' and in 1295–6 John de Neville was paid for acting as the king's serjeant for his pleas 'in all places in Ireland'.[137] William of Bardfield is known to have pleaded on the king's behalf in the 1301 eyres of counties Louth and Cork as well as in the Bench, the justiciar's court and the exchequer; Richard le Blund of Arklow in the 1301 eyre of Co. Louth as well as in the Bench, the justiciar's court and the exchequer.[138] Other evidence of serjeants' activity in the eyre is disappointingly sparse. We do hear of Robert of Bristol and William of Bardfield being adjudged one hundred shillings in the 1307 Tipperary eyre for services to John de Cogan in the previous eyre held by the same justices in Co. Meath.[139] We also know that both John Plunket and John of Staines were present at the 1322 Meath eyre, where they stood surety for the prior of Llanthony Secunda (and presumably also acted in a professional capacity as serjeants).[140] In England reports of cases heard in the eyres in this period show that the serjeants who practised in the eyre were largely (but not exclusively) drawn from those who practised in the Bench. The same was very probably also true in Ireland. There is no certain evidence of professional attorneys practising in the eyre in Ireland.

There were certainly professional lawyers practising in the lower courts of the Irish lordship as well. As early as 1272 William Picot was complaining of being unable to obtain a 'narrator' or 'consultor' (by which he clearly means a serjeant) for litigation in the court of the city of Dublin because of the influence of his opponent in the case, Richard of Exeter, a justice of the Bench.[141] This suggests that already by this date there may have been a small group of professional serjeants practising in the court whose

137. PRO E 372/139, m. 9; E 372/144, m. 28.

138. Bardfield: (i) in eyres: PROI RC 7/8, pp. 61, 215; (ii) in the Bench: RC 7/5, pp. 441–3; RC 7/6, pp. 15–6; RC 7/9, pp. 379–81, 441; RC 7/10, pp. 136, 602–3; RC 7/11, pp. 309–10, 353–5; RC 7/13/2, p. 1; RC 8/2, p. 168; (iii) in the justiciar's court: *Cal. justic. rolls, Ire., 1295–1303*, pp. 383–5, 445; *Cal. justic. rolls, Ire., 1305–7*, pp. 155, 162, 302–4, 305; (iv) in the exchequer: PROI RC 8/2, p. 136. Blund: (i) in the eyre: PROI RC 7/8, pp. 9, 13–4, 215 and PRO C 47/10/17, no. 2; (ii) in the Bench: PROI RC 7/5, p. 367; RC 7/7, pp. 216, 509; RC 7/8, pp. 98, 163; RC 7/9, p. 311; RC 7/10, p. 273; (iii) in the justiciar's court: *Cal. justic. rolls, Ire., 1295–1303*, p. 411; *Cal. justic. rolls, Ire., 1305–7*, pp. 10, 101–3; PROI KB 1/1, m. 48; (iv) in the exchequer: PROI RC 8/4, pp. 450–1; RC 8/9, pp. 591–2.

139. PROI RC 7/13/2, pp. 3–4, 9–10.

140. PRO C 260/43, no. 10.

141. PRO C 47/10/13, no. 8. (cited by Hand in *Eng. law in Ire.*, at p. 139).

services a litigant could normally expect to obtain. There is also a provision in the custumal of the city of Dublin, which seems to belong to this period, as to the penalty to be imposed when someone was 'disavowed' in litigation. The person disavowed is here specifically called 'un countour'.[142] It is not possible to be sure whether or not this is a reference to a professional serjeant rather than just 'one who makes a count for someone else'; but the former seems the more likely. In England we know that there were professional serjeants practising not just in the city courts in London but also in the courts of smaller towns such as Shrewsbury, King's Lynn and Oxford. It would be surprising if Dublin did not also have its own professional serjeants.

Reports of cases heard in the Warwickshire county court in the early fourteenth century indicate that there were then at least five or six professional serjeants practising in the court; and it is possible to show that there were also professional serjeants in a number of other English county courts. In Ireland it is only the fortuitous survival of a single piece of evidence which allows us to see that in 1306 there were already professional serjeants practising in at least one county court, that of Co. Louth.[143] A lessee had been distrained for arrears of the rent owed by his lessor to that lessor's feudal lord. He asked the lessor to take appropriate steps to deal with the matter. The lessor claimed that the rent had been paid and told the lessee to contest the justice of the distraint through an action of replevin in the county court. He would himself, he said, pay for the litigation and find a serjeant. However, when the case came on for hearing at the county court the lessor failed to provide a serjeant and the lessee was non-suited in his plea for lack of one. The reference is surely to a professional serjeant. If there were professional serjeants in the county court of Co. Louth by this date then it seems reasonable to assume that professionals were also by then active in other Irish county courts though not necessarily in all.

By 1300 there seems also to have been a group of professional serjeants practising in the court of the liberty of Kilkenny. In 1302 John son of William de Poer complained that when his father William had assigned a debt of £100 owed him by John to Master Thomas of Quantock, chancellor of Ireland, and Master Thomas had brought litigation in the court to secure payment of his debt John had been unable to get 'right, grace and favour' or even a

---

142. Above, note 5.
143. *Cal. justic. rolls, Ire., 1305–7*, pp. 182–3.

serjeant in the court because of the influence of his opponent.[144] There were presumably professional serjeants by this date in the other liberty courts of Ireland as well.

VI

In England the evidence for the existence of professional (or perhaps more precisely proto-professional) lawyers goes back to the early thirteenth century. Doris Mary Stenton noticed that some fourteen men occurred on the plea-rolls of the king's courts during the reign of King John with sufficient frequency as attorneys and sureties to suggest that they may have been professional lawyers; and we know that at least one of these men (John Bucuinte) also on occasion acted as a serjeant. It is of interest to note that at least two of the fourteen men (Roger Huscarl and Richard Duket) also went on subsequently to serve as justices in Ireland: thus the link between the English legal profession and the Irish judiciary was one forged very early in the history of both institutions.

During the following reign (that of Henry III) we first get clear evidence of a distinct group of professional serjeants active in the Westminster Bench and by the end of the reign it is clear that the normal assumption is that litigants in the court will have professional serjeants speaking on their behalf. It is also during the latter part of the same reign that we first begin to get evidence pointing to the existence of professional lawyers in Ireland. The Record Commission calendars show John of Athy, father of the later Bench serjeant William of Athy, suing on behalf of the king in the 1260 eyre of Co. Cork and the 1261 eyre of Co. Dublin.[145] In the early 1270s we find the same man acting as deputy seneschal of the liberty of Kildare.[146] John is also to be found *c*.1258–64 witnessing a confirmation of a grant to the abbey of St Thomas in Dublin in company with two royal justices (Wellesley and Exeter) and *c*.1260–5 witnessing a quitclaim to the archbishop of Dublin in company with the same two justices and the treasurer of Ireland.[147]

144. *Cal. justic. rolls, Ire., 1295–1303*, pp. 392–3 (and transcribed in full in PROI RC 7/9, pp. 514–8).

145. PROI RC 7/1, pp. 248, 260, 323, 327.

146. *P.R.I.rep.D.K.36*, p. 23.

147. *Register of the abbey of St Thomas, Dublin*, ed. J.T. Gilbert (Rolls Series, 1889), pp. 52–3; *Alen's reg.*, p. 138.

There is no definite proof here that he was a professional lawyer; but the evidence is at least suggestive of such a conclusion. Clearer evidence is provided by a petition of Roger Oweyn dating from the 1270s.[148] In it Roger claimed that he had been appointed to act as serjeant for the king (then the lord Edward) at the time when Richard de la Rochelle was justiciar of Ireland and Fromund le Brun chancellor (between 1261 and 1266). Despite the promises which had been made to him, he said, he had received no payment for his services. If he had not been in the king's service, he went on to assert, he could have received large fees from the magnates of Ireland ('ubi dictus Rogerus magnum sallarium de magnatibus Hibernie potuit recepisse'). Roger is himself clearly a professional serjeant, though apparently a disappointed one.[149] What he has to say suggests that there were also other professional serjeants in practice in Ireland. It was presumably the large salaries which they had received from the Irish magnates which led Roger to talk of the large salaries which he could have received if he had not been in the king's service. And the most likely context for the lord Edward retaining a serjeant full-time to act on his behalf in the first place is a well-established practice of other litigants utilising the services of other professional serjeants for their litigation. This evidence suggests, therefore, that by the early 1260s at latest professional serjeants had become a normal feature of the Irish courts.

In England it is the reign of Edward I (1272–1307) which first brings much fuller evidence of the existence and activities of professional lawyers; and some of that evidence entitles us to begin describing them as members of a legal profession. The same period also brings much fuller evidence of the existence and activities of professional serjeants in Ireland. In addition to the serjeants retained by the king (Roger Oweyn and his successors Robert of St Edmund's and John fitzWilliam)[150] we also find during the 1280s a number of serjeants being paid by the earl of

---

148. PRO C 47/10/13, no. 6 (printed but with several errors and omissions in Richardson & Sayles, *Admin. Ire.*, p. 230).

149. For evidence of his activity on behalf of Edward in the 1269 and 1278 Dublin eyres see PROI RC 7/1, pp. 427, 473, 475, 480–1; RC 8/1, p. 31. For evidence that he was retained by at least one private client (the chapter of St Patrick's cathedral in Dublin) see *Crede Mihi: the most ancient register of the archbishop of Dublin before the reformation*, ed. J.T. Gilbert (Dublin, 1897), p. 113, no. cxxii.

150. Richardson & Sayles, *Admin. Ire.*, pp. 174–5. For evidence of annuities paid to Robert of St Edmund's by private clients see PROI RC 7/4, p. 53.

Norfolk for their services in the Irish courts: William of Weston, Ellis of Ibstone and David of Pembroke.[151] A note of material from the now lost Bench plea-roll of Trinity term 1282 shows the same William of Weston and an otherwise unknown Richard Basset being amerced half a mark for 'chattering and speaking foolishly' but being pardoned the half mark, apparently in return for providing breakfast for the clerks of the court.[152] There is a marginal annotation opposite the entry 'castigatio narratorum' ('punishment of serjeants'), and the entry clearly relates to some kind of unacceptable behaviour on the part of the two serjeants which the court subsequently forgave. The earl of Norfolk also made a single payment of sixty shillings to the English serjeant (and future chief justice of the English court of king's bench) Gilbert of Thornton during the same period. This was for his service in the earl's litigation with Philip of Stanton. Philip was claiming the manor of Old Ross but the litigation ended (in part, at least, thanks to Gilbert's assistance) with the earl retaining the manor.[153] Gilbert had been sent over to Ireland in the autumn of 1284 to act for the king in *quo warranto* proceedings in the Dublin Bench against Thomas fitzMaurice. These concerned the shrievalties of the counties of Waterford, Cork and Kerry and the lands of Decies and Desmond.[154] Gilbert's return to England in June 1285 (to resume his role as king's serjeant on one of the English eyre circuits) created a major problem in the Decies and Desmond proceedings. When the litigation started it had been envisaged that Gilbert would remain in Ireland until the plea was over. The justiciar had therefore given permission for 'all the good serjeants of Ireland' ('quasi omnes bonos narratores Hibernie') to act for Thomas. He had then retained them to act for him and thus all of them knew his strategy for the litigation ('qui sciunt totum consilium predicti Thome in hac parte'). When Gilbert left Ireland before the litigation ended it was no longer possible to engage any of them to act on the king's behalf in his place. The solution eventually adopted, perhaps the only solution possible in

151. PRO SC 6/1239, nos. 1–9. David of Pembroke was only paid once, and then for not acting against the earl in a particular case. The earl also paid the king's serjeant, John fitzWilliam, for his assistance during the same period.

152. RIA, MS. 12.D.12, p. 9.

153. PRO SC 6/1239, no. 4.

154. *Cal. pat. rolls, 1281–92*, pp. 134, 136; PRO C62/60, m. 2; *Cal. doc. Ire., 1252–84*, nos. 2310, 2319; PRO C 47/10/14, no. 22 (printed in *Anal Hib*, no. 1 (1930), 209–12).

the circumstances, was for the case to be transferred to England. This case suggests that as yet, in the mid-1280s, the number of expert professional serjeants in Ireland may have been quite small, no more than a handful of men. It also suggests, in the way that these professionals are described as 'serjeants of Ireland', that already as later these serjeants could probably be found acting for clients in any of the main Irish royal courts, the Dublin Bench, the justiciar's court and eyres.

We have already seen that there were probably professional attorneys in the Dublin Bench by 1290 but apparently in much smaller numbers than in the Westminster Bench.[155] It is of course possible that there were more professional attorneys than the two identified but the amount of business coming to the court suggests that there cannot have been many. The earl of Norfolk's Irish accounts of the 1280s record payments to attorneys, but none of them seem to be professional attorneys practising in the main Irish courts. Some are men sent over from England by the earl and paid expenses in crossing the channel and two pence a day while in Ireland.[156] Others seem to be officials of the administration of the earl's liberty of Carlow or their close relatives.[157] These arrangements suggest that there may not as yet have been many professional attorneys practising in the Irish courts whom the earl could engage on his behalf. The real development of professional attorneys in Ireland probably only came after 1290; even then they were probably always much less numerous than their counterparts in England.

VII

By 1300 there was a legal profession in Ireland whose members provided specialist legal assistance to those with litigation in the courts of the lordship of Ireland. That legal profession seems to have borne a close resemblance to the legal profession which had recently emerged in England. It too was split into two separate branches (serjeants and attorneys) and the members of those two branches appear to have performed much the same services for

155. Above, p. 39.
156. E.g. Richard Faucun and Ardern sent to Ireland for the Old Ross case in 1284: PRO SC 6/1239, no. 3.
157. E.g. Ralph Wade, probably a relative of Thomas Wade the treasurer of Carlow, and William Cadel, seneschal of Carlow, both paid for acting as attorneys in different cases in 1284–5: PRO SC 6/1239, no. 4.

their clients as their English counterparts. A sizable minority of the Irish serjeants of the late thirteenth and early fourteenth centuries themselves came from England; and there is evidence suggesting that others as well received part of their professional education in England (though there is also evidence pointing to the availability of some legal education in Ireland). The two legal professions were, however, distinct entities. There is no evidence of professional lawyers practising on a regular basis in both countries or of them transferring their practice from one country to the other; and the promotion of English serjeants to the Irish bench was a one-way phenomenon. There were, moreover, certain distinctive features of the Irish legal profession which are not paralleled in England: the courts' ability to require individual serjeants to act for clients who sought the court's assistance (presumably a by-product of the relatively small number of serjeants); the failure of the Irish serjeants to gain a monopoly over appointments to the higher judiciary; and (probably) the relatively small size of the 'lower branch' (attorneys) in proportion to the number of serjeants in Ireland. The Anglo-Irish legal profession in its early years bears a close resemblance to its English counterpart, but they are by no means identical twins; and for the historian the differences between them are perhaps at least as instructive as the resemblance.

APPENDIX

Irish serjeants, 1290–1350

This list contains the names of all persons who are specifically described in official records of the period as being serjeants. Each entry gives the earliest and latest dates at which they are to be found so described (though their careers as serjeants must in many cases have been much longer than those here given) and also the sources for this information.

Ashbourne, Roger of: serjeant, 1299–1307: PROI RC 7/6, p.11; *Cal. justic. rolls, Ire., 1305–7*, p.392.

Athy, William of: lately a serjeant, 1305: *Cal. justic. rolls, Ire., 1305–7*, p.35.

Bagod, Thomas: serjeant, 1318 (but only in the court of the justiciar): PROI KB 2/10, p.46.

Bardfield, William of: king's serjeant, 1297–1308: PRO E 372/144, m. 28d; PROI RC 7/13/2, p.1.

Barford, Edmund of: king's serjeant, 1347–60: Richardson & Sayles, *Admin. Ire.*, p.178.

Beningbrough, Henry of: serjeant, 1302–1308: *Cal. justic. rolls, Ire., 1305–7*, p. 406 (and PROI RC 7/9, p. 299); PROI RC 7/3/3, p. 130.

Blund, Master David le: serjeant, 1303–5: PROI RC 8/2, pp. 278–9; PROI RC 7/11, pp. 25–6.

Blund, Richard le, of Arklow: king's serjeant, 1297–1322: Richardson & Sayles, *Admin. Ire.*, pp. 174–6.

Bridgwater (Ponte), John of: king's serjeant, 1292–1300: PRO E372/ 139, m.9; *Cal. justic. rolls, Ire., 1295–1303*, pp. 238, 316–17.

Bristol, Robert of: serjeant, 1303–9: PROI RC 7/13/2, pp. 9–10 (though not specifically described as such); PROI RC 7/13/4, p. 56.

Brown, Hugh: king's serjeant, 1331–46: Richardson & Sayles, *Admin. Ire.*, p. 176.

Cardiff, John of: king's serjeant, 1327–30: Richardson & Sayles, *Admin. Ire.*, p. 177.

Cardiff, Nicholas of: serjeant, 1317 (apparently in the court of the justiciar): PROI RC 7/12, pp. 139–41.

Carmarthen, John of: serjeant, 1306: *Cal. justic. rolls, Ire., 1305–7*, pp. 321–3 (but only in the court of the justiciar).

Carrick, Philip of: serjeant, 1305: *Cal. justic. rolls, Ire., 1305–7*, pp. 67–70 (but only in the court of the justiciar).

Chaumflour, Nicholas de: serjeant, 1317 (apparently in the court of the justiciar): PROI RC 7/12, pp. 139–41.

Dallinghoo, Robert of: serjeant, 1299–1306: *Cal. justic. rolls, Ire., 1295–1303*, pp. 319–321: PROI RC 7/6, p. 11; PROI RC 7/11, pp. 426–7.

Dent, Thomas of: king's serjeant, 1331–4: Richardson & Sayles, *Admin. Ire.*, p. 177.

Edgfield, Nicholas of: serjeant, 1307: *Cal. justic. rolls, Ire., 1305–7*, p. 361 (but only in the court of the justiciar).

FitzRichard, Simon: serjeant, 1317: PROI RC 7/12, pp. 139–41; and king's serjeant, 1322–31: Richardson & Sayles, *Admin. Ire.*, p. 177.

Forester, Henry: serjeant, 1317 (apparently in the court of the justiciar): PROI RC 7/12, pp. 139–41.

Forester, Simon: serjeant, 1336: PROI RC 8/19, pp. 478–80.

Galeye, Adam de la: serjeant, 1333: PROI RC 8/17, pp. 328–9.

Gernoun, John: king's serjeant, 1327–30 and 1334–8: Richardson & Sayles, *Admin. Ire.*, pp. 176–7; and serjeant, 1343: *Account roll of Holy Trinity, Dublin*, pp. 45–6.

Gerveys, John: serjeant, 1317–8 (but only in the court of the justiciar): PROI KB 2/9, p. 22; PROI KB 2/10, p. 55.

Glen, Roger of: serjeant, late Edward I: *Cal. justic. rolls, Ire., 1308–14*, pp. 42–3.

Grantchester, John of: serjeant, 1312–8: PROI RC 8/6, pp. 406–7; PROI RC 7/12, p. 380.

Hanwood, Matthew of: king's serjeant, 1310–5: Richardson & Sayles, *Admin. Ire.*, p. 175; PROI RC 8/10, p. 546.

Horton, John of: serjeant, 1299: *Cal. justic. rolls, Ire., 1295–1303*, p. 267 (but only in the court of the justiciar).

Kinton, John of: serjeant, 1344: *Account roll of Holy Trinity, Dublin*, p.44.

Laffan: see Lessayn.

Lenfaunt, Robert: serjeant, 1313: PROI KB 1/1, m. 42 (but only in the court of the justiciar).

Lessayn, William: serjeant, 1318: PROI KB 2/10, p. 55 (but only in the court of the justiciar) and note that PROI KB 2/9, pp. 107 and 120 suggest that Lessayn may be a misreading for Laffan.

Locard, Richard: serjeant, 1305–8: *Cal. justic. rolls, Ire., 1305–7*, pp. 337–8; *Cal. justic. rolls, Ire., 1308–14*, p. 62 (but only in the court of the justiciar).

McCotyr, Reginald: serjeant, 1312–3: PROI KB 1/1, mm. 6, 37 (but only in the court of the justiciar).

Neville, John de: king's serjeant, 1293–6: PRO E 372/139, m. 9; PRO E 372/144, m. 28.

Petit, William: king's serjeant, 1334–48: Richardson & Sayles, *Admin. Ire.*, pp. 177, 179.

Plunket, John: serjeant, 1310–17: PROI RC 8/5, p. 251; PROI RC 7/12, pp. 139–41.

Ponte, John de: see Bridgwater.

Preston, Robert of: king's serjeant, 1348–58: Richardson & Sayles, *Admin. Ire.*, p. 179.

Reading, John of: serjeant, recently murdered in 1316: PROI KB 2/7, p. 63 (not associated with any particular court).

Snitterby, Nicholas of: serjeant, 1316; PROI RC 8/111, pp. 827–8.

Staines, John of: king's serjeant, 1319–27: Richardson & Sayles, *Admin. Ire.*, pp. 176–7.

Staines, Nicholas of: serjeant, 1312: PROI RC 8/6, pp. 443–4.

Sully, William of: serjeant, 1305: *Cal. justic. rolls, Ire., 1305–7*, p. 16 (but only in the court of the justiciar).

Sotton, Michael de: serjeant, 1291: PROI RC 7/3, pp. 169/70.

Stapenhill, William of: serjeant, 1344: *Account roll of Holy Trinity, Dublin*, p. 103.

Threekingham, Hugh of: serjeant, 1307: *Cal. justic. rolls, Ire., 1305–7*, p. 413 (but only in the court of the justiciar).

Vincent, Walter: serjeant, 1313: PROI KB 2/5, pp. 108, 109 (but only in the court of the justiciar).

The brehons of later medieval Ireland

KATHARINE SIMMS

THE WORD BREHON is simply an anglicisation of the Irish *breitheamh*, or judge. It did not originally define the nature of the law administered by such a man, whether civil or canon law, native Irish custom or English common law. Indeed the vernacular law tracts and Latin canon laws of early Christian Ireland show such a marked interdependence that Ó Corráin has suggested: 'It may yet be possible to show that the two streams had flowed together and that effectively there was only one legal profession with a broad spectrum of individual interests and special skills, but a great deal more research needs to be done before such a hypothesis can be proved or disproved.'[1] In the first essay in the present volume Liam Breatnach has considerably strengthened this case by drawing attention to the passage in *Uraicecht Becc* on 'a judge of three judgments, namely, in matters concerning the laity, the poets and the church' and further texts indicating the competence of early Irish lawyers in both lay and ecclesiastical causes.[2]

Apart from the internal evidence of the law tracts, the annals confirm that many pre-Norman churchmen were experts in Irish law,[3] and during the eleventh and twelfth centuries some highly placed ecclesiastics actually bore the formal title of *an brethem* (the judge). The judge O Mancháin who died in 1095 was abbot, perhaps lay abbot, of Glendalough, where his family had long

1. D. Ó Corráin, 'Irish law and canon law' in *Irland und Europa/Ireland and Europe: the early church*, ed. P. Ní Chatháin and M. Richter (Stuttgart, 1984), p. 157.

2. See above, p.7.

3. D. Ó Corráin, 'Nationality and kingship in pre-Norman Ireland', in *Nationality and the pursuit of national independence* (Historical Studies XI), ed. T. W. Moody (Belfast, 1978), pp. 14–15; K. McCone, 'Dán agus Tallann', in *Léann na Cléire* (Léachtaí Cholm Cille xvi), ed. P. Ó Fiannachta (Maynooth, 1986), p. 12.

held ecclesiastical offices of one kind or another.[4] The judge O Rebacháin (d. 1106), from a Lismore ecclesiastical dynasty, was erenagh or superior of Mungret, Co. Limerick,[5] and in 1158 we are told that the judge O Duilendáin was erenagh of Ballysadare, *ollamh* or master of *fénechus* (traditional law), and also chieftain of his local territory or *tuath*.[6] These men, however, were living on the eve of a revolution in the Irish church.

The year 1098 saw the death of a doyen of the Irish hierarchy (who owed his position largely to the patronage of the O Briain high-kings), Bishop Domnall O hEnna of the Dál gCais. A marginal addition to the *Annals of Ulster* describes him as 'eminent in both laws, that is, Roman and Irish'.[7] Two letters addressed to Bishop Domnall by Lanfranc and Anselm, successive archbishops of Canterbury, suggest that his reputed expertise in Roman 'law' was not unconnected with his efforts to bring the Irish church into closer contact with the Gregorian reform then taking place on the Continent.[8]

The whole emphasis of the Gregorian movement lay in enforcing a standardised and codified version of canon law, the first widely accepted comprehensive collection being the *Decretorum libri XX* of Burchard of Worms, compiled 1008–12, followed by the *Decretum* of Ivo of Chartres (1093–5) and ultimately by the *Concordantia discordantium canonum* of Gratian of Bologna *c*.1140, which was to form the official basis of canon law in the catholic church for the rest of the medieval and early modern periods. By these yardsticks the Irish church was found wanting. In 1074 Archbishop Lanfranc wrote to the high-king, Toirdelbach Mór O Briain:

some things have been reported to us which are not pleasing. It is reported that in your kingdom a man will abandon his lawfully wedded wife at his own will, without any canonical process taking place . . .

4. *AFM* (*Annals of the kingdom of Ireland by the Four Masters*, ed. J. O'Donovan, 7 vols. (Dublin, 1851)), 1095. For other members of the family see ibid., 964, 965, 1002, 1050. Annals are cited by A. D. date of entry, unless otherwise stated.

5. *AI* (*Annals of Inisfallen*, ed. S. MacAirt (Dublin, 1951)), 1106. For other members of this family see ibid., 1041, 1090, 1129.

6. *AFM*, 1158 (and see ibid., 1230).

7. 'sui in uird cechtardha .i. Roman ⁊ na nGoeidhel', *The Annals of Ulster (to A.D. 1131)*, ed. S. MacAirt and G. MacNiocaill (Dublin, 1983), pp. 534–5. This is not a reference to civil law. The word *ord* could signify order, ecclesiastical rule, regulation or even ritual.

8. A. Gwynn and D. F. Gleeson, *A history of the diocese of Killaloe* (Dublin, 1962), i, 105–8.

according to a law of marriage which is rather a law of fornication; that bishops are consecrated by one bishop only; that many bishops are ordained in towns and cities; that at baptism children are baptized without consecrated chrism; that holy orders are conferred by bishops for money.

All these practices and any others like them are contrary to the teaching of all the orthodox Fathers who have gone before us: as is well known to all who have even a little theological knowledge . . . command the bishops and religious to come together in unity, show your own presence with your nobles to this holy assembly and strive to rid your kingdom of all these evil customs and all others contrary to the laws of the church.[9]

Among the practices criticised by Lanfranc only those involving marriage, divorce and concubinage could be seen as originating in secular custom,[10] the others clearly reflected shortcomings in the existing Irish canon law, and all were to be remedied by decrees of a church synod. The confrontation did not lie between the church and the pre-Christian traditions of secular lawyers, but between the long-established practices of Irish churchmen themselves and the more stringent demands of the new canon law system that was even then still struggling to assert itself on the Continent. As a consequence of this pressure the existing Irish system of three interlocking 'judgments' was to be replaced by a clear-cut twofold division, between the reformed 'laws of the church', based on a fixed series of Latin texts stemming from the Continent on the one hand, and on the other *fénechus*, the customs of the Irish laity.

Twentieth-century scholars have expressed some puzzlement because the native Irish reforming synods, while they legislated on the need for clerical celibacy and defined forbidden degrees of consanguinity and affinity within which sexual intercourse became incest, failed to tackle the customs governing marriage, divorce and concubinage which were being so fiercely criticised by Lanfranc, Anselm, St Bernard of Clairvaux and Popes Adrian IV and Alexander III.[11] However, this becomes a perfectly natural omission if we assume that marriage customs among the laity were seen as

9. J. Watt, *The church in medieval Ireland* (Dublin, 1972), pp. 6–7.

10. Even here the influence of the church may have been stronger than is sometimes supposed: see D. Ó Corráin, 'Marriage in early Ireland', in A. Cosgrove (ed.), *Marriage in Ireland* (Dublin, 1985), p. 5.

11. A. Gwynn, *The twelfth century reform* (A history of Irish catholicism, gen. ed. P.J. Corish, ii, fasc. 1, Dublin, 1968), pp. 16–19; Watt, *The church in medieval Ireland*, p. 9; K. Simms, 'The legal position of Irishwomen in the later middle ages', in *Ir Jur*, x (1975), 97–8.

pertaining to *fénechus,* now a separate discipline, whereas the synods were confined to reforming 'the laws of the church'.

An immediate practical problem resulting from this switch from a threefold to a twofold system of laws was the ambiguous status of the poets, and at the first synod of Cashel in 1101 the seventh decree which established the separation of ecclesiastical from civil jurisdiction asserted that poets shared the clerics' immunity from lay judgment.[12] As the reorganisation of the church progressed, however, the reform party among the native Irish clergy were not only to disown the poets, but under Primate David Mag Oireachtaigh (d. 1346) a provincial synod of Armagh legislated against poets, together with harpers, tympanists, mimers, jugglers and kernes, or mercenary soldiers.[13] The fourteenth-century bardic poets reacted indignantly by defying those whom they identified as an anglicising party among the clergy to produce justification for their attitude in standard canon law:

No book in Rome speaks of an action to diminish our privilege; it is in Ireland itself that you got the legal formula which has ordained it . . . the learning of Paris has not instigated the interdict which it was sought to put on us . . .

They cannot (impose) an interdict on us according to the judgment of any book of theirs; it is right that we should be dealt with justly according to the seven books of learning.[14]

The learning (*léigheand*) that clerics speak of and our own truly wise art (*ealadha*) are two streams from one fountain-head, although they say we should be rejected.[15]

If the somewhat doubtful attribution of the poem *A theachtaire thig ón Róimh* to Giolla Brighde MacConmidhe (d. *c.*1272) is correct, this clerical rejection of the poets may have started as early as the mid-thirteenth century.[16] That it was considered appropriate in 1101 to extend ecclesiastical immunity to all poets in right of their profession speaks volumes for the monolithic nature of learning in pre-Norman Ireland, a unity nostalgically recalled in the verse quoted above.

12. A. Gwynn, 'The first synod of Cashel', in *IER,* lxvii (1946), 109.

13. *The register of Primate John Swayne,* ed. D. A. Chart (Belfast, 1935), p. 11.

14. This seems to be a reference to the corpus of canon law, reckoned as the five Decretals, the Liber Sextus and the Clementinae, the latter issued in 1317.

15. B. Ó Cuív, 'An appeal on behalf of the profession of poetry' in *Éigse,* xiv (1972), 92, 96.

16. Ibid., at 88–90; N. J. A. Williams, *The poems of Giolla Brighde Mac Con Midhe* (Dublin, 1980), pp. 204–13, 339–44.

The fact that fourteenth-century bardic poets could so confidently invoke the contents of the seven books of canon law, and the work of the Parisian commentators, highlights a more cosmopolitan trend in Irish scholarship from the twelfth century onwards. The anonymous cleric in Killaloe who wrote the Lives of SS Flannán and Mochulla had travelled in France and the Rhineland for some years *c*.1141, studying medicine above all, but also literature and law, both civil and canon.[17] In 1133, Flann or Florentius O Gormáin left Ireland to study sacred and secular learning for twenty-one years in France and England before returning in 1154 to spend a further twenty years 'directing the schools of Ireland' as chief lector (*ardfherléighinn*) or chief master (*ardmaighistir*) of Armagh.[18] His nationwide influence and close association with the reform movement were attested when the synod of Clane (1162) agreed 'that no one should be lector in a church in Ireland except an alumnus of Ard-Macha'.[19] Then, in 1169, Ruaidhri O Conchobhair, as high-king of Ireland, granted a stipend of ten cows a year in perpetuity to the lector of Armagh (Florentius) and his successors 'to give lectures (*ac léighinn do dhenamh*) to students of Ireland and Scotland'.[20]

Besides this official recognition, Florentius O Gormáin may have received additional support through membership of an eminent dynasty of ecclesiastical scholars, all connected with the monastic reform. Finn O Gormáin (d. 1160), bishop of Kildare and for a time abbot of the Benedictine (?) foundation at Newry, was a joint compiler of that compendium of traditional Irish learning, the Book of Leinster.[21] Maolmuire O Gormáin, abbot of the Augustinian canons of Knock, Co. Louth, composed the *Martyrology of O Gormáin c*.1166–74,[22] while Maolchaoimhghin O Gormáin (d. 1164), abbot of the Augustinian canons at Termon-

---

17. D. Ó Corráin, 'Foreign connections and domestic politics: Killaloe and the Uí Briain in twelfth-century hagiography', in D. Whitelock, R. McKittrick, D. Dumville (ed.), *Ireland in early medieval Europe: studies in memory of Kathleen Hughes* (Cambridge, 1982), pp. 222–4.

18. *AU* (*Annals of Ulster*, ed. W.M. Hennessy and B. MacCarthy, 4 vols. (Dublin, 1887–1901)), 1174; *Ann. Tig.* ('The Annals of Tigernach', ed. W. Stokes in *Rev Celt*, xvi–xviii (1895–97)), 1174.

19. *AU*, 1162.

20. Ibid., 1169.

21. W. O'Sullivan, 'Notes on the scripts and make-up of the Book of Leinster' in *Celtica*, vii (1966), 26–7; A. Gwynn and R. N. Hadcock, *Medieval religious houses: Ireland* (London, 1970), p. 142.

22. J. F. Kenney, *The sources for the early history of Ireland: ecclesiastical* (New York, 1929; repr. Dublin, 1979), pp. 482–4.

feckin, and later *magister* or master of the school at the larger Augustinian house of Louth, was eulogised as 'chief sage of Ireland' (*ardshaoi Erenn*), by the Four Masters.[23] This pattern of a hereditary family of learned clerics gaining added learning and further promotion as a consequence of the reform movement was not unusual in the twelfth century. The most obvious example is that of the brothers Malachy and Christian O Morgair, sons of an earlier lector of Armagh, who were appointed between them to three of the newly formed territorial dioceses,[24] but the O Dubhthaigh family from Clonmacnoise were also extremely successful at acquiring high office under the new dispensation.[25] As Ó Corráin has commented: 'This is paradoxical only in a very superficial sense: none had greater need to swim with the tide of reform than the professional ecclesiastical families, and when it ebbed (as ebb it did in a very short time) they quickly reverted to type.'[26]

A number of factors combined to end this period of honeymoon between the hereditary church families with their traditional mixture of Irish and Latin learning and the Gregorian reform. In the first place, those clerics who responded literally to the novel insistence on celibacy left no direct heirs. Then, too, Ó Corráin has remarked of a text stemming from the twelfth-century reform that 'dynasty and diocese are powerfully identified'.[27] Local ecclesiastical families might find their claim to the bishopric shouldered aside by a relative of the secular ruler, an O Briain at Killaloe or an O Tuathail at Glendalough,[28] with no commitment to the traditional learning of the pre-reform monasteries. This 'disinheritance' of the old families was exacerbated after the Norman conquest, when the English kings maintained control over appointments to all bishoprics and abbeys located in or bordering on lands occupied by the Anglo-Normans, and displayed some reluctance to appoint native Irish candidates.[29] Within the new religious orders the gradual ousting of traditional Irish learning is signposted by the failure of one monastery after another to

23. *AFM*, 1164.

24. *St Bernard of Clairvaux's life of St Malachy of Armagh*, ed. H.J. Lawlor (London and New York, 1920), pp. 6–7, 36, 53, 62–3, 66, 89n.

25. *AFM*, 1136, 1150, 1168, 1174, 1200, 1209, 1223.

26. D. Ó Corráin, 'Mael Muire Ua Dunáin 1040–1117' in P. de Brún, S. Ó Coileáin and P. Ó Riain (ed.), *Folia Gadelica* (Cork, 1983), p. 52.

27. Ó Corráin, 'Foreign connections' (as above note 17), p. 230.

28. Ibid.; *AFM*, 1127, 1128, 1153, 1162.

29. J. A. Watt, *The church and the two nations in medieval Ireland* (Cambridge, 1970), pp. 72–84, 165, 193–4, 207.

maintain and update their Irish annals.[30] This last development poses a problem for the modern historian. Although the annalistic texts were eventually copied and continued by hereditary historians working under secular patronage, the transfer was not always instantaneous, and coverage is scanty for the key period of transition, the later thirteenth century.

It is consistent with this general picture that we find no brehons named in the annals between 1232 and 1309, and the contrast between these two entries epitomizes a wider change. Tiobraide O Braoin, who died in 1232, came from an eminent ecclesiastical family, many of whom are recorded as holding office in Roscommon and Clonmacnoise from the tenth century on, and as excelling in both Latin learning and Irish history and poetry. He himself is described as 'coarb of St Comán [of Roscommon], who was learned in theology, history and law (*saoi cléircechta, sencusa 7 breithemhnassa*)'.[31] He was, however, the last distinguished representative of his dynasty. In 1234, the annals record the death of Giolla na Naomh son of Art O Braoin, erenagh of Roscommon, a term beginning to signify simply hereditary lay administrator of church lands,[32] and the only other member noted thereafter was Bran O Braoin, 'an eminent tympanist', perhaps a professional musician, who died in 1364.[33] Two other brehons are recorded as contemporaries of Tiobraide O Braoin, whose surnames do not recur in a legal context thereafter, though their ecclesiastical connections are less obvious. One was Giolla Earnáin O Martain, 'ollam of Ireland in jurisprudence (*i mbreitheamhnacht*)' and eminent in many [poetic] arts (d. 1217/18),[34] and the other was the judge O Mionacháin, whose son Eachtighearn, a follower of Aodh, king of Connacht, was slain in a skirmish in 1230.[35]

Then, after a seventy-seven year silence in the records, comes the first obit, that is, notice of the death of a MacAodhagáin brehon.

30. B. W. O'Dwyer, 'The Annals of Connacht and Loch Cé and the monasteries of Boyle and Holy Trinity' in *RIA Proc*, lxxii (1972), sect. c, 83; *AI*, pp. xxviii–xli.

31. *AFM*, 1232, and see ibid., 987, 1088 and 1187.

32. *AFM*, *AU*, *ALC* (*The Annals of Loch Cé*, ed. W. M. Hennessy, 2 vols. (London, 1871; repr. Dublin, 1939)), 1234. On the changing significance of the term 'erenagh' see J.A Watt, 'Gaelic polity and cultural identity' in A. Cosgrove (ed.), *A new history of Ireland, ii* (Oxford, 1987), pp. 338–40.

33. *AU*.

34. *AFM*, 1216; *AU*, 1217; *ALC*, 1218. An O Martain bishop of Clogher died in 1431 (*AFM*).

35. *AFM*, *AC* (*Annála Connacht: the Annals of Connacht*, ed. A.M. Freeman (Dublin, 1944)), 1230.

In all, some forty members of Clann Aodhagáin are named in the annals, the overwhelming majority described as experts in Irish customary law (*féineachas*), secular jurisprudence (*breitheamhnas tuaithe*) or the like. They are one of the great secular learned dynasties of later medieval Ireland, dominating the lawyers as the Uí Dhálaigh dominated the poets or the Uí Mhaolchonaire the historians, but the steps by which they rose to this eminence are somewhat obscure.

According to the 'Customs of Hy Many', Clann Aodhagáin had been a tribute-paying sept under the O Ceallaigh chiefs of Uí Mhaine (east Co. Galway) before acquiring the office of chief's *ollamh*,[36] presumably his *ollamh* in law. Throughout the thirteenth-century annals they figure as warriors. In 1225, during a succession struggle in Connacht between Aodh son of Cathal Croibhdhearg O Conchobhair and his cousin, Aodh son of the high-king Ruaidhri, MacAodhagáin was raided by the followers of Aodh son of Ruaidhri and fought back with some success,[37] an indication that he was associated with Aodh son of Cathal Croibhdhearg (king of Connacht 1224–8). In 1249, during the insurrection of the 'king's sons' against the English conquerors of Connacht, Baothghalach MacAodhagáin fell with Aodh son of Aodh son of Cathal Croibhdhearg in an unsuccessful attack on Athenry, repulsed by Jordan d'Exeter, sheriff of Connacht.[38] In 1273, the same Jordan d'Exeter fought off an assault by the 'king's sons' in Corann (south Co. Sligo) in which Oireachtach MacAodhagáin was killed, possibly in association with the Clann Mhuircheartaigh Uí Chonchobhair.[39] These were cadets of the O Conchobhair family, supported in the later thirteenth century by the FitzGerald lords of Sligo against both the O Conchobhair kings and the de Burgh lords of Connacht.[40] Although the wording of the annals is somewhat ambiguous, it seems to have been in the service of the same Clann Mhuircheartaigh, now dispossessed after the expulsion of the FitzGeralds from Connacht, that Giolla na Naomh Mac-Aodhagáin was killed in 1309, in a murderous attack on the king of Connacht, Aodh son of Eoghan O Conchobhair.[41]

36. *The tribes and customs of Hy-Many*, ed. J. O'Donovan (Dublin, 1843 repr. Cork, 1976), p. 62.
37. *AC*, 1225 (30).
38. *AC*, 1249 (9), (10).
39. *AC, AU, ALC, AFM*, 1273.
40. *AC*, pp. 93 n.5, 161 n.2; K. Simms, 'Nomadry in medieval Ireland: the origins of the creaght or *caoraigheacht*', in *Peritia*, v (1986), 382.
41. *AC, AFM, AU*, 1309; G. MacNiocaill, 'Aspects of Irish law in the late thirteenth century' in *Historical Studies:X*, ed. G.A. Hayes-McCoy ([Indreabhán Co. Galway], 1976), p. 30.

Up to this point, there had been no explicit references to the family's links with the legal profession, so it comes as something of a shock to find the martial Giolla na Naomh termed 'ollamh of Connacht in law (*re fénechas*)', or even 'ollam of Connacht and Ireland', 'a universal master equally skilled in all arts'.[42] His date and his eminence combine to identify this man in the genealogies as Giolla na Naomh mac Duinnshléibhe Mhic Aodhagáin, 'chief master of *fénechas* jurisprudence', author of an unusual law tract in Early Modern Irish and ancestor of the MacAodhagáin of Ormond.[43] While the most illustrious, he was not the only lawyer in his generation. In 1316, Eoin MacAodhagáin, judge to Feidhlim O Conchobhair, king of Connacht, fell with his master in the battle of Athenry. The next year, Maol Iosa Ruadh MacAodhagáin, 'most eminent in Ireland in *féineachas* jurisprudence', and second cousin to Giolla na Naomh, died.[44] In 1320, Giolla na Naomh's third cousin, Maol Iosa Donn MacAodhagáin, described by the Four Masters as 'chief ollamh of Connacht', was captured on the shores of Lough Key, when the new king of Connacht raided the home of MacDiarmada, chief of Magh Luirg (north Co. Roscommon).[45] The comparatively distant relationship between three of these sages suggests that law had been studied in the MacAodhagáin family for some generations before 1300, in spite of the annals' silence. *An Giolla Suasanach* MacAodhagáin (d. 1235), grandfather of Maol Iosa Ruadh and great-uncle of Giolla na Naomh, may have earned the brief notice of his death in the *Annals of Connacht* as a man of learning rather than as a minor chieftain.

42. *AC, ALC, AU.*

43. C. Ní Maol-Chróin, 'Geinealaigh Clainne Aodhagáin' in *Measgra i gCuimhne Mhichíl Uí Chléirigh*, ed. S. O'Brien (Dublin, 1944), pp. 135, 138 and table; G. MacNiocaill, 'The interaction of laws' in J. Lydon (ed.), *The English in medieval Ireland* (Dublin 1984), pp. 105–6, and 'Aspects of Irish law' (above note 41).

44. *AC*, 1316 (5), 1317 (9). The mid-fourteenth-century O Cianáin miscellany, NLI MS. G 2, f. 25(24)r contains the earliest recension of the MacAodhagáin genealogies, of whose existence C. Ní Maol-Chróin was apparently unaware (in the absence of a catalogue). This leads with the name of Maol Iosa Ruadh and interlinear additions state that both he and Maol Iosa Donn had grandsons called Solamh mac Saorbhreathaigh whose identities were confounded in all subsequent recensions. This weakens Ní Maol-Chróin's argument ('Geinealaigh', p. 132) that the 'Solamh' who wrote in the *Leabhar Breac* belonged to the Connacht rather than the Ormond branch of the family, since Maol Iosa Ruadh was of the Ormond branch.

45. *AC, AU, AFM*, 1320; *AC, AU*, 1330; *AFM*, 1329; Ní Maolchróin, 'Geinealaigh', pp. 136, 138–9; MacNiocaill, 'Aspects of Irish law', p. 29.

Clann Aodhagáin were not the only hereditarily learned family in the later middle ages who originated as lay nobles rather than ecclesiastical tenants or the descendants of a pre-Norman professional class, whether clerical or lay. The Uí Dhálaigh poets of the twelfth century included one who was also chieftain of the two territories of Corca Raoidhe and Corca Adhain in West-meath,[46] and in the fifteenth century the head of the O Cobhthaigh family in Meath combined praise poetry with military leadership (*sai fhir dána 7 sai cinn-fhedhna*).[47] Cú-chairn or Cú-charad O Cobthaig, a mercenary soldier who murdered Domnall Got, king of Meath, in 1030,[48] may have been a remote ancestor. The Mac or O Duinnshléibhe physicians of Tír Conaill have been claimed as descendants of the thirteenth-century MacDuinnshléibhe kings of Eastern Ulster, though in this case the facts are difficult to establish.[49]

By contrast, the O Breisléin brehons of Fermanagh, also first recorded in the early fourteenth century, were hereditary church tenants, sharing the erenaghy of Derryvullen with the Uí Luinín, who were poets and historians, and the Uí Bhanáin whose most distinguished members were diocesan clergy.[50] Other hereditary lawyers, such as the Munster MagFhlannchadha and the Leinster O Deoradháin families, have less identifiable origins, but the fifteenth-century Mac-an-Bhreitheamhan *ollamh* to Muinntear Maolruain in Roscommon[51] was very possibly a descendant of one of those eleventh or twelfth-century dignitaries styled '*an Breit-heamh*' in the annals, and the Ulster surname MacBiorrthagra,[52] literally 'son of sharp pleading', suggests a longstanding connec-tion with the legal profession. As already hinted, this threefold pattern of recruitment, from church tenants, minor nobility and pre-Norman professionals, applies not only to the brehons but to all the hereditary exponents of native Irish learning in the later

46. *AFM, ALC*, 1185.
47. *AU, AC, AFM*, 1446.
48. *Ann. Tig., AFM*, 1030.
49. *AFM* iv, p. 742 n.f. The physicians' family is called O Duinnshléibhe rather than MacDuinnshléibhe in the annals, while the MacDuinnshléibhe kings of Ulster were not completely dispossessed by John de Courcy as O'Donovan assumed, but were still using their title in 1273 (*Cal. doc. Ire., 1252–84*, no. 953).
50. *AU, AFM*, 1447, 1495 (O Breisléin erenaghs): *AU*, 1396, 1441, 1477 (Uí Luinín); *AFM*, 1319; *AU*, 1420 (Uí Bhanáin). See Hadcock and Gwynn, *Medieval religious houses: Ireland*, p. 379.
51. *AFM*, 1483.
52. *AC, ALC*, 1529.

middle ages.[53] Class solidarity is demonstrated by their marriage patterns. On three occasions the O Breisléin judges are recorded as intermarrying with MagUidhir clerics, junior members of the ruling dynasty of Fermanagh, and once with the poetic family of O Fialáin.[54] Brian MacAodhagáin, law-ollamh for Breifne (d. 1390), married Gormlaith, daughter of David O Duibhgeannáin, 'a noble ollamh of history' and erenagh of Kilronan, Co. Roscommon.[55]

These social ties are matched by academic contacts between the various professions. Maghnus O Duibhgeannáin, compiler (*c.*1384–94) of the Book of Ballymote, which includes the law-tract *Uraicecht Becc*, refers in a marginal note to his 'beloved tutor', the MacAodhagáin,[56] and in 1432 Gregory O Maolchonaire, a potential 'sage in history', died while attending school at the house of MacAodhagáin of Ormond.[57] Adam O Cianáin, a cel-ebrated scribe and historian of the fourteenth century, got his kinsman Seaán O Cianáin to copy out for him the Bodleian manuscript Rawlinson B. 506, containing, besides genealogies and place-name lore, what amounts to a Middle Irish recension of the *Senchus Már*.[58]

Besides the historians, many praise-poets air their knowledge of laws and court procedure. Most frequently, this occurs in metaphors, referring to the prosecution and defence of their souls on Judgment Day,[59] or the poet's plea in self-defence against the anger of a temporal lord whom he has offended.[60] However, sometimes the bard cites specific precepts from the law books: that a younger, better qualified candidate may inherit the kingship

53. This pattern of recruitment is also suggested by a passage from the *Bretha Nemed*: 'for he who is not the child of a noble, or a poet, or a learned churchman, sues for only half honour-price until he serve learning doubly' (*Uraicecht na Ríar*, ed. L. Breatnach (Dublin, 1987), p. 46).
54. *AU*, 1459, 1475, 1478, 1479.
55. *AC*, 1437 (4); *AU*, *AFM*, *Ann. Clon.* (*The Annals of Clonmacnoise*, ed. D. Murphy (Dublin, 1896)), 1398.
56. T. Ó Concheanainn, 'The Book of Ballymote' in *Celtica*, xiv (1981), 21, where the MacAodhagáin in question is identified as MacAodhagáin of Ormond.
57. *AU, AFM*.
58. I am indebted to Liam Breatnach for this description of the text.
59. E.g. *Aithdioghluim Dána*, ed. L. McKenna (vol. i, text, Dublin, 1939, vol. ii. translation, Dublin, 1940), nos. 59 vv. 6–7, 11, 17, 20–1, 24, 29; 63 v. 1; 66 vv. 1, 3; 67 vv. 1, 15, 32, 38–9; 68 vv. 1, 3–4, 12, 16, 21; *Dán Dé*, ed. L. McKenna (Dublin [1922]), nos. iii vv. 1–2, 9–10, 12, 18; iv vv. 1–3, 6; viii vv. 7, 9–11, 15; ix vv. 13, 19; xv vv. 1–3, 14; xxi vv. 24, 26–7.
60. C. Ó Lochlainn, 'A poem by Tadhg mac Dáire', in *Éigse*, i (1939), 4; *Aithdioghluim Dána*, no. 40 v. 15; *Leabhar Branach*, ed. S. MacAirt (Dublin, 1944), p. 112, line 2949.

in preference to his elder kinsman;[61] that possession is nine points of the law;[62] that the road to a royal feast must be cleared;[63] and, somewhat mysteriously, that a carpenter is entitled to wound his own fist,[64] a principle it is tempting to see as derived from the lost tract *Bretha Luchtine*, the regulations governing carpentry.[65]

According to a passage of commentary on *Uraicecht Becc*, those engaged in the four practical professions, the braziers, carpenters, physicians and smiths, had a financial interest in studying the customary laws applying to their own skills, named respectively the *Bretha Créidine*, *Bretha Luchtine*, *Bretha Déin Chécht* and *Bretha Goibnenn* after the pre-Christian 'gods' of those arts. A craftsman who was thus learned was qualified to pass judgment himself regarding the payments he was entitled to as the reward of his labour, as long as the proceedings were witnessed by a trained lawyer. Unlearned craftsmen needed a brehon to pass judgment for them, and the judge then obtained a twelfth part of the whole as his traditional fee.[66] As one consequence of this vested interest, the only complete copies of two law tracts in Old Irish relating to physicians, *Bretha Crólige* and *Bretha Déin Chécht*, survive today in a fifteenth-century medical manuscript, with no more than brief excerpts from them to be found in strictly legal compilations.[67] The fact that we do not have comparable texts of *Bretha Créidine*, *Bretha Luchtine* and *Bretha Goibnenn* may indicate that hereditary artisans in the later middle ages had less book-learning than their monastic counterparts of the early Christian period, when the *ollam suad saeir*, the 'master wright', had an honour-price (*lóg n-enech*) approaching that of the 'judge of three judgments'.[68]

61. *Leabhar Cloinne Aodha Buidhe*, ed. T. Ó Donnchadha (Dublin, 1931), pp. 59–60. See *CIH*, iii, 797.12, iv, 1232.25, 1289.1.

62. *Aithdioghluim Dána*, no. 17 v. 1; this looks like an optimistic reading of *CIH*, vi, 1962. 13–18 'Buna fides . . . Iustus tidulus . . . Tempus continetur' etc., five grounds of lawful ownership clearly based on Roman civil law (see *Inst.* 1. 6 and *D*. 41.3 on 'usucapio'.)

63. *Aithdioghluim Dána*, no. 64 v. 13; see D. A. Binchy, 'Aimser chue' in J. Ryan (ed.), *Féilsgríbhinn Eoin Mhic Néill* (Dublin, 1940), pp. 19–20.

64. *Aithdioghluim Dána*, no. 84 v. 10. Other apparent precepts or maxims are found in *Dán na mBráthar Mionúr*, ed. C. Mhág Craith (Dublin, 1967) i, no. 39 v. 1 (see *CIH*, vi, 2068.19–20); *Dán Dé*, no. xxviii, vv. 10–12 (see D. A. Binchy (ed.), *Studies in early Irish law* (Dublin, 1936), p. 90); *Duanaire Mhéig Uidhir*, ed. D. Greene (Dublin, 1972), nos. xii v. 11, xiii v. 17.

65. D. A. Binchy, 'Bretha Déin Chécht' in *Ériu*, xx (1966), 2.

66. *Anc. laws Ire.*, v, 99; *CIH*, v, 1614, vi, 2330–1; and see passages edited by L. Breatnach above, pp 8, 9, 10.

67. D. A. Binchy, 'Bretha Crólige' in *Ériu*, xii (1934–8), 1–2.

68. *CIH*, vi, 2329.7; *Anc. laws Ire.*, v, 93. On the *lóg n-enech* or honour-price see L. Breatnach above, p.1.

Interdisciplinary connections were by no means one-way. The statement in the annals that Giolla na Naomh mac Duinnshléibhe Mhic Aodhagáin, law-ollamh of Connacht (d. 1309) was 'a sage equally skilled in every art' is to some extent borne out by the existence of two long poems on legal topics with final verses which name him as author. In particular, his poem in *rannaigheacht mhór*, 'Take my advice, gentle youth' (*Gabh mo chomhairle a mheic mhin*), discusses recommended reading of the rising law student. In addition to the law-tracts themselves, he advises study of the Old Irish kingship tracts, the Teachings of Cormac mac Airt and the *Audacht Morainn*, together with the cultivation of history and poetry. One recension of the poem ends with the exhortation: 'Be expert in every art . . . you whom all learning profits.'[69]

The wisdom of this advice seems vindicated by the success and widespread employment of brehons from the two lawyer dynasties of MacFhlannchadha and MacAodhagáin,[70] whose schools taught both *féineachas* and *filidheacht* (law and poetry), in contrast to the more localised influence of the O Deoradháin, O Duibhdabhoireann, Mac an Bhreitheamhan, MacBiorrthagra and O Breisléin families, whose members are described by the annalists as qualified in law only.[71] It should be noted, however, that *filidheacht* in the post-Norman annals did not refer to the full-blown art of the

69. M. Ní Dhonnchadha, 'An address to a student of law' in D. Ó Corráin, L. Breatnach, K. Mc Cone (ed.), *Sages, saints and storytellers: Celtic studies in honour of Professor James Carney* (Maynooth, 1989), pp. 159–177. I am very grateful to Máirín Ní Dhonnchadha for allowing me to consult her article while still in typescript.

70. As well as being *ollamhain* of Thomond or Dál gCais (*AFM*, 1483, 1492, 1576), MagFhlannchadha brehons served the earl of Desmond (*AFM*, 1578), the earl of Ormond (*Ormond deeds*, ed. E. Curtis, iii (Dublin, 1935), 49–50) and the Poers of Waterford (H. Hore and J. Graves, *The social state of the southern and eastern counties of Ireland* (Dublin, 1870), p.199). There were MacAodhagáin *ollamhain* of Connacht (*AFM*, 1329), Conmhaicne (*AFM*, 1354), North Connacht (*AFM*, 1378), Breifne (*AC*, 1390 (11)), Ormond and Uibh Fiachrach (*AC*, 1399 (4)), Uibh Failghe and Ceineál Fhiachach (*AC*, 1401 (7)), Teathbha, Anghaile, Ely O'Carroll, Clanrickard (*AFM*, 1409; *AU*, 1438, 1487; 'The Annals of Ireland by . . . Duald MacFirbis', ed. J. O'Donovan, *Miscellany of the Irish Archaeological Society* i (Dublin, 1846), 198–302, 1451) and many more territories.

71. However an ambiguous reference to Séamas son of Ruaidhri MacBiorrthagra describes him as a *mac fuirmhigh* (normally a poetic grade) 'of his own art' (*ALC*, 1529), and the legal poem 'Einecland na tri secht ngrád' (RIA MS. 1234 (C/i/2), f.4) is ascribed to one Muirghius O Dubhdabhoireann. Individuals from lesser families may have attended the larger law-schools, and obtained a poetic education there, or the annalists' distinction may have reflected only the degree of emphasis on *filidheacht*.

praise poet, known as *dán*, though is did imply an ability to compose in the bardic metres.[72] Indeed, some heads of these hybrid schools of law and literature seem to have earned more fame as *literati* than lawyers. In 1529, the MacAodhagáin of Ormond was called 'head of the learned of Leth Modha in knowledge and poetry' (*cend éigsi Leithe Modha ar éigsi ocus ar fhilidecht*),[73] and, in 1483, the MagFhlannchadha ollamh of Thomond was described as 'a man accomplished in literature and poetry' (*saoi dersccaighthe i n-eiccsi ⁊ hi filidheacht*).[74] In neither entry was there explicit reference to the ollamh's legal qualifications. The literary traditions of both these schools combined to produce the delightful skit on a judge's summing-up composed by Tadhg an Ghadhraigh MacAodhagáin as the closing contribution to the fourteenth-century (?)[75] poetic contention over the River Shannon. This was couched in the loose form of *ae freislighe* metre commonly used by scholarly amateurs, and the last verse refers to the MagFhlannchadha law-ollamh of Thomond as the author's former tutor.[76] One or two of Clann Aodhagáin are said to have been accomplished musicians,[77] a skill that may also have been practised by those of the family known as 'sages in every art'.[78]

Some of these additional studies can be seen as being of practical value to the brehon lawyer. While Middle Irish recensions of classical texts like the *Senchus Már* and the *Uraicecht Becc*[79] presumably facilitated comprehension for the junior or 'fettering

---

72. The historian Torna O Maolchonaire, ollamh of *seanchas* and *filidheacht* (d. 1468) was apparently attacked by the bard Tuathal O hUiginn as incompetent to compose praise-poetry: see K. Simms, '"Gabh umad a Fheidhlimidh"—a fifteenth-century inauguration ode?' in *Ériu*, xxxi (1980), 137–9.

73. *ALC*.

74. *AFM*.

75. The firmest grounds for dating the contention are Tadhg MacAodhagáin's references to the 'Diarmaid' who wrote the first little poem in *óglachas* 'A Shionainn Bhriain Bhóroimhe' (O. Bergin, *Irish bardic poetry* (Dublin, 1970), no. 12) as 'O Briain' and 'high-king of Munster' (below, note 76). Only two O Briain kings were called Diarmaid in the post-Norman period—Diarmaid *Cléireach* (d. 1311) and Diarmaid son of Toirdhealbhach Mór (d. 1364). The latter is otherwise known to have had literary interests: see B. Ó Cuív, 'An appeal' (above, note 15), 90–1.

76. B. Ó Cuív, 'The poetic contention about the River Shannon' in *Ériu*, xix (1962), 89.

77. *AFM*, 1369 (compare *AU*); *AFM*, 1399.

78. *AC*, 1309 (2); *AFM*, 1430, 1443.

79. *Uraicecht na Ríar*, ed. L. Breatnach (Dublin, 1987), p. 6; and see above, note 58.

advocates' (*glasaighneadha*), greater familiarity with the original Old Irish wording befitted a teaching ollamh or commentarist, and the linguistic training of the bardic poet [80] had a part to play here. The mythical judgments often cited as precedents in the texts presupposed knowledge of the old tales and saga cycles,[81] while, in disputes over boundaries and land titles, it was customary in the later middle ages to invoke the evidence of professional historians as expert witnesses.[82]

There was also, however, a theoretical basis for this liberal education. On the one hand, both the Old Irish text and the later commentary of the tract *Uraicecht Becc* state that the honour-prices and privileges associated with the various arts and crafts accumulate for a man of more than one skill, to endow him with a higher status in law. 'Who has one art, let him have one *díre*; he who has many arts, let him have many *díres:* it increases nobility'.[83] In this context the commentary mentions an 'advocate whom judgment encounters' (*aigne frisnindli breth*), who was also a *dos*, or poet of the third grade, and whose honour-price was raised in consequence from nine to twelve cows.[84] Within the legal profession itself, the same commentary indicates that the learning of the junior 'fettering advocates' might be limited to the law tracts themselves, such as the *Cetharslicht Athgabála* or the *Bretha Déin Chécht*, but the 'court advocate' was required to be flush with knowledge of both customary law and poetry—in so far as it touched law—and was equated with the Old Irish *breithem berla feni ⁊ filidiacta* (judge both in matters concerning the laity and the poets), while the senior 'advocate whom judgment encounters' was equated by the commentarist with the Old Irish *breithem tri mberla* (judge of three speeches—law, poetry and [Latin] learning).[85]

We have seen that the evidence of post-Norman verse compositions and annals substantiates the existence in later times of the 'poet-lawyer' as outlined above, but since this threefold hierarchy of advocates is already to be found in ninth-century glosses to the *Senchus Már*,[86] and since the commentary which

80. B. Ó Cuív, 'The linguistic training of the medieval Irish poet' in *Celtica*, x (1973), 114.

81. E.g. *CIH*, ii 406–7; *Anc. laws Ire.*, i, 250–5.

82. *CIH*, i, 50.24, 190.16, v, 1622.2–6, vi, 1961.3(?).

83. *Anc. laws Ire.*, v, 109 (*CIH*, vi, 2333.30–2).

84. *CIH*, vi, 2328.28–34; *Anc. laws Ire.*, v, 93.

85. *CIH*, vi, 2330–1; *Anc. laws Ire.*, v, 99, 101. For the various grades of judge and advocate in the Old Irish period see L. Breatnach above, pp. 7–13.

86. See L. Breatnach above, p. 10.

accompanies the text of *Uraicecht Becc* may date in whole or in part to as early as the eleventh century,[87] it must remain open to question whether the *ollamhain* and the most senior advocates educated in the secular law-schools of later medieval Ireland were still 'judges of three languages', knowing Latin and using canon and civil law texts as well as the Irish tracts on customary law.

From the twelfth century onwards,[88] Irishmen who wished to study civil and canon law or medical science to the highest level could travel abroad to obtain degrees as bachelors, masters or doctors at the various universities of medieval Europe. In the society of Gaelic, as opposed to Anglo-Norman, Ireland, this university-style learning normally became hereditary in certain families, at first those associated with church reform, but, as time went on, Latin scholars seem to have made no attempt to practise the celibacy the canon law preached,[89] and they became less sharply distinguished from the home-educated practitioners of poetry, history and law.

The first dynasty of Latin scholars noted by the post-Norman annalists was the Uí Ghibealláin. In the early thirteenth century two of their number were monks in the Premonstratensian house of Trinity Island, Lough Key, while in the next generation Florentius O Gibealláin (d. 1287) was archdeacon of Elphin, 'a philosopher of wisdom and knowledge and discernment and divinity'.[90] Then, in 1328, we hear of Maurice O Gibealláin 'chief master of Ireland in law both old and new, civil and canon, a learned and erudite philosopher, accomplished in poetry and Ogham lore (*sai ndana ⁊ n-ogmorachta*) and many other arts, a choral canon at Tuam and at Elphin and at Achonry and at Killala and at Annadown and at Clonfert, Official and general judge of the archdiocese [of Tuam]'.[91] The wording of this eulogy is somewhat ambiguous. Given Maurice's skill in bardic arts, it is conceivable that he was a master of *four* laws, the new common law and the old *fénechas* together with canon and civil law, but a

87. I am indebted to Liam Breatnach for this information.
88. See above, note 17, and F. Shaw, 'Irish medical men and philosophers' in B. Ó Cuív (ed.), *Seven centuries of Irish learning* (Dublin, 1961), p. 87.
89. See *AU*, ii, p. 564, iii, pp. 152, 162 (MacGiolla Coisgle); *AC*, 1413 (2) (Mac an Oglaigh), and below, note 103.
90. *AC*, 1234 (11), 1236 (20), 1287 (4).
91. *AC*, 1328 (13); H. F. Berry, 'Some remarks on a notice in *Revue Celtique* of Maurice O'Gibellan, a fourteenth-century canonist, in connexion with his knowledge of Ogham' in *RSAI Jn*, xxxii (1902), 158. On the term 'Official' see below, note 111.

more natural interpretation would be to understand the 'new law' as canon law, and the 'old law' as civil law. Belonging to the same period and category were Master Thomas O Naan, archdeacon and bishop-elect of Raphoe (d. 1306) and Trinity O Naan, 'a high master in many arts, in civil and canon law' (d. 1336).[92]

From non-annalistic sources we learn details about an inter-connected group of hereditary clerics in the province of Cashel, the Uí Ogáin coarbs of Ardcroney, Uí Ghráda coarbs of Tuam-graney and the Uí Chormacáin and Mhic Chearbhaill who supplied respectively three bishops to Killaloe and four archbishops to Cashel during the thirteenth and fourteenth centuries. Not only did members of these families obtain degrees in canon law (from Oxford, in those cases where a university is named),[93] but they appear to have shared a hostility towards brehon law.

In 1280, David MacCearbhaill, archbishop of Cashel, Matthew O hOgáin, bishop of Killaloe and David O'Cusby (?), bishop of Emly, offered King Edward I the sum of ten thousand marks in the name of all the Irish of Ireland:

In order to put an end to the evil law and the disaffection which is in the land of Ireland concerning the Irish tongue, to maintain the law of God and to serve our lord the king and his heirs loyally for ever . . . in order to have the common law which the English have and use in Ireland and to be treated as such Englishmen are treated, alive or dead, in body and in real and personal property . . . Moreover, the aforesaid prelates guaran-tee . . . that they will expel from the church all the Irish who will not receive and hold this law . . . and they will interdict their lands and suspend and deprive of their benefices all chaplains who sing mass for them, except the prelates and friars preachers and minors and others who will preach to them to hold the same law.[94]

When, in the course of the negotiations that ensued from this pro-posal to extend English law to the native Irish, the king stated that 'the laws which the Irish use are detestable to God and so contrary to all laws that they ought not to be called laws', he may have been echoing the words of Archbishop MacCearbhaill's petitions.[95]

92. *AC*, 1306 (5), 1336 (11).
93. Watt, *The church and the two nations in medieval Ireland*, p. 211 n. 3; idem. 'Gaelic polity and cultural identity', in *A new history of Ireland, ii*, pp. 336–8; Gwynn and Gleeson, *A history of the diocese of Killaloe*, i, 315–6, 369–70.
94. J. Otway-Ruthven, 'The request of the Irish for English law', in *IHS*, vi (1949), 269; see A. Gwynn, 'Edward I and the proposed purchase of English law for the Irish', in *R Hist Soc Trans*, x (1960), 111.
95. A. J. Otway-Ruthven, *A history of medieval Ireland* (London, 1968), p. 189.

The proposal to extend English law came to nothing, probably frustrated by the opposition of the Anglo-Irish parliament, but in 1366 three Gaelic-Irish prelates attended the parliament summoned by Prince Lionel of Clarence which passed the Statutes of Kilkenny, ordering *inter alia* clerics holding benefices among the colonists to use the English language, forbidding the admission of native Irishmen to cathedrals, collegiate churches or monasteries in Anglo-Irish areas, and outlawing the use of march or brehon law by the king's subjects. These three men were Thomas MacCearbhaill, archbishop of Cashel, Thomas O Cormacáin, bishop of Killaloe, and Eoin O Gráda, archbishop of Tuam, representing in a later generation the same nexus of clerical interests as those who petitioned for common law in 1277–80.[96]

The period in question, from the late thirteenth to the mid-fourteenth century, and the pressure group involved, an anglicizing party among the Gaelic-Irish clergy, even their location in the province of Cashel, coincide strikingly with the circumstances surrounding the attempt to impose an ecclesiastical ban on bardic poets noted earlier,[97] so that it is possible to argue that the 1277–80 incident represents not merely a movement in favour of common law, with the equality of protection and security of land tenure this offered, but a movement against brehon law, in a logical continuation of the twelfth-century reform.[98]

However, this clerical antipathy to bards and brehons collapsed after the mid-fourteenth century. Gaelic-Irish prelates who wished to form an alliance with the English administration in Ireland received little encouragement in the years following the enactment of the Statutes of Kilkenny. 'Pure Irish' scholars attending Oxford or other schools in England or the English area of Ireland were suspected as enemy spies,[99] clerical proctors entitled to take their seats in the Anglo-Irish parliament were excluded on the same grounds,[100] and the see of Armagh was monopolised by men of English blood after the death of Primate David MacOireachtaigh

---

96. Watt, *The church and the two nations*, pp. 210–11.

97. See above, notes 15 and 16. The poem cited there was addressed to King Diarmaid O Briain of Thomond, while allusions to the controversy occur in two further bardic poems by the Munster bard, Gofraidh Fionn O Dálaigh (Bergin, *Irish bardic poetry*, no. 16; E. Knott, 'Filidh Eireann go haointeach' in *Ériu*, v (1911), 50).

98. Otway-Ruthven, *A history of medieval Ireland*, p. 189.

99. *Documents on the affairs of Ireland*, ed. G.O. Sayles (Dublin, 1979), p. 225.

100. H. J. Lawlor, 'A calendar of the register of Archbishop Fleming' in *RIA Proc*, xxx (1912–13), sect. c, 130, no. 119.

in 1346.[101] A rather different style of canonist is represented by Bishop John O Corcráin, Benedictine monk and doctor of decretals of the monastery of St James Würzburg, who succeeded to the diocese of Clogher in 1370.[102] His son, Thomas O Corcráin, who died in 1385, is described as a public notary by imperial authority, an alien qualification subject to official disapproval in England since 1320.[103] In subsequent generations, besides Master Feidhlimidh O Corcráin, 'a cleric eminent in canon [law] and in versifying and in grammar',[104] the family produced two expert harpists and the bardic praise-poet Brian O Corcráin, author of the prose romance, *Eachtra Mhacaoimh-an-Iolair.*[105]

The title 'master' may not always guarantee that its owner had graduated in some foreign university, since it seems clear that hereditary Latin scholars taught university subjects in local schools, just as the hereditary physicians did. In 1384, we hear of Master John MacGiolla Choisgle, 'erenagh and parson of Airech-Brosga [in Fermanagh], an approved lecturer of both laws and especially of the canon law',[106] and, in 1416, of Thomas Mac-an-Oglaigh, 'erenagh of Killery [Co. Sligo] and chief master of law in Connacht'.[107]

Richard Stanihurst, writing in 1577, apparently referred to these local schools of civil and canon law when he remarked of the wild Irish:

Without eyther preceptes or obseruation of congruitie, they speake Latin lyke a vulgar language, learned in their common schooles of leachecraft and lawe, whereat they begin children and hold on 16 or 20 yeres, connyng by rote the Aphorismes of Hypocrates, and the ciuill institutes, with a fewe other paringes of those faculties. In their schooles, they groouel vpon couches of straw, their bookes at their noses, themselues lye flat prostrate, & so they chaunt out with a lowd voyce their lessons by peecemeale, repeating two or three wordes 30 or 40 tymes together.[108]

101. Above, note 13; see K. Simms, 'The archbishops of Armagh and the O'Neills 1347–1471' in *IHS*, xix (1974), 38.

102. A. Theiner (ed.), *Vetera monumenta Hibernorum et Scotorum* (Rome, 1864), p. 349.

103. *AU*, 1385; E. R. O'Connor, *The Irish notary* (Oxford, 1987), pp. 6–7.

104. *AU, AFM*, 1522.

105. *AU*, 1433, 1496; O. Bergin, *Irish bardic poetry*, p. 63.

106. *AU.*

107. *AC*, 1416 (8); and see note 89 above.

108. *Holinshed's Irish chronicle 1577*, ed. L. Miller and E. Power (Dublin, 1979), p. 114.

When going on to speak of the brehons, he distinguishes them clearly from the above:

Other lawyers they haue lyable to certaine families, which after the custome of the countrey determine & judge causes . . . The breighon (so they call this kinde of lawyer) sitteth on a banke, the lordes and gentlemen at variance round about him, and then they proceede.[109]

There was nothing to prevent a student of brehon law attending one of the Latin schools, especially since many members of brehon families entered the church. The genealogies of Clann Aodhagáin mention that the eminent Giolla na Naomh mac Duinnshléibhe Mhic Aodhagáin (d. 1309) had a son Fiachra who became dean of Clonfert, that the *ardollamh féineachais* Saorbhreathach mac Siomóin also had a son who was a dean, and *c.*1400 the family boasted two priors, of Roscommon and Rindown, besides a Domhnall *cléireach* and an Aodh *cléireach*.[110] In December 1390, the annals record the murder of Seán 'the Official' MacAodhagáin, a title signifying the officer who presided over church courts as representative of the bishop of the diocese, a function hardly to be performed without a knowledge of canon law.[111]

Against this social and educational background, it is not surprising to find that some of the brehon law commentarists of the later middle ages did have a knowledge of canon law. Liam Breatnach has identified many sources of scattered Latin quotations in the corpus of the vernacular law tracts, some of these occurring in the Old Irish texts themselves and many drawing on the Bible and the *Collectio canonum Hibernensis* of the early Christian period, but the commentaries also contain citations from later canon law, particularly the Sext, Liber V, tit. xii (*De regulis juris*), promulgated in 1289.[112] These Latin tags are used to clarify and resolve problems arising in the application of secular law, the brehon commentarists appealing to their authority side by side with citations from the Old Irish law tracts,[113] apparently ascribing equal validity to each body of teaching as a guide to just

---

109. Ibid., pp. 114–15.
110. Ní Maol-Chróin, 'Geinealaigh' (above, note 43), pp. 138–9; Hadcock and Gwynn, *Medieval religious houses: Ireland*, p. 215.
111. *AC*, 1390 (12); A. Gwynn, *The medieval province of Armagh 1470–1545* (Dundalk, 1946), pp. 84–5, 95–7.
112. D. Ó Corráin, L. Breatnach and A. Breen, 'The laws of the Irish' in *Peritia*, iii (1984), 437 n.1; D. A. Binchy, '"De fontibus iuris Romani"' in *Celtica*, xv (1983), 13 n.1.
113. Ó Corráin, Breatnach and Breen, 'The laws of the Irish', 437 para. ii.

judgments in later medieval Ireland. Canon law was useful as a familiar source for maxims ultimately derived from the less familiar corpus of civil law.[114]

This willingness to use thirteenth and fourteenth-century canon law to remodel what is sometimes thought of as the sacrosanct and immemorial corpus of traditional Irish custom (*féineachas*) was quite compatible with the Old Irish system of 'three judgments', and with the assertion at the beginning of *Uraicecht Becc*: 'The judgment of a lord, however, it is based on them all, on maxims and precedents and scriptural citations.'[115] According to the writers of the Old Irish tracts, those pre-Christian customs of the Irish people which had been accepted by Patrick and handed on to later generations were based on natural law (*recht aicnid*), that is, on God's moral order as intuitively perceived by 'just men' before the Faith.[116] This view is maintained in the later commentaries,[117] crediting native Irish custom with an underlying universality which meant it could be usefully discussed and analysed in terms of the *ius commune*, the internationally accepted standards of civil and canon law.

The practical consequences of this approach appeared when in the later fifteenth century we find two of the most powerful Gaelic chieftains employing canon lawyers rather than hereditary brehons as the 'lord's judge' in secular matters. Canon Arthur MacCathmhaoil, of the Armagh cathedral chapter, was judge to Henry O Néill, captain of his nation and prince of the Irish of Ulster 1455–83, while Feidhlimidh MagUinseannáin (d. 1507) was judge to O Domhnaill and also Official, or presiding officer, of the ecclesiastical court of Raphoe diocese.[118] The potential advantage for a secular chief in employing a man with this training is suggested in 1537 when the jurors of the city of Waterford complained that Edmund Butler, archbishop of Cashel, 'hath

114. Binchy, '"De fontibus"', 13.

115. K. McCone, 'Dubthach maccu Lugair and a matter of life and death in the pseudo-historical prologue to the *Senchas Már*' in *Peritia*, v (1986), 12; Ó Corráin, Breatnach and Breen, 'The laws of the Irish', 386–7.

116. McCone, 'Dubthach maccu Lugair', pp. 10–12.

117. *CIH*, i, 240.26, 241.17; *Anc. laws Ire.*, v, 481, 483.

118. K. Simms, 'The concordat between Primate John Mey and Henry O'Neill (1455)' in *Archiv Hib*, xxxiv (1976–7), 73, 78–9; *AU*, 1507. A kinsman of Feidhlimidh, Brian son of Tadhg Mag Uinseannáin, was Official of Clogher diocese (*AFM*, 1509). He is possibly to be identified with the Barnardus McGincenane sentenced to be unfrocked *c.*1470 for forging a letter in the name of Prince Henry O Néill (Belfast PRONI, Register of Primate Octavian, vol. i, f. 18b (p. 36)).

retayned one called Dyrmond Doff for his officiall and counsaillor or commissary which entertayneth the kyngs people by colour of canon lawe that there can be no more extorcyon committed by any Irish brehowne'.[119]

Canon law was not, of course, the only external model to exercise an influence on later medieval brehons. If Irish customs were understood as local expressions of a universal moral order, it seems the precepts of English common law could also be legitimately drawn upon as a source of universally applicable principles. About the year 1300, within a generation of Edward I's pronouncement that Irish customs were 'so contrary to all laws that they ought not to be called laws',[120] the multi-talented Giolla na Naomh mac Duinnshléibhe Mhic Aodhagáin wrote a brief treatise which purported to be simply an adaptation of difficult Old Irish law tracts into a more modern Irish idiom, but was in fact a handbook of contemporary Irish custom, showing some important borrowings from English institutions.[121] By the close of the middle ages the brehons' indebtedness to English common law went beyond simple imitation. In disputes over land titles it became necessary to accommodate within the system claims based on common law charters granted to Irishmen by their Anglo-Irish lords, and to weigh their validity against counter-claims based on Irish customary 'laws of gavelkind', past mortgages and so forth.[122] The brehon charters of the sixteenth century are riddled with terms and concepts borrowed from common law, as 'heirs and assigns', 'livery of seisin', 'feoffment' and 'reversion'.[123] Criminal law could hardly escape the same influence. The Anglo-Irish lords of the southern and eastern counties of Ireland in the late fifteenth and early sixteenth centuries used Irish brehons to try criminal cases involving not only native Irish tenants but the 'king's subjects' in their areas.[124] In the case of Garret Og, ninth earl of Kildare, it was alleged 'he used two lawes, our prince's lawes and brehens lawes, which he thought most beneficiall, as the case did require . . . And every commandement or proclamacion that he caused to be made it was taken for a lawe'.[125] It is

119. Hore and Graves, *Social state of the southern and eastern counties*, p. 203.
120. Above, note 95.
121. MacNiocaill, 'The interaction of laws' (above, note 43), pp. 105–9.
122. E.g. *CIH*, v, 1622. 10–18.
123. MacNiocaill, 'The interaction of laws', p. 115.
124. Curtis, *Ormond Deeds*, iii, 49–50; Hore and Graves, *Social state of the southern and eastern counties*, pp. 186, 189, 192, 199, 201–2, 204, 245.
125. Hore and Graves, op. cit., p. 162.

hardly surprising, then, to find an English lawyer and administrator of the early seventeenth century stating that the brehons,
when they gave judgment, were 'assisted by certen sgollers whoe
had learned manie and civill rules of the common lawe rather by
tradicion then by readinge'.[126] The Great O Néill, Shane the
Proud (d. 1567), employed as his judge one William Fleming,[127]
who may perhaps have been a common law scholar of this sort.

The occasional appearance of non-hereditary judges in the
service of Irish chieftains at this time points to a growing
distinction between the ollamh, or master teacher of a law school
and the practising 'lord's judge', a distinction reflecting that
between the *doctor legum* of the universities and the royal judges
on the continent of Europe. Conversely, the existence of separate
Latin schools of canon and civil law in Gaelic Ireland and the
presence of independent specialists in common law argues for the
purity of the *féineachas* tradition in the brehons' schools, as
opposed to the hybrid conglomeration of old custom, recent
borrowings, local proclamations and march law which the judges
had to administer in practice.

Even in the Old Irish period the law tracts emphasize that their
own *fénechus* teaching is only one strand in the body of law
enforced in practice.[128] *Cairde*, the treaties regulating relations
between the subjects of two or more neighbouring *tuatha*, were a
kind of forerunner of the later medieval march law, while *cána*
were royal or ecclesiastical proclamations. The king enforced
obedience to these by distraining offenders' chattels after a three
days' delay (*athgabáil treise*) 'for ignoring thy *cáin*, for ignoring thy
cairde'.[129] In the post-Norman period Giolla na Naomh mac
Duinnshléibhe Mhic Aodhagáin (d. 1309) warned the rising law-
student to distinguish between custom and enactments: 'Customary law, treaty and statute—(deserving) greatest deference from
us—do not confuse them with each other in obscurity, extract
only the winning judgment.'[130]

This longstanding and fundamental distinction between
customary law as taught in the schools and analysed in their textbooks, and the body of customs, ordinances and regulations

126. San Marino, California, Huntington Library MS. 7042, p. 11. I owe this
    reference to the kindness of Robert Hunter, of the New University of
    Ulster.
127. *Cal. S. P. Ire., 1509–73*, p. 229.
128. *Críth Gablach*, ed. D. A. Binchy (Dublin, 1941), pp. 20–1, 104.
129. D. A. Binchy, 'Distraint in Irish law' in *Celtica*, x (1973), 40.
130. See above, note 69.

administered by a brehon in a particular territory at a particular time, reduces the contrast for us between the early Christian lawyers and the brehons of the later middle ages. It seems hardly fair to accuse the latter of having 'carried conservatism to unheard of lengths'[131] because they collected and preserved the earliest available written accounts of Irish customary law and studied them by means of glosses and commentary, as was the practice of civilians and canonists in law schools and universities throughout Western Europe at that time. If there was a decline in intellectual standards after the twelfth century, it came about through the separation of ecclesiastical and secular learning consequent on the Gregorian reform of the church. Elsewhere in Western Europe the narrowness of church schools led to the foundation of universities as independent corporations, but medieval Ireland never developed a university. Realistically then, the most prestigious law schools of MagFhlannchadha and MacAodhagáin were only equipped to educate judges of 'two speeches' or 'two judgments', poetry and customary law, though some brehon commentarists seem to have been acquainted with *léigheann* or Latin learning 'insofar as it relates to *fénechus*'.[132] Stanihurst's reference to Irish brehons as 'very unskilled in civil and canon law'[133] presupposes a partial knowledge of this kind.

Within Gaelic Ireland the secular schools of the brehons, historians, poets and physicians easily maintained a reputation for learning at least equal to that of the rural Latin schools. For the most prestigious centres of each profession, *filidheacht*, the study of Irish literature, language and metrics, provided a common basic curriculum,[134] equivalent to the Latin *trivium* and *quadrivium* of the universities. This appears to have operated as an effective

131. D. A. Binchy, 'Lawyers and chroniclers' in B. Ó Cuív (ed.), *Seven centuries of Irish learning* (Dublin, 1961), p. 60.
132. *CIH*, v, 1612, vi, 2329; *Anc. laws Ire.*, v, pp. 92–3. See above, notes 112 and 113.
133. R. Stanihurst, *De rebus in Hibernia gestis* (Antwerp, 1584), p. 37.
134. For the cultivation of *filidheacht* as opposed to *dán* by the praise-poets themselves, see *AC*, 1315 (22), *AU*, 1349, 1350, *AFM*, 1507; for the study of *dán*, *seanchas* and *filidheacht* see *AU*, 1528, *AFM*, 1602; for *seanchas* and *filidheacht* see *AC*, 1301 (4), 1310 (2), 1385 (15), 1468 (11), 1482 (3), 1506 (3), 1543 (9), *ALC*, 1495, *AU*, 1520, *AFM*, 1347, 1492, 1565; for *féineachas* and *filidheacht* see *AFM* 1436, 1483, 1575, *ALC*, 1529 (above, notes 73 and 74). That *filidheacht* might be studied in schools of leechcraft can only be inferred from occasional poems by members of medical families. A late thirteenth-century genealogical poem on the ruling families of Breifne in RIA MS. 471, ff. 1–5, claims part authorship by Giolla Bearaigh, *saoi leighis* or 'sage in leechcraft'.

mental discipline, involving analysis and criticism as well as memory work[135] and encouraging precision of language. The modern reader of bardic poetry or brehon commentaries is conscious of encountering an educated mind, if not always an original thinker.

Because the brehons' studies were pursued in the vernacular, they were more accessible to laymen than the legal science of the universities. In the late sixteenth century Richard Stanihurst remarked of the Irish gentry that 'the tyme they have to spare from spoyling and preding, they lightly bestow in parling about such matters',[136] while Edmund Spenser admitted it was not easy to get the better of Irishmen in disputes over legal titles to property: 'they are for the most part so cautelous and wily headed, especially being men of so small experience and practice in law matters, that you would wonder whence they borrow such subleties and sly shifts'.[137] In 1607, the freeholders of Fermanagh and Cavan were to show themselves very alive to the dangers of having their titles wrongly defined by Sir John Davies.[138]

A fortiori, the brehons themselves were as well equipped as any members of Gaelic society to adapt to the changes brought about by the Tudor reconquest. In 1591 the brehon Patrick MacAodhagáin of Carrickbeg, Co. Longford, was appointed by the crown seneschal of Carrickbeg, with licence 'to prosecute and punish by all means malefactors, rebels, vagabonds, rymors, Irish harpers, idlemen and women, and other unprofitable members'.[139] In 1575, Aodh son of Baothghalach MagFhlannchadha, 'professor of the feineachas and of poetry', appears to be described as a wine merchant also in his obit.[140] His son Baothghalach, 'a man fluent in the Latin, Irish and English languages', was elected as one of the two knights of the shire for Co. Clare in the Anglo-Irish parliament of 1585.[141] There were limits, however, to what could be achieved by adaptability alone. King James I's proclamation of

135. Bergin, *Irish bardic poetry*, nos. 42 vv. 7, 11; 48 vv. 5–12.

136. *Holinshed's Irish chronicle*, ed. Miller & Power, p. 115.

137. *A view of the present state of Ireland, by Edmund Spenser*, ed. W. L. Renwick (Oxford, 1970), p. 23.

138. H. Morley (ed.), *Ireland under Elizabeth and James I* (London, 1890), pp. 348, 375–6, 386–7.

139. *Fiants Ire., Eliz.*, nos. 5528, 6658.

140. *AFM*, 1575. The phrase 'a purchaser of wine' (*ceannaighe fiona*) could perhaps be interpreted as a complimentary allusion to his habits of hospitality, but it would be an unusual application of the term.

141. *AFM*, 1585, 1598.

common law throughout Ireland in 1605 ended the brehons'
profession, and subsequent confiscations and plantations were to
deprive many of them of their lands.[142] Their age has passed away,
but left us with imposing monuments in the wealth of medieval
and early modern paper and vellum manuscripts with their texts,
glosses, commentaries and lexicons of Irish customary law.

142. E.g. T. D. Costello, 'The ancient law school of Park, Co. Galway' in
    Galway Arch Soc Jn, xix (1940–41), 98–9.

The king's serjeant at law in Tudor Ireland, 1485-1603

A. R. HART

THE OFFICE OF THE KING'S (or queen's) serjeant at law in Ireland had its origin in the need of the king, as lord of Ireland, to retain a pleader to represent his interests in the royal courts, and from about 1265 when Roger Owen was retained to act on the king's behalf,[1] it was usual for one or more 'narratores' or pleaders to be retained, variously styled 'serviens domini regis' as in Owen's case or 'servientes narratores nostri' as in the cases of Hugh Brown and William Petyt in 1343.[2] By the late fourteenth century the king's serjeant had emerged as a recognised legal office although there were generally at least two at a time, and indeed additional appointments were made as circumstances demanded, usually because the disturbed condition of various parts of the lordship and the difficulties experienced in travelling made it necessary. Thus in 1380 Walter Cottrell was appointed to act as 'narrator regis' in Munster and the counties of Kilkenny and Wexford 'by reason that John Tyrell could not attend his duty in these parts, on account of the dangers of the road etc., and his then being employed in the other parts of Leinster'.[3] Tyrell had been one of the king's serjeants since 1366 and Cottrell had also acted as king's serjeant in 1374 in Wexford and Waterford, and acted again in 1381 and 1385.[4]

That the duties of the king's serjeant expanded during the fourteenth century from being a pleader in court to an officer of state may be illustrated by comparing the description of his duties by Owen in a petition to Edward I in 1274 or 1275 when he said he

1. H. G. Richardson and G. O. Sayles, *The administration of Ireland 1172–1377* (Dublin, 1963), p. 40.
2. C. J. Smyth, *Chronicle of the law officers of Ireland* (London, 1839), p. 182.
3. Ibid., p. 183.
4. Ibid., p. 184.

was required 'to prosecute and defend the king's pleas in Ireland',[5] with Cottrell's patent a century later when he was 'to arrest or make stay of ships, take inquisitions and hold sessions'. In addition, with John Keppock, chief justice of the justiciar's court, and William de Karlell, baron of the exchequer, 'he was employed to inquire of hidden treasure in Co. Wexford for 14 days'.[6]

What one might call the regular king's serjeants such as Tyrell, as opposed to temporary appointments such as Cottrell, by this time had evolved from simple pleaders of the royal causes before the courts to principal law officers of the king; they were also established members of the council and, as such, were summoned to attend parliaments or great councils. Tyrell was summoned in 1375, 1378 and 1380, and in 1375 Richard Plunkett was also summoned, having been a king's serjeant since 1358, but Cottrell was not, presumably because his was only an ad hoc appointment.[7]

During the fifteenth century it would seem that only one king's serjeant was appointed at a time, and the king's serjeant was the junior member of, and the only law officer in, the inner council of seven ministers who were the ministerial advisors of the chief governor of the day.[8] In 1423, for example, Christopher Barnewall, described as the king's serjeant at law in Ireland, was one of seven ministers summoned to the meeting of the council held at Drogheda.[9] The burdensome nature of such attendance—parliaments or great councils were held regularly at this time—is evidenced by the granting to Barnewall upon the renewal of his patent in 1432, besides his customary annual fee of £10, of 'an additional sum of £5 as he was obliged to attend all parliaments and councils at his own expense, wheresoever they were held in Ireland'.[10]

Why by this period only one king's serjeant at a time was appointed cannot be stated with certainty, but the reason is probably a diminution in the volume of business with which the king's serjeant had to deal to such an extent that only one was needed: after the late fourteenth century the area of effective royal jurisdiction contracted until it was confined to the Pale and one

5. Richardson & Sayles, *Admin. Ire.*, p. 230.

6. Smyth, *Chronicle of the law officers of Ireland*, p. 184.

7. William Lynch, *A view of the legal institutions, honorary hereditary offices, and feudal baronies established in Ireland during the reign of Henry II* (London, 1830), pp. 321–33; H. G. Richardson and G. O. Sayles, *The Irish parliament in the middle ages* (Philadelphia, 1952), pp. 302–5.

8. Richardson & Sayles, *Ir. parl. in middle ages*, pp. 164–5.

9. Ibid., pp. 312–7.

10. Smyth, *Chronicle of the law officers of Ireland*, pp. 184–5.

or two outlying areas such as the ports of Wexford, Youghal, Cork, Kinsale, Limerick and Galway. Outside these areas lay the earldoms of Kildare, Butler and Desmond, covering in effect the rest of Leinster and Munster, in which there was little, if any, royal administration of justice, the earls enjoying virtually complete control over the administration of justice within their possessions.

By the beginning of the Tudor period, the king's serjeant had thus existed as an office for two centuries, and for the greater part of that time had been one of the leading officers of state, outranking the king's attorney (or attorney general, as he became known) who was also required to maintain and defend the king's pleas. The earlier part of the period covered by this study, between 1485 and 1532, is characterised by a scarcity of references to the king's serjeant in such contemporary documents as have survived, and as a result little is known of his precise functions at that time; indeed, it has not been possible to identify the holders of the office between 1487 and 1497 or between 1513 and 1532 as may be seen from the gaps in the succession list contained in Appendix I. For these years we are almost entirely dependent upon volume 1 of Ball's *The judges in Ireland, 1221–1921*. Unfortunately, although a good deal is known about those whom Ball identified as holding the office of king's serjeant at law, such information as is available largely relates to their careers after they were elevated to judicial or other senior offices. Moreover, as the fragmentary references in contemporary documents refer to the serjeants as members of the council, it is not until a later period that we can construct a more detailed, though still incomplete, picture of the functions of the king's serjeant. Yet, for all these difficulties, we would probably be justified in assuming that during this period the role of the serjeant was much as we know it to be in later years and as it had been before.

At the beginning of the reign of Henry VII in 1485, the Irish council and the administration of the medieval lordship were dominated by the justiciar, Gerald, eighth earl of Kildare, who had first been elected in 1478 by the seven members of the council following the unexpected death of his father and who remained chief governor for most of the period from 1479. The king's serjeant at law at that time was John Estrete who, together with the other six ministerial members of the council, had been assured tenure of his office for life by virtue of an act confirming the statute of Henry FitzEmpress passed by the Irish parliament at Kildare's instigation in 1485 to ensure that, in the event of a change of dynasty, Kildare, through the council, could ensure the continuity of his power.[11] Estrete clearly was a trusted adherent of

Kildare who dispatched him to London in 1486 to negotiate confirmation of Kildare's authority to govern Ireland on behalf of Henry VII.[12] Estrete appears to have remained king's serjeant until he was appointed deputy chief baron of the exchequer in 1487.[13] The next known appointment as king's serjeant is that of Thomas Kent in 1497. The parliament summoned by Sir Edward Poynings between December 1494 and April 1495 passed an act providing that the seven chief officers of state should no longer hold office for life but at pleasure, so we may assume that Kent was appointed upon that basis. A native of Drogheda, Kent had held the minor office of escheator of the exchequer since November 1495 and became chief baron in 1504.[14] Poynings' policy had been to appoint English-born officials and Kent's appointment accordingly marked its reversal: Kildare was by now lord deputy again, and had obtained from Henry VII the right to make all appointments except that of chancellor, a right generally reserved by the king in order to place a check on the power of the chief governor of the day.[15] Kent's background as a lawyer of Irish birth and his previous service in a lesser post before his elevation were typical of the serjeants throughout this period.

One of the most striking features in any study of the leading legal figures in Ireland during the Tudor period is the frequency with which the same Old English families appear as holders of legal or judicial office: John Barnewall, Kent's successor as serjeant, exemplifies this tradition of involvement in public affairs and royal service in the lordship. The great-grandson of the Christopher Barnewall mentioned earlier, John Barnewall was the son of Robert Barnewall, Lord Trimleston. He was a pleader at the Irish bar when he was appointed king's attorney in 1504 and, later in the same year, king's serjeant at law and solicitor general. In the course of a long public career, he was to become second justice in the king's bench, deputy treasurer, treasurer and, in 1534, chancellor,[16] in which year his nephew Patrick Barnewall became king's serjeant and solicitor general.[17]

11. Richardson & Sayles, *Ir. parl. in middle ages*, pp. 169, 330–1.

12. Ibid., p. 328.

13. F. E. Ball, *The judges in Ireland 1221–1921* (London, 1926), i, 187.

14. Ibid., p. 191.

15. S. G. Ellis, *Tudor Ireland: crown, community and the conflict of cultures 1470–1603* (London, 1985), p. 78.

16. Ball, *Judges*, i, 193.

17. Ibid., p. 204.

John Barnewall's tenure as king's serjeant was brief, being succeeded in the office by Clement Fitzleones in 1505, and he does not appear to have held further office until he became a justice of the king's bench in 1514. Fitzleones had acted as deputy chief baron in 1493 and as king's attorney in 1502.[18] It is not known whether Fitzleones continued to act as king's serjeant until 1509 when Patrick Finglas was appointed, nor whether Finglas in turn continued as serjeant until the appointment of Thomas Rochfort in 1511.[19] Finglas, like Barnewall, was to fill many judicial offices until his death in 1537. In common with many of the serjeants, Finglas was appointed soon after he embarked upon a legal career; he had entered Lincoln's Inn in 1503.[20]

Thomas Rochfort's appointment was unique during this period: he was a cleric, having become precentor of St Patrick's cathedral in 1502 and dean in 1506. He went on to become keeper of the rolls in 1513. Rochfort's clerical background was clearly not a handicap but merits some notice: although it was still common for the chancellor to be a cleric, it was by now unusual to find a cleric acting in the common law courts, something later evidence suggests that the king's serjeant was required to do. However, it is not known how many of the serjeants received their training in the common law during the early Tudor period. Of the six serjeants who can be named between 1485 and 1513, only two, Barnewall and Finglas, have identifiable common law backgrounds before their appointment—Barnewall as a narrator and Finglas at Lincoln's Inn.

From Rochfort's appointment as keeper of the rolls in 1513 until the appointment of Thomas Luttrell in 1532 the identity of the king's serjeant (or serjeants) is unknown, and all that can therefore be said about the period from 1485 until 1532 with any confidence is that such evidence as there is suggests that the king's serjeant was still the principal law officer and one of the leading members of the council which ruled the lordship under the chief governor of the day. The appointment of Thomas Luttrell as king's serjeant at law and solicitor general in September 1532 provides a convenient starting-point for the next part of this study because not only is it possible to identify all of the king's (or queen's) serjeants from that date onwards, but there is also a markedly greater volume of contemporary documentary evidence about the various functions which the king's serjeant performed. Especially is this so in the

18. Ibid., p. 188.
19. Ibid., p. 192.
20. Ibid., pp. 193–4.

period from 1532 to 1554 when there were three king's serjeants and one of the three, Patrick Barnewall, was, albeit briefly, a highly significant figure in one of the most important episodes in the Tudor period. As a result, a picture emerges which, although necessarily shadowy in some areas, is considerably more detailed than at any time since the fourteenth century.

Luttrell's appointment in September 1532 was directly due to the influence of Thomas Cromwell who marked him out for advancement, and in October 1534 Luttrell became chief justice of the common pleas (then called the common bench or common place), replacing Richard Delahide, a Geraldine supporter. However, during his period of office, which largely coincided with the final term of office as deputy of Gerald, ninth earl of Kildare, Luttrell was not a member of the council, a major departure from the practice which had continued for over one hundred and fifty years.[21] We do not know why this occurred but it may be that this was symptomatic of a focussing of attention upon the major offices, as happened in 1529 and 1530 when a secret council of three was entrusted with the powers of deputy in the absence of the lieutenant, the infant duke of Richmond who was the king's illegitimate son.[22]

Cromwell's close and continuing interest in Irish affairs resulted in his advancing to high legal office those whom he believed would further the policy of reform in Ireland upon which he had embarked. As part of this policy, he appointed Luttrell's brother-in-law, Patrick Barnewall, king's serjeant and solicitor general in 1534.

Barnewall, the nephew of John Barnewall himself a former king's serjeant who was now lord chancellor, had entered Gray's Inn in 1527.[23] When appointed, he was a pleader in the courts and, like other lawyers who reached high office at this time, his legal activities involved him with the affairs of leading magnates and monastic institutions. Together with his uncle, Barnewall was steward of seven estates in north Co. Dublin held by the English abbey of Kentsham,[24] and, in addition, he was the agent for the Irish estates of Sir Thomas Boleyn, earl of Wiltshire and father of the queen. That this involved him in what might today be called a

---

21. D. B. Quinn in Art Cosgrove (ed.), *A new history of Ireland*, ii (Oxford, 1987), p. 682.
22. Ellis, *Tudor Ireland*, p. 119.
23. Ball, *Judges*, i, 204.
24. Brendan Bradshaw, *The dissolution of the religious orders in Ireland under Henry VIII* (Cambridge, 1974), p. 53.

conflict of interest can be seen by his interceding with Wiltshire in April 1535, saying that many of Wiltshire's tenants alleged that they had supported Silken Thomas in the recent rebellion in order to protect their lives.[25] Although one might have expected a prominent royal official to be unsympathetic to those who had lent aid and comfort to a rebellious subject, Barnewall's action illustrated the dilemma all too frequently faced by royal officials in Ireland who had to combine loyalty to the king's policies which were formulated in England with their anxiety to alleviate the plight of their neighbours and those with whom they had business links. It may also be seen as a forerunner of his position in 1536 and 1537 during the so-called reformation parliament. Barnewall also acted on behalf of a number of monastic houses and in later years was granted several annuities secured on their revenues by these houses, some of which were clearly made in anticipation of their being suppressed but some of which may have been in recognition of past services; for example, in October 1537 the abbot of the Cistercian house of St Mary's, Dublin granted him an annuity secured on its revenues.[26] Barnewall was not alone in combining such activities as a steward or agent with his other duties; so did Thomas Luttrell and Robert Dillon, king's attorney between 1534 and 1555.[27]

As we have already seen, the first pleader retained by the king in the reign of Edward I was John Owen who was retained to 'prosecute and defend the king's pleas in Ireland', and this appears to have continued to be the role of the king's serjeant thereafter, judging by a letter which Barnewall wrote to Cromwell in April 1538. Between July 1537 and April 1538 four commissioners appointed by the king and led by Sir Anthony St Leger represented the king in Ireland and were engaged in a thorough investigation into all aspects of the Irish administration and they appear to have considered increasing the role of the king's attorney or attorney general at the expense of the king's serjeant, prompting Barnewall to write in the following terms:

Part of the commissioners was minded, amongst other things, to order that the king's attorney should maintain and confess pleas for the king; where that the king's serjeant, for the time being, has always used to

25. R. D. Edwards, 'The Irish Reformation Parliament of Henry VIII', *Historical Studies: VI*, ed. T. W. Moody (London, 1968), p.62.

26. Bradshaw, *The dissolution of the religious orders in Ireland*, p. 88.

27. Ibid., p. 53. Robert Dillon was attorney general 1534–55, second justice of the king's bench 1555–9 and chief justice of the common pleas 1559–80: Ball, *Judges*, i, 206.

maintain pleas, and confess the same, for the king's highness, as the case did require; as by the records thereof plainly may appear, for this two hundred years and more.[28]

Since the king's attorney had also maintained and defended the king's pleas since the first such appointments early in the four-teenth century,[29] it would seem that the commissioners may have contemplated the abolition of the office of king's serjeant, perhaps to save money or because the post appeared to be an anomaly or both. In any event, the details of this proposal are unknown and as the office of king's serjeant survived, Barnewall's plea appears to have been successful.

However, Barnewall had been less successful in 1536 and 1537 in defending his position which was challenged in several ways by Robert and Walter Cowley. Robert Cowley, aptly described as 'an ambitious mischief-making adherent of the Butlers',[30] and his son Walter had long been intimate with the earl of Ormond, were amongst Cromwell's most indefatigable Irish correspondents and were constantly intriguing to advance their fortunes, often at Barnewall's expense. In June 1535 Barnewall added the post of customer of customs for Dublin and Drogheda to his responsi-bilities but this no doubt lucrative post was quickly removed from him, Robert Cowley becoming customer of Dublin, and Walter of Drogheda, in December of the same year.[31] By August 1536 Barnewall clearly felt that his hold on the office of king's serjeant and solicitor general was threatened, to judge by the abject terms in which he wrote to Cromwell:

Till I may know your lordship's further pleasure I shall be contented that Master Cowley enjoy my office, and for no right he hath to the same, but only during your pleasure, which without fail I shall accom-plish in everything, to my power, during my life. If it shall be your pleasure that I may appoint such a person for the exercising of my office, as shall be well known here to be of more better learning and experience than I am, so that I may have licence to repair to my learning, I trust in God to do the king, in my office, the better service.[32]

28. *S. P. Hen. VIII*, ii, 510.

29. Richardson & Sayles, *Admin. Ire.*, p. 41.

30. Edwards, 'The Irish Reformation Parliament of Henry VIII', p.70.

31. *Patentee officers in Ireland, 1173–1826*, ed. J. L. J. Hughes (Dublin, 1960), pp. 7 and 33; Bradshaw, *The dissolution of the religious orders in Ireland*, p. 58.

32. *S. P. Hen. VIII*, ii, 359.

Nothing came of this move then, although, as we shall see later, a new post was created for Walter Cowley in 1537, and Barnewall remained king's serjeant and solicitor general. That Barnewall had to appeal to his patron illustrates the manner in which Cromwell and Henry VIII were now directly making and changing appointments in Ireland, whereas in the early years of Henry's reign, under the Kildare domination, such interest was spasmodic and irregular. The letter also shows that the king's serjeant's activities were not necessarily confined to the courts or the council chamber because Barnewall wrote from Limerick where he was in attendance upon Lord Deputy Grey who was campaigning at the time against the O'Briens and their supporters.

Barnewall was soon to emerge for a short time as a significant political figure, in part because he was the king's serjeant, playing a pivotal role in the activities of the reformation parliament which sat intermittently from May 1536 until December 1537 and during which highly contentious legislation was brought before the Irish parliament to reform the customs, raise taxes and suppress the monasteries. The royal proposals received a severe set-back at the hands of determined opponents, and Barnewall was alleged to be the leading spirit amongst the opposition. It is beyond the scope of this study to examine the history of this parliament in detail and the wider significance of Barnewall's actions. These have been fully considered elsewhere, notably by Dr Bradshaw in his books, *The Irish constitutional revolution of the sixteenth century* and *The dissolution of the religious orders in Ireland under Henry VIII*, but no survey of Barnewall's career as king's serjeant would be complete without some reference being made to these events.

We have already seen that Barnewall was closely involved with the financial affairs of Irish monastic institutions, links which would be threatened by the proposal to suppress the monasteries and take their possessions into royal hands. By the early sixteenth century the monasteries in Ireland, and in particular those within the Pale and the lordships of Kildare and Ormond, had in general fallen victim to a secular malaise which had resulted in the communities dwindling in size to a point where they often consisted of less than half a dozen members, if not completely derelict, and with little evidence of spiritual intensity. In addition, they possessed much more landed wealth than they were able to cope with, much of which had passed into the hands of the laity by various means such as alienations and leases.[33] The royal proposals thus threatened the interests of the Old English lawyers of the Pale

33. Bradshaw, *The dissolution of the religious orders in Ireland*, pp. 33–9.

who were intimately involved, both professionally and personally, in the existing state of affairs. Barnewall's position as serjeant and a leading representative of this class was clearly a difficult one since his private interests and connections were at variance with his role as a leading royal official. Certainly by October 1536 he and Robert Dillon, the king's attorney, had been selected by the Irish commons to go to London to place their objections to each of the royal proposals before the king. In doing so, Barnewall and Dillon were in a difficult, not to say dangerous, position at a time when opposition to the king's wishes might result in the opponent's death if opposition was pressed too far, particularly if Henry considered that his vital interests were threatened. We are solely dependent for a description of Barnewall's views at this moment upon a long letter written to Cromwell early in October 1536 by Robert Cowley, in which he characteristically sought to portray his rival's actions in the most unfavourable light. After referring to the opposition in the commons to the bills and the decision to send Barnewall and Dillon to England, he contended that they were

to persuade, and if they could, inveigle the king's council to defeat and reject the king's advantage and profit by feigned suggestions. Of which two, Patrick Barnewall, the king's serjeant, is one principal champion, who, and in effect of all his lineage of the Barnewalls, have been great doers and adherents, privy counsellors to the late earl of Kildare.[34]

Given that later in the letter Cowley asked that he might be granted the manor of Holmpatrick at a yearly fee if it were suppressed, a monastic property in north Co. Dublin where the Barnewalls' estates and interests were particularly concentrated, and given the rivalry concerning Patrick Barnewall's offices, it may be justifiable to treat Cowley's suggestions with some reserve, particularly the allegation that Barnewall was an intimate supporter of the Kildares. As we have already seen, both Patrick Barnewall and his uncle, the lord chancellor, had been advanced by Cromwell to their present offices in 1534, and although the lord chancellor's long official career started under the lord deputyship of the eighth earl, and the ninth earl appointed him treasurer in September 1524 shortly after the ninth earl was re-appointed lord deputy, a contemporary chronicler suggested that their relations were poor in 1520 to 1522.[35] However, Cromwell was prepared to rely upon

34. *S. P. Hen. VIII*, ii, 370–2.
35. *Cal. Carew MSS, 1515–74*, p. 191.

the lord chancellor who survived an allegation that during Silken Thomas' siege of Dublin in September 1534 he had tried to bribe the constable of Dublin castle to surrender the city to the rebels[36] and in 1536 he did much to prove his loyalty when, with Brabazon, the under-treasurer, he led an expedition which expelled the O'Connor from Offaly where he had been attacking Anglo-Irish settlements,[37] and, as we have already seen, in August of the same year Patrick Barnewall was with Lord Deputy Grey at Limerick when O'Brien's bridge was destroyed.

Nevertheless, in setting out on his journey to England at the end of 1536, Patrick Barnewall was embarking upon a very important, delicate and possibly dangerous mission as he might be seen not merely as an emissary but as a leading opponent of the king whose servant he was. Cowley, in the October letter quoted earlier, told Cromwell:

the said Patrick Barnewall, serjeant, who now repaireth thither, said openly in the commons house, that he would not grant that the king, as head of the church, had no large power as the bishop of Rome; and that the king's jurisdiction therein was but a spiritual power, to reform or amend the enormities and defaults in religious houses, but not to execute men's laws, nor to dissolve abbeys, or to alter the foundation of them to any temporal use.[38]

Whilst one might question whether he expressed his views quite so plainly, nevertheless Barnewall's appointment as one of the two emissaries is indicative of his sympathy, if not his support, for the opposition to these contentious measures. He and Dillon remained in England until well into 1537 and they succeeded in persuading Henry to abandon the plan to extract additional revenue and to grant a general pardon to those involved in the revolt of Silken Thomas. Their success may be seen by the grant (rarely given) of permission to purchase a grant of inheritance in monastic properties which they had leased at a discount of five years upon the price of twenty years purchase.[39]

However, despite the success of his mission to London, and the high regard in which he was held in Dublin—the under-treasurer, Brabazon, writing to Cromwell that 'such an earnest officer cannot here be spared'[40]—Barnewall's career received a set-back when he

36. Ellis, *Tudor Ireland*, p. 127.
37. *DNB*, i, 1180.
38. *S. P. Hen. VIII*, ii, 370–2.
39. *S. P. Hen. VIII*, iii, 298.
40. *L. & P. Hen. VIII*, xii(1), 470.

failed to become chief baron upon the death of Chief Baron
Finglas despite a recommendation to the effect by the lord deputy
and council in August 1537, the post going instead to Richard
Delahide who had been removed as chief justice of the common
pleas in 1534.[41] In September of 1537 his position as king's
serjeant and solicitor general was altered to some extent (though
not to his financial disadvantage) with the appointment for the
first time of a separate principal or chief solicitor in the person of
Walter Cowley. Upon his appointment as king's serjeant Barnewall, as had John Barnewall, Rochfort and Luttrell before him,
also became solicitor general. Appointment to both offices was
made by the same letters patent which provided that the holder
was to receive a single annual fee. Thus, on Luttrell's appointment, he received a salary of twenty marks a year to be paid
equally by the treasury and the sheriff of Drogheda, illustrating
the perennial difficulty which the royal administration faced in
securing funds, even to pay such a senior official.[42] Although
Cowley is generally referred to by writers on this period as being
the solicitor general, it is clear that the existing title of solicitor
general continued to be enjoyed by the king's serjeant and Cowley
was described as the principal or chief solicitor, being appointed
by a patent dated 7 September 1537 at an annual fee of £10.[43] As
the existing administration in Dublin was dependent upon a small
number of officials at this time, the creation of a separate post of
principal solicitor no doubt served a dual purpose of rewarding
Cowley and enabling the considerable administrative burden
involved in the projected dissolution of the monasteries to be
shared more widely. Despite the creation of the new post, Barnewall not only continued to be described in official documents as
'king's serjeant and solicitor general' until his appointment as
master of the rolls, but he also continued to be paid for the office,
probably in addition to his annual fee of twenty marks, since in
1542 a payment is noted 'to Patrick Barnewall, the other solicitor,
for his reward 4l'.[44]

Although he had been instrumental in persuading the king to
modify his plans to raise additional revenue etc., Barnewall did
not continue his opposition to the proposed suppression of the
monasteries, opposition which was ultimately confined to the

41. Bradshaw, *The dissolution of the religious orders in Ireland*, p. 185.
42. *Cal. pat. rolls Ire., Hen. VIII—Eliz.*, p. 5. Twenty marks = £13.6s. 8d.; one
    mark = 13s. 4d. The attorney general received £12 p.a.: ibid.
43. Smyth, *Chronicle of the law officers of Ireland*, p. 172.
44. *Cal. S. P. Ire., 1509–73*, p. 62.

spiritual lords in the upper house and the clerical proctors who still had a place in the house of commons. However, in September and October 1537 even this opposition collapsed and the proctors were henceforth excluded from parliament.[45] By this time the writing was clearly on the wall for the monasteries, the more far-sighted of which were doing what they could to ensure their future by rewarding those who had been linked to them in the past and who might be of assistance in the days to come, Barnewall himself being the recipient of such an annuity in October, granted by the Cistercian abbot of St Mary's, Dublin.[46]

Apart from the grant of a licence to himself and Dillon to purchase grants of inheritance in the monastic lands which they had leased, and obtaining annuities, Barnewall did not, contrary to what is generally inferred, immediately profit to any significant extent from the dissolution of the monasteries during the first phase of their suppression in 1537 and 1538.[47] Indeed, although he and another lawyer, Thomas Houth, had taken a lease for thirty-five years from the king of lands which had formerly belonged to the English priory of Cartemell, it was declared void, prompting Barnewall to write to Cromwell in April 1538 asking that the lease be confirmed.[48]

Fifteen thirty-nine to 1541 saw Barnewall playing a prominent part in the final phase of the suppression of the monasteries. The machinery created to carry out this policy involved the appointment of commissioners, who visited each institution in turn and received a formal surrender of the abbey, priory or convent from its members, together with all of its estates and possessions. The commissioners were accompanied by assessors who witnessed the surrenders and presumably ensured that the necessary legal formalities were complied with. Robert Cowley, by now master of the rolls, and Barnewall are frequently found acting as assessors, and in July 1539 Barnewall was present at the surrender of the Augustinian convent of St Brigid of Odder, Co. Meath, on the 16th, on the 25th at the much wealthier St Thomas Court near Dublin and on the 26th at the surrender of the Augustinian

45. Bradshaw, *The dissolution of the religious orders in Ireland*, p. 64.

46. Ibid., p. 89.

47. His name is not to be found in the list of beneficiaries of the distribution of properties which is set out in Bradshaw, *The dissolution of the religious orders in Ireland*, at pp. 233–5. In this respect, Barnewall is thus to be distinguished from several other officials of the period.

48. *S. P. Hen. VIII*, ii, 570; *L. & P. Hen. VIII*, xiii (1), 259; *Cal. S. P. Ire., 1509–73*, p. 9.

foundation of St John the Baptist at Naas, Co. Kildare.[49] Between October 1540 and January 1541, he is recorded as acting as assessor in surveys of various monastic properties,[50] and, ultimately in July 1541, he purchased the nunnery of Gracedieu, Co. Dublin. As can be seen from the details enrolled in the patent and close rolls, the properties held by the nunnery were scattered through six parishes in north Co. Dublin, and as well as land included mills at Portmarnock.[51]

Undoubtedly, Barnewall did very well out of his part in the dissolution of the monasteries, but as can be seen from the details in Appendix I of Bradshaw's *The dissolution of the religious orders in Ireland under Henry VIII*, so did other leading royal officials of the time, magnates such as the earls of Desmond and Thomond, merchants and gentry. Indeed, others such as his brother-in-law Thomas Luttrell, chief justice of the common pleas, and Thomas Cusack, master of the rolls, did as well, if not better, in obtaining leases and grants of valuable properties. It is certainly arguable that, whilst Barnewall in due course shared in the spoils, he did so primarily in 1541 and not as an immediate consequence of his mission to London in 1536–7.

Barnewall's prominence in the reformation parliament of 1536–7 may give a false impression of the importance of the office of king's serjeant at law at this time. There can be little doubt that his emergence as a spokesman for the opposition to the initial royal proposals was due to his position as a leading royal official and to his legal expertise. Nevertheless, Barnewall's political significance was short-lived and, with his return to Ireland in 1537, the office of king's serjeant resumed its familiar place in the Irish official hierarchy of the time: of lesser importance than the lord chancellor, the chief justices and chief baron, or even of the vice-treasurer and the master of the rolls, though clearly ranking above the other law officers of the day and so continuing to play a major role in both legal and political affairs. Unfortunately, the comparative wealth of contemporary material relating to Barnewall's activities as a royal official in the political and in the administrative or quasi-legal sphere is in sharp contrast to the scarcity of material about the functions of the king's serjeant in the purely legal sphere, a scarcity which only allows glimpses of his role in the law courts of the Pale.

49. *Cal. pat. rolls Ire., Hen. VIII—Eliz.*, pp. 134–5.
50. *Extents of Irish monastic possessions, 1540–1541*, ed. Newport B. White (Dublin, 1943), pp. 177 and 183.
51. *Cal. pat. rolls Ire., Hen. VIII—Eliz.*, pp. 73–4.

In 1538 Barnewall had asserted that it had been the function of the king's serjeant to maintain and confess the king's pleas, thereby inferring perhaps that this was solely the function of the king's serjeant, no doubt mainly before the king's bench, although if he was unavailable presumably the king's attorney would act in his place since the latter had also prosecuted and defended the king's affairs from the creation of that office.[52] A letter to Cromwell of November 1537 from one John Bolter, a goldsmith, suggests that Barnewall was also engaged in cases before the lord chancellor, though whether in his official capacity as king's serjeant or as a pleader or even perhaps as a litigant, is unknown. Bolter complained that he could have 'no furtherance in his causes before the lord chancellor, but is driven from term to term by the importunity of Patrick Barnewall, the king's serjeant'. Given Barnewall's involvement in affairs of state at this time, it is hardly surprising that he was unable to attend to his cases before the lord chancellor, although 'his consanguinity with the judges', as Bolter alleged, may well have helped him to have his cases delayed.[53]

Apart from his functions in the courts of law, it is clear that the king's serjeant was constantly called upon, as were the king's attorney and the principal solicitor, to assist in the resolution of matters which came before the king's council in its judicial role. As Richardson and Sayles have shown, in the fourteenth and fifteenth centuries the medieval Irish parliament constantly acted as a judicial forum for the resolution of disputes, the parties to which either could not or were unwilling to litigate through the courts of law.[54] During the Tudor period when parliaments were only summoned at infrequent intervals, the council assumed the judicial role formerly performed by parliament. The common procedure was for the council to appoint a number of commissioners who would investigate the matter, hear the parties, and examine witnesses and then report their conclusions to the council which would act accordingly. The general pattern was that two or three commissioners would be appointed, of whom at least one would be a judge of the common law courts and another would be one of the law officers, generally the king's serjeant, though occasionally the attorney or solicitor would be included. Two examples illustrate the type of dispute which came before the council at this time. In 1547 Lord Protector Somerset directed Sir Thomas Luttrell, chief justice of the common pleas,

52. Richardson & Sayles, *Admin. Ire.*, p. 41.
53. *Cal. S. P. Ire., 1509–73*, p. 34.
54. Richardson & Sayles, *Ir. parl. in middle ages*, pp. 216–17.

Walter Kerdiff, justice of the common pleas, and Barnewall to investigate a petition in which the widow of the earl of Clanrickard claimed a third of his estate. The commissioners were appointed under the great seal and required 'to hear and examine the petition of Piers Marten and wife, to call witnesses before them, and to determine some better decisions than heretofore has been pronounced', as the matter had already been referred to the lord deputy and council and the complainant 'could obtain no final order from them'.

The commissioners duly reported that as the earl's first wife was still alive when he married the petitioner, the later marriage was void, and so she was not entitled to one third of his estate. However, she was entitled to £300, being the amount of a bond entered into as part of the marriage settlement, together with various items of plate. That this decision took the form of a binding judgment may be inferred from the fact that it was enrolled as a decree, and the commissioners also provided that the widow was to be at liberty to seek to have the earl's first marriage annulled, in which case she should be entitled to one third of the earl's possessions and lands.[55] A similar form had been adopted in 1545 when it was decreed by Gerald Aylmer, chief justice of the king's bench, Thomas Houth and Walter Kerdiff, justices, and Barnewall in a suit between the portrieve and commons of Cashel 'that the corporation, their successors and assigns, should have and possess "the commons" and every part thereof, without let or interruption'.[56]

Barnewall's long tenure of the office of serjeant came to an end when he was appointed master of the rolls in 1550 in place of Sir Thomas Cusack who became chancellor. Barnewall's successor was one John Bathe, who was called to the bar at Lincoln's Inn in 1539 and had been the principal solicitor since 1546. From Co. Meath, he was related to James Bathe, chief baron, and was at one time recorder of Drogheda.[57] The importance attached by the king and his advisers to the major legal offices in Ireland may be gathered from the fact that these appointments were all communicated to the lord deputy and council by a letter from Edward VI, the terms of which make it clear that whilst the lord deputy had advised the appointments, the final say rested with the king in London and, as we have seen in the case of Patrick Barnewall in 1537, the recommendations from Dublin were not

55. *Cal. pat. rolls Ire., Hen. VIII—Eliz.*, pp. 170–1.
56. Ibid., p. 36.
57. Ball, *Judges*, i, 206; *Cal. pat. rolls Ire., Hen. VIII—Eliz.*, pp. 166–7.

always followed. Bathe was duly appointed serjeant at law and solicitor general, but by separate patents both dated 16 October, and whilst Barnewall had held both offices for life, Bathe's patents appointed him as serjeant at law for life but as solicitor general during pleasure,[58] no doubt because the separation of the offices of serjeant and solicitor general foreshadowed by the appointment of a principal solicitor was at least envisaged as a possibility. This indeed may have occurred in 1553 when Richard Finglas became solicitor general. That at least would appear to be the case as an undated patent appointing Finglas (who had been principal solicitor since 1550) solicitor general is included amongst the calendar of patent and close rolls for that year. However, Smyth in his *Chronicle of the law officers of Ireland* records that Bathe was continued in office as solicitor general by Mary by a patent dated 12 February 1554, Finglas also being continued as principal solicitor by a patent of the same date. From this it would appear that the undated patent has been incorrectly attributed to 1553 and that Bathe did in fact continue to enjoy both offices until his appointment as chief justice of the common pleas in 1554.[59] Bathe's successor, Richard Finglas, it would seem, also continued to hold the offices of serjeant and solicitor general until his death in 1574, having received a fresh patent as solicitor general in 1566 from Elizabeth,[60] although in contemporary documents it was customary to refer to him as simply the serjeant and the principal solicitor of the day as the solicitor or solicitor general.

During his tenure as serjeant, Bathe continued to act as his predecessors had, appearing occasionally as a member of judicial commissions, as a commissioner of gaol delivery and being named in the commission of the peace for Dublin. He appears to have impressed by his legal knowledge as well as by his diligence, discretion and loyalty.

Bathe's successor as serjeant and solicitor general, as previously noted, was Richard Finglas, principal solicitor since 1550, and who was destined to hold both offices until his death in 1574. Unlike Bathe, Finglas was appointed serjeant during good behaviour, a highly unusual stipulation at this time when even judges were appointed at pleasure, and this unusual provision is almost certainly the reason why his patent was not renewed upon the accession of Elizabeth, it being the custom to issue fresh patents to all such office-holders by a new sovereign.

58. Ibid., pp. 220–1.

59. Ibid., p. 313; Smyth, *Chronicle of the law officers of Ireland*, p. 173.

60. Hughes, *Patentee officers*, p. 49; but see T. W. Moody, F. X. Martin and F. J. Byrne (ed.), *A new history of Ireland, ix*, pp. 518 and 520 n. 11.

As mentioned earlier, it had long been part of the serjeant's duty to plead and defend the king's pleas. By the reign of Mary, the need to diligently attend to royal business before the queen's bench and common pleas was such that a blistering rebuke was administered to the Irish judges and law officers in 1556 by the queen herself. This was in words which illustrate both the financial benefits which were expected to accrue to the crown from the administration of justice as well as the failure of those addressed to administer justice impartially:

And where in times past, justice being ministered and executed, much profit, besides the common quiet of our realm, hath been made to the use of the crown by the seals and process of those courts, we now understand that of all escheats by forfeiture of recognizance, attainders, escapes, breach of peace, riots, unlawful assemblies, false verdicts, forfeitures upon penal statutes, false recoveries, fines, amerciaments, and such like, little profit or none hath accrued and been answered to us, the default whereof is to be chiefly ascribed to negligence of officers; our pleasure therefore is, that our said deputy and council shall command and diligently call upon our judges of either bench, our serjeant, attorney, solicitor, and other officers from henceforth to use good diligence in their several offices, not only in ministering justice to all men without respect indifferently, the lack whereof hath caused many mischiefs and disorders in that realm, but that also they shall most diligently see to our profit, and that we lose no duties, as we specially trust them; requiring our said deputy to declare unto them and every of them that we are not now ignorant of the ill husbandry in times past used in those courts, which we trust shall from henceforth be amended.[61]

That these defects were not confined to the queen's bench and common pleas was emphasized in the letter, equally trenchant criticism being directed at the failure of the exchequer to ensure that royal rents and revenues were collected. Indeed, at regular intervals throughout Elizabeth's reign complaints were made, frequently in the most forceful terms, about the inability of the Irish judges and law officers to perform their duties, and requests were frequently made that they be replaced by English lawyers. An example occurs in 1597, when, upon the death of Serjeant Corye, a request was made to Sir Robert Cecil that he

might consider some fit man from England to supply his place. This may greatly advantage the revenues and exchequer causes, which for want of good assistance, have hitherto grown to no small disorder and

61. *Cal. Carew MSS, 1515–74*, p. 254.

prejudice through her officers, among whom the solicitor only hath taken more care and pains than all the rest.[62]

On occasion law officers were appointed from England, such as Thomas Snagge who was appointed attorney general in 1578,

her majesty observing that the public service had not been a little hindered through the default and insufficiency of the officers in the law previously appointed; for redress whereof her majesty thought that a person well-chosen in England might be sent over to exercise the office of attorney general.[63]

Thus it would seem to be clear that the serjeant, together with the attorney and solicitor, was responsible for the conduct of all royal business before the superior common law courts, as well as representing the royal interest elsewhere as necessary, an obligation that led to Serjeant Finglas being granted an annuity of £10 Irish 'in recompense of his labour, diligence, and attendance had and to be had in the castle chamber before the privy council, from time to time, as often as should be requisite and fit...'.[64] As this was expressed to be at pleasure, it was presumably an additional payment over and above the normal emoluments which the serjeant could expect to receive.

Given the importance which the Tudors attached to the law and the constant warfare associated with the efforts made to extend effective royal control over the whole of Ireland throughout Elizabeth's reign, one might have expected that the law officers, and the serjeant in particular, would feature more prominently in official records as representing the royal interest, but that is not always the case. The explanation lies in a combination of several factors. The situation may be due in part to the reliance placed upon the judges to protect the royal interest in the manner that Mary clearly expected for instance in 1556. Or it may be due to the destruction of so many legal records which inevitably leads to a reliance upon contemporary documents which survived either because they were removed from Ireland by holders of high offices upon their return to England or were correspondence with English officials and which may not therefore convey a complete picture of the law and law officers in action. Yet another factor may be that as the Tudor era progressed, detailed control was

---

62. *Cal. S. P. Ire., 1596–7*, pp. 390–1.

63. *Cal. pat. rolls Ire., Eliz.*, p. 11.

64. Smyth, *Chronicle of the law officers of Ireland*, pp. 185–6.

exercised directly over Irish affairs from London, thereby reducing the importance of Irish officials other than the major officers of state.

One important occasion where we catch a glimpse of the serjeant in action occurred during Sir Henry Sidney's second term as lord deputy in 1577. This was in the course of the controversy over cess, when a petition or bill was brought before the lord deputy and council challenging the legality of impositions placed upon the inhabitants of the Pale, whereby they were required to provide and transport supplies for the soldiers at prices fixed by the government which were well below the market price. A substantial number of landowners complained, and as they were not prepared to accept the lord deputy's views, they petitioned to be allowed to go to London to press their case. But before they did so, Sidney referred the matter to the lord chancellor, Gerrard, who conducted a hearing at which the petitioners were represented by counsel. After they had been heard, because it was 'the queen's cause he called her majesty's serjeant (Fitzsimon) and attorney and willed them to consider of it, and the morrow after to say in maintenance of her majesty's prerogative what they could'.[65]

Fitzsimon had succeeded Finglas who died in 1574. Fitzsimon (or Fitzsymon) had been attorney general since 1570 and was to equal his predecessor's tenure of office, remaining serjeant for twenty years until his death in 1594. A native of Dublin, he entered the Inner Temple in 1555 and became justice of the liberty of Wexford in 1563.[66] Like his predecessors, he acted on occasion in a quasi-judicial or inquisitorial role, an instance occurring in 1584 when he was one of a number of commissioners inquiring as to all persons attainted in counties Dublin, Kildare, Meath, Westmeath, Louth, Waterford and Carlow, and all their possessions. Similarly, in 1588, he was one of several commissioners sitting at Sligo to ascertain what lands O'Connor Sligo held of the queen.[67]

In 1578, Fitzsimon was appointed to act as master of the rolls in place of Nicholas White. This is one of the earliest known occasions when the serjeant was called upon to perform a judicial office, a practice that became common from the seventeenth century until the office of serjeant ceased to exist in Ireland.

65. *Anal Hib*, no. 2 (1931), 132; Ellis, *Tudor Ireland*, pp. 272–3; N. P. Canny, *From reformation to restoration: Ireland, 1534–1660* (Dublin, 1987), pp. 94–7.

66. Ball, *Judges*, i, 219.

67. *Cal. pat. rolls Ire., Eliz.*, pp. 71 and 145.

Few examples have survived of the serjeant acting as a general legal advisor to the crown in the manner of law officers in later times. One of those that has involved Fitzsimon who, a few months after his appointment, was asked to give his opinion as to the adequacy of a commission concerning reformation of her majesty's customs at Chester, presumably because of the importance of Chester in the context of trade to and from Ireland. However, he declined to give his opinion because the bearer would not leave the commission until the next day and Fitzsimon could not give his opinion in such a short time.[68]

As we have seen in the case of Patrick Barnewall, the office of serjeant was one which enabled its holder to accumulate considerable wealth, and there is some evidence to suggest that other serjeants were also men of substance if the position of Christopher Fitzsimon was representative. The son of Serjeant Fitzsimon and a student at the Middle Temple, in December 1575 he wrote to Burghley asking that a warrant for the very substantial sum of £100 which had been sent to him by his father be paid,[69] although as Fitzsimon had only become serjeant the same year he had presumably acquired such means earlier in his career. Christopher Fitzsimon again appears in 1581 as a recusant, writing to his father from London that he had temporarily withdrawn from his studies in the Temple because

by virtue of a commission not only sent thither but also to all other houses of court and chancery for the trying and finding out of those that would not go to church and [receive communion] I separated myself from them, lest being unknown, by being called before them in examination I should be known.[70]

Like many other students from Old English Pale families in London at this time, the serjeants's son was obviously a conscientious roman catholic and, understandably in the climate of the time, not anxious that his religious beliefs should be discovered.

It has been established that the serjeant acted on behalf of the monarch in all the common law courts, defending or prosecuting cases involving the royal interest as required and in addition playing a leading part in the judicial role of the council and generally acting as a law officer of the crown. It is also plain that the serjeant at law was the senior law officer throughout the

68. *Cal. S. P. Ire., 1574–85*, p. 76.
69. Ibid., p. 87.
70. Ibid., p. 286.

Tudor period. He was a member of the council in the early Tudor period whilst the attorney was not, and his annual fee in mid-Tudor times was greater. In addition, where both are mentioned in the same document, the serjeant is almost invariably named first, and this pattern is so consistent that it clearly demonstrates that the serjeant was viewed then as the senior office: this is underlined by three of the serjeants in this period serving as attorney immediately before they became serjeant (John Barnewall, Fitzleones and Fitzsimon) whereas no serjeant became attorney afterwards. As will be apparent from the details in Appendix II, in the early Tudor period the office of serjeant was usually a stepping-stone to the bench as it was in later times, but in the half-century from the appointment of Serjeant Finglas in 1554 to the accession of James I in 1603 no serjeant achieved permanent judicial office. However, this was due in part at least to two factors. First of all, some of the judges showed considerable longevity and there were not a great many vacancies as a result. Secondly, Elizabeth's dissatisfaction with the quality of the Irish bench led her to appoint English judges or lawyers on many occasions when vacancies did occur.

There are some signs towards the end of the Tudor period that the serjeant at law was no longer in reality the predominant law officer in Ireland although he was to retain formal precedence over both the attorney general and the solicitor general until the office of prime serjeant (as it had become known) was abolished in 1805. This change (which may well only be apparent with hindsight) can perhaps best be illustrated by comparing the official salaries which the holders of the respective offices enjoyed. In 1606 Serjeant Kerdiff received £27 6s. 8d. p.a. whereas Sir Charles Calthorpe, the attorney general, and Sir John Davies, the solicitor general, each received £159 6s. 8d. p.a., compared with a salary of £133 6s. 8d. p.a. received by the puisne judges of the king's bench and common pleas and the barons of the exchequer.[71] That such salaries had been paid to the attorney general and the solicitor general for some years is apparent from the request in 1601 by Saxey, chief justice of Munster, that he might have the same fee as the attorney and solicitor, who each received a yearly fee of £200 as well as what they might make in practice.[72] However, this disparity in salaries is not the whole story as the serjeant was entitled to 'the accustomed fees and perquisites'[73]

71. *Cal. S. P. Ire., 1603–6*, pp. 429–30.

72. Ibid., p. 301.

73. *Cal. pat. rolls Ire., Eliz.*, p. 466: the patent of Serjeant Loftus in 1597.

which unfortunately cannot now be completely identified. One profitable area was wardship of minors: in 1538 Serjeant Barnewall mentioned in a letter to Thomas Cromwell that he had purchased a king's ward for £200, although the ward turned out to have only £18 in possession so it was not as profitable as he had anticipated.[74] It would appear that 'the accustomed fees' included the right to charge fees on the making of grants in the exchequer, a complaint being recorded in 1597 against the then solicitor general, Sir Roger Wilbraham, that 'he takes the making of all grants, both from the serjeant, attorney and remembrancer, who ought to have the making of them all'.[75] As such fees were the recognised method of remunerating judges and officials, we may be justified in assuming that the serjeant could be handsomely remunerated. Nevertheless, the disparity in the salaries is striking and the salaries paid to the attorney general and the solicitor general certainly emphasize the significance of these offices at the close of the Tudor era, an era which started with the king's serjeant at law firmly established as one of the oldest Irish legal offices as well as the senior Irish law officer. Whilst the status of the office of serjeant was eroded to some extent towards the end of the Tudor period, it nonetheless had survived a threat of extinction and, despite undergoing changes and a reduction in prestige and status in the future, was to survive until this century.

APPENDIX I

Succession list of the serjeants at law, 1478–1609

1478–87	John Estrete	1534–50	Patrick Barnewall
1497–1504 (?)	Thomas Kent	1550–4	John Bathe
1504–5	John Barnewall	1554–74	Richard Finglas
1505– ?	Clement Fitzleones	1574–94	Edward Fitzsimon
1509–11 (?)	Patrick Finglas	1594–7	Arthur Corye
1511–13 (?)	Thomas Rochfort	1597–1601	Edward Loftus
1532–4	Thomas Luttrell	1601–9	Nicholas Kerdiff

74. *S. P. Hen. VIII*, ii, pt. iii, 570–1.
75. *Cal. S. P. Ire., 1596–7*, p. 497.

APPENDIX II
Biographical notes *

JOHN ESTRETE	king's serjeant 1478; deputy chief baron 1487
THOMAS KENT	king's serjeant 1497; chief baron 1504–11
JOHN BARNEWALL	attorney general, king's serjeant and solicitor general 1504; second justice of the king's bench 1514; deputy treasurer 1522, treasurer 1524; chancellor 1534–8
CLEMENT FITZLEONES	deputy chief baron 1493; attorney general 1502; king's serjeant 1505
PATRICK FINGLAS	king's serjeant 1509; second justice of the common pleas 1519; chief baron 1520; chief justice of the king's bench 1534–5; chief baron 1535–7
THOMAS ROCHFORT	king's serjeant and solicitor general 1511; master of the rolls 1513–21
THOMAS LUTTRELL	king's serjeant and solicitor general 1532–4; chief justice of the common pleas 1534–54
PATRICK BARNEWALL	king's serjeant and solicitor general 1534–50; master of the rolls 1550–2
JOHN BATHE	recorder of Drogheda, principal solicitor 1545–50; king's serjeant and solicitor general 1550–4; chief justice of the common pleas 1554–9
RICHARD FINGLAS	principal solicitor 1550–4; king's (later queen's) serjeant and solicitor general 1554–74
EDWARD FITZSIMON	attorney general 1570–74; queen's serjeant 1574–94; deputy master of the rolls 1578
ARTHUR CORYE	queen's serjeant 1594–7
EDWARD LOFTUS	queen's serjeant 1597–1601
NICHOLAS KERDIFF	queen's (later king's) serjeant 1601–09

---

* These details are taken from vol. 1 of F. E. Ball, *The judges in Ireland 1221–1921* (London, 1926) and from the *Calendars of patent rolls (Ireland)*.

The regulation of the admission of attorneys and solicitors in Ireland, 1600-1866

W.N. OSBOROUGH

I

THE RULES GOVERNING ADMISSION to the lower branch of the legal profession form an integral part of the system of statutory control exercised over it that remains a feature of the law in the two jurisdictions of modern Ireland.[1] This system of control may be traced back to legislation enacted in medieval and early modern England. In a recent survey of the lower branch in England, C.W. Brooks has recalled that one post-restoration reader at the inns of court claimed that attorneys were dealt with in more regulatory statutes than any other occupational group in the realm.[2] Mention of two will suffice here. The ordinance De Attornatis et Apprenticiis of 1294 stipulated that the judges should appoint a limited number of qualified men to act as attorneys. The much-rehearsed statute 4 Henry IV, c. 18, passed by the English parliament in 1402, is more detailed, and at the same time a model of succinct expression:

For sundry damages and mischiefs that have ensued before this time to divers persons of the realm by a great number of attornies, ignorant and not learned in the law, as they were wont to be before this time; it is ordained and established, that all the attornies shall be examined by the justices, and by their discretions their names put in the roll, and they that be good and virtuous, and of good fame, shall be received and sworn well and truly to serve in their offices, and especially that they make no suit in a foreign county; and the other attornies shall be put out by the discretion of the said justices; and that their masters, for whom

---

1. Solicitors Act 1954, Solicitors (Amendment) Act 1960; Solicitors (Northern Ireland) Order 1976.
2. C.W. Brooks, *Pettyfoggers and vipers of the Commonwealth: the 'lower branch' of the legal profession in early modern England* (Cambridge, 1986), p. 19.

they were attornies, be warned to take others in their places, so that in the mean time no damage nor prejudice come to their said masters. And if any of the said attornies do die, or do cease, the justices for the time being by their discretion shall make another in his place, which is a virtuous man and learned, and sworn in the same manner as afore is said: and if any such attorney be hereafter notoriously found in any default of record, or otherwise, he shall forswear the court, and never after be received to make any suit in any court of the king . . . [3]

Remarkably—and it is eloquent testimony to the enduring strength of the common law—reliance was placed on the words of the statute of Henry IV in the Irish court of exchequer as late as 1844, when A.R. Symes, the law reporter and former barrister, sought, by way of special concession, an abridgement of his period of apprenticeship and to be admitted an attorney much sooner than was customary.[4] In applications of this kind it doubtless helped to be in a position to demonstrate that the bench had long retained a discretion to act which moreover was expressly sanctioned by statute. Fortunately, other evidence exists to show that the statute 4 Henry IV, c.18 was recognised as having legal effect in Ireland, and at a considerably earlier date. The explanation is standard in the case of medieval English statute law: the statute became operative under the provisions of Poynings' Act of 1495 (10 Henry VII, c.22) which extended to Ireland the generality of the pre-existing statute law of England. Thus John Merick, in a collection published in Dublin in 1617 of English statutes which he reckoned applied in Ireland, includes 4 Henry IV, c. 18. Edward Lee does likewise in his guide of 1734; so too do Bullingbrooke and Belcher in their abridgement of 1754. There is also reference to the statute in the preface to a practitioner's manual brought out by Gorges Edmund Howard in 1759.[5]

Mention in the writings of Howard, inclusion in compendia of statute-law brought out in the seventeenth and eighteenth centuries and resurrection for purposes of an isolated lawsuit in the nineteenth hardly constitute compelling proof however that

3. *Stat. realm*, ii, 138-39.

4. *In re Symes* (1844) 7 Ir Eq R 339.

5. John Merick, *A compendious collection and breefe abstract of all the auncient English–statutes . . . which now are in force within this kingdome of Ireland . . .* (Dublin, 1617), p. 53; Edward Lee, *The statute-law of Ireland common-placed . . .* (Dublin, 1734), p. 24; Edward Bullingbrooke and Jonathan Belcher, *An abridgement of the statutes of Ireland . . .* (Dublin, 1754), p. 28; G.E. Howard, *A compendious treatise of the rules and practise of the pleas side of the exchequer*, 2 vols. (Dublin, 1759), i, xx.

the statute 4 Henry IV, c.18 continued throughout to have significant practical impact. The question is an instructive one to air at the outset. Although the statute of Henry IV had the capacity to provide the sinews of the regulatory framework for the admission of attorneys at the point where this survey commences in 1600, if the statute actually did so then or in subsequent years corroborative evidence in either respect is wholly lacking. In a petition to parliament of 1858 the recently founded Law Society deals cursorily with the law determining entry to the solicitors' profession that antedated the passing of the seminal Irish act of 1733. Before that date, the petition recalls,

the right to exercise the profession of attorney-at-law in Ireland was attained by persons binding themselves to, or placing themselves in the office of, some admitted attorney for a certain period, and afterwards applying to one of the courts of law in Ireland for liberty to practise as an attorney in such court.[6]

Baron Pennefather of the Irish court of exchequer is the author of another foray into history in his judgment on Lyons' controversial application to be admitted an attorney that came before the courts on several occasions between 1834 and 1839:

Before the statute of the 7 Geo.II, c. 5, Ir. [the act of 1733], this court and the other superior courts in Dublin exercised, under certain regulations, the power of admitting attornies as their own officers, to discharge the duties of the respective courts. It was thought right, however, by the legislature, that certain rules should be laid down by legislative enactments, reserving to the superior courts the power of exercising their original jurisdiction in such cases as, in their discretion, it might seem fit so to do.[7]

On the historical perception of rules and procedures on entry to the profession these two extracts are illuminating both as to what they say and as to what they omit. In the latter connection, the absence of any express reference to Henry IV's legislation is noteworthy.

Two explanations for this neglect of the early legislative precedent may be tentatively advanced. The first is indicated by Brooks when assessing the evidence for England.[8] Until the mid-sixteenth century, he argues, the available information shows that the regime envisaged by the act of 1402 was in regular use.

6. Daire Hogan, *The legal profession in Ireland 1789-1922* (Dublin, 1986), p. 15.

7. *In re Lyons* (1839) 1 Ir Eq R 267 at 272.

8. Brooks, *Pettyfoggers and vipers*, p. 19f.

Thereafter the pattern alters, as a result, Brooks maintains, of changes in the general procedures of the common law courts. These changes were linked to the rise in influence of the prothonotaries and their clerks. It is Brooks' contention, in the case of the court of king's bench for instance, that by the late sixteenth century the majority of attorneys were not admitted in the fashion contemplated by Henry IV's statute: this was for the simple reason that, in a technical sense, so many had become clerks of the chief prothonotary of the court. In chancery the early dominance of the six clerks and their underclerks had brought about a concentration in their hands of functions the equivalents to which elsewhere fell to be carried out by attorneys—thus leaving a residue of functions to be performed by a motley group of practitioners who were to acquire in the course of time the denomination of solicitors. Only in common pleas, ultimately, were the attorneys destined to remain independent of clerks and their underclerks and to discharge tasks of the traditional procedural variety on behalf of their several clients. The inference one is invited to draw from these disparate developments is that the manner in which the English system of courts chose to evolve rendered the act of 1402 an increasingly unsatisfactory instrument for the purpose for which it had been originally engineered. Falling first into disuse, the act sank eventually into oblivion.

A second possible explanation is of a different calibre, being confined to circumstances peculiar to Ireland: it is concerned generally with the matter of the knowledge of past law possessed by subsequent generations of administrators and judges in the country. The contention being put forward is that reliable, rounded knowledge of the actual content of Irish law in previous centuries was invariably a commodity in short supply. The absence of what today would be termed adequate library resources—the unavailability of copies of Irish and English statutes for instance—must be counted a principal cause. But there were other problems and technical complications too that made it difficult to discover not only what the law had been in the past but also more seriously what it amounted to in the present.[9] With facilities for the proper

---

9. Consider for instance this defence by Edward Lee of his decision to include within the body of statute law in force in Ireland certain post-Poynings' Act English legislation. The prose is awkward but the sense is plain (*The statute-law of Ireland common-placed*, p. vii): 'Some English statutes made since Poynings's law, tho' Ireland, not expressly mentioned, yet in regards they (to particular purposes) bind the people of Ireland, are here set down, some of which see in title, Egyptians, petitions, etc.' And see generally my 'In praise of law books', *Ir Jur*, xxi (1986), 326 at 351.

practice of the profession so depressing, exactitude on matters of indigenous legal history was neither encouraged nor indeed did it come to be expected. The upshot deserves to be contrasted with the much-vaunted durability of the common law: precise historical recollection could not and did not survive.

Whatever the explanation, a void opened up and to one facet of this void special attention needs to be drawn. A certain vagueness came in time to surround the practical operation of the rules governing admission to the lower branch of the legal profession in Ireland. The date at which this vagueness first manifested itself is not immediately obvious. More germane to the present purpose is to observe the long-term consequences flowing from it. A concomitant of any intelligible regime for controlling the admission of attorneys and solicitors (indeed, the admission into any profession) was the furnishing of answers to such questions as who had the authority to sanction entry, what the requirements on entry were and how exactly entry was to be effectuated. Answers to these questions were vital and they were in fact to emerge, but they emerged somewhat haphazardly. What occurred was that at intermittent intervals and in varying circumstances a succession of initiatives was taken. Some new 'rule' was the outcome in each instance. The authors of these initiatives fell into one of four groups. First, there were the two parliaments, the English as well as the Irish. Secondly, as also might have been anticipated, there were the judges. From a study of their involvement however it is helpful to distinguish between the three roles that members of the judiciary filled: that as judges simpliciter (sitting in court, deciding matters arising there), that as draftsmen of rules of court (for the courts to which they were attached), and, finally, that as benchers of their inn of court (in effect, of the society of King's Inns). Third, there were sundry senior court officers. And fourth, there were the masters of apprentices (ordinarily court clerks or attorneys themselves) who prescribed the terms of the indentures of apprenticeship.

Over time, the outcome of this sequence of haphazard regulatory initiatives was the transformation of the regime on admissions into a world of almost byzantine complexity. Development tended to take this direction in particular because of the relative infrequency with which any attempt was made to relate each successive initiative to the pre-existing rules. This world survived far into the modern period undoubtedly alike constituting a discouragement to the faint-hearted and posing a trap for the unwary. That it survived the length of time it did appears, superficially, something of a puzzle, given that from the 1770s onwards at least the trend was perceptibly towards the 'professionalisation' of the lower branch.

It is this modernizing movement that culminates in major changes in the 1860s. In 1860 itself the decision is reached to introduce written examinations.[10] Six years later parliament transfers important regulatory functions to the new representative professional body, the Law Society.[11] Together, these two events may be said to mark the birth of the modern Irish solicitors' profession. By comparison, the removal of the remaining vestiges of the distinction between solicitors and attorneys which followed a decade later as one of the consequences of the enactment of the Judicature Act is a minor footnote.[12]

The persistence of the confusion and obscurity which the reforms of the 1860s and later were designed to expunge is exemplified by an episode that took place in the rolls court in the early 1830s, to which some publicity has already been accorded.[13] In the course of a lawsuit a dispute surfaced as to whether a solicitor, prior to the receipt of his professional licence, was obliged to subscribe an oath, traditionally subscribed by all attorneys at the period, not to permit any person to practise in his name.[14] A solicitor named Smith claimed not to have subscribed any such oath and he was criticised in consequence in open court by the then master of the rolls, Sir William McMahon. Sir William considered that the oath was both appropriate and prudent. But was the subscribing of it legally mandatory? Smith had investigated the matter and he was satisfied that he had been entitled to decline to subscribe it. A rule of court of 1791 merely required the presentation of a certificate signed by the senior master and by the registrar that the aspiring solicitor was a fit and proper person; there was no mention of an oath. Sir William was forced to admit he had made a mistake and apologised. Happily, the solicitor left on record an explanation of how this abuse of insisting on an unnecessary oath had originally come to be perpetrated:

Many gentlemen do not wish to take the same trouble to inform themselves, but prefer applying to some of the subordinate clerks in the six clerks' office, who have an interest in making a mystery of the

10. Hogan, *Legal profession in Ireland*, pp. 109-11.

11. Attorneys and Solicitors (Ireland) Act, 1866: 29 & 30 Vict, c. 84.

12. Supreme Court of Judicature (Ireland) Act, 1877: 40 & 41 Vict, c. 57.

13. Hogan, *Legal profession in Ireland*, p. 99.

14. *Birch* v. *Oldis* (1831) Glascock 351.

manufacturing of solicitors, and in this way I can account for the introduction of the objectionable and unnecessary clause, through the ignorance of some clerk who had obtained some hearsay notion of the oath taken by attorneys (originally framed in reference to the then popery acts), of which the present version is a clumsy imitation.[15]

II

In the absence of hard data, the arrangements that governed the admission of attorneys in Ireland in 1600 can only be matter for speculation. It is legitimate to infer, however, that a system of apprenticeship operated and that some test, however cursory, preceded formal admission to the pertinent common law court, king's bench, common pleas or exchequer. Who administered that test remains problematic.

Parliamentary intervention, redolent of the statute 4 Henry IV, c.18, continued in England. In 1605 an act superimposed a degree of specificity upon the existing rules regulating the entry of attorneys there: the latter were to be brought up in the courts or to be well practised in the soliciting of causes and to be found by their dealings to be skilful and of an honest disposition.[16] No equivalent Irish act ensued: sittings of the Irish parliament were still relatively infrequent at this time. To move on several years, it would seem, to judge from an entry in the Irish commons' journal for 1641, that some kind of legislative initiative, of which, however, the details do not survive, was at that stage in contemplation.[17] Under the Commonwealth, it is true, specific measures were adopted to drive catholics out of practice.[18] But otherwise there was no formal intervention in the field in Ireland.

Matters were not left as before, however—whatever that might have involved—for significant modifications were effected in other ways in the Ireland of the seventeenth century. These originated in the activities of the Irish inn of court, the society of King's Inns, which had been revived in 1607, and in the increasing preparedness of the Irish courts of law, certainly from around 1670 onwards, through the drawing up of rules of court to proceed to regulate both the admission and the activity of attorneys.

15. At 355-6.
16. 3 Jas I, c. 7; Robert Robson, *The attorney in eighteenth century England* (Cambridge, 1959), p. 53.
17. *Commons' jn. Ire.*, i, 252: 10 July 1641.
18. Colum Kenny, 'The exclusion of catholics from the legal profession in Ireland, 1537-1829', *IHS*, xxv, no. 100 (Nov. 1987), 337 at 349.

In 1806 Bartholomew Duhigg, the first historian of King's Inns, contended that the right of the benchers to regulate the lower branch through insistence on compulsory membership was first asserted in 1793.[19] The claim cannot be supported. Hogan has explained that the new rules of 1793 merely enshrined 'an old obligation which, with effect from the first day of Hilary term 1794, was enforced with a new vigour'.[20] The testimony of the Black Book of King's Inns too is unchallengeable. Attorneys were amongst the categories of legal practitioner admitted to the Inns on the latter's revival in 1607. And in 1629 there occurs the first recital of a crucial new rule to the effect that no one was to be admitted an attorney in any of the courts of Dublin unless he had first been admitted to membership of the society. A corollary adopted at the same time obliged existing attorneys who were not already members of the society to present themselves for admission early in the next ensuing Hilary term; otherwise they were to be struck off. Every attorney was equally required to keep one week's commons at the society in each law term.[21] This basic rule was restated in 1656, in 1683 and again in 1710. The restatement of 1683 went further: it insisted that proof of the payment of the Inns admission fine (originally in the case of attorneys set at 13*s.*4*d.*, and shortly to be raised to £2 13*s.*9*d.*) had to be presented as a preliminary to admission as an attorney in any of the common law courts.[22]

The unequivocal character of the rule on compulsory membership of the Inns notwithstanding, the pages of the Black Book reveal that there were many defaulters among the ranks of attorneys. Membership had been made compulsory for barristers too and lists of defaulters in both categories were ordered to be brought forward in 1629, 1663, 1674, 1698 and 1704. The entry for 1698 singled out attorneys who 'never pay any respect to the courts where they are sworn but live in the country' and unfairly monopolised assize business.[23] Failure to pay for commons and to contribute to the fund for pensioners was another regular complaint—in 1657, 1663, 1667 (when the complainant is one Abigail Swift, the widow of the recently deceased steward), 1698

19. Bartholomew Duhigg, *History of the King's Inns* (Dublin, 1806), p. 459.

20. *Legal profession in Ireland*, p. 22.

21. T. Power, 'The "Black Book" of King's Inns: An introduction with an abstract of contents', *Ir Jur*, xx (1985), 134 at 180 (Black Book, ff.181r-181v).

22. Ibid., pp. 167 (f. 116r (1656)); 165 (f. 87v (1683)); 208 (f. 329r (1710)).

23. Ibid., pp. 180 (ff. 181r-181v (1629)), 186 (f. 197r (1663)), 195 (f. 258v (1674)), 202 (ff. 282r-283r (1698)), 206 (ff. 319r-319v (1704)).

and 1704.[24] To meet this latter problem a rule adopted in 1710 required all new members, attorneys included, to lodge a bond with the treasurer of the Inns and to provide sureties that they would at all times observe the rules of the society.[25] Denial of the right to practise was the standard sanction, though a less draconian form of punishment appears to have been in force around 1704.

The prominent position occupied by the society of King's Inns in the scheme of regulation is indicated by other evidence. An Irish statute of 1715 which conferred rights of practice in the assize courts on attorneys who had been admitted to the superior courts in Dublin stipulated that such attorneys should first have paid their 'commons and other duties to the stewards of the Inns'.[26] A second revival of King's Inns towards the end of the eighteenth century brought a spate of new rules of court that re-affirmed yet again the obligation of prior membership of the society. In 1789, four years before the benchers adopted the regulation to which Duhigg took such grave exception, the court of common pleas insisted, as a preliminary to entry, on proof of payment of one's admission fine to the society.[27] In 1785 king's bench followed suit: where common pleas had been content with a receipt however, they demanded a certificate.[28]

III

There was nothing novel about compulsory membership of the Inns being dealt with in this fashion in the rules of the various courts themselves. The existence of this further mode of regulation was expressly acknowledged by Baron Pennefather in 1839,[29] and the legacy itself went back to 1671, the date of the first set of rules of court for the Irish common law courts thought to have

24. Ibid., pp. 168 (ff. 120r–121v (1657)), 186 (f. 197v (1663)), 190 (f. 209v (1667)), 202 (ff. 282v–283r (1698)), 206 (ff. 319r–319v (1704)).

25. Ibid., p. 208 (f. 329r).

26. 2 Geo I, c. 11 (an act for reviving and amending an act intituled an act for recovery of small debts in a summary way, before the judges of assize), s. 12.

27. Order of 22 June 1789: R. S. Moore and T. K. Lowry, *A collection of the general rules and orders of the courts of queen's bench, common pleas and exchequer of pleas in Ireland* (Dublin, 1842) (hereafter *Moore & Lowry*), app. I, p. 61.

28. Rules and orders of the court of queen's bench in Ireland, lxxxvii (20 June 1795): *Moore & Lowry*, p. 138.

29. *In re Lyons* (1839) 1 Ir Eq R 267 at 272.

survived. This set emanated from common pleas and began with a re-assertion of the Inns' own contemporary regulations: existing attorneys were to become members of the Inns prior to the start of the next ensuing Michaelmas term; new attorneys would in future be obliged to become members of the Inns in the course of the same law term in which they were admitted to practice; all were to attend commons at the Inns one week in each term at least. There was one additional requirement: each attorney of the court was to notify the steward of the Inns of his place of residence.[30]

The common pleas rules of 1671 touched on many other facets to the work of the court's attorneys. Rule iii in a group headed 'concerning attorneys and officers', for example, prescribed what had to be done to preserve one's right to practise in court.[31] Of most interest however is the information that the rules furnished as to the regime then in force that governed entry to the profession. A period of apprenticeship 'of 5 years at the least' was prescribed; so too were the categories of possible master and the mode of conduct of the 'moral examination' of apprentices. All these matters were dealt with in rule vi of the group headed 'concerning attorneys and officers':

That none be admitted an attorney of this court, unless he hath served or shall serve by the space of 5 years at the least, as a clerk to some judge, serjeant at law, practising counsellor, attorney, clerk or officer of one of his majesty's courts at Westminster or Dublin unless his master die or give over his practice, and he also upon examination be found of good ability and honesty for such employment and that sufficient proof, to be put into writing, be made of such service upon a desire of admittance, and filed with the clerk of the warrants without fee, and taking the oath of supremacy in open court; that every minister and officer of this court shall in like manner take and receive the said oath, according to the statute made in the second year of Elizabeth upon his admission into his office, ministry or service.[32]

A complementary group of rules, headed 'concerning the better preservation of order among the officers and clerks', completed the picture:

---

30. Rules and orders of his majesty's court of common bench in Ireland, of Trinity term, in the 22nd year of King Charles II—concerning attorneys and officers, i: *Moore & Lowry*, app. I, pp. 4-5.

31. *Moore & Lowry*, app. I, p. 5.

32. *Moore & Lowry*, app. I, p. 6.

rule i   That the court do once in every year, in Michaelmas term, nominate and appoint three or more able and credible practitioners in the court, to continue for the year following, for these purposes following:

rule ii   That they, or any two of them, examine such persons as desire to be admitted attorneys, and appoint convenient times and places for the same; and in order thereunto, that such persons as shall desire to be admitted attorneys, first attend the prothonotary with his proof of service, then to repair to the persons appointed to examine attorneys, and being approved, to be presented to the court with his approbation, and then to be sworn in open court, unless some just exception be against him.

rule iii   That they give information to the court from time to time upon their oaths, of breaches of order, and miscarriages of officers, attorneys and clerks.[33]

Unfortunately, no evidence appears to be available as to the manner in which any of the rules from either of the two groups operated in practice. The dearth of any data at all for the other common law courts is another serious lacuna.

IV

The major legislative intervention in the affairs of the lower branch in Ireland that starts to unfold at the end of the seventeenth century has to be set in the context of contemporary political events. In Ireland the victory of William III over James II at the Boyne in 1690 ushered in an era of penal laws where religious affiliation was the yardstick of political loyalty. The class that had suffered during the short reign of James made it their business, once the tables had been turned and their fortunes had revived, to ensure that none other than loyal protestants should taste political power or hold legal or administrative office. The 'protestantising' of the Irish legal profession was a direct outcome, a policy carried through in respect of the lower branch by legislative measures spanning the years 1691 to 1733 and which were effectively in force until 1792. This chapter in the story of Irish law has been related before but not always so as to underline the impact of the policy on entry to the lower branch.[34]

33. *Moore & Lowry*, app. I, p. 9.

34. Colum Kenny, 'The exclusion of catholics from the legal profession in Ireland 1537–1829', *IHS*, xxv, no. 100 (Nov. 1987), 337; T.P. Power, 'Conversions among the legal profession in Ireland in the eighteenth century' in this vol., post, p.153; Hogan, *Legal profession in Ireland*, pp. 14-15.

An act passed for Ireland by the English parliament in 1691 served as the harbinger of what was to follow. A fresh test of political reliability was imposed on all aspirants to public office in Ireland, a category broad enough to include barristers, attorneys and clerks of the courts. Such aspirants were required to sub-scribe the oath of allegiance and the oath of abjuration and to make the declaration against transubstantiation.[35] The only test of loyalty demanded by the common pleas rules of 1671 was preparedness to subscribe the oath of supremacy that went back to the reign of Elizabeth.[36] Clearly, the English act of 1691 displayed features that were bound to cause offence to catholic practitioners. One category alone was exempted: those (lawyers included) who managed to bring themselves within the terms of the religious concessions contained in the articles of Limerick and later, by extension, of Galway too.

The English act of 1691 was aimed at many others besides attorneys. The Irish act of 1698 on the other hand boldly proclaimed itself 'an act to prevent papists being solicitors'.[37] The preamble set forth a justification for the passing of so severe a measure,[38] and the act itself inserted, by way of addition to the earlier proofs of loyalty, on the giving of an undertaking to educate one's children as protestant. The two oaths, the declara-tion and the undertaking were expressed to be required of all persons seeking 'to act as solicitor in any court of law or equity, or as agent or manager in any cause or suit in law or equity, or as seneschal, or solicitor in all or any of the courts or offices in this kingdom'.[39]

The provisions contained in a further act of 1707 were designed to strengthen the act of 1698.[40] Penalties were increased, 'reputed papists' as well as 'papists' simpliciter were brought within its scope; and the courts and activities that were prohibited to catholics were individually listed: the four courts in Dublin, the courts of the Tipperary palatinate, 'any court of record in this

---

35. 3 Will & Mary, c.2 (an act for abrogating the oath of supremacy in Ireland and appointing other oaths).

36. Concerning attorneys and officers, vi: *Moore & Lowry*, app. I, p.6.

37. 10 Will III, c.13.

38. See T.P. Power, 'Conversions among the legal profession in Ireland in the eighteenth century', post, p.153 at p.154

39. 10 Will III, c.13, ss. 1 and 2. Exceptions applied in the case of solicitors pursuing their own lawsuits (s.3) and such solicitors as fell within the terms of the articles of Limerick (s.4).

40. 6 Anne, c.6: an act to explain and amend an act intituled, an act to prevent papists being solicitors.

kingdom', any ecclesiastical or admiralty court and service as clerk in any sheriff's office or in any commission issued by a court of equity.[41] Section 3 enabled informers to interrupt legal proceedings and intimate to the presiding judge their suspicions regarding the religious persuasion of any practitioner present in court. Failure by such practitioner to subscribe the necessary oaths and pass the other tests that had been prescribed compelled the judge to treat the former as a 'popish solicitor convict'. The act shut out catholics from apprenticeship; it also deprived solicitors who benefited from the terms of the articles of Limerick of their right to continue in practice unless they subscribed the oath of abjuration.[42] As these and other penal law measures progressed through the Irish parliament, a number of petitions were presented on behalf of individuals who sought special concessions. These were presumably catholic attorneys and solicitors: such petitions for instance were received from Oliver Weston in 1704 and 1707 and from Francis Glascock, Robert Ridge and Peter Daly, all in 1707.[43]

A further turn of the screw occurred in 1727. Legislation adopted that year was aimed at legal practitioners who were either converts to protestantism or born of popish parents. It stipulated that aspirant barristers and attorneys falling within either category should adduce proof that they had been protestants for at least two years prior to applying for admission.[44] The judges of the court of common pleas adopted a rule of court two years later to guard against the risk that the 1727 measure might become a dead letter. An additional affidavit was demanded of all aspirant attorneys falling within either of the suspect classes. The examiners of apprentices were additionally enjoined to 'enquire into these particulars and certify how they find the same'.[45]

There was legislation yet again in 1733.[46] Henceforth aspirant attorneys and solicitors had to demonstrate that they had been

41. Ss. 1 and 2.

42. Ss. 6 and 8.

43. *Commons' jn. Ire.*, ii, 431 (22 Feb. 1704) and 508-9 (25 July 1707).

44. 1 Geo II, c.20: an act for regulating the admissions of barristers at law, six clerks, and attornies, and of other persons, into offices and employments; and for preventing papists practising as solicitors; and for further strengthening the protestant interest in this kingdom.

45. Order of Michaelmas term, 3 Geo II, 1729 (Lord Chief Justice Reynolds, Mr Justice Gore and Mr Justice Bernard): *Moore & Lowry*, app. I, p.47.

46. 7 Geo II, c.5: an act for the amendment of the law in relation to popish solicitors; and for remedying other mischiefs in relation to the practitioners in the several courts of law and equity.

protestants from the age of 14 or for at least two years before commencing their apprenticeship.[47] Section 6 facilitated conviction on charges connected with breach of the act by describing the tasks then commonly understood to be performed by the Irish solicitor and which accordingly were forbidden to catholics. It is an invaluable contemporary check-list. Any person would be deemed to be acting as a solicitor who

draws, dictates or abbreviates, pleadings or transcribes or abbreviates any depositions or other evidence in order to be made use of in any suit either at law or in equity or takes upon himself the direction or management in any cause or suit or the defence thereof in the said Four Courts, or any of them, wherein he is not a party, nor concerned in interest.

Over the plight of catholic would-be practitioners vain protests continued to be mounted. One such protest was presented to the Irish commons in 1734 from a group headed by Sir Edmund Butler, bart., and including William Purcell of Crumlin, John Reilly of Dublin, two Dublin merchants Francis Lynch and Augustus Clark, and a Dublin brewer, one Richard Mathews.[48] No other details are available.

V

The act of 1733 had a dual importance. It served to strengthen the existing legislation aimed at preventing catholics from entering the legal profession. But the majority of the act's provisions constituted, in effect, as Baron Pennefather recalled in 1839,[49] the first indigenous statutory framework for detailed regulation of the lower branch to be adopted in Ireland. This framework duplicated much of what was already prescribed by the common pleas rules of 1671, and it would be misleading to deduce from its adoption at this time the existence of any new-found determination to advance professional standards. Equally, however, the decision to cast in a statutory mould an approximation to the best in contemporary practice cannot be dismissed as bereft of significance. The principle of the exercise of statutory control over the workings of the lower branch had been reasserted and this was to have major long-term implications.

47. S.2.
48. *Commons' jn. Ire.*, iv, 137 (3 April 1734).
49. *In re Lyons* (1839) 1 Ir Eq R 267 at 272.

An English act of 1729 was the immediate inspiration.[50] That act had laid down, as had the Irish common pleas rules of 1671, an apprenticeship period of five years: the Irish act of 1733 introduced an identical clause. The inventory of categories of master at liberty to take apprentices that the act went on to furnish represented a change from those authorised under the terms of the common pleas rules of 1671: henceforth these were to be only six clerks in chancery, attorneys or licensed solicitors. Such masters could possess an English qualification or an Irish: in short, the Irish apprentice could enter into indentures with an English master. Prior to admission, the apprentice had to procure an affidavit that he had completed his period of service and this had to be presented in the appropriate court and filed in the manner prescribed.[51] The indentures had to be registered by each master, although it was the apprentice himself who was obliged to pay the fee, fixed by statute at one shilling.[52] The size of the profession was also an object of concern: in an attempt to keep numbers down the maximum number of apprentices any master could have simultaneously was fixed at three for attorneys and solicitors and at six for six clerks in chancery.[53] A further clause dealt with the problem that could arise where a master died before the five-year period of apprenticeship had concluded.[54] Section 7 inaugurated a system for licensing solicitors. Aside from the standard requirements as to religious persuasion, no particular criteria were laid down or restrictions envisaged. Publicity however was to be accorded to the names of those licensed as solicitors for the whole of the law term next ensuing.[55]

Though the extent to which these various arrangements represented a true departure can be exaggerated, it is undeniable that a degree of structural reform within the lower branch was being attempted. Simultaneously, deliberate cultivation of new traditions of professionalism may have been projected. In this latter regard, the drawing up in 1740 by the three judges of the court of common pleas—Lord Chief Justice Singleton, Mr Justice Gore and Mr Justice Lindsay—of the terms of a fresh professional oath that was ordered by them to be subscribed by every attorney

50. 2 Geo II, c.23 (Eng.): an act for the better regulation of attornies and solicitors.
51. 7 Geo III, c.5, s.2.
52. S.3.
53. S.9.
54. S.14.
55. S.8.

of the court prior to admission is of more than passing interest.
Statute law had originally demanded the subscription of the oath
of supremacy; at the outset of the penal law era this had been
superseded by the oath of allegiance and the oath of abjuration.
From scrutinising the terms of the supplementary oath of 1740
(that was ordered to be administered in open court by the prothonotary or his clerk), it is plain that the preoccupation of its
authors was with matters of a different sort:

You shall do no falsehood or deceit, nor consent to any to be done
within this court, and if you shall know of any to be done, you shall give
notice thereof to the lord chief justice, or other his brethren justices of
this court, that it may be reformed.
You shall delay no man for lucre or malice.
You shall increase no fees, but you shall be contented with the old
accustomed fees.
You shall plead no foreign plea, nor sue any foreign suits unlawfully to
the hurt of any man, but such as shall stand with the order of the law
and your own conscience.
You shall seal all such process as you shall sue out of this court, with the
seal thereof, and see the king's majesty and chief justice discharged for
the same.
You shall not wittingly or willingly sue or procure to be sued any false
suit, or give aid or consent to the same, on pain to be expelled this court
for ever.
And further, you shall truly use and demean yourself in the office of an
attorney within this court according to your learning and discretion. So
help you God.[56]

In certain respects, the wording of this oath follows that
prescribed by the English court of common pleas in the late
Tudor period and which is reproduced by Brooks:[57] the Irish
common pleas oath of 1740 cannot therefore pretend to be
original. Similar if somewhat shorter oaths were administered to
attorneys on their admission to practise in the other courts, whose
provenance is equally likely to have been English. One of these,
that used in the Irish court of exchequer in the middle of the
nineteenth century, is reproduced by Plunkett:

You and each of you shall well and truly and faithfully behave yourselves
in the office of attorney in this her majesty's court of exchequer; you
shall do no falsehood or rasure or cause or consent to the doing of any;
nor to the rasing of any records, pleadings, writings or memoranda of

56. Order of Hilary term, 14 Geo II, 1740: *Moore & Lowry*, app. I, p. 50.
57. Brooks, *Pettyfoggers and vipers*, p. 119.

this court, whereby the court of the queen or her subjects may be hindered or prejudiced, and if you know of any to be done shall give speedy knowledge thereof to the lord chief baron or the barons of this court, that thereby the same may be redressed and reformed. You shall delay no man for lucre or malice, and rightfully and truly you shall do unto all men in that which belongeth you to do by reason of your place and office of an attorney.[58]

The practice of administering such oaths fell into disuse after the enactment of the Judicature Acts in the 1870s. Plunkett did not mourn their passing. 'The young attorneys', he wrote, 'who stood up in open court to repeat these oaths on the threshold of their professional careers might have been excused if they had reflected like Carlyle—"Where we are we know; where we are going no man knoweth".'[59] On the publicising of the terms of the new common pleas oath of 1740, comparable heterodox opinions may have been expressed, though these are not now traceable. Apart altogether from the question of its practical efficacy, the oath itself deserves to be probed into a little further. The terms of it strongly indicate one line of inquiry that is surely worth pursuing. Those terms are redolent of ideas of contemporary professional virtue. Is it conceivable that the oath's judicial progenitors could have planned to launch an assault on the phenomenon of professional vice?

This is not the place to attempt a survey of the virtues and vices of attorneys and solicitors in eighteenth-century Ireland, either individually or collectively. Research has not advanced sufficiently to enable even a start to be made. Yet some mention of the matter in a brief sketch is warranted: questions of professional ethics are a focus of concern in the regime governing entry to any profession that is worthy of the name. They were a focus of concern in the regulations relative to attorneys in the common pleas rules of 1671, and the character of aspiring attorneys remained throughout the particular preoccupation of the examiners deputed by each court, more especially after the reforms of 1773.

Occasional glimpses reveal individual members of the lower branch going about their daily routine. From these it is a reasonably safe conjecture that the majority led unremarkable lives. Though the redoubtable Gorges Edmund Howard is a witness to the contrary, it is also a reasonably safe conjecture that

58. E.A. Plunkett, 'Attorneys and solicitors in Ireland' in *Record of the centenary of the charter of the Incorporated Law Society of Ireland, 1852–1952* (Dublin, 1953), p. 38 at pp. 64-65.
59. Plunkett, loc. cit., p. 65.

in the process that majority helped to maintain, even to consolidate, rough and ready standards of professional respectability. A few achieved a modicum of fame. Elizabeth Bowen in her family history, *Bowen's court*,[60] left a pleasing vignette of the Dublin attorney Richard Chester, her forebears' mid-century family confidant, factotum and general legal adviser. Staying in Dublin but passing down the years, there was William Deane, a solicitor in whose honour a medallion commemorating his prominence in contemporary scientific pursuits was struck by the celebrated Dublin medallist, William Mossop, in 1785;[61] Archibald Hamilton, too, an attorney who flourished at the turn of the nineteenth century, and who is to be espied in his dual extra-curricular roles of impress officer for Ireland and council member of a prominent charity, the Sick and Indigent Roomkeepers' Society.[62]

But black sheep flourished as well. The penal laws directed at catholic landholding which were maintained in full vigour between 1704 and 1778 provided scope for collusion, fraud and general sharp practice on a grand scale. From the scattered pieces of evidence surviving, such vices were undoubtedly practised by a number of attorneys that it remains possible to identify. Three of those who can be named—Farrell, Daly and Franks—were all attorneys in the court of exchequer. Exchequer attorneys were far and away the largest group and the explanation for any relative predominance in the ranks of villainy is probably to be found in that circumstance rather than in any procedure peculiar to the exchequer court which could have facilitated the perpetration of abuses.[63]

60. Elizabeth Bowen, *Bowen's court* (2nd ed., London, 1964; repr. London, 1984), pp. 174-82. The vignette is based on letters sent by Chester between the early 1760s and the mid-1770s. Chester was admitted an attorney of the court of exchequer in 1756: *King's Inns admission papers, 1607-1867*, ed. Edward Keane, P.B. Phair and T.U. Sadlier (Dublin, 1982), p. 84.

61. Deane's scientific interests lay principally in the establishment of works to make bottles and window glass. At his death in 1793 he bequeathed both his chemical apparatus and his planetarium to Trinity College, Dublin. See further William Frazer, 'The medallists of Ireland and their work', *RSAI Jn*, xvii (1886), 443 at 448. Deane was admitted an attorney of king's bench in 1732 (*King's Inns admission papers*, p. 126) and was subsequently licensed as a solicitor. A.E. J. Went's *Irish coins and medals* (Dublin, 1978) reproduces Mossop's commemorative medallion.

62. Archibald Hamilton, 'A treatise on impressing', *Ir Jur*, viii (1973), 117; Deirdre Lindsay, 'The Sick and Indigent Roomkeepers' Society', in David Dickson (ed.), *The gorgeous mask: Dublin, 1700-1850* (Dublin, 1987), p. 132 at p. 136. Hamilton was admitted an attorney of the court of exchequer in 1796: *King's Inns admission papers*, p. 208.

63. See my 'Catholics, land and the popery acts of Anne' in Kevin Whelan and T.P. Power (ed.), *Endurance and emergence: catholics in Ireland in the eighteenth century* (Dublin, 1990), p. 21.

Aside from the temptations held out by the penal laws, there was the lucrative side to the work of an attorney retained by a large landed family. This could have proved the undoing of William Beauman, admitted in 1794. He had kept estate papers, title deeds and counterparts of tenant's leases as a lien on costs incurred by him in connection with lawsuits undertaken at the family's behest and as security for loans advanced to them. The pack of cards came tumbling down in 1828, nearly thirty years after the commencement of the first in a series of intricate and seemingly interminable lawsuits, when Beauman was ultimately ordered to surrender all the various documents. Suspiciously, six years later, Beauman himself was struck off.[64]

The severest strictures directed at any identifiable eighteenth-century Irish attorney were probably those pronounced on Thomas Kenney by Chief Baron Yelverton in 1796. Kenney had elected to sue a client called Browne, an erstwhile sailor, for reneging on a bargain he was convinced was lawful and proper. Yelverton was astounded at Kenney's conduct which he condemned out of hand as

a complete tissue of imposition from its commencement to its determination. It is a case which originated, continued and ended in fraud. It is the case of an attorney obtaining from his client pending the cause an unconscionable bargain, without any consideration—for extraordinary acts of friendship never performed—services never done—or, if done, more than amply rewarded.[65]

VI

Irrespective of whether the act of 1733 or the oath of 1740 truly displayed a commitment to a new professional ethos, the refrain itself was taken up by the Irish house of commons in the ensuing decades. In 1749 and again in 1764 initiatives were brought forward for the better regulation of the lower branch. The heads of bill of 1749 were approved but were swiftly lost to sight. Those of 1764 were approved, progressed to the bill stage but thereupon they too were doomed to sink without trace. Intriguingly, in the process, the title of the measure had been altered. The original heads of bill had been expressed to be 'for better regulating agents,

64. *Gifford* v. *Hart* (1804) 1 Sch & Lef 386; *Lansdowne* v. *Beauman* (1828) 1 Molloy 89; *King's Inns admission papers*, p. 29.
65. *Kenney* v. *Browne* (1796) 3 Ridg P C 462 at 521.

receivers and attornies'; the bill that emerged was entitled merely
a measure 'for better regulating stewards, agents and receivers'.[66]

The refrain had also been taken up by that self-appointed
scourge of his own profession, G.E. Howard. Howard devoted
the major part of the preface to his treatise on the pleas side of the
exchequer, published in 1759, to criticism of the Irish attorney's
profession mid-century. The profession was overcrowded and too
many attorneys enjoyed insufficient annual income. Nor could it
harbour any delusion that it was 'learned': a preponderance of
recent entrants were 'hackney clerks' and educational attainments
in Latin, mathematics and the rudiments of book-keeping were all
depressingly low. Howard took particular exception to the statutory reform under which Latin was replaced by English as the language of record for the courts, castigating it as 'a deadly stroke to
learning'. There was a further evil over which Howard 'would fain
have drawn a veil': the profession's over-indulgence in alcohol.
He repeated the reputation that the Irish profession had come to
enjoy amongst the members of the English: 'they seemed to them
to do nothing but walk the courts the whole morning, and to
devote whole evenings to the bottle.'[67]

These abortive parliamentary initiatives and the scattershot
from Howard can scarcely be dignified as a 'campaign'. The result
nevertheless in 1773 was a legislative measure that gave the reformers much of what they were seeking. The statute, 13 & 14 Geo
III, c.23, 'an act for the better regulation of the admission and
practice of attornies' underwent only minor modifications during
its ninety-year existence. It was to prove of singular importance in
connection with entry requirements through its insistence that for
the last three years of the stipulated five-year period of apprenticeship the aspiring attorney would have to attend for two terms at
the least in every year at the Four Courts in Dublin.[68]

The reasons for the change were itemised in sections 1 and 6.
There existed, section 1 declared,

a frequent practice among the inferior class of attornies of the said courts
to take apprentices of low education, whose circumstances or condition
of fortune frequently induce them to be guilty of mean and improper
practices to the dishonour of the profession, and to the great injury and
damage of their clients and the public in general.

66. *Commons' jn. Ire.*, v, 66, 68, 69, 80; vii, 285, 294, 329, 330.
67. G. E. Howard, *A compendious treatise of the rules and practise of the pleas side of
    the exchequer in Ireland* (2 vols., Dublin, 1759), i, preface, passim.
68. 13 & 14 Geo III, c.23, s. 6.

Section 6 portrayed the legislature's anxieties no less vividly. It cited the 'many inconveniences and mischiefs' that had frequently arisen and daily arose,

by reason that persons, who have been legally admitted attornies of the courts, but who afterwards resided entirely or for the most part in the country, do there in like manner take apprentices from amongst the lower class of the people without education as aforesaid, or any means of subsisting themselves, and cause them to be sworn attornies of the said courts, where it often happens they never after appear, but become common barreters or promoters of suits especially amongst labouring and industrious poor people, to the impoverishing and ruin of them and their families.

Howard in 1759 had attributed the new practice of attorneys taking up residence in the country to their comparative penury. Whatever the reason, movement into rural areas did take place and the countryside perhaps inevitably came to be treated as a new theatre of operations. The development was not always to the liking of the local gentry. A not untypical attitude perhaps was captured in a newspaper advertisement, later to achieve a degree of notoriety:

To be let, from the 1st November, 1779, the house and demesne of____, situated near the town of H__d, in the co. of Galway. There is a rookery on the lands, good sportage, and *not an attorney* within 12 miles on any side.—Apply to ____etc.[69]

Where the gentry's fears over the development may have been largely indeterminate, Howard's were clear-cut and forcibly expressed. He dreaded the promotion of a needless litigiousness and the collapse of an established social peace. 'From their poverty', many attorneys, Howard wrote,

are under a necessity of settling in the country, to the absolute ruin and oppression of the lower kind of people, and the embroiling of whole countries. In short, it is letting out a drove of wolves and tygers to devour mankind; for it is unknown, what mischiefs an evil-inclined attorney can produce, and create in the neighbourhood he dwells in; he has this advantage of the rest of mankind, that he can torment, perplex, and impoverish, without being himself at any cost or expense, nay, sometimes to his gain and profit.[70]

69. Reproduced in Oliver J. Burke, *The history of the lord chancellors of Ireland from A.D. 1186 to A.D. 1874* (Dublin, 1879), pp. 205-06.
70. Howard, *A compendious treatise . . .*, i, preface, p. iv.

The thrust to section 6 was plainly influenced by perceptions such as Howard's; whether the principal remedy envisaged by parliament—compulsory attendance at the courts in Dublin—would make any difference remained to be seen.

Section 4 of the act represented another attempt to contribute to the solution of the immediate difficulty. It restated in an expanded form the task of the examiners deputed by each court to vet all aspirant attorneys: these examiners were to enquire into the morals and qualifications of the latter and to report accordingly. The innovation was no dead letter, for the names of the first five common pleas examiners appointed for this purpose under the terms of the act are preserved in an order of that court made in Trinity term 1774. Apart from the prothonotary (the hon. Barry Barry) or his deputy (Hector Graham), these were to be the following practising common pleas attorneys: William Lane, Crosdail Moloney, John Carroll and William Lyster.

Several other aspects of entry procedure were touched on. Section 5 stipulated that all apprentice-applicants had to furnish their names, those of their master and their parents, and also details of their place of residence. Two matters were left entirely to the discretion of the judges. Section 7 acknowledged their right to grant exemptions from the rule of compulsory attendance in court. Section 9, re-echoing perhaps a provision to be found in the statute 4 Henry IV, c.18, confirmed the possession by the judges of all three common law courts of a broad dispensing power. Nothing, the wording of the section ran, was to prevent the judges or the barons respectively from conducting their own examination into the character and qualifications of such persons as applied,

or from admitting or refusing to admit such persons in such manner and with discretion, as the said judges and barons respectively have heretofore in that behalf lawfully used.[71]

Section 9 thus retained in the judiciary the power to regulate a large number of matters. It was under section 9 that the judges of the several courts purported to act when allowing suppliants to abridge the period of their apprenticeship. Predictably, as will be demonstrated, use of section 9 for such purposes was to prove extremely contentious. It was under powers implicit in the same section too that the judges promulgated and later varied the rules that governed the admission in one common law court of an

71. *Moore & Lowry*, app. I, p. 55.

attorney already admitted to practice in either of the remaining two. But section 9 could be utilised for the promotion of some more immediate educational objective and on at least one occasion there is evidence that this happened. In Easter term 1782 the judges of the court of common pleas—Lord Chief Justice Paterson, Mr Justice Lill and Mr Justice Hellen—drew up the following order:

The judges observing that inconveniences have frequently happened (which must necessarily increase if not prevented) by clerks having neglected to learn to write and read the court and text hands,
To remedy which, they give public notice, that the officers and examiners appointed by law to certify the qualifications of clerks, previous to their being admitted attornies, shall require if such clerks can read and write the court and text hands well, and shall certify the same.[72]

It is known that the judges, in their capacity as benchers of King's Inns, discussed the same problem in that forum at this time.[73] It is not improbable therefore that the judges of king's bench and the barons of the exchequer adopted a stance identical to that of their colleagues in common pleas on this particular educational difficulty.

The act of 1773 spawned one major controversy. In 1781 attorneys with offices in Cork presented a petition to the Irish house of commons, seeking the exemption of their apprentices from the rule contained in section 6 that made a period of attendance at the courts in Dublin mandatory. The petitioners averred:

that on account of the great trade and business carried on in the city of Cork it is absolutely necessary that there should be at all times attornies resident in the said city to advise and conduct the affairs of the merchants, traders and others, and also to conduct and manage suits at law in the court of record of the said city where causes of very great consequence, particularly relative to trade, are carried on and determined, and petitioners flatter themselves that they have conducted the business of the said city for a number of years past with credit and advantage to their clients and the public.

They continued:

That for the well conducting their business, it is necessary, and has been the custom, time out of mind, to take apprentices who have been heretofore constantly admitted attornies of some or one of the superior

72. *Moore & Lowry*, app. I, p. 57.
73. Colum Kenny, 'The history of the King's Inns Dublin, to 1800' (unpublished Ph.D. thesis, University of Dublin 1989), pp. 255-6.

courts of law but that on account of [the act of 1773] the petitioners labour under great difficulties in getting their apprentices admitted attornies of the said superior courts, although the petitioners conceived that by the preamble of the said act it was merely intended for attorneys residing in the country parts of this kingdom and not practising in the profession, and not meant to extend to attorneys residing and practising in large cities.[74]

The Cork attorneys' petition was presented in December 1781 and initially appears to have met with a degree of support. However, when the heads of a bill were brought forward to give the Cork attorneys the concession they had sought, a group of Dublin attorneys counter-petitioned that it would be wisest to make no change. It was their contention that the act of 1773:

hath already been attended with the most essential advantages to the public and been the means of preventing many exceptionable and improper persons from being admitted members of that profession.

They concluded 'that a variation from, or repeal of any part of the said act . . . would be of the most dangerous consequences to the community'.[75] This may have been hyperbole but it clinched the argument. Matters for the moment were allowed to rest.

The adoption by the benchers of King's Inns of new rules in 1793 reopened the same broad issue. Rule vi prescribed that any attorney applying to take apprentices should state 'his place of abode, and whether he attends the courts in Dublin or not'.[76] An inference that it became possible to draw from this form of wording was that attorneys who were not resident in Dublin might not be permitted by the benchers to take any apprentices at all—plainly, from the point of view of attorneys resident in Cork and else-where, a retrograde step. Two Cork attorneys tested the waters in 1795. According to Duhigg, the benchers discussed the issue at length and, on being satisfied that for the final years of their articles, the apprentices in question would be in attendance at the courts in Dublin as the act of 1773 insisted should be the case, approved the application. In 1802 however, for reasons that are not immediately apparent, the benchers contemplated a shift of position: they declined to give any decision on a number of appli-

---

74. *Commons' jn. Ire.*, x, 273: 7 Dec. 1781.

75. *Commons' jn. Ire.*, x, 315: 5 Mar. 1782.

76. The rules are set out in an appendix to Duhigg's *History of King's Inns*, at p. 581.

cations presented to them, referring the issue to a sub-committee of five.

The impasse drew forth the wrath of Duhigg whose *History of King's Inns* was published four years later, before, apparently, that impasse had been resolved. Duhigg made no secret of his view that the rules of 1793 in more than one particular were ultra vires. He contended that it was intolerable if rule vi conferred legitimacy on the course of action followed by the benchers in 1802 in regard to the applications from Cork: the outcome of the delay was that 'no apprentices can be taken by Cork residents, whereby that ancient city may be said to lye in a state of legal blockage'. The Cork attorneys had not acquiesced lightly either in this sinister turn of events. Their memorial to the benchers went over much the same ground as the earlier petition addressed to the Irish house of commons in 1781. According to Duhigg's summary, that memorial stated:

Cork to be a city opulent, commercial and populous. That there are generally thirty resident attornies, who are all admitted of the superior courts; the greater number of whom served apprenticeships to attornies resident in Cork. That there is a court of record which sits once a week, the jurisdiction of which is unlimited in personal actions. That quarter sessions sit to try misdemeanours weekly, whereby apprentices have an opportunity of practical improvement in civil and criminal business. That much conveyancing is done in the city of Cork, which they go through with the assistance of their apprentices, but except resident attornies are permitted to take apprentices, it will be impossible to do.

It has not been possible to establish when exactly the impasse was finally resolved.[77]

VII

Legislation of 1792, the statute 32 Geo III, c.21, set aside the restraints and disabilities to which catholics had been subject and henceforth entry to either branch of the legal profession in Ireland was in effect open to all. Promotion of catholic barristers to the rank of king's counsel or appointment of catholics to judgeships still had to await Emancipation in 1829 and advancement of a catholic to the lord chancellorship further legislation in 1867.

77. The foregoing account is based on that supplied by Duhigg in his *History of King's Inns*, at pp. 550-5.

The early 1790s inaugurated a number of important if little publicized changes which also helped to shape the future development of the lower branch. For instance, the common law courts set out to improve supervision of the attorneys attached to each through a system of registration of names and addresses.

It is not easy to establish what degree of supervision of this latter type had existed previously. Under the act of 1773 apprentices had had to supply their names and addresses, and the names of their masters as well. The benchers too through the assumption by them of the power to vet the taking of apprentices by attorneys would have amassed an amount of this kind of ephemeral information in addition. The common pleas rules of 1671 insisted that all of its attorneys who wished to be regarded as in active practice had to make a personal appearance in court every term not later than the seventh day. Common pleas attorneys were also obliged to take 'dwellings in some convenient place' and to inform the steward at King's Inns where their 'chambers and habitations' were.[78] The requirements of the other courts in these latter respects are not known.

Starting in 1791, the exchequer of pleas introduced a novel system of registration that the other courts were to copy. Henceforth a book would be kept in the office attached to the court and in it each attorney would be obliged to enter up his place of residence. King's bench made provision to similar effect in 1798 (repeating the rule in 1803), and common pleas in 1799. The exchequer of pleas required its attorneys to enter their place of residence in the city of Dublin; king's bench and common pleas insisted on a place of abode that fell geographically 'within the Circular Road'.[79] Proximity to the Four Courts therefore was made not only virtuous but imperative. All these various provisions undoubtedly conditioned members of the lower branch to the routine of regularly entering up their names and addresses in an official register. From the perspective of government, such conditioning must have enabled the introduction of the requirement of an annual practising certificate that was to occur shortly to proceed with comparative smoothness.

It is not improbable that these new provisions stemmed from decisions arrived at earlier by the judges acting in their role as benchers of King's Inns. Other regulations promulgated directly

78. 13 & 14 Geo III, c. 23, s. 5: rule vi of the general rules of King's Inns of 1793 (Duhigg, *History of King's Inns*, p. 581); *Moore & Lowry*, app. I, p. 5.

79. *Moore & Lowry*, app. II, p. 38 (exchequer of pleas); pp. 153-4 (king's bench); app. I, p. 66 (common pleas).

by the judges in this latter capacity had an even more fundamental impact. Rule v of the general rules of the Society issued in 1793 altered yet again the requirements in regard to prospective masters: only attorneys—and Irish attorneys at that—it stipulated, could take apprentices. In the century and more that had elapsed since 1671 it is possible, through study of the alterations in these requirements, to chart the stages in the process by which the Irish lower branch was to be given certain of its distinctive characteristics.

First, the profession became exclusively 'Irish'. The common pleas rules of 1671 and the act of 1733 had expressly contemplated the possibility that an apprenticeship might be served with an English master in England. Plainly at this stage recruitment of persons born in England and undergoing training there was both sanctioned and welcomed. Few obstacles even would appear to have been placed in the way of more senior English expatriates who wished to transfer to Ireland. The case of Richard Goodenough happens to be documented; how many similar such cases there were must await future investigation. Goodenough served as under-sheriff of London at the time of the Popish Plot and was instrumental in securing the conviction and execution for treason of Cornish, the sheriff. Cornish's innocence soon after appearing, Goodenough was himself imprisoned. There is mention of this unsavoury customer in Gilbert Burnet's *History of his own time* and Dean Swift, in his copy of that book, notes that, following his final release, Goodenough retired to Ireland where he practised as an attorney. This latter detail is confirmed by the *King's Inns admission papers* which record both Goodenough's membership of the society (unfortunately, undated) and his death in December 1708.[80]

Entry into the Irish profession for English expatriates was made much more difficult following the adoption of the statutory requirement in 1773 that each apprentice should spend part of his apprenticeship in attendance at the courts in Dublin. Nor did rule v of the King's Inns rules of 1793 signal any relief. The notion that the English practitioner might somehow insinuate himself into the ranks of the Irish profession—as easily perhaps as Goodenough had done—was not immediately abandoned however. And it appears to have been only in 1863 that the Irish Law Society first successfully objected in an Irish court to the association of an English attorney with an Irish lawsuit.[81]

---

80. Gilbert Burnet, *History of his own time* (Everyman ed., London, 1979), pp. 235-6; *King's Inns admission papers*, p. 192.

81. *Scovell* v. *Gardner* (1863) 16 ICLR 84n.

Concentration of apprentices in the hands of attorney-masters was a development of no less significance. The prospect that an apprentice might enter into articles with, in effect, a member of the bar was terminated by statute in 1773. Articles entered into with a court officer simpliciter (a six clerk) were similarly forbidden under the terms of the King's Inns rules of 1793.[82] Rule v thus represented the culmination to an evolutionary trend, one doubtless assisted by changes in legal procedure and in the Irish legal system generally, which reflected an adherence to the virtues of specialisation and of a more pronounced division of labour. It read shortly and simply:

That no person shall be admitted a member of this society, in order to his becoming an attorney, who has not served twenty whole terms as an apprentice, to an attorney, a member of this society.

Rule vii of the same rules of 1793 governed the procedure for the admission of aspiring attorneys to the Inns. It again was an innovation:

That before any attorney's clerk or apprentice shall be admitted into this society, in order to his being sworn an attorney, he shall be examined publicly in the dining-hall of the society in the presence of the benchers and the society, then there assembled, by the same officers who now examine such persons, and by any other member of the society there present, who may think fit to do so.

A further rule, rule viii, obliged a master who refused a favourable reference to give his reasons. Rule vi, as we saw earlier, appeared to sanction the refusal of the benchers to let attorneys based in Cork take apprentices. Neither escapes Duhigg's bitter censure.[83] Over rule vii the invective is even more uncontrolled:

If this dominion over attornies was ancient and legal, still truth ought to accompany its enforcement. The preceding mummery was never intended for serious exhibition; without a character, how could it be enforced? Yet legal practicers have been hitherto such tame and voluntary vassals, that there seems no law or usage necessary to consecrate their servitude.[84]

82. On the position of apprentices to six clerks see *In re Lyons* (1839) 1 Ir Eq R 267. Six clerks were only finally barred from practising as solicitors and attorneys themselves in 1823: 4 Geo IV, c. 61, s. 12. The office itself was abolished in 1836: 6 & 7 Will IV, c. 74.
83. On rule viii Duhigg commented, 'There is not a scintilla juris scripti aut inscripti to warrant this innovation': *History of King's Inns*, p. 586.
84. *History of King's Inns*, p. 585.

Aside from the legislation of 1792, the principal emphasis to legislative intervention at this period related to financial matters. Stamp duty was leviable on each set of indentures of apprenticeship from 1790 onwards.[85] The provisions stipulated that portion of the income was to be transferred to King's Inns. After 1866 attorneys ceased to be obliged to become members of the King's Inns but portion of the stamp duty was still transferred to the Inns. The continuance of this arrangement soured relations between the Law Society and the Inns in the last third of the nineteenth century.[86]

The rules of the common law courts had long laid down what had to be done by an attorney to be permitted to continue in practice and to continue to enjoy the privileges of an attorney. A new—and in the eyes of members of the profession—an unwelcome development was the introduction of the requirement that each attorney and solicitor obtain a practising certificate annually and that this be paid for.[87] The requirement first surfaced in England in 1785. It appears to have been introduced in Ireland in 1806,[88] though it is commonly asserted that introduction did not occur until 1816.[89] Different rates applied, depending on the number of years the attorney or solicitor had been in practice: qualified practitioners with less than three years' experience paid at the lower rate of £3. The higher rate was £8. Although it can scarcely have been anticipated, this financial levy was destined to leave a mark on practice and procedure generally with regard to the system of admitting attorneys in the common law courts.

In 1715 statute made admission as an attorney in any one of the common law courts a prerequisite to the exercise of any right to practise as an attorney in regard to civil business at the assizes.[90] In 1851 a similar monopoly was conferred on attorneys with

85. Hogan, *Legal profession in Ireland*, p. 126.

86. Charles Gamble, *Solicitors in Ireland 1607–1921* (Dublin, 1921), pp. 44 et seq.

87. There was a not unimportant quid pro quo: the establishment of the conveyancing monopoly.

88. By s. 24 of 46 Geo III, c. 64: an act to repeal the several duties under the care of the commissioners for managing the duties upon stamped vellum, parchment, and paper in Ireland, and to grant new and additional duties in lieu thereof; and to amend the laws relating to the stamp duties in Ireland.

89. See ss. 65-68 of 56 Geo III, c. 56: an act to repeal the several stamp duties in Ireland, and also several acts for the collection and management of the said duties, and to grant new stamp duties in lieu thereof; and to make more effectual regulations for collecting and managing the said duties.

90. 2 Geo I, c. 11, s. 12.

respect to the assistant barrister's courts (the future county courts).[91] In the light of such statutory concessions it remained anomalous that admission as an attorney in one common law court bestowed no right to practise in the other two. That the anomaly actually existed is amply confirmed by a glance at the Dublin almanacks for the 1760s. These give names of all Dublin attorneys with an indication of the court or courts by which they had been admitted. The vast majority are identifiable as attorneys of one court alone and within that majority the preponderance is invariably of attorneys attached to the court of exchequer. Very few indeed had been admitted in more than one court and there is no record that any had been admitted in all three. Within a generation, however, as another glance at the Dublin almanacks will show, the pattern had changed: by 1802 for instance there was a sizeable number of attorneys who had been admitted to practice by all three courts and that number was to increase with the passage of the years.[92]

The act of 1773 had effectively restated the existing law that admission as an attorney was admission to practise in a single common law court. Already however a slight modification was in operation whereby an attorney admitted to one court could practise in another with the consent of an attorney of that other in regard to any lawsuit of which the latter had carriage. So much is clear from rules of court drawn up by both common pleas and exchequer in 1776 which sought to terminate the modification and which indeed appeared to accord better with the philosophy espoused by section 8 of the 1773 act. By 1786, however, common pleas had again changed its mind, reverting to the status quo ante.[93]

The court of king's bench seems to have done most to enforce the rigour of the 1773 act. A rule adopted in 1775 affirmed that 'for the better and more regular manner of carrying on business' attorneys from other courts who desired to practise in king's bench would have to be admitted in the ordinary fashion. Another rule the following year stressed that any such attorneys could not expect to be exempted from the scrutiny of the court's own examiners, and a further rule of 1784 even went so far as to

---

91. By s. 13 of 14 & 15 Vict, c. 57: an act to consolidate and amend the laws relating to civil bills and the courts of quarter sessions in Ireland, and to transfer to the assistant barristers certain jurisdiction as to insolvent debtors.

92. See Watson's *Dublin Almanack* for the years 1762 and 1802 respectively.

93. *Moore & Lowry*, app. I, pp. 56 and 58: orders of 19 June 1776 and Michaelmas term 1786 (common pleas); app. II, p. 38: order of 26 June 1776 (exchequer).

lay down the period of notice that had to be given by attorneys from other courts who sought admission.[94]

The introduction of annual practising certificates on a permanent basis from 1816 onwards meant that these various arrangements now assumed a different complexion. The certificate was a certificate to practise in the court to which one had been admitted as an attorney; it did and could not confer any right to practise in all. If the individual practitioner sought such a right he would have to seek admission in all three courts and pay three times over for the privilege, i.e. for three practising certificates. This financial impediment to the emergence of a single, comprehensive right of practice became increasingly difficult to defend in the face of the emergence within the legal system of a general rapprochement between all the courts. In a show of obduracy each maintained a different stance on the procedures associated with the striking off of an attorney prior to his call to the bar;[95] with equal stubbornness each adhered to a different time-table for the swearing in of attorneys in each law term.[96] But the substantive law they all recognised was virtually the same and rules of procedure became very similar too, especially under the impetus of legislation of 1831 which authorised the three courts to draw up uniform rules of court, the so-called 'general rules' of the epoch preceding the Judicature Act.[97]

Individual attorneys continued to fall foul of the strict legal position. In a succession of cases reported in the 1830s it is commonplace to read of an attorney who had been admitted in common pleas and exchequer alone seeking to move an execution in king's bench in the name of an attorney of that court and with the latter's consent.[98] This was of course a fraud on the Stamp Act of 1816 as the court in question did not hesitate to point out. The serious side to such manoeuvres was that proceedings handled by the technically unauthorised risked being dismissed as a nullity. In 1833 the court of exchequer, when faced with clear evidence of the perpetration of just this kind of abuse, reacted with remarkable equanimity, and charity: it elected to excuse the practitioner involved on grounds of his youth and of the fact that he did 'a lot of business'.[99]

94. *Moore & Lowry*, pp. 124 (rule of May 1775), 125 (rule of 25 June 1776), 135 (rule of 29 Nov. 1784).

95. See *In re Smith* (1838) Crawf & Dix 611.

96. *Moore & Lowry*, p. 233. The data there supplied presumably represents the then current situation in 1842.

97. By s. 5 of 1 & 2 Will IV, c. 31: an act to improve the administration of justice in Ireland.

98. E.g., *Murphy* v. *Rafferty* (1837) 5 Law Rec ns 148.

99. *Dinnon* v. *Aubrey* (1833) 1 Law Rec ns 38.

The law on this contentious question had been changed in England in 1815 but no equivalent measure was immediately forthcoming for Ireland. To the average member of the Irish lower branch at the time it must have seemed that somewhere there was a determination to add insult to injury when in 1836 the benchers adopted a new rule that henceforth any future applicant to take apprentices had to be not only an attorney admitted in all three common law courts but a solicitor in addition. The following year the benchers contemplated a retreat.[100] In fact the pressure to bring Irish law into line with that in England on the financial side to the question was now proving irresistible. Finally in 1840 the overdue legislative reform was enacted. Where the practitioner paid stamp duty on securing his admission to practice in any one of the four superior courts (chancery and the three courts of common law) he would be entitled to be admitted to the three others without the payment of any additional duty.[101]

VIII

Another facet to the benchers' decision of 1836 and to the remedial legislation of four years later deserves to be noted: both contributed in different ways to the achievement of a merger of the ranks of attorneys and solicitors and thus in a sense anticipated the joint educational programme of the 1860s and the final union proclaimed by the Judicature Act of 1877. Historically, admission to the ranks of solicitor had been organised very differently—where it was organised at all. Their separate story can be briefly recounted.

In the common law courts the attorneys oversaw the critical procedural stages in litigation. A residue of tasks, in particular the drafting of documents, came to be discharged, not only in relation to common law litigation, but also in relation to that in the equity courts, chancery and equity exchequer, by a practitioner with the different title of solicitor. Solicitors were not covered by the regulatory legislation of the medieval and early modern periods. Though lawyers of multifarious descriptions 'solicited' causes in the various courts, no legal training of any kind was insisted upon—there appears to have been no apprenticeship system, for instance—and the attack on a number of them as 'sundry varlets' which

100. Hogan, *Legal profession in Ireland*, p. 97.
101. 3 & 4 Vict., c. 79: an act to amend the law relating to the admission of attornies and solicitors to practise in the courts of law and equity in Ireland.

Brooks records for the England of 1577[102] may indeed have been thoroughly deserved.

The first attempt to regulate them occurs at the start of the eighteenth century and is linked exclusively with the penal laws directed at catholics. A formal licensing system was introduced in 1733. Thereafter, no one could practise as a solicitor in any of the four courts, who, in addition to satisfying the requirements as to religion, had not served the minimum of a five-year apprenticeship.[103] That apprenticeship was described in identical terms to that demanded by the same legislation of the aspiring attorney. It appears to have been envisaged that the ranks of solicitors should be filled in much the same way as the ranks of attorneys themselves. In 1791 this in fact was insisted upon in a chancery rule drawn up that year which is of considerable significance. This rule provided:

That no person shall presume to practise as a solicitor of the court of chancery, who shall not have been first duly sworn and admitted an attorney of his majesty's court of king's bench, common pleas or exchequer, and who has not a fixed place of residence in the city of Dublin, and that from and after the last day of Hilary term 1791, no such attorney shall be allowed to practise as a solicitor of the said court, unless he shall first obtain a certificate, signed by the senior master and the registrar of the court, or his deputy, that he is a fit and proper person to be admitted a solicitor of the court and that he has a fixed place of residence in the city of Dublin . . . [104]

What constituted another important structural reform in the Irish legal profession in the 1790s was almost certainly the achievement of Clare, the lord chancellor. Unlike certain other of his initiatives of the period, this particular change was to endure. And, unsurprisingly, as a result, the numbers of solicitors showed a marked increase.

Administratively, there came to exist the temptation to treat solicitors on a par with attorneys. Over the matter of the oath that convention was to dictate solicitors should subscribe, this was a mistake as, it will be recalled, a solicitor with the name of Smith managed to persuade Sir William Mc Mahon, the master of the rolls, in the case of *Birch* v. *Oldis*, firmly relying on the text of the 1791 chancery rule.[105] In other contexts, the perceived equivalence

102. Brooks, *Pettyfoggers and vipers*, p. 26.

103. 7 Geo II, c. 5, s. 7.

104. H.G. Hughes, *Practice of the court of chancery in Ireland* (Dublin, 1837), pp. 429-30: rule of 1 Jan. 1791.

105. *Birch* v. *Oldis* (1831) Glascock 351.

of function was close enough to the mark. And the decision to apply the rules on the annual practising certificate to each attorney and solicitor willy-nilly made sound sense. Efforts continued to be made nonetheless to emphasise the distinctiveness of the role of the solicitor. In a case in 1824 an attorney with the name of Barrett was discovered to have used the name of a solicitor called Tobin in defending a suit in equity. The court was not prepared to ignore what had been done. The manoeuvre flouted the rule of 1791 on attorneys becoming solicitors; it constituted, moreover, a fraud on the Stamp Act.[106] The next year the lord chancellor had occasion to point out that only a solicitor recognised as such by the court would be entitled to costs in any equity suit.[107] Plainly one ignored these demarcation rules at one's peril.

The comparison with the predicament of attorneys seeking without proper authority to maintain a presence in all three common law courts is striking. Even the experience of shared misfortune therefore had a levelling tendency. As occurred in relation to attorneys, the benchers' resolution of 1836 and the reform of the law on the annual practising certificate served to bring much closer the emergence of a unified lower branch. Within a few short years only the notaries public, the licensed conveyancers and the proctors of the ecclesiastical courts failed to fit neatly into the pattern of what was unfolding.

IX

In 1821 parliament sanctioned a reduction in the period of apprenticeship from five years to three for graduates of the three universities of Oxford, Cambridge and Dublin (Trinity College).[108] This move, whilst it connoted a welcome preoccupation with the educational attainments of aspiring attorneys, a preoccupation that was to intensify as the century progressed, by no means commanded universal support at the time. A London practitioner told the house of commons select committee in 1821 for instance that it could not be claimed that a university education was absolutely necessary for the profession of an attorney or a solicitor.[109] Three years earlier an attorney in the north of England had been asked to advise a Mrs Munby of York whether she should consider send-

106. *Lawrence v. Sharp* (1824) 1 Hogan 85.
107. *French v. Morgan* (1825) 1 Hogan 230.
108. 1 & 2 Geo IV, c. 48: an act to amend the several acts for the regulation of attornies and solicitors.
109. Hogan, *Legal profession in Ireland*, p. 92.

ing her son to university as a first step to his becoming an attorney. In forthright terms he had pronounced against: 'It would not only defeat all that you had planned for his future introduction into business; but would most probably be ruinous to him.'[110] She was urged instead to send her offspring to a respectable academy.

Parliament pressed ahead regardless. The resultant legislation contended that the present five-year period of apprenticeship, a feature of both English and Irish statute law, was from its undue length likely to deter the graduate and that it was expedient that entry to the profession should be facilitated 'in consideration of the learning and abilities' requisite for the taking of a university degree.[111] The concession was surrounded by a number of restrictions set out in section 3: in order to profit from it the arts graduate had to acquire his degree within six years of matriculation, the law graduate within eight; and indentures had to be entered into within four years of graduation.

The act of 1821 was not well drafted. On one reading, section 3 seemed to say that law graduates obtaining their degree within eight years of matriculation were to be excluded from the concession—the reverse of what was intended. An act passed in 1822 sought to rectify the error.[112] The terms of this short remedial act were themselves unsatisfactory however, for the measure conveys the unmistakable impression that a uniquely English problem was being attended to. The explanation for this of course lay in the fact that the draft of the bill of what became the act of 1821 had originally contemplated the conferment of the new privileges on graduates of the universities of Oxford and Cambridge alone and that it was only at an advanced stage that the bill's scope was widened to embrace graduates of the university of Dublin. Further legislative provision in 1827 gave the act of 1821 retrospective effect so as to confer an entitlement to claim admission on persons graduating before 1821 who had served three years' apprenticeship in the interim.[113] This entitlement, however, was

110. Quoted in Robert Robson, *The attorney in eighteenth century England* (Cambridge, 1959), p. 45.

111. 1 & 2 Geo IV, c. 48, s. 1.

112. 3 Geo IV, c. 16: an act to amend an act, made in the last session of parliament, for amending the several acts for the regulation of attornies and solicitors.

113. By s. 5 of 7 Geo IV, c. 44: an act to allow, until the tenth day of October 1826, the enrolment of certain articles of clerkship; to prevent attornies and others from being prejudiced in certain cases by the neglect to take out their annual certificates; to prohibit the stamping articles of clerkship after a certain time; and to extend the period for taking out certificates after matriculation at the universities.

expressly limited to persons seeking admission to the profession in England: no equivalent statute appears to have been deemed necessary or desirable for Ireland. In 1851 the general scheme of concessions in favour of graduates, originally confined in the case of Ireland to graduates of Trinity College, was extended to cover graduates in arts and law of the new Queen's Colleges at Belfast, Cork and Galway.[114]

The year 1851 witnessed the introduction of another major concession, this time in favour of the undergraduate student. Apprenticeship was reduced from five years to four for two categories of student: those studying simultaneously for a university degree and those pursuing simultaneously a course of recognised study extending over two years at either Trinity College or the Queen's Colleges.[115]

These various concessions in favour of graduates, undergraduates and persons pursuing a prescribed course of university education represented a major shift in attitude by the profession. The particular concessions were to become part of the permanent educational arrangements governing entry to the lower branch. They also signalled the start of the involvement of the Irish universities in professional legal education which was destined to become a dominant feature in the twentieth century. As is about to be demonstrated, in the early years the judges were to place interesting glosses upon certain of these concessions, generally acting under the broad discretionary powers conferred upon them by section 9 of the act of 1773.

X

Considerable light is shed on the actual procedures governing the entry of attorneys and solicitors in the pages of Irish law reports from the late 1820s onwards, the precise point when local law reporting becomes both more comprehensive in coverage and more avowedly professional in tone. A short résumé of this body of case-law will not therefore be out of place.

One group of cases examines diverse aspects of the law on indentures of apprenticeship. The technical legal position was that at the same time as the apprentice was bound to his master his indentures had to be enrolled and the stipulated stamp duty

114. By s. 1 of 14 & 15 Vict, c. 88: an act for amending the several acts for the regulation of attornies and solicitors.
115. 14 & 15 Vict, c. 88, s. 2.

paid. A flexible stance would apparently be adopted however where, due to the negligence of some clerk of the master's, for instance, the indentures had not been enrolled in the prescribed office at the prescribed time: the apprentice would not be placed at a disadvantage. One such case was referred to the court of king's bench in 1835 and the judges there, having first called for a report on what had occurred from their examiners, had no compunction over granting, three years after the apprentice had first been bound, a motion for the enrolment of his indentures *nunc pro tunc*.[116]

By contrast, where stamp duty had not been paid, altogether different considerations generally would seem to have applied. In a case of 1830 from king's bench the judges there, it is true, chose to be remarkably lenient. Stamp duty had not been paid until the five-year period of apprenticeship had all but expired. The court heard that the apprentice in question very shortly after he had been bound had got embroiled in an equity suit which had drained him of every shilling and he had only lately enjoyed the fruits of ultimate success. The court went on to grant a *nunc pro tunc* motion despite an initial reluctance to do anything of the sort.[117] In the exchequer a much more hostile attitude was evinced towards comparable applications presented there even when it was arguable that the apprentice himself was not at fault. In a case from 1828 the apprentice had given his master the money to pay the stamp duty but the latter had applied it to his own purposes and the prescribed duty was only finally paid a year later: the court refused an application to antedate the commencement of the period of apprenticeship to 1823.[118] In a similar case heard in 1842 the barons of the exchequer again refused the relief sought. Baron Pennefather pointed out that apprentices could themselves ensure that they were not defrauded—and their entry into the profession accordingly delayed—by seeing to it that the stamp duty was actually paid before the indentures were signed. Baron Lefroy was perturbed that the master involved, William Barlow, solicitor to the Ordnance at the time, should in such fashion have managed to deceive both the apprentice, one William Fry, and the latter's father, a military officer. He advised the father to take steps against Barlow either before the court or before the benchers of King's Inns.[119] Whereas in the king's bench case of 1828 the court

116. *Anon.* (1835) 2 Law Rec ns 140.
117. *Anon.* (1830) 4 Law Rec 258.
118. *Anon.* (1828) 2 Law Rec 36.
119. *In re Fry* (1842) Long & Town 679.

indicated that they were satisfied that the applicant had not sought to evade the Stamp Act, by 1834 the exchequer had refused to accept that this was in any way germane.[120]

Departure, illness or death of a master during the currency of an apprenticeship occasioned a number of difficulties. A fresh master had to be found, one who was at liberty to take another apprentice, that is, was still within quota, in appropriate instances the erstwhile master's consent to the reassignment was required, and in all cases that too of the benchers of King's Inns, following the adoption by the latter of a rule to that effect.[121] In a case from 1832 where the master had simply disappeared and it was not known if he would ever re-appear, the court was successfully applied to for consent to a reassignment in principle.[122] In a further case from 1839 the apprentice's first master had died in July of the previous year and the apprentice had only managed to find himself a new master by the middle of the November following. He applied successfully to the court of exchequer to be given credit in respect of the 'lost months'.[123]

Eight years later the same court was faced with a more difficult problem in *Stewart* v. *Davis*.[124] The brothers Davis were attorneys and partners. James operated the Belfast end of the practice, and lived there; William resided in Dublin. Stewart was apprenticed to James and was based in Belfast. James died during the currency of Stewart's apprenticeship. William decided to move to Belfast to manage the practice from there, but since he already had the maximum number of apprentices allowed, Stewart had to be re-assigned. Stewart's family proposed the name of another Belfast attorney, Suffern. William, however, demurred, suggesting rather an attorney in Dublin called Cusack. It emerged from further contact between the parties that William would not consent to the option that Stewart be placed with Suffern unless he received a payment of £100. Stewart's family in turn sought a partial refund out of the £195 they had earlier paid over to James when Stewart had been apprenticed to him.

It is not easy to explain the conduct of William Davis and the barons of the exchequer, once they had been made familiar with

120. *Ex p. Kinder* (1834) 1 Jones 43. Kinder was four and a half years into his apprenticeship when he vainly endeavoured to secure a *nunc pro tunc* ruling in his favour.

121. On the importance of obtaining the benchers' permission see e.g. *Anon.* (1828) 2 Law Rec 74 and *Stewart* v. *Davis* (1847) 11 Ir LR 34.

122. *In re William Hitchcock* (1832) 5 Law Rec 222.

123. *In re Powell* (1839) 1 Ir Eq R 328.

124. (1847) 11 Ir L R 34.

the evidence in the case, did not find it easy either. The Belfast end to the practice had been operated separately and no part of the £195 paid to James had ever found its way into William's pocket. William admittedly was concerned to provide for his brother's widow and his many children.

In the result the barons of the exchequer ordered William to reassign Stewart's indentures; they also required the examiner to report on the refund, if any, properly payable to the Stewarts. Chief Baron Pigot elected not to take his leave of the brothers Davis and the financial arrangements of their firm without a few parting shots. 'Theirs', he observed,

was a partnership conducted as most are, one partner residing in a populous town in the country, and the other in town (Dublin); both take a share in the apprentices bound to each; one partner dies, then the other partner becomes the owner of the entire concern, taking the benefit of, what may perhaps be the most beneficial portion of the partnership property, the depending suits; he therefore must take the benefit cum onore, and, therefore, with regard to the liability to refund a portion of the fee taken on the apprenticeship of the son of the petitioner, it is but just that he should bear the burthen, if the officer should hold that it ought to be refunded.[125]

With respect to the period of apprenticeship itself, the rules on attendance at the courts in Dublin—the rules that had provoked the remonstrance from the attorneys of Cork—underwent some further elaboration. The statute of 1773 insisted on two terms attendance in each of the last three years of the apprenticeship. In Crowley's case the king's bench admitted the apprentice despite the fact that he had kept two terms in his third year, none in his fourth and four in his fifth and last. Ill-health was the explanation and on that basis the ordinary rules were waived as indeed the statute itself expressly authorised.[126]

The question whether master and apprentice were obliged to keep the same terms in attendance at the courts in Dublin was raised in John Julian's application in 1832. Julian had graduated from college in 1829 and was entitled therefore to be admitted after a three-year apprenticeship. His master, one Pollock, and Julian had not kept the same terms in Dublin. Pollock had frequent business down the country and it was Pollock's son who had been in attendance with Julian. It was a misapprehension, the court of exchequer ruled, that master and apprentice had to

---

125. 11 Ir L R at 43.
126. *In re John Crowley* (1827) 1 Law Rec 168; 13 & 14 Geo III, c. 23, s. 7.

attend together. Indications to that effect to be found in a book of precedents containing a standard affidavit of an apprentice to ground admission as an attorney were not warranted by law.[127]

In relation to the conduct of the apprentice during the currency of his apprenticeship a variety of problems surfaced.

First, there arose, prior to the intervention of parliament in 1851, the question of the acceptability of concurrent university study. The question arose in this way. The act of 1821 had introduced the concession of a reduced period of apprenticeship for the university graduate. Might it be possible for the under-graduate to claim the benefit of the same concession? The point of statutory interpretation involved was authoritatively settled by the court of exchequer in Carmichael's case in 1831. The conclusion accorded with the more intelligent reading of the clause: the concession was directed at graduates alone and the corollary entailed that graduation had to precede apprenticeship. Carmichael had become apprenticed early in his undergraduate career, and the barons of the exchequer, perhaps somewhat inconsistently in view of the interpretation they had just placed on the act of 1821, permitted an abridgement of the period of apprenticeship to occur. Chief Baron Joy yielded one hostage to fortune when, in support of his decision, he observed:

It is true that the order of time may be of importance; but it is nevertheless the duty of the court, to support the respectability of the profession, and to encourage those who have had a collegiate education.[128]

The possession of a university degree remained a factor in a number of cases falling outside the scope of the act of 1821 where abridgement of the customary period of apprenticeship was to secure court sanction. But in the case of undergraduates, the actual decision in Carmichael's case can be counted something of an aberration. Once the matter of statutory construction had been settled the courts seem to have been determined to set their minds against further concessions. Archibald Colville, another apprentice flush from success in concurrent undergraduate study which had earned him a degree, sought in 1838 the immediate concession that had been accorded Carmichael a mere seven years before, only to receive this reproof from Baron Richards:

---

127. *In re John Julian* (1832) 5 Law Rec 315. For the remarkable reply of the author of the book of precedents, W. Stewart, see ibid., at 317.

128. *Ex parte Thomas Carmichael* (1831) 1 Hayes 138.

As the applicant was going on with his college course and learning his profession at the same time, the statute is clear on that point, and according to that the apprenticeship must commence after taking out a degree.[129]

It was a lesson that had to be repeated more than once before the four-year period of apprenticeship for undergraduates was introduced in 1851 and all transitional difficulties were disposed of.[130]

Blotting one's copy-book by means of concurrent undergraduate study was easy enough to identify. Other blemishes in the careers of prospective attorneys were much harder to pinpoint. Three affairs, spanning the years 1827 to 1849, were the subject of special reports by the 'moral examiners' which were then in turn evaluated by the courts. In the case of Bamfield in 1827, the examiners reported against his admission as an attorney of the court of common pleas. Whilst an apprentice he had acted in his master's name and had been privy with others to extorting a bond from a person whose arrest he had contrived when so acting. The court of exchequer had even gone so far as to issue an attachment against him. The chief justice, Lord Plunket, endorsed the findings of the examiners: as guardians of the public interest, the judges were obliged to be careful; moreover, Bamfield had added to his villainy by making payments out of moneys that belonged to his wife and family.[131]

Dowling whose case was adjudicated upon in 1835 was more fortunate. Here again it was alleged that an apprentice had in fact acted as an attorney. For good measure, details of a number of alleged disreputable transactions were furnished. The moral examiners investigated the general background, found that Dowling had perhaps been imprudent but did not recommend against his admission. The Law Society who had taken an interest in the proceedings were not so hesitant: they opposed Dowling's admission outright. Taking their cue rather from the conclusions of the examiners, the barons of the exchequer nevertheless decided to admit Dowling.[132]

The affair of William Coates in 1849 disclosed a somewhat unusual but perhaps not unparalleled situation. A man of some

---

129. *In re Archibald Colville* (1838) 6 Law Rec ns 121. Compare *In re Collum* (1839) 1 Ir Eq R 278, where a graduate of three-years standing was permitted an abridgement even though he had commenced articles before he became a graduate and had not been bound de novo.

130. *In re Foot* (1855) 4 ICLR 499.

131. *In re Bamfield* (1827-28) 1 Law Rec 12.

132. *In re Dowling* (1835) 3 Law Rec ns 198.

wealth, he appears to have been brought in to help rescue a failing practice. Technically the apprentice, Coates seemed to possess more power than his master, certainly in regard to money matters. Objecting to Coates' admission, a Mr Kenny alluded to these financial arrangements—those evidenced by one document in particular—and also brought forward an undifferentiated complaint against Coates for sharp practice. Though plainly they did not like what they uncovered during their examination of the firm, the moral examiners once again did not recommend against admission. The Law Society did not appear before the examiners, but when the matter was aired again before the barons of the exchequer they both put in an appearance and announced their opposition to Coates' admission. A great deal of detail is gone into at all stages of the investigation into Coates and his master's practice. Eventually, the barons by a majority decided to admit Coates.[133] Baron Richards lodged a strong dissent. The deed at the centre of the controversy, he declared,

makes the apprentice the master; enables him to deny him a pair of shoes to his feet, clothes on his back, or a shilling in his pocket. With this deed before me, I cannot think service under it such service as the law requires.[134]

At the heart of all these controversies, including that associated with the status of the undergraduate student, was the fundamental question of what a legal apprenticeship was for and what was supposed to be happening in the course of it. Unfortunately, the notion of apprenticeship itself was rarely delineated with anything approaching precision, not even where—alas, too infrequently—individual indentures of apprenticeship from the years before 1866 have survived and their texts can be studied.[135] Presence in an office, attendance in court, gradually, from experience, from watching others or as a result of personal instruction, learning 'the tricks of the trade': no contemporary, invited to put flesh on the bones, would have been likely to have been more specific than that. This recurring vagueness about an element so crucial to the whole process of securing entry to the profession made it possible of course for markedly different attitudes to be manifested towards applicants for entry whose personal circum-

133. *In re Coates* (1849) 13 Ir LR 235.

134. At 245.

135. Irish indentures from 1790 and 1865 are quoted in Hogan, *Legal profession in Ireland*, p. 108.

stances diverged from those of the normal run of candidates. Nowhere were these attitudes to prove more contradictory than in the case of applicants for admission who whilst apprenticed to the traditional type of master simultaneously held down a job as salaried clerk to an officer of the court. Apart from the biblical-sounding question as to whether such individuals could satisfactorily serve two masters at the same time, concern was inevitably expressed at their possession of an independent source of income. A further factor that entered into the equation was the circumstance that such individuals almost certainly did manage to acquire, from the strange routes their careers had assumed, considerable knowledge of the law and the practice of the courts: could that, consistently with the standards that the lower branch sought to espouse, actually be held against anyone?

The suppression of a range of court offices in the 1820s and '30s threw a number of such salaried clerks out of a permanent job, and the issue of their admission into private practice became acute. Eventually one of their number, Timothy Lyons, after several rebuffs, managed in 1838 to persuade Lord Plunket, by this stage lord chancellor, that there was no insuperable opposition to his admission as a solicitor. Exchequer soon followed suit, sanctioning Lyons' admission as an attorney of that court a few months later.[136]

Throughout the Law Society had opposed the application not because, they hastened to say, they were against Lyons personally but because he belonged to

a class of persons whose admission . . . would do away with the general rule against mock apprenticeships and leave the profession open to those mischievous consequences which must ever ensue from the admission into it of incompetent and irresponsible persons.[137]

Their objection in short was grounded on the belief that a person who held down two jobs at the same time was necessarily a risky investment. Lyons indubitably could not be regarded as having followed the normal route in his apprenticeship. None of this special pleading prevailed with Lord Plunket. Lyons had had a responsible job as clerk to one of the six clerks in chancery; he could not but have acquired a sound grasp of the law and of the practice of that court. As to other possible grounds of objection,

136. *In re Timothy Lyons* (1837) 6 Law Rec ns 116n, (1838) 1 Dr & Walsh 327, (1839) 1 Ir Eq R 267.
137. 1 Dr & Walsh at 331.

the lord chancellor was content to observe that Lyons was a young man who had 'acted with the greatest propriety', was 'of unimpeachable moral character', and had 'applied himself with the utmost diligence to the duties of his profession, meritoriously endeavouring at the same time to give assistance to a family depending upon him'.[138]

It is not known how many members of the group of ex-salaried clerks to which Lyons had belonged sought, and were granted, admission as attorneys and solicitors in the wake of Lyons' final success after a struggle lasting five years. Perhaps not very many. It seems probable even so that the Law Society would not have lightly abandoned the fight against what they had chosen to label 'mock and colourable' apprenticeships.

Applications to abridge the normal five-year period of apprenticeship were probably already in contemplation when the Irish parliament chose to confirm the dispensing power of the judges in enacting section 9 of the act of 1773. They were destined to become comparatively frequent, so frequent in fact that special rules of court were drawn up to regulate the manner of their presentation. Contemporaneously with the promulgation of section 9, G.E. Howard had expressed his concern lest the power bestowed by it might not be 'too indulgently exercised'.[139] As events were to show, that concern was soundly based.

The case-law from the late 1820s onwards amply demonstrates that exercise of this dispensing power could be requested for any one of a number of different reasons. It might be called in aid to secure the regularisation of the position of some apprentice where his indentures had not been enrolled, or stamp duty paid, at the specified time. Most commonly however it was resorted to in order to obtain the sanction of the court to the abridgement of the length of an individual apprenticeship. One instance is recorded of the court sanctioning such an abridgement in order to facilitate an apprentice on the point of emigrating to Australia.[140] But the background in the overwhelming majority of such applications was very different: another member of the apprentice's family already an attorney would have died and the application for an abridgement presented by the apprentice would be designed to enable him to succeed to the family practice with the least possible delay.

138. 1 Dr & Walsh at 334.

139. *Moore & Lowry*, pp. 232-33: king's bench rule of 26 Nov. 1832; Hogan, *Legal profession in Ireland*, p. 96 (quoting Howard).

140. *Ex parte Bushe* (1854) 4 ICLR 434.

Succession to an uncle, brother or brother-in-law might be sought in this fashion, but it was the death of a father that precipitated most of the applications.[141] In cases recorded from before 1835 the courts seem to have been prepared to sanction an abridgement by as much as four years. Thereafter, however, they seem to have insisted that at least three years had to be served before application could be made. At the same stage too they drew the line at sanctioning an abridgement that would have enabled anyone to become an attorney under the age of 21.[142] So far as the actual merits of the individual application were concerned, years of service in the attorney-relative's practice prior to formal apprenticeship created a favourable impression, as did the possession of a university degree. Support from within the profession was also likely to prove of assistance. A remarkable degree of support from this quarter was forthcoming at the hearing of White's application in the exchequer in 1829: every attorney and barrister in practice on the particular circuit expressed themselves in favour, after White's father had died, leaving a widow and nine children. The circumstances of this particular application elicited an instructive observation from Baron Smith:

I would be disposed to lay most stress on the petition of the solicitors who pray that a rule might be relaxed which had been adopted to protect them and who therein show they would willingly give up the emoluments they would otherwise receive if this young gentleman was not now admitted. The compassion of the case can have nothing to do with it.[143]

Compassion indeed does seem to have had little to do with it. Even after the courts had appreciably stiffened the requirements for an abridgement, it is plain that their principal concern was to attempt to achieve, by means of the exercise of this power they possessed, protection of the interests of the clients of what were so many one-man practices.

The case-law also sheds welcome light on an aspect to admission procedures that has so far escaped scrutiny: the position with

141. Death of uncle: *In re Jameson* (1834) 3 Law Rec ns 72.

Death of brother: *Ex parte Carmichael* (1831) 1 Hayes 138; *In re McNally* (1853) 3 ICLR 518.

Death of brother-in-law: *Ex parte Fitzgibbon* (1830) 1 Hayes 139n.

Death of father: *In re White* (1829) 3 Law Rec 34; *In re Nolan* (1833) 1 Law Rec ns 199; *In re Armstrong* (1834) 3 Law Rec ns 72; *In re Charles Hughes* (1838) 6 Law Rec ns 120; *In re Mulhall* (1861) 12 ICLR app. xxi.

142. *Ex parte Robinson* (1838) 2 Jones 622.

143. 3 Law Rec 34.

regard to members of the bar who endeavoured to become attorneys. Transfers of this sort occurring at any stage after the differences between the two branches of the profession took final shape are almost impossible to quantify. Duhigg asserts that in the middle of the eighteenth century a sizeable number of attorneys switched to being barristers,[144] but information in respect of traffic proceeding in the opposite direction is virtually non-existent. For the early nineteenth century however it is possible to detect the emergence of what may indeed be a new pattern: the barrister seeking to become an attorney in order to take over some family practice that would, following the death of some close male relative, almost certainly otherwise have gone under.

In the cases of Symes and McNally reported at length in 1844 and 1853 both barristers sought admission as attorneys following the deaths of their respective brothers. The cases had different outcomes but on both occasions the barons of the exchequer announced at the outset that they were obliged to follow a ruling of long standing made by the benchers that no barrister could be admitted an attorney until he had first been disbarred and then entered into indentures of apprenticeship. Only then could any question of the abridgement of the period of apprenticeship be entertained. This latter represented a concession which the Law Society, in observations addressed to the court over Symes' application, were clearly loath to accept. 'It is very important,' they declared, 'that all should enter into the profession of attorney on nearly equal terms; that one should not have to undergo great expense and a long preparation, which another is spared'.[145]

Over Symes' application the barons of the exchequer stood their ground and admitted Symes almost at once. He had in fact been exceptionally well qualified. A graduate who had served in the office of the assistant clerk of the rules in the court of queen's bench, he had been in the chambers of a distinguished Lincoln's Inn conveyancer, Mr Malins, and had been in practice at the Irish bar for seven years. In addition, in conjunction with Jebb, Symes had brought out a set of reports of Irish queen's bench decisions.

McNally's application presented in 1853 looked remarkably similar. He had been in practice at the bar for twelve years. Prior to that he had been in the chambers of an eminent pleader, Mr Molyneux. McNally sought another swift transfer after his brother, an attorney, had been killed in a railway accident. The attorney general of the day appeared on behalf of the Law Society in order

144. Duhigg, *History of King's Inns*, p. 313.
145. *In re Symes* (1844) 7 Ir Eq R 339 at 342.

yet again to oppose an application for a major abridgement in the period of apprenticeship. Once more however the barons of the exchequer were unimpressed and they voted to authorise McNally's admission. On this occasion, however, the instinct of the Law Society proved sounder. Five months after admitting McNally the barons of the exchequer vacated their order on the strength of evidence of disreputable conduct on McNally's part which had subsequently come to light. His undoing was a series of financial dealings with his brother's widow—there had been assigned to him the costs due the brother at the time of the latter's death and all of the widow's interest in the outcome of lawsuits that had then been pending.[146]

The basic rule governing applications in this area—that there had to be disbarment and then a period of apprenticeship—was regularly operated on a number of subsequent occasions. Publicity over its terms could still be required however as the circumstances of Hilliard's application in 1858 made clear.[147]

A last group of cases focus on the final stages of the process of gaining entry to the lower branch: the filing of the application to be admitted an attorney by the pertinent court. The act of 1773 and accompanying rules of court had set the requirements: notice had to be given in all the common law courts, though admission was being sought in only one; and notice had to be served by the prescribed date in the preceding law term. The judges were consistent in their insistence that these requirements be scrupulously observed. An aspiring common pleas attorney who had omitted to post his notices in the other two courts experienced this rebuke from Torrens J. in 1839: 'The attorneys of the other courts are entitled to notice as well as those of this court. It would be going behind their backs to admit this gentleman.'[148] Seven years earlier, in 1832, the exchequer refused to excuse an aspiring attorney who had posted his notices late, after the law term in fact had terminated: 'For aught we know a hundred persons might have been in attendance during last term to oppose his admission.'[149] In a second common pleas case, heard in 1831, where yet another aspiring attorney had omitted to post his notices in the regular fashion, Mr Justice Moore touched on somewhat different

---

146. *In re McNally* (1853-54) 3 ICLR   518 (decision to admit) and 576 (vacating of order).

147. *Ex parte Hilliard* (1858) 7 Ir Ch R 63.

148. *Anon.* (1839) Smythe 87.

149. *Ex parte Black* (1832) Hayes 206n, following *Ex parte Thompson* (1831) Hayes 206.

considerations, in moving the rejection of the application for special treatment:

I own I have a strong difficulty in assisting any apprentice who is not strictly regular in everything required, when I consider, that from the records of the King's Inns, there is an average application of 130 persons to be admitted, in every year. For their own sakes, apprentices should wish the utmost strictness to be attended to.[150]

XI

An element in the litigation summarised in the foregoing survey was the increasingly important contribution registered by the society which had been founded in 1830 specifically to advance the interests of members of the lower branch. The Law Society with its headquarters in Dublin was to grow perceptibly in influence and prestige as the century advanced, a high point being reached in 1852 when the society was granted its charter.[151]

In its formative years the Law Society came to hold a 'watching brief' in those cases where application was made to the courts for an abridgement of the period of an apprenticeship: the various applications of Lyons in the 1830s and the applications involving barristers like Symes and McNally furnish instances. Simultaneously, the society sought to apply pressure to the judges and to the benchers of the King's Inns on a range of topics connected with the maintenance of standards and the well-being of the professions of attorney and solicitor generally, pressure that, naturally in the course of time, was to extend to mooted reforms of the rules governing entry. By 1835 the courts had recognised the right of the Law Society to be heard to object to an application for admission as an attorney. Four years earlier they had listened too when the society took the initiative in proposing that two attorneys convicted of felony should be struck off the rolls. In 1863 the society scored a victory that was as complete as it was symbolic when the Irish courts upheld its contention that an attorney who had merely qualified in England should not be permitted to appear in an Irish lawsuit.[152]

Equally critical was the adoption of the new rule by the benchers in 1843—again as a result of pressure—that copies of

---

150. *Anon.* (1831) 4 Law Rec 187.

151. Hogan, *Legal profession in Ireland*, ch. 7.

152. *In re Dowling* (1835) 2 Law Rec ns 198; *In re Michael White, In re Jeremiah O'Brien* (1831) Glascock 55; *Scovell* v. *Gardner* (1863) 16 ICLR 84n.

memorials of all persons seeking to be apprenticed to attorneys should also be lodged with the society.[153] Baron Pennefather spelt out a crucial corollary four years later: an attorney who had voluntarily got himself struck off and who sought re-admission would first have to give notice to the Law Society.[154] 'He ought', the baron insisted,

to give them the same notice as a person seeking originally to be admitted; as though this applicant may be most correct and proper in his conduct, still he has been after a long time out of the control of the court as one of its officers, and a person might have done something in the meantime which would render it desirable that he should not be again admitted.

Prompted by developments in England, the Law Society from the beginning pressed the benchers for reforms in the system of education for aspiring attorneys and solicitors.[155] Apprenticeship, attendance at the courts in Dublin, possession of a university degree, exposure to scrutiny by the moral examiners, recital of a solemn oath, membership of King's Inns: none of this, so it was contended, quite reflected the proper image the profession now held of itself or guaranteed that the correct decisions on the admission of individual candidates were assured. The remedy was thought to lie in a two-tiered system of written examinations—an intermediate examination to be sat by all aspiring apprentices and a final to be sat during the concluding stage of apprenticeship. Change along these broad lines was introduced in England in the 1830s, but the benchers in Dublin were not satisfied that this constituted the right way forward. Thus was battle joined.

In the early 1830s the attorneys and solicitors of Ireland had made common cause to challenge an interpretation on the impact on the level of their fees of the Irish currency change introduced in the previous decade.[156] It is not impossible that from the lessons learned then there evolved the instinct for concerted effort and passion for unrelenting politicking that become such conspicuous features in a new, more assured and less self-effacing generation of practitioner. The claim advanced by this generation that it was motivated exclusively by the best interests of the profession may have been dismissed out of hand by certain contemporary critics, though equally it would have delighted earlier critics such as

153. Hogan, *Legal profession in Ireland*, p. 115.
154. *Anon.* (1847) 10 Ir LR 111.
155. Hogan, *Legal profession in Ireland*, ch. 8.
156. *Case of Solicitors and Attorneys* (1835) Lloyd & Goold temp. Sugden 349.

Howard and Duhigg who had regularly upbraided Irish attorneys for their pusillanimity. However this may be, a series of developments, some of them, interestingly and perhaps paradoxically, the achievement of the judiciary, undoubtedly helped to buttress this claim, which was advanced, first of all, by informal groupings and then after 1830 more publicly by the Law Society. In 1828 the then lord chancellor, Sir Anthony Hart, denied that under Irish law any attorney could be exempted from arrest for debt, in refusing a claim for the issuance of a writ of protection in favour of the particular attorney.[157] Over twenty years previously, in 1807, in another symbolic break with the privileged era of past years, the courts adopted a new general rule to the effect that attorneys litigating in a personal capacity would have to pay the same fees as other litigants.[158]

The battle fought by the Law Society to induce the benchers to introduce written examinations was greeted with final success in 1860. Six years later legislation terminated the rule that members of the lower branch were obliged to become members of King's Inns and, in acknowledgement of the new role of the Law Society, transferred to that body certain functions connected with the regulation of the affairs of the lower branch. To preserve a degree of continuity with earlier arrangements, however, the benchers were confirmed in their role as supervisors of the programme of education for aspiring attorneys and solicitors.[159] This programme, despite the significant reforms of 1860, continued to attract an amount of criticism[160] but the Law Society only became master in its own house when this residual link with the benchers was finally sundered in 1898.[161]

Throughout the course of this warfare over the perceived educational needs of the lower branch, the Law Society laid regular emphasis on its own respectability and on its commitment to the interests of the profession. Three years before parliament passed the act of 1866, thus endorsing the reforms of 1860, the members of the Irish court of queen's bench had seized the opportunity to express a view on the position of the attorney in the Ireland

157. *Anon.* (1828) 1 Molloy 76.
158. *Moore & Lowry*, app. I, p. 76.
159. 29 & 30 Vict, c. 84: an act to amend the laws for the regulation of the profession of attorneys and solicitors in Ireland, and to assimilate them to those in England.
160. Mark S. O'Shaughnessy, 'On legal education in Ireland', *JSSISI*, vi (1871-76) 124 at 152 et seq.
161. 61 & 62 Vict, c. 17: an act to amend and consolidate the laws relating to solicitors and to the service of indentured apprentices in Ireland.

of the period, a view against which educational controversies of both then and later years deserve to be set. An attorney engaged by the defendant in a pending lawsuit changed sides, provoking the client in question to lodge a protest over the attorney's conduct in a frank letter that he despatched to the Law Society. Was the occasion a privileged one or was it not? A majority of the court had little difficulty in deciding that privilege attached. A passage in Mr Justice Hayes' concurring judgment touched on weightier matters to which the circumstances of the litigation had tempted him to give voice. The upshot is a picture of the lower branch at a time when one radical departure had recently been inaugurated and policies designed to 'professionalise' the profession in all its aspects were plainly in the ascendant:[162]

The good conduct of the profession, collectively and individually, is one of the most precious possessions of the public, and one of the best guarantees of public liberty and safety. It is to our attorney that we confide the inmost secrets of our heart, in confidence that they will not be betrayed; and it is from our attorney that we expect the advice which is to regulate our conduct in the most important concerns of life. The profession of an attorney is not then to be compared with other, the ordinary callings and avocations in life, and the laws which regulate that profession very clearly demonstrate that; for while other professions and businesses are allowed, in a great measure, to regulate themselves, very special enactments apply to the attorney.

There is much more in similar vein. In the inventory that is appended, Mr Justice Hayes, however, omits the rules of varying date and varying provenance that had been drawn up to regulate, in the detail that they had, entry to the attorney's profession. In retrospect, this can only be regarded as an extraordinary omission.

162. *Hamerton* v. *Green* (1863) 16 ICLR 77 at 99.

Conversions among the legal
profession in Ireland
in the eighteenth century

T.P. POWER

THE BROAD OUTLINES of the experience of conversion among catholics in eighteenth-century Ireland are now reasonably clear.[1] That experience exhibited a pragmatic response by members of the catholic upper class and by other sections of catholic society to the strictures of penal legislation. What emerged in the course of the century was a hybrid class of crypto-catholics who had conformed in order to maintain or improve their landed status, career prospects, or political opportunities—a development which gave them an important influence locally and nationally.

In this context, a study of conversions among members of the legal profession is important for four reasons. First, it permits concentration on a well-defined group of catholics, thereby enabling the precise dimensions of the conversion experience for this specific group to be established. Second, it can reveal interesting patterns so far as career trends are concerned. Third, it is important in relation to an assessment of law enforcement, particularly of the penal legislation itself. The final importance of such a study derives from the wider influence that these particular converts exerted on eighteenth-century Irish society. While certain broad aspects of this question have recently been addressed,[2] greater consideration needs to be given to the relationship between conversions among catholic lawyers and initiatives in the legal domain (both statutory legislation and court judgment) and to their chronological spread over the century, and to such other issues as social background, regional distribution, and the pattern

1. T.P.Power, 'Converts' in T.P. Power and K.Whelan (ed.), *Endurance and emergence: catholics in Ireland in the eighteenth century* (Dublin, 1990).
2. C.Kenny, 'The exclusion of catholics from the legal profession in Ireland, 1537-1829', *IHS*, xxv, no.100 (Nov.1987), 337.

of attendance at the London inns of court, and how these may have influenced the timing of conversion.

The materials for such a study consist of a published list of converts, manuscript notes on individual converts, and contemporary directories.[3] Although there are problems in the use of such sources, from the point of view of completeness and full identification, they undoubtedly permit determination of overall trends. Utilising these sources, one can identify 229 converts in the legal profession for the period 1704–78.[4] Despite the evidence of alarm raised by the primate, Hugh Boulter, in the 1720s as to the great increase of convert lawyers, there were only 49 for 1704–27, with the greatest incidence of conformity actually occurring in 1728–36 with 55 and in the 1760s with 53 (see Appendix).

The articles of Limerick and Galway, made at the conclusion of hostilities between the Jacobite and Williamite armies in 1691, included provision for catholic lawyers, qualifying under these articles, to continue the practice of their profession. The liberality of these provisions, however, was shortly to be circumscribed due to the exertions of an expatriate group of Irish protestants who obtained a new law requiring Irish catholic lawyers and aspirants to the profession to subscribe certain oaths. Catholics found such oaths objectionable on grounds of conscience and faith, and so were disinclined to subscribe them. Increasingly, therefore, qualification under the articles of Limerick or Galway, for those who could lay claim to it, was becoming the criterion whereby catholic lawyers might practise openly.[5]

The access of other catholics to the profession was further restricted by an act (10 Will III, c.13) of 1698 which cited two reasons. The first was that 'papist solicitors have been and still are the common disturbers of the peace and tranquillity of his majesty's subjects in general' (s.1). This emphasises the security consideration which was to be the characteristic motivation behind the passage of the penal laws. Secondly, that 'at this time there are a great number of papist solicitors and agents practising within the

---

3. E.O'Byrne, *The convert rolls* (Dublin, 1981) (hereafter *Rolls*); Irish Genealogical Research Society, London: Fr Wallace Clare, 'Notes on the converts' (hereafter *Notes*); *Wilson's Dublin directory 1765* (Dublin, 1765).

4. This figure is arrived at as follows: the *Rolls* and the Clare ms notes give a total of 186 (17 of whom conformed twice), so giving a net figure of 169; from the *Dublin directory* of 1765 a further 60 converts can be identified, consisting of attorneys (43), barristers (14), and solicitors (3), supplementary to the above; thus giving a total of 229.

5. For the foregoing see Kenny, 'Exclusion of catholics', 350–1.

several courts of law and equity in this kingdom, by whose numbers and daily increase of them, great mischiefs and inconveniences are likely to ensue to the prejudice and disquiet of his majesty's subjects' (s.1). This statement highlights the over-representation which was to be a general feature of the profession in the eighteenth century. Together these two elements—security and over-representation—were to be mutually reinforcing factors in government attempts to control catholic access to the profession thereafter.

In pursuance of its objective, the act of 1698 reiterated the requirement concerning oaths of loyalty to King William, a disavowal of papal power, and a declaration concerning transubstantiation (s.1). Practising catholic solicitors, having taken these oaths, were required to educate their children as protestants (s.2). Although those in practice during the reign of Charles II and those qualified under the articles of Limerick were exempt from these provisions (s.4), it was obvious that within a generation this immunity would no longer persist. This process of attrition and the restrictions on access to the profession would in combination serve to reduce and ultimately eliminate catholic influence in the area of the law. This reductionist approach duplicates that taken towards the catholic clergy during this period also.

Significantly, however, within a brief time the act of 1698 was judged to be ineffective. By 1707 an amending act (6 Anne, c.6) was passed which sought to rectify the deficiencies in the earlier act: first, that catholics simply continued to act openly as solicitors despite a penalty of £100 which was now deemed too low, 'in respect of the great gains they make by their practice'; and secondly, as the act itself declared, because of 'the difficulties attending the prosecution thereof' (s.1). In response to this evasion, the new act specified in more detail the different courts wherein catholic solicitors might not function (s.1); it added the oath of abjuration denying the Stuart succession, to those oaths already required (s.1); the penalty for non-compliance was doubled to £200 (s.2); an informer system was introduced (s.3), and, in association with this, it was enacted that 'no barrister, attorney, officer, or other practiser in law or equity', was to be exempt from giving testimony (s.4).

Further, the act stipulated that attorneys, solicitors, and other legal practitioners in the courts concerned were forbidden to take catholic apprentices henceforth (s.6). The exemption of those who practised in the reign of Charles II or who came under the articles of Limerick was reiterated, but all of these were now obliged to take the oath of abjuration (s.8). This condition would have been objectionable to many of those concerned as it further curtailed the concessions which the articles of Limerick gave to certain catholic lawyers. Finally, catholics were not to be selected for grand jury service unless there was an insufficient number of protestants available (s.5).

All in all, the act of 1707 further restricted access to legal practice for catholics, by penalising those already enjoying this privilege through requiring them to take a politically sensitive oath, and by imposing a variety of other conditions, which together indicated that the political establishment was moving closer to an outright insistence that catholics must convert to anglicanism before they could practise.

In fact, the Act to prevent the further growth of popery (2 Anne, c.6) of 1704 introduced a range of provisions whereby inducements to conformity were held out to catholics. For a brief period catholics were able, by various devices, to avoid the act's more repugnant clauses. Expressive of this was an upsurge in litigation in the courts, by which catholic lawyers fought cases on behalf of those affected by the new act, especially landowners.[6] The act of 1707, while in part an attempt to strengthen the earlier act of 1698, was directed at curbing this growth in litigation. Because of the ability of catholics to circumvent the act of 1704, the compulsion on them to conform was reduced. This created a need for a more comprehensive and unambiguous law, and this came with the act of 1709 (8 Anne, c.3). This contained clauses tightening up the process whereby conversions were registered, and it obliged members of the legal profession who conformed to educate their children under fourteen years of age at the time of conversion, in the protestant faith (s.12).

The act of 1709 was to be decisive in compelling a greater degree of official conformity among catholics. Only two persons of legal background are on record as having conformed prior to the 1709 act: Richard Malone of Westmeath (1704) and James Farrell of Longford (1708), both resident in Dublin at the time of conversion.[7] But in 1709 six conformities are recorded: Gerald Burke, Denis Daly jnr., and Patrick French all of Galway, Cornelius O'Callaghan of Cork, Terence Geoghegan of Westmeath, and Terence Quin.[8] In 1710 Darby Egan of Tipperary and Mathias

---

6. R.E. Burns, 'The Irish popery laws: a study of eighteenth century legislation and behavior', *Review of politics*, xxiv, no.4 (1962), 498–9.

7. *Rolls*, pp. 95, 192. Farrell is described as 'councellor at law' at the time of his conformity.

8. Ibid., pp. 66, 303, 304, 305; *Notes*, pp. 45, 338. The Denis Daly jnr. of Park, Co.Galway, who had his certificate of conformity enrolled 16 Dec. 1709, is probably the same person as Denis Daly, French Brook, Co.Mayo, who took the oath 22 Dec. 1709 (*Rolls*, pp. 66, 304).

Reilly of Dublin conformed.[9] Thus by the end of the first decade of the century 10 conversions of persons of legal background had been obtained, and these persons came from some important catholic families.

Even though official conversions among catholic lawyers were not substantial again until the 1720s—being 17 for 1711–22 inclusive (Appendix)—the impact of the first group of convert lawyers was significant. The general intention in having catholics convert was to bind them more intimately to the political and religious outlook of the protestant establishment, and thereby enhance the landed and security balance within the state. While individual catholics were prepared to conform in the early decades of the century, the expected transformation in religious and political preferences did not necessarily follow. In relation to convert lawyers the result was cogently outlined in 1714 by the author of *The conduct of the purse of Ireland*:

These persons, till the very moment of their being called to the bar, or till they have certain expectation of other advantage . . . continue in the profession of the Romish religion.
They frequently, after their conversion, retain their former intimacy with the papists, and are as well and as cordially received by them as ever. They never make or endeavour to make any new acquaintance or alliance with the old protestants; they rejoice with the papists and when they are cast down it is so with them also. . . . In a word, excepting that they sometimes go to church, they remain in all respects to all appearance the very same men they were before their conversion.[10]

This observation identifies in embryo a section of the hybrid group in Irish society which was to become more numerous and characteristic as the century progressed. Thus these convert lawyers came to possess a dual capacity: they conformed officially and occasionally outwardly, but on the whole retained their catholic allegiance and connections. The emergence of such a class of convert lawyers came to be influential in relation to law enforcement.

By the 1720s it was realised in official circles that the penal legislation was not achieving its desired end of a neutralisation of catholicism. Indeed, the contrary was the case, as it was recognised that catholicism was vibrant, and that convert lawyers were using their position to defeat the application of the law. In 1723 a report

9. *Rolls*, pp. 88, 240.
10. Quoted in W.E.H. Lecky, *History of Ireland in the eighteenth century* (5 vols., London, 1892), i, 283 (1912 ed.).

to the Irish house of commons from a committee of enquiry
into the state of catholicism admitted that there was widespread
evasion of the laws; that this was in part due to the neglect of the
magistrates in enforcing the laws sufficiently; and that a situation where persons in state employment had catholic wives was
prejudicial to the proper application of the laws.[11] In addition,
those who had converted were identified as having contributed to
the ineffectiveness of law enforcement. At an earlier date it had
been thought prudent to appoint qualified, recent converts to
positions in the commission of the peace as a means of allowing
them to become part of the establishment.[12] But by the 1720s it
was recognised that the optimism of such materialising was over-
hasty and self-defeating, as such appointees simply favoured their
former co-religionists in the application of the law.[13] A similar
criterion applied to the activities of convert lawyers, and the
report recommended that in future such persons not be allowed
to practise until seven years following their conformity.[14]

These recommendations did not come to fruition until four years
later. It came in the context of an admission that the number of
all catholic conversions obtained in the period 1703–27—494—
was not impressive, did not meet with expectations, and were, on
the whole, insincere.[15] In response to this critical situation a more
active evangelisation was forced on the Church of Ireland by
1730. This took two forms: the first was one of expansion,
whereby leading figures in church and state sponsored the
foundation in 1733 of the Incorporated Society for Promoting
English Protestant Schools in Ireland (later known as the charter
schools), for the purpose of an active conversion of catholic
children. The second form was one of limitation whereby in the
period 1727–34 a series of laws were passed, inspired by the
primate Hugh Boulter, which further restricted catholics and
converts functioning as openly as formerly in various areas of
political and professional life, including the law.

Boulter's influence in the formulation of this legislation was
decisive. His analysis of the critical position in relation to converts
in the legal profession is instructive. In 1727 he wrote to the duke
of Newcastle that:

11. *Commons' jn. Ire.*, iii, pt.i, 346.

12. Power, 'Converts' (note 1, above).

13. Ibid.; *Commons' jn. Ire.*, iii, pt.i, 346.

14. *Commons' jn. Ire.*, iii, pt.i, 346.

15. Power, 'Converts', Table I.

The practice of the law from the top to the bottom, is at present in the hands of new converts, who give no further security on this account than producing a certificate of their having received the sacrament in the Church of England or Ireland, which several of them, who were papists at London, obtain on the road hither, and demand to be admitted barrister in virtue of it at their arrival; and several of them have popish wives, and mass said in their houses, and breed up their children papists. Things are at present so bad with us, that if about six should be removed from the bar to the bench here, there will not be a barrister of note left that is not a convert.[16]

Boulter's remarks may seem exaggerated when one considers the number of convert lawyers up to the time he wrote. As indicated, there were 10 for 1704–10, 17 for 1711–21, and 21 for 1723–7, being 48 in all (Appendix). These numbers were not overbearing as it would have taken many practitioners some years to become established before having expectations of being raised to the bench, as suggested by Boulter. Nevertheless it is true that in the 1720s a greater number of conversions were occurring in a shorter period than previously. However, the interesting aspect that Boulter's remarks bring out is that many of these lawyer converts obtained their certificates of conversion in England before arriving in Ireland, and hence are not reflected in the official Irish conversion returns.

The second dimension to Boulter's observation is that lawyer converts had been negligent in fulfilling the requirement under the acts of 1698 (s.2) and 1704 (s.12) that they raise their children under fourteen years as protestants. They were able to do so because of a technicality: they interpreted the relevant clauses as not affecting children born *subsequent* to their conversion as these were not under fourteen years *at the time* of conversion.[17] The implications were clear: such converts were free to marry catholics and raise their families as catholics without legal impediment. Due to this technicality, the practice became widespread, with the obvious detrimental results for the objectives of the penal legislation in general and for the laws against catholic lawyers in particular. The protestant interest suffered as a result.

The third, and perhaps most crucial element in Boulter's analysis was his declaration concerning the infiltration of the legal establishment by recent converts. In a further letter he was more specific on this point, stating that:

16. *Letters written by his excellency Hugh Boulter, D.D., lord primate of all Ireland* (2 vols., Dublin, 1770), i, 182. Significantly, a similar outline of the problem was given by Boulter to the bishop of London (ibid., p.184), in whose diocese, no doubt, many of the Irish received their certificates of conformity, and who, therefore, would need to be alerted to the problem.

17. Boulter, *Letters*, i, 184.

Much the greatest part of the attorneys, solicitors, deputy officers, sub-sheriffs, sheriffs' clerks, are new converts and the old protestants are every day more and more working out of the business of the law, which must end in our ruin.[18]

This development, though it is difficult to quantify the accuracy of the assertion, is highly significant for an interpretation of the enforcement of the penal laws. Traditionally, in the catholic-nationalist school of historical writing, best represented by W.P. Burke, the contention was that those laws were applied to the letter.[19] More recently, a revisionist school of writing represented in the work of M.Wall, L.M.Cullen, and S.J. Connolly, has stressed that the rigorous enforcement of the penal laws was not axiomatic, and that much depended on the administrative resources of the eighteenth-century state, and the vagaries, personalities, and conditions in particular localities.[20] To the factors militating against the full operation of the laws, must now be added that of the infiltration of the legal profession by converts, who by virtue of their position were able to compromise the application of the penal statutes. The magnitude of that influence cannot be easily quantified, but what is important is that establishment figures like Boulter by the late 1720s perceived the threat to be serious, all the more so because its dimensions were inter-related: insincere conversion by lawyers for the purpose of professional qualification and advancement, their marriage to catholic women, and the raising of their children as catholics together undermined the intent of the penal laws.

Boulter's resolution in the matter resulted in the passing of an act of 1727 (1 Geo II, c.20) for regulating admission to the legal profession, and particularly for the prevention of catholic practitioners.[21] It enacted that from 1 August 1728, before any lawyer (whether barrister, attorney, solicitor, or other) be admitted to practice, they must first take the required oaths and make the declaration as laid down by the act 2 Anne, c.6, while converts seeking to be admitted must, in addition, prove that they were practising protestants for two years prior to such application (s.1).

18. Ibid.
19. W.P. Burke, *The Irish priests in the penal times, 1660–1760* (Waterford, 1914; repr. Shannon, 1969).
20. M.Wall, *The penal laws, 1691–1760* (Dundalk, 1961); L.M.Cullen, 'Catholics under the penal laws', *Eighteenth century Ireland*, i (1986), 23; S.J.Connolly, *Priests and people in pre-famine Ireland, 1780-1845* (Dublin, 1982).
21. Froude is incorrect in his statement that Boulter was unsuccessful in getting the bill he sponsored passed in 1727(Froude, *English in Ireland* (3 vols., London, 1881), i, 580).

Boulter had originally wanted this period to be five years and to apply to all categories, but the act applied the five-year rule only to sub-sheriffs or sheriffs' clerks (s.4).[22]

The deficiency in earlier legislation concerning the education of children in the protestant religion by converts was rectified. Henceforth, converts were to educate their children as protestants irrespective of whether they were under fourteen years of age at the time of conversion, or whether they were born later. This was to apply to existing converts and to those who might convert in future (s.2). Those comprehended as coming within the articles of Limerick or Galway were to be exempt (s.5), a ruling which must have increasingly become inapplicable as the generation it affected began to die off.

The immediate effect of the act was to occasion a sharp rise in conformities in 1728 to 9, the highest annual figure recorded thus far. Amongst those who conformed were Ignatius Blake and John Dillon, both of Galway, Charles Callaghan of Dublin, James Sexton of Limerick, Matthew Lyster of Roscommon, Robert Dillon of Dublin (for the second time), and Patrick Brady also of Dublin.[23] In addition to new converts there is evidence that the two-year rule requiring persons to show that they were practising protestants was being enforced before converts would be admitted to the Irish bar. In 1729, for instance, the bench of King's Inns requested such proof from James Roche, which he was able to provide from Robert Allen and Ignatius Hussey, the latter of whom was himself a convert in the law since 1718.[24]

Subsequent developments in Ireland concerning legal converts were influenced by changes in the rules of legal practice and apprenticeship made in England at this time. In 1729 the British parliament passed an act that required attorneys and solicitors to take a professional oath before admission to practice, and from 1 December 1730 an apprenticeship or clerkship of five years was obligatory before admission.[25] The act was to be a milestone in

22. Boulter, *Letters*, i, 182, 185.

23. *Rolls*, pp. 14, 20, 76, 77, 170, 253; *Notes*, p 61.

24. T.P. Power, 'The "Black Book" of King's Inns: an introduction with an abstract of contents', *Ir Jur*, xx (1985), 211; *Rolls*, p.140. Roche does not appear in the official roll of converts.

25. 2 Geo II, c.23 (Eng.), ss.1, 2, 5, 7. The oath was: 'I AB do swear that I will truly and honestly demean myself in the practice of an attorney [or solicitor] according to the best of my knowledge and ability' (s.13). The act was in force for an initial period of nine years from 1 June 1729, but was renewed again in 1739 (12 Geo II, c.13) and in 1749 (22 Geo II, c.46), which continued it until 1757.

the evolution of the lower stratum of the legal profession in terms of the advent of formal control by parliament over it, and in laying down a specific training period.[26] In the Irish context, the parliamentary control of the profession inevitably at this point meant regulating access by converts and catholics. Although the secondary purpose of an act of the Irish parliament in 1733 (7 Geo II, c.5) was to prevent 'obscure and ignorant persons from practising as attorneys and solicitors' (s.1), its primary objective was to rectify the continuing problem of catholic influence in the area of the law. Not merely were the earlier acts of 1698 and 1707 deemed to have been ineffective in this respect, but also, as the preamble stated, 'by means of such popish solicitors, the acts against the growth of popery have been and daily are greatly eluded and evaded' (s.1).

At this stage the problem of such influence must be viewed in the context of the overall threat which protestants believed an irrepressible catholicism posed. It was clear that by 1730 the penal laws had failed to achieve their purpose; indeed the contrary was the case as catholicism was virulent in many areas. For instance, so high was the level of participation of catholics as voters in the general election of 1727, that an act of 1728 (1 Geo II, c.9, s.7) specifically deprived them of the parliamentary franchise. Moreover, the report on the state of catholicism commissioned by the house of lords in 1731 revealed a well-organised church, in terms of its personnel, physical fabric, attendance, and open functioning. In this context, the position of convert lawyers was of key importance, since the effectiveness of the penal laws depended, in large part, on the state's ability to obtain successful prosecutions in the courts. This applied not merely to the wider catholic population, but more specifically to catholic legal practitioners. When the laws against the latter were deemed ineffective, the consequence was a diminution in the effectiveness of the legal system as a whole. In endorsing the sentiments of the house of commons in this matter, the lord lieutenant, the duke of Dorset, in his transmission of the bill which became the act of 1733, stated that:

the influence of the popish lawyers has been heretofore found so fatal, that several acts have passed since the Revolution to prohibit their practice but have all proved so ineffectual by reason of the obloquy and danger of inforcing publicly against such offenders, that the protestant professors of the law observe with concern the great share of business

26. B.Abel-Smith and R.Stevens, *Lawyers and the courts: a sociological study of the English legal system 1750–1965* (London, 1967), pp.19–21.

which is thrown by means of these solicitors into the hands of the converts.[27]

From this statement three facts are apparent. Firstly, catholic lawyers had established such an entrenched interest as to make the laws against them unenforceable. Secondly, they channelled much legal business into the hands of convert associates who used their special position to oppose the penal laws in the courts, where it was said in 1739 that 'two thirds of the business of the Four Courts consists of popish discoveries'.[28] In this context, it is noteworthy that catholic lawyers who had conformed, such as Richard Burke (conformed 1723), father of Edmund Burke, were to establish their reputations and wealth at this time, due to the amount of business diverted their way. Thirdly, protestant practitioners suffered in consequence and, by extension, so did the entire apparatus of the law.

The act of 1733 attempted to deal with this critical situation by the introduction of further restrictions on the licensing of lawyers and by making the definition of 'protestant' more comprehensive. It enacted that from the end of Michaelmas term 1734, no solicitor was to practise in the Four Courts unless properly licensed; masters and six clerks in chancery, attorneys and officers in the Four Courts, their clerks and apprentices were exempted (7 Geo II, c.5, s.1). A stringent admission procedure had to be followed henceforth before a lawyer was admitted to practice. The act stipulated that none were to be admitted an attorney or licensed as a solicitor, unless he was a protestant from the age of fourteen, or for two years before being admitted an apprentice, and who had served an apprenticeship of five years to a six clerk in Ireland or England, to an attorney, or to a licensed solicitor, and be able to produce evidence of such (s.2). Indentures of apprenticeship had to be registered (s.3); a new oath had to be taken by practitioners whereby they declined to allow disqualified lawyers to act on their behalf in the courts, or to take catholic apprentices as solicitors or clerks (s.4); and the number of such apprentices was to be limited (s.9).

Practitioners (with the exception of those subject to the articles of Limerick) who married catholic women or who educated their present or future children as catholics, would be considered to be legally catholic themselves, and would be disqualified from

27. Dorset to Newcastle, 17 Jan.1733 (PRO, S.P. Ire., Eliz–Geo III, vol. 397).

28. Quoted in P.F.Moran, *The catholics of Ireland under the penal laws in the eighteenth century* (London, 1899), p. 7.

practising unless such wives converted within a year (s.12).[29] In 1734 a further act (7 Geo II, c.6) reinforced this clause on marriage and education by enacting that converts with catholic wives or educating their children as catholics were to be excluded from acting as justices of the peace, and be subject to a fine of £100 and one year's imprisonment for non-compliance.[30]

This legislation of 1727 and 1733 was comprehensive and unambiguous. The response to it in subsequent years was marked. The number of converts climbed to 12 in 1731, 10 in 1734—the year following the 1733 act—and 8 in 1736 (Appendix). Indeed the period 1728–36, during which the most determined effort was made to purge the legal profession of catholic or convert influence, saw the highest number—55—for a period of similar duration in the entire century, even for the 1760s. From the mid-1730s until 1760 conversions among lawyers were only a trickle.

The upsurge in conversions again in the 1760s is related to wider forces. The key event was a judgment handed down in a case between a protestant discoverer and Edward O'Farrell, a lawyer and Longford landowner, who had conformed in 1741 and who had been admitted to the Middle Temple in 1747.[31] The judgment, delivered in December 1759 and upheld on appeal in the British house of lords in 1761, decreed O'Farrell's property to the discoverer on the basis that O'Farrell had completed the registration of his conformity within six calendar months instead of six lunar months (the shorter of the two), as required by law.[32] Because of this difference of a few days, O'Farrell was judged to be still legally a catholic and therefore not entitled to the full benefits of conformity. The insecurity created as a result accounts for the high number of conversions, or re-conversions in many cases, as individuals desired to have their conformity fulfil the proper legal requirements.

Such conversion was also high for lawyers in the 1760s, reaching a peak with 12 in 1763 (Appendix). Among those who conformed as this time were Philip Barry, Cork (1761), Martin Blake, Mayo (1765), Thomas Coffey, Longford (1765), Patrick Corbett, Dublin

29. If his wife died and he survived her, then the disqualification would cease (s.13).
30. The description of the act given in T.W.Moody, F.X.Martin, and F.J.Byrne (ed.), *A new history of Ireland, viii: a chronology of Irish history to 1976* (Oxford, 1982), p. 266 is inaccurate. It should read: 'Apr.29. Act (7 Geo II, c.6) prohibits converts to established church, who have catholic wives or educating their children as catholics, from acting as justices of the peace'.
31. *Rolls*, p. 61; *Notes*, p. 138.
32. For further details see Power, 'Converts'.

(1761), Daniel Feely, Dublin (1761), Charles Doyle, Kilkenny (1762), and John Murphy, Cavan (1761). Those who re-conformed included Edward O'Farrell himself (1761), Dominick Sarsfield (1759), Patrick Brady (1759, 1762), and Thomas Fitzgibbon (1761). Sarsfield, who was admitted to the Middle Temple in 1733 and who was called to the Irish bar in 1749, conformed in Cork on 4 May 1740, obtained the bishop's certificate of conformity on 30 May, had it enrolled on 4 July, took the oaths on 21 October, and had his certificate enrolled accordingly on 24 October.[33] With a lunar month equivalent to 28 days, Sarsfield had not filed his certificate within six lunar months, and therefore, in the light of the 1759 judgment, would have been technically still a catholic, and subject to all the disabilities this entailed. On 17 November 1759 Sarsfield, by then a well-established barrister, conformed in Dublin, before the outcome of the O'Farrell case was known, but obviously as a precaution.[34] On the same day he initiated a collusive discovery in order to protect leasehold property he held in Cork, his title to which he assumed was safe under his 1740 conformity, but which now appeared precarious. Thus, for Sarsfield, a timely re-conformity and a discovery proceeding helped to forestall any potentially debilitating effects from the O'Farrell judgment.

In the 1770s conversions among catholic lawyers declined, in common with the overall fall in conversions after 1770 (Appendix).[35] The relaxation of the penal laws from 1778 substantially accounts for this drop. The relief acts of 1778 (17 & 18 Geo III, c.49) and 1782 (21 & 22 Geo III, cc.24, 62) contained no specific concessions in relation to catholic legal practice. Rather, the change must be viewed in terms of the chronology of reform within the legal profession as a whole in the last two decades of the eighteenth century. Already an act of 1774 (13 & 14 Geo III, c.23) had tried to ensure against growing malpractice by having attorneys being admitted to the courts screened more closely, and by having a stricter probationary period for their apprentices. Within a decade, another act (21 & 22 Geo III, c.32) dealt with the other half of the profession, by stating that none were to be admitted as barristers unless they attended King's Inns for five years (s.1). More specifically the act declared that none were to be admitted to the Inns who were not protestant (s.2). This act was subsequently overridden, however, when the powers of King's Inns were confirmed

33. NLI D.25,483; *Rolls*, p.250; *Notes*, p.360.
34. Ibid.
35. Power, 'Converts'.

by letters patent in 1792.[36] In the same year, the restrictions imposed on catholic lawyers and converts by the acts of 1698, 1707, 1727, 1733 and 1782 were repealed by a catholic relief act (32 Geo III, c.21). Henceforth, the oaths required by those former acts were repealed and replaced by the more acceptable oath of allegiance of 1774 (13 & 14 Geo III, c.35). Those taking the oath were entitled to be admitted as barristers and to practise as attorneys and solicitors, though they could not become king's counsel (s.1). They did not have to conform to the Church of Ireland (ss.5, 6, 7, 8). They could now take catholic apprentices and clerks who subscribed the oath (s.2); they could have catholic wives without penalty (ss.3, 9); and they were no longer required to educate their children as protestants (s.4). Despite these important concessions, the higher legal offices in the state such as prime serjeant, attorney general, solicitor general and chief justice, were still to remain the preserve of protestants (33 Geo III, c.21, s.9). Nevertheless, the restrictions which had operated for almost a century were now gone, and no longer did the ordinary lawyer have to resort to conformity as a method of professional advancement.

The vast majority who conformed over the century did so to practise as attorneys, solicitors, or other court officials. Of the barristers, attendance at an English inn has been identified in 92 cases, divided as follows:

Middle Temple	68
Gray's Inn	17
Lincoln's Inn	4
Inner Temple	3

From these figures it is clear that, despite the restrictions pertaining to the profession in Ireland, it was still possible for catholics to attend the English inns of court, as they had done in the past.[37] That this was the case is supported by Boulter's remark in 1727, quoted above, where he referred to the fact that the converts 'were papists at London'.[38] In the majority of cases such persons did not conform until their return to Ireland, usually within seven years on average of their admission to an English inn. In a few cases, exceptionally long periods elapsed between admission to an English inn and conformity following their return to Ireland. For instance, the period was in excess of 20 years for John Aylward of

36. 32 Geo III, c.18. By 33 Geo III, c.44 (1793), the act confirming the patent was repealed.

37. Kenny, 'Exclusion of catholics' (note 2, above), 340, 351.

38. See above p.159.

Galway, Richard Dease (given as of Dublin, but probably of Meath), Darby Egan of Tipperary, and Valentine Quin of Limerick.[39] But all of these persons were eldest sons and heirs who conformed primarily to inherit property and whose attendance at the inns reflected the initial, rather than the ultimate, career choice of catholic gentry families. A good example of this is Richard Kirwan of Galway, who had originally attended St Omer in pursuit of a medical career, but the death of an elder brother caused him to return to Ireland; in 1756 he entered the Middle Temple, he conformed in 1764, and although he did not practise, he proceeded to a distinguished career devoted to science and theology.[40] Although it is uncertain what proportion of those qualified to practise actually did so, it is likely that since the majority of Irish conformed within a decade of entering the English inns, most proceeded to practise at the bar, and that the small minority who conformed in the longer term were not primarily concerned with the pursuit of the law as a first choice of career.

In 25 instances candidates conformed before entry to the English inns, usually within a year prior to admission or in the same year. This again suggests a commitment to practise, and prior conformity was the case with individuals from well-known legal families such as Thomas Fitzgibbon, Thomas Rice, Dominick Rice, Thomas Duhigg, John and Matthew Ryan.[41] Ignatius Hussey of Kildare, who, as noted above, attested to the protestantism of James Roche in 1729, is recorded as having entered Gray's Inn in 1705 and Middle Temple in 1719, but conformed in 1718 before the bishop of London, and when he formally registered his certificate of conformity in Dublin in 1724, he is described as 'late of [the] Middle Temple'.[42]

In 31 instances there is a record of converts who had attended English inns being called to the Irish bar. Three such persons— Felix O'Neill, Dominick Rice, and John Taaffe—were also called to the English bar. In one case, that of Richard Dease, there was a call to the English bar alone.

The bulk of those who conformed came from well-established catholic, landed gentry families. These included those of Blake, Daly, Burke, French and Martin of Galway; Carroll, Dwyer, Egan and Ryan of Tipperary; O'Farrell of Longford; Fitzgerald

39. *Notes*, pp.5, 105, 130, 338.
40. Ibid., p.232; A.Webb, *A compendium of Irish biography* (Dublin,1878; repr. New York, 1970), p.277.
41. *Rolls*, p.140; *Notes*, pp.208–9.
42. *Notes*, pp.123, 152, 347, 350, 356–7.

and Stackpoole of Clare; Fitzgibbon and Quin of Limerick; Geoghegan of Westmeath; Meade and Barry of Cork; Rice of Kerry; Savage of Down; and Taaffe of Louth. Some were from titled families. For instance, Ulick Burke entered the Middle Temple in 1738, was called to the Irish bar in 1743, conformed in 1748, and succeeded as eighth baronet of Menlo in 1749, yet was a practising barrister in Dublin in 1765.[43] Similarly with Edmund Butler who conformed and entered the Middle Temple in 1744, was called to the Irish bar in 1749, was a practising barrister in Dublin in 1765, and succeeded as tenth viscount Mountgarret.[44] At least four converts are described as the sons of merchants: Robert Dillon and James French, both of Dublin, David Power of Limerick, and George Stackpoole of Cork.[45]

Where regional identification is possible, the vast majority of converts came from Dublin (56), followed by Galway (27), Cork, Limerick, and Clare (11 each), Mayo (8), Tipperary (7), Kilkenny and Kerry (5 each), Westmeath and Longford (4 each), Roscommon, Kildare, Louth, and Derry (2 each), and one each for Meath, Carlow, Queen's, Waterford, Wexford, Cavan, and Down. This broadly reflects the catchment area where the catholic interest was strongest in the century.

The statements made by Boulter in the 1720s attest to the wider influence convert lawyers had in Irish society: not merely were they dominating the legal profession, but their actions were serving plainly to diminish the effectiveness of the penal laws. As Professor Burns has shown, those laws became the focus for catholic agitation in the courts when parliament denied catholics the customary form of political expression.[46] As a generalisation, this contention is true and adequately reflects the situation of the first generation of convert lawyers. However, even though the courts became the centres of catholic effort, that did not mean that parliament was entirely outside their realm of influence. For instance, of the nine converts elected to serve in the 1713 parliament, four—Cornelius O'Callaghan, Darby Egan, Patrick French, and Denis Daly—had a legal background.[47] Egan, who sat for Kilkenny city 1713–15, held the important position of recorder of the corporation of that city from 1705 until 1736, and

43. *Notes*, p.27; *Wilson's Dublin directory 1765*, p.18.
44. *Notes*, p.53; *Wilson's Dublin directory 1765*, p.18.
45. *Notes*, pp.111, 162, 332, 373.
46. Burns, 'Popery laws' (note 6, above), 498–9.
47. E.M.Johnston, *Ireland in the eighteenth century* (Dublin,1974), p.65.

was among the pro-tory faction that dominated it until 1715.[48] Egan was involved in the re-acquisition of former family property in Co.Tipperary associated with the break-up of the Ormond estate there in the early part of the century.[49] A similar process of land purchase operated in the case of O'Callaghan who in the 1720s acquired the bulk of the heavily indebted Everard estate in south Tipperary.[50] The conversion experience was important not only in gaining access to the landed class for the family (it was granted a peerage as Lord Lismore in 1785), but it also helped to determine and shape the family's political position: it came to have an influence in the borough of Fethard, Co.Tipperary. And though it supported protestant settlement on the estate in the 1740s, in the long term the family favoured catholic emancipation.[51] Estate acquisition is also known to have featured in the case of two attorneys of the exchequer: Patrick Brady, who accumulated a large fortune and purchased an estate in Co. Carlow, and Terence Geoghegan of Westmeath.[52]

In addition to the above, there are other instances of political participation by converts of legal background. Another Kilkenny member of parliament was Nicholas Aylward of Shankill, Co. Kilkenny, an eldest son who was admitted to the Middle Temple in 1706, conformed in 1711, was admitted to King's Inns, was MP for Thomastown, Co. Kilkenny from 1727 until his death in 1756 (of which corporation he was also recorder), and, in addition, was high sheriff of the county in 1742.[53] Other instances of membership of parliament include: James Brown, MP for Jamestown, a lawyer and son of viscount Westport; Denis Daly, MP for Co. Galway; Cornelius O'Callaghan, MP for Fethard; and Windham Quin, MP for Kilmallock.[54]

Within the legal profession itself there are some impressive examples of advancement by catholics due to conformity. For instance, James Fitzgerald of Co. Clare, who conformed in 1767,

48. Kilkenny Corporation minute book, 1730–60, p.122. See also T.P. Power, 'Parliamentary representation in county Kilkenny in the eighteenth century' in W.Nolan (ed.), *Kilkenny: history and society* (Dublin, 1990).

49. *Notes*, p.130; T.P. Power, 'Land, politics and society in eighteenth century Tipperary' (unpublished Ph.D. thesis, University of Dublin, 1987), pp.11, 32–9, 85–92.

50. Power, 'Tipperary' (note 49, above), pp.39–42.

51. Ibid., pp.101, 121–2.

52. *Notes*, pp.34, 177–8.

53. G.D.Burtchaell, *Members of parliament for the county and city of Kilkenny* (Dublin, 1888), pp.132–3; *Notes*, p.7; Power, 'Kilkenny' (note 48, above).

54. D.Large (ed.), 'The Irish house of commons in 1769', *IHS*, xi, no.41 (Mar.1958), 30, 32, 38, 39.

was by 1779 a third serjeant at law.[55] Arthur Dougherty, who
conformed in 1757, was by 1767 public notary and deputy registrar
for the diocese of Derry, and was also an MP for Londonderry.[56]
Others progressed to achieve advancement professionally outside
Ireland, the two most outstanding examples being Andrew
Arcedeckne of Galway and Bryan Finucane of Clare.

Arcedeckne, who was born *c*.1691, entered Gray's Inn in 1710
and conformed in 1712.[57] Moving to Jamaica—the West Indies
being a traditional destination for Galway families in the seventeenth century though by now declining in importance—he acted
as attorney general there, 1716–17.[58] In 1718 he was elected to
the local assembly, a position he was to hold for the next forty
years. That assembly was dominated by planters, and by 1750
Arcedeckne was the second largest landowner in the assembly,
owning over 12,000 acres.[59] This landed wealth gave him great
political influence, which the British administration on the island
tried to malign in the 1730s by referring to him as a papist, and
the governor, Robert Hunter (1729–39), also complained of 'a
turbulent faction of Irish lawyers', a reference to Arcedeckne and
his associate, Dennis Kelly, chief justice of Jamaica and an
assembly man also.[60] Significantly, this complaint was made to,
amongst others, the duke of Newcastle in London, who at this
time was also receiving representations from Boulter on similar
matters of concern. In Arcedeckne's case, when the charge
against him was brought before the assembly for debate, the
assembly declared him a 'loyal protestant', a sign of the influence
he could exert in that house.[61]

Finucane, who was born in 1737, came from a leading catholic
family of Co.Clare. After reaching his majority in 1758, he
conformed in April 1758, was admitted to the Middle Temple in

55. *Rolls*, pp.100, 281 n.15.

56. *Rolls*, p.83; *Notes*, p.120.

57. *Notes*, p.3.

58. F. Cundall, *The governors of Jamaica in the first half of the eighteenth century*
    (London, 1937), pp.xix, 70; L.M.Cullen, 'Galway merchants in the outside
    world, 1650–1800' in D. O'Cearbhaill (ed.), *Galway, town and gown
    1484–1984* (Dublin, 1984), p.70.

59. E. Brathwaite, *The development of Creole society in Jamaica 1770–1820*
    (Oxford, 1971), p.40. By 1820 the Arcedeckne estate had 717 slaves, the
    largest on the island (ibid., p.121).

60. G. Metcalf, *Royal government and political conflict in Jamaica 1729–1783*
    (London, 1965), pp.38, 93, 93n.3). Kelly does not appear in the convert
    rolls. Other Irishmen who held positions of importance were Matthew
    Concanon, attorney general, and Nicholas Bourke, speaker of the assembly.

61. Ibid., p.93n.3.

1759, and in 1764 was called to the Irish bar.[62] The influence of the secretary of state, Lord George Germain, through his connections in the Irish legal establishment, was instrumental in securing the appointment of Finucane as chief justice of Nova Scotia in 1776, the only Irish-born person to hold that office. Until his death in 1785, Finucane wielded considerable influence by virtue of his office: he acted to get a fellow Irishman, John Parr, appointed governor of the province; he advanced Richard J. Uniacke (from the Co. Cork family, which had cónformed in the seventeenth century), to the position of solicitor general, who was to advocate the cause of catholic emancipation in Nova Scotia until his death in 1830; and he promoted the interests of a group of Halifax Irish merchants, getting one of their number, Thomas Cochran, elected to the council.[63] The final person whose overseas career can be traced is Edward Savage of Co. Down, who entered the Middle Temple in 1749, conformed in 1754, was called to the Irish bar in 1760, was a practising barrister in Dublin in 1765, and subsequently became a judge in South Carolina.[64]

These represent the exceptions: those who advanced to high careers in the law in British overseas possessions where Irish communities already existed, but, in the case of Finucane and Arcedeckne, making use of their position achieved through conversion, to challenge the British establishment. For the most part, however, the first generation of catholics conformed in order to advance professionally in the law, and to use their position to challenge the clauses of the penal laws in the courts. In this, they enjoyed some success. The next generation brought the process a stage further by a more active political participation, especially on the central issue of catholic relief.

This can be best illustrated by an examination of key legal families. Richard Malone of Westmeath conformed in 1704, having been called to the Irish bar in 1703, and proceeded to establish a lucrative practice.[65] The next generation of the family built upon the achievement of the first and were to have distinguished careers in the law. Thus Anthony Malone was called to the bar in 1726 and progressed to being king's first counsel at law; Edmond

62. *Notes*, p.142; *Rolls*, p.98.
63. For the foregoing see B.Cahill, 'The career of chief justice Bryan Finucane', *Collections of the Royal Nova Scotia Historical Society*, xlii (1986), 153; B.C. Cuthbertson, 'Uniacke and the struggle for patronage in Nova Scotia', in C.J.Byrne and M.Harry (ed.), *Talamh an Eisc: Canadian and Irish essays* (Halifax, 1986), 148.
64. *Rolls*, p.251; *Notes*, p.362.
65. *Notes*, p.273.

Malone was called to the bar in 1740, and became second serjeant at law; and Richard Malone was called to the bar in 1758, and with the two others was a practising Dublin barrister in the 1760s.[66] Not only did the family advance professionally, but it also came to achieve influential political office. Thus, following his call to the bar, Anthony Malone became MP for Westmeath in 1727 (a seat he held until 1760); he was later made prime serjeant (1740–54) and chancellor of the exchequer (1757–61).

Malone was closely involved in the political crisis brought about by the money bill dispute in 1753 on the side of a faction led by Henry Boyle, speaker of the commons, opposed by the Castle administration and its followers. One of the main protagonists for the Castle side was George Stone, archbishop of Armagh, who in 1752 presented the following view of Malone to the duke of Newcastle:

. . . there is a growing disinclination to the speaker's influence here, as he has been for some few years under the sole direction of Mr Malone, a name extremely unpleasing to the protestant and whig interest in Ireland; and as he was born and bred in a popish family, and as many of his nearest relations still remain in those connections, his own conversion (it being necessary to his appearing in his profession of the law) does not give such full satisfaction to zealous protestants as not to make them greatly averse to the thoughts of his arriving to the principal possession of power here which he is known to aim at, and which, with his own talents, with his constant leaning to an Irish interest (which name will always have a popular following after it) with his absolute dominion over the speaker, and with a dominion over the lord lieutenant also, he could not fail to acquire.[67]

This comment bears witness to the position of political influence which Malone acquired by virtue of professional advancement obtained through conversion, and how he retained a sympathy with the catholic interest.

Another example is Richard Burke, who conformed in March 1723, was admitted an attorney in June 1723, and proceeded to establish a respectable legal practice. His son, Edmund Burke, following a period of study at Trinity College in the 1740s, entered the Middle Temple. From the 1760s onward, following his alignment with the Rockingham party in England, Burke advanced his political reputation, and was particularly influential

66. *Wilson's Dublin directory 1765*, p. 21.
67. Stone to Newcastle, 3 Mar. 1752 (C.L.Falkiner, 'Correspondence of Archbishop Stone and the duke of Newcastle', *EHR*, xx (1905), 512).

in promoting the cause of catholic relief. His son Richard was agent to the Catholic Committee in the 1790s.

While, in the cases of Malone and Burke, eminence in the law in the first generation propelled the second generation into the mainstream of political life on the catholic side, a contrary outcome resulted in the case of the Fitzgibbons. John Fitzgibbon of Co. Limerick conformed in 1731, the same year as he was called to the Irish bar, and gained a fortune from his practice. His son, also John, proceeded to have a more illustrious career in the law paralleling that of the Malones, being called to the bar at the young age of twenty-three in 1772. From June 1772 to June 1798 he reputedly earned almost £46,000 from legal practice.[68] In the 1780s and 1790s, his political career advanced rapidly, Fitzgibbon attaining the office of attorney general (1783–9) and lord chancellor (1789–1802), and in 1795 being raised to the peerage as earl of Clare. On the political issues of the day Fitzgibbon was a staunch supporter of the Anglo-Irish ascendancy, and, in particular, he was a strong opponent of catholic emancipation.

The laws which gave a legal basis to the traumatic changes of the seventeenth century and the penal legislation of the period 1695–1728, together created a situation where Ireland became an extremely litigious nation. The result was a growth in the demand for legal services leading to an over-representation in the legal profession. Catholics were able not merely to participate in the fulfilment of this demand—despite policies of professional exclusion imposed by the state—but also to utilise their position to challenge the penal laws in their application in the courts and, in a subsequent generation, in addition, to stimulate the movements in favour of catholic emancipation.[+]

68. Webb, *Compendium*, p.196.

+ I am grateful to Colum Kenny for comments on an earlier draft.

APPENDIX
*Yearly figures of conversions by catholics of
legal background, 1704–78*

Year	Number	Year	Number	Year	Number
1704	1	1735	3 (1)	1758	3 (3)
1708	1	1736	5 (3)	1759	4 (1)
1709	6	1737	(1)	1760	2
1710	2	1739	2 (2)	1761	4 (3)
1711	2	1740	1 (2)	1762	5
1712	1 (1)	1741	2 (2)	1763	9 (3)
1715	1	1742	1 (2)	1764	3
1716	2	1943	3 (1)	1765	5 (3)
1717	1 (1)	1744	1	1766	1
1718	2 (1)	1745	(2)	1767	5
1719	3	1746	2 (2)	1768	4
1721	2	1747	(2)	1769	3
1723	4 (2)	1748	2 (1)	1770	3
1724	4	1749	2 (1)	1771	3
1725	5 (1)	1750	3 (2)	1773	6
1726	3	1751	2	1774	1
1727	1 (1)	1752	2 (2)	1775	2
1728	8 (1)	1753	1 (5)	1776	2
1730	3	1754	3	1777	3
1731	9(3)	1755	1	1778	2
1732	4 (1)	1756	3 (1)		
1734	7 (3)	1757	3 (1)		

Figures in brackets are for those who are likely to have been of legal background.

Source: E.O'Byrne, *The convert rolls*; Clare, Notes on converts; *Wilson's Dublin directory 1765.*

Two eighteenth-century provincial attorneys:
Matthew Brett and Jack Brett

C.E.B. BRETT

ON 11 DECEMBER 1724, the Rev. Jasper Brett[1] wrote to his barrister cousin, Michael Ward,[2] in Dublin, seeking advice regarding a legal embarrassment he had suffered:

I wrote to my son Matthew who is clerk to Mr Anderson in the Cheife Remembrancers office, to see if possible to get of a ffine of five pd. imposed upon me by my good friend Justice McCartney for Bayling a man barely suspected of ffelony, & whether it would be worth the cost & pains to attempt. I ordered him to wait on you for yr advice but have had hitherto no return from him. If yr affairs will permit pray let him have yr advice.[3]

Young Matthew's failure to obey his father's command was ominous enough; but, eighteen months later, much worse was to follow; and on 25 April 1726, Jasper Brett wrote again to his cousin:

My son Matthew who was bound apprentice to Mr Francis Anderson, Cke in the Chiefe Remembrancer's Office, has by repeat'd Misbehavr provokd his Master to turn him off in the Last Year of his Apprenticeship his Term ending next Michaelmas at which time I hoped to have him sworn Attorney. Upon a long tryal of discipline & his repeated vows & promises to amend his Life, I have been prevaild upon to send him once more to Dublin at my great Expence & trouble, tho' Mr Anderson

1. Rev. Jasper Brett, 1665-1736, was at this date vicar of Rathmullan, and curate of the parishes of Bright and Tyrella, all in Co. Down; eldest son of William Brett and Thomasene Ward.
2. Michael Ward, 1683-1759, of Castleward, Strangford, Co. Down, barrister-at-law, Dublin, appointed judge of the king's bench, 1729.
3. PRONI, D 2092/1/3, p.35.

won't let him into his house or Office (for wh I can by no means blame him), yet if he behave himself well for the 2 next terms, and diligently write for him in a Lodging of his own and at his own Expence, he may be prevaild upon to certifie for him that he may be sworn when his term is out. Without wh I have lost both my money & my son. My earnest request is that you woud give him yr advice & speak a word in his far. to his Mr on condition of his future good behavr. I have never seen the young man since his last revolt, and am fully determined never to see him hereafter or to make any farther tryal of him, unlisse he retreive the favr of his Mr and end his service with credit. I have desir'd the favour of Cos. Vere Ward (having no other freind in Dublin whom I could with Confidence trouble) to see him put into some lodging near the office, where he may have diet for wh I must pay (& God knows how well I am able) & hope both you and he will excuse this trouble wh I can't avoid putting upon you. I have sad Bills to pay his Mr what he owes him, & his other debts tho' they who trust Minors in their apprenticeship don't deserve, in my humble opinion, to be pd.[4]

Matthew, whose misdeeds must have been egregious, seems eventually to have been admitted around 1734[5] and practised in the exchequer court in Dublin. In 1762 he announced in the *Belfast News Letter*[6] that he had removed to Down (Downpatrick), and had 'taken Commission out of said Court of Exchequer, King's Bench and Common Pleas, for taking affidavits in the County of Down'. By this date he must have been in his fifties, and his father had been dead for nearly thirty years. At some earlier date, apparently about 1730, he had married one Ellen Graham of Killough or Tyrella, by whom he had six children, of whom the eldest, Jasper, died unmarried in the West Indies; John followed his father as an attorney; Mary, Lucretia and Isabella appear never to have married; and the youngest, Ann, married William Johnston of Ballykilbeg.

According to Pilson,[7] 'Matthew Brett lived at Killough in extremely confined circumstances. He came to town (i.e. Downpatrick) on Manor Court days, and pleaded trifling causes before the Seneschal for as trifling fees. His son John probably learned law from his father's practice, for the graduating of an Attorney in those days was neither laborious nor expensive'.

4. PRONI, D 2092/1/3, p.84.

5. *King's Inns admission papers*, p.53.

6. *Belfast News Letter*, 5 Jan. 1762.

7. Aynsworth Pilson, 'Memoirs of notable inhabitants of Downpatrick, 1838,' transcribed R.W.H. Blackwood 1930, Linenhall Library, Belfast.

John Brett (commonly known as 'Jack') was born at Killough in June 1736. He may have spent some time in Dublin, for he was admitted an attorney of the king's bench and exchequer courts only in 1771[8], when he was 31. He set up immediately in practice in Downpatrick, and for many years 'engrossed the whole business' of the county town, having no competitors till well after 1790. He secured several agencies, including the management of the affairs of Dean Annesley, the Savages of Hollymount, and the Mauleverer family; but much the most important was the agency of Lord Downshire's Downpatrick estates. It does not appear when he was appointed, but in 1790 he resigned the post of seneschal (an appointment made by Lord Downshire) of the manors of Hillsborough, Kilwarlin, Castlereagh, and Scatnailes.[9] He acted as solicitor to the Grand Jury for the county, was appointed clerk of the peace in 1797, and 'through the sole influence of Arthur, second Marquis of Downshire', was appointed county treasurer in 1800.

As Colonel Johnstone[10] later remarked, 'Treasurer of the County was in his time a very lucrative appointment as he was *really* the treasurer, and himself banker; having the custody of the money, and use and interest of it, between each assizes'. John Brett prospered: the several agencies brought in £1,000 a year, the county treasurership another £1,000. He was able to make substantial investments in land and buildings in the town of Downpatrick. In 1777 he built himself a handsome stone Georgian house in English Street which still stood until it was demolished, in the 1950s, to make way for the new county planning office: a wanton and inexcusable act of official vandalism, from an architectural point of view; a sad loss from the point of view of family sentiment; I paid the house a visit just before its demolition, and it was just such a house as I should wish to live in myself.

He was 'very fond of curiosities, and spent about £5,000 or £6,000 in collecting a museum, which he had in his house at Downpatrick'. He was a convivial man; R.H. Wallace[11] records that he was one of the sixteen founder-members of the 'Downpatrick Social Club', in 1780.

8. *King's Inns admission papers*, p.53; *Belfast News Letter*, 17 May 1771.

9. *Belfast News Letter*, 14 Sept. 1790.

10. Letter from C.G. Johnstone, late Lt Col 5th R.I.R. (brother of Johnston of Ballykilbeg) to Charles H. Brett, solicitor (the author's great-grandfather) of 10 Oct. 1904: PRONI, D 33093/12/J/3.

11. Col. the Rt Hon R.H. Wallace, 'Historical collections relating to Downpatrick,' transcribed R.W.H. Blackwood 1937, Linenhall Library, Belfast.

The Club met generally in a tavern in Scotch Street, known as 'The Four Alls', kept by Edward Connolly. The cognomen was applied to the house because of a flying sign which it had, having thereon:

> The King favours all,
> The Parson prays for all,
> The Soldier fights for all,
> But the Farmer pays for all.

The Club met together every Tuesday evening, at seven o'clock, for social enjoyment and recreation, each member wearing a silver medal, having on one side two right hands joined, surrounded by the word 'Unanimity', while the obverse side bore the figure of an hour-glass with the motto 'Swift fly the hours by wit and friendship blest'. Any member who did not appear in the club-room before eight o'clock was fined 4*d.*, and in case of non-attendance a fine of 6½*d.* was inflicted. It does not appear that there was much literary food provided. The principal business was indulging in the flowing bowl. Rule three provided that the president should call for the landlord's bill as soon as each member had expended 8*d.* for liquor, and in case this sum was exceeded the president was compelled to pay the surplus. A note to this rule says, 'The expense of Oysters and eating not included in the regulation'.

Notwithstanding his convivial habits, he was a pious churchman; in 1788 he had been appointed registrar for the diocese of Down[12]; and it appears that he was 'chiefly instrumental' in carrying out the restoration of Downpatrick cathedral in 1789-1812; 'when a new organ was put in ... in 1853, the old one was found, with the address to John Brett Esq. D'patrick'[13]. According to Colonel Johnstone, 'the Marquis of Downshire always stayed with him, when he visited Downpatrick, and on one occasion when the Lord Lieutenant was on a visit to Hillsboro' Castle, the Marquis tried to induce old John Brett to visit the castle for the purpose of being knighted, but failed: perhaps if he had been married it would have been different'.

Pilson[14] says that 'Mr Brett, though in easy circumstances and without family, having never married, saw very little company. He drank largely of wine for many years of his latter life, and in the evenings often made himself ridiculous. He is supposed never to have had commerce with the other sex. He was of middle stature, but very light frame, hair almost white in his age, snuffed to excess, was generally healthy, and died very suddenly upon the

12. *Belfast News Letter,* 31 Oct. 1788.

13. C.G. Johnstone, op. cit.

14. Aynsworth Pilson, op. cit.

roadside in the country, when out in his carriage for exercise'. Colonel Johnstone[15] adds that 'he was very fond of touring, and went all over the three kingdoms, posting in his own "chariot" '. He had made his will in 1808; his sudden death took place in November 1810; he was buried at Rathmullan. By his will he left £300 Irish (£276.18s.5½d.) to the Dean and Curate of Down to be invested, and the interest applied to making a distribution of Bread and Mutton on Christmas Eve each year to the poor, principally housekeepers of Downpatrick. In 1837, eight sheep and 104 sixpenny loaves were so distributed, but 'either from dishonesty or carelessness' of later deans the fund was allowed to dwindle away. The rest of his estate, including his collection of curiosities, to a total value of some £10,000, he left to his grand-nephew William Johnston.

To a later generation of un-Orangemen it seems a little ironical that on the one hand the remnants of the family estate in Lecale, on the other hand the modest fortune amassed by Jack Brett by his own efforts, should both have passed to the Johnston family—a family best known to history for the Orange exploits of William Johnston of Ballykilbeg.[16]

15. C.G. Johnstone, op. cit.
16. The foregoing notes were compiled in connection with the research for *Long Shadows Cast Before: Nine Lives in Ulster, 1625-1977*, published by Bartholomew in 1978. In that work, I noted the names of seventeen predecessors (mostly of the same blood, but some of the firm rather than the blood) in the legal profession in Ireland, of whom the earliest was my great-great-great grandfather, Charles Brett, attorney, of Killough, 1698-1758; nephew of the Rev. Jasper Brett, and first cousin of Matthew Brett, referred to above. In the end, it was decided to discard this material from the book since it related to the senior branch of the family, now (I believe) extinct, rather than to the cadet branch, which was the subject of the book; and which still carries on the profession in Belfast.

The legal profession and the defence of the *ancien régime* in Ireland, 1790-1840

JACQUELINE HILL

I

ON 15 JANUARY 1793 the grand jury of Co. Dublin assembled for the opening of the winter quarter sessions. As usual, there was an address from the chairman before the judicial proceedings began. On this occasion, however, the opening charge went beyond conventional observations about the duties of magistrates. The jury was asked to reflect on the benefits of reposing 'under the shade of the British constitution', with its provision for civil liberty; its protection for the innocent and punishment of the guilty; the security provided for life, liberty, property and reputation through the civil and criminal codes, and trial by jury; and the fact that no distinction was made before the law between the prince and the pauper. These qualities, said the chairman, guaranteed that 'the life and liberty of an Irishman are sacred'. But such benefits were not always appreciated as they should be; and he went on to deplore what he called delusions of 'equality'.[1]

A decade earlier, Edmund Burke, in a speech in which he denounced systematic schemes of parliamentary reform, had produced a similar panegyric on the British constitution:

In that constitution, I know, and exultingly I feel, both that I am free, and that I am not free dangerously to myself or to others. I know that no power on earth, acting as I ought to do, can touch my life, my liberty, or my property.[2]

1. *Faulkner's Dublin Journal*, 22 Jan. 1793. The immediate background was the defiance by certain Dublin Volunteers of a government ban (3 Dec. 1792) on associations of persons under arms, and the activities of the Defenders in south Ulster and north Leinster in the winter of 1792/3. See Marianne Elliott, *Partners in revolution: the United Irishmen and France* (New Haven and London, 1982), pp. 39-44.
2. Speech in (British) house of commons in 1782, quoted in Isaac Kramnick (ed.), *Edmund Burke* (New Jersey, 1974), p. 36.

It is not the intention of this paper to examine the validity or otherwise of these judgments on the British constitution, which attracted its share of detractors as well as defenders in the age of the American and French revolutions. Rather, the focus is on the central place of the law in that constitution, and the prominence of members of the legal profession among those who struggled against revolution and radical reform for almost half a century. While the war with revolutionary France lasted (1793–1815) the strength of counter-revolutionary values kept the radical challenge in check, or forced it underground; but with the return of peace the struggle commenced again, reaching a climax in the period 1828–32, when some of the most characteristic constitutional features of the old regime in Britain and Ireland were overturned. Protestants lost their monopoly of political office; the monarchy lost its real claim to freedom of action; the idea of 'fundamental laws', impervious to constitutional reform, was undermined; and corporate values were displaced in favour of the representation of numbers in the political process. Finally, during the 1830s these changes at national level were paralleled at local level by municipal reform measures for both England and Ireland, which had the effect (in Ireland) of placing control of urban corporations outside Ulster in catholic hands.

For Ireland we know something of the importance of the legal profession in the challenge to the *ancien régime*, thanks to numerous studies made of the barrister Daniel O'Connell, several of which have drawn attention to the significance of O'Connell's training and role as a lawyer.[3] It is well known, too, that other barristers were prominent in the campaign for catholic emancipation: Denys Scully, for instance, and Richard Lalor Sheil.[4]

3. See for instance, Maurice R. O'Connell, 'O'Connell: lawyer and landlord' in Kevin B. Nowlan and Maurice R. O'Connell (ed.), *Daniel O'Connell: portrait of a radical* (Belfast, 1984), p. 107; Kevin B. Nowlan, 'The meaning of repeal in Irish history' in *Historical Studies IV*, ed. G.A. Hayes–McCoy (London, 1963), p. 1.

4. Denys Scully, 1773-1830, called to the bar in 1796; practised on the Leinster circuit; made an important contribution to the debate on the catholic question in the early 1800s, especially with his *A statement of the penal laws which aggrieve the catholics of Ireland*, pts. I and II (Dublin, 1811-12). See *DNB*, and Brian MacDermott (ed.), *The catholic question in Ireland & England 1798-1822: The papers of Denys Scully* (Dublin, 1988).

Richard Lalor Sheil, 1791-1851, called to the bar in 1814; admitted to the inner bar, 1830 (one of the first catholics to gain that distinction). Played an important part in the emancipation movement during the 1820s. Sheil is accessible through his printed works; for instance, *The speeches of the right honourable Richard Lalor Sheil*, with memoir by Thomas MacNevin (Dublin, n.d.).

Although the theme has not been fully developed, attention has been drawn to the links between certain legal circuits in Ireland and the spread of support for emancipation during the 1820s. The role of the Irish intelligentsia (including the legal profession) in Irish nationalist movements in the 1840s has also received some attention.[5] But the lawyers active in the emancipation campaign and in the repeal movement were mostly catholics, and catholics represented only a minority of the Irish legal profession: perhaps as little as one-fifth down to the early 1820s, rising to around one-third by the time of the 1861 census.[6] The majority of lawyers throughout this period were protestants, and, while some of them certainly joined catholics in the emancipation campaign and the subsequent reform and even repeal movements, they did not represent the bar and the profession as a whole. In fact, the legal profession supplied several of the most articulate and influential defenders of the constitution against emancipation and reform. Such figures included Patrick Duigenan (appointed king's advocate general of the high court of admiralty in 1790); William Saurin (attorney general, 1807–22); Henry Joy (solicitor general, 1822–7, attorney general 1827–31); Thomas Lefroy (first serjeant, 1822–30); Francis Blackburne (attorney general, 1831–5); Joseph Jackson (second serjeant, 1835–1841); and Isaac Butt (whose ability as a young barrister in the late 1830s induced Dublin corporation to retain him as counsel against the municipal reform bill in 1840). While several (though not all) of these lawyers attained very high office, it is noteworthy that all of them were born and bred in Ireland.[7]

See also Thomas Wyse's evaluation of the role of catholic lawyers in the emancipation movement in his *Historical sketch of the late Catholic Association of Ireland*, 2 vols. (London, 1829), i, 143-6, 152.

5. See Fergus O'Ferrall, 'The growth of political consciousness in Ireland, 1823-47: a study of O'Connellite politics and political education' (unpublished Ph. D. thesis, University of Dublin, 1978), p. 221; Jacqueline R. Hill, 'The intelligentsia and Irish nationalism in the 1840s' in *Stud Hib*, xx (1980), 73.

6. Hill, 'The intelligentsia and Irish nationalism', 76. The estimate for the early 1820s is based on Sheil's evidence to the 1825 select committee on the state of Ireland, *Dublin Evening Mail*, 28 Mar. 1825.

7. Patrick Duigenan, 1735-1816. Born O'Duibhgeannain, in Co. Leitrim, converted to established church. Graduated B.A. from TCD in 1757; M.A. and fellow, 1761; called to the bar, 1767; regius professor of feudal and English law in TCD, 1776–1816; bencher, King's Inns, 1784; appointed king's advocate general in the high court of admiralty, 1790; MP for Old Leighlin 1790–98, Armagh 1798–1816. See *DNB*.

During the 1820s and 1830s O'Connell counted such lawyers among his most formidable opponents. His correspondence contains many references to Saurin, Joy, Lefroy, Blackburne and Jackson, and reveals his chagrin when any of them held public office.[8] Yet we know next to nothing about their views, save for the impression given by modern historians that their outlook was bigoted and negative; they are rarely allowed to speak for themselves.[9] A characteristic approach is that adopted by David Thornley, in an otherwise valuable study of Isaac Butt:

The youthful Butt had first risen to prominence in the early 1840s when as a brilliant young lawyer and a distinguished graduate of Trinity

William Saurin, 1757–1839. Of Huguenot extraction, son of the vicar of Belfast. Graduated B.A. from TCD 1777; called to the bar in 1780; granted patent of precedence after the prime serjeant in1798; offered the post of solicitor general in 1798 but rejected it on account of his opposition to the union. Moved the resolution of the Irish bar against the union, which led to him being stripped of his silk gown; attorney general 1807-22. See *DNB*.

Henry Joy, 1763–1838. Youngest son of Henry Joy of Belfast. Made first serjeant in 1817; solicitor general 1822–7; attorney general 1827–31; appointed chief baron of the exchequer, 1831. See *The correspondence of Daniel O'Connell*, ed. Maurice R. O'Connell (hereafter O'C. *Corr.*), 8 vols. (Dublin, 1972-80), iii, letter 1387, n. 5.

Thomas Langlois Lefroy, 1776–1869. Eldest son of Anthony Lefroy of Newton Perry, Co. Limerick. Graduated B.A. from TCD in 1793; called to the bar 1797; king's serjeant 1808; first serjeant 1822-30; MP Dublin University 1830–41; appointed baron of the exchequer, 1841 and chief justice of queen's bench, 1852. See *DNB*, and Thomas Lefroy (jun.), *Memoir of Chief Justice Lefroy* (Dublin, 1871).

Francis Blackburne, 1782–1867. Born Co. Meath; graduated from TCD, called to the bar in 1805; attorney general, 1831-35; master of the rolls, 1842–6; chief justice of queen's bench, 1846–52; chancellor, 1852, 1866–7; lord justice of appeal, 1856–66. See *DNB*, and Edward Blackburne, *Life of the rt hon Francis Blackburne* (London, 1874).

Joseph Devonsher Jackson, 1783-1857. Son of Strettell Jackson of Peterborough, Co. Cork. Graduated B.A. from TCD; called to the bar in 1806; serjeant 1826; M.P. for Bandon 1835-42; judge of common pleas 1842–57. See O'C. *Corr.*, v, letter 2170, n. 2.

Isaac Butt, 1813–79. Only son of Revd Robert Butt of Stranorlar, Co. Donegal. Graduated B.A. from TCD in 1835; held chair of political economy in TCD, 1836–41; called to the bar 1838; inner bar 1844; defended William Smith O'Brien at the state trials in 1848; launched home rule movement, 1870. See *DNB*, Terence de Vere White, *The road of excess* (Dublin, 1946), and David Thornley, *Isaac Butt and home rule* (London, 1964).

8. See O'C. *Corr.*, iii, letter 1389; iv, letters 1598, 1849; v, letters 2100, 2107, 2108, 2109, 2114, 2118, 2119, 2120, 2228, 2229; vi, letter 2383.

9. Of the seven lawyers under consideration here, only Butt has been treated to a modern biography; Lefroy and Blackburne were the subject of filial *Lives* by their sons (see note 7 above).

College Dublin he appeared the most promising of the younger conservatives. Even at this early stage some of his work as editor of the *Dublin University Magazine* . . . had demonstrated that his conservatism rested upon two pillars, an emotional sympathy with the grievances of the peasantry, and the conviction that this and other weaknesses in the Irish economy were essentially imperial problems. But in public controversy he found as yet no inconsistency in conducting himself as a violent Orange bigot. Sir William Gregory . . . recalled him in this period as 'the very type of ultra-domineering, narrow-minded, protestant ascendancy'. When the municipal reform measures of the whig administration in 1840 threatened to destroy this citadel of ascendancy, Butt's combination of bigotry and legal brilliance caused him to be chosen to argue the case of the old Dublin corporation before the house of lords. His career as a conservative spokesman reached its zenith when in 1843 he was chosen to put forward the conservative reply to O'Connell in the great corporation debate on repeal. By this time, however, a natural breadth of mind and generosity of spirit, a love of country and a susceptible emotional nature, had stripped much of the bigotry from his politics . . . [10]

It is not only the Irish defenders of the *ancien régime* whose principles have received such perfunctory treatment. The fate of those in Britain has not (until recently) been much better. One historian who has set out to analyse these principles has commented:

The protestant constitutionists have probably received a worse press than any other party in the history of the English church and state. Ridicule and contumely were their lot even while their great principle was still intact. It was fashionable to laugh at them for being behind the times. It was easy to be bored with their repetition of the same arguments year after year. It was not difficult to arraign them of that unpopular quality, intolerance, with all its implications of moral arrogance, and overtones, in those days, of *ancien régime* cruelty. . . . The protestant tories have been variously presented as wicked, bigoted, foolish and stupid.[11]

Yet, as G.F.A. Best has pointed out, those who supported the ultra-tories in resisting catholic emancipation included (among others) the poets Robert Southey, S.T. Coleridge and William Wordsworth; and the churchmen (and founders of the Oxford movement) John Keble and John Henry Newman.[12] Such names

10. Thornley, *Isaac Butt and home rule*, pp. 15-16.

11. G.F.A. Best, 'The protestant constitution and its supporters, 1800-1829', in *R Hist Soc Trans*, 5th series, viii (1958), 105 at 107.

12. Ibid., 108.

alone lend credibility to Best's argument that there was more to
the defence of the protestant constitution than sheer bigotry.

If sectarianism, which was to become so prevalent in nineteenth-
century Ireland, is to be understood, it is particularly important to
examine the outlook of the Irish champions of the *ancien régime*.
Because the position they defended was eventually defeated, their
case has largely gone by default, and their opponents' verdicts on
them have been accepted at face value. The result is that our
understanding of Irish political culture in the first half of the
nineteenth century is incomplete. No systematic study can be
attempted here; but it is hoped that by analysing opposition from
leading lawyers to two key measures, catholic emancipation and
municipal reform, it will be possible to gain insight into their
arguments and outlook.

II

Between 1789 and 1792 extraordinary changes took place in
France. Feudalism was abolished and the 'rights of man' proclaimed; church property was confiscated and the catholic clergy
transformed into servants of the state; the titles and status of
hereditary nobility, along with guilds and monopolies, were
suppressed; the monarchy was abolished and a republic declared.
Help was promised to subject peoples wishing to be free. To put
the seal on all this, on 21 January 1793 (within a week of the
meeting of the Co. Dublin quarter sessions referred to above)
King Louis XVI was executed.[13]

These revolutionary events in France had admirers in other
countries, who were quick to argue that the 'French' principles of
liberty, equality and fraternity were, in effect, the natural rights of
man. Throughout western Europe, wherever a degree of freedom
of the press existed, a debate began about 'revolutionary principles'. The rights of established churches; privileges based on
birth, custom or royal charters; indeed, privilege itself, of a political
and religious kind—all were looked at with a new and critical eye.
However, the dissemination of the new ideology in turn prompted
champions of the *ancien régime* to spring to its defence: champions
like Edmund Burke, whose counter-revolutionary tendencies, evi-

---

13. A useful chronology of the main events associated with the French
    revolution is contained in J. M. Roberts, *The French revolution* (Oxford,
    1978), pp. 166-72.

dent even before the revolution, crystallised in his *Reflections on the revolution in France* (1790). Burke's defence of the existing institutions of monarchy, aristocracy and established church are well known; but the assumptions which lay behind them are worth drawing out. Referring to those who invoked the 'rights of man', Burke wrote:

Whilst they are possessed by these notions, it is vain to talk to them of the practice of their ancestors, the fundamental laws of their country, the fixed form of a constitution whose merits are confirmed by the solid test of long experience and an increasing public strength and national prosperity. They despise experience as the wisdom of unlettered men; and as for the rest, they have wrought underground a mine that will blow up, at one grand explosion, all examples of antiquity, all precedents, all charters, and acts of parliament. They have 'the rights of men'. Against these there can be no prescription, against these no agreement is binding . . . [14]

The key ideas here are custom ('the practice of their ancestors'), fundamental laws, prescription—the concepts that underlay the system of privilege, not only in Britain but in all *ancien régime* countries. With such themes Burke helped to rally opponents of the 'rights of man' behind existing institutions, and against systematic plans for reform. But in one area his concern for the preservation of those institutions led Burke to adopt a position which, ironically, proved divisive among the very people whose outlook was, in other respects, identical with his. This was the question of catholic political rights.

This is not the place to examine in detail either the evolution of Burke's own thought on the catholic question, or the stages by which the British government arrived at its historic new Irish policy in the winter of 1791/2. A number of points, however, may be made. According to the view taken by Burke, adopted by Lecky, and still generally accepted by historians, the relaxation of the penal laws against Irish catholics represented a continuous process, beginning in George III's reign. But Burke was out of touch with Irish protestant views. Contemporaries drew a sharp distinction between penal laws relating on the one hand to land and freedom of worship (by 1782 these had been repealed, without provoking serious opposition), and on the other to those which concerned political rights. Because of the still prevailing understanding of 'popery' as a political system, the question of political rights for catholics was extremely sensitive, and most

14. Quoted in Kramnick, *Edmund Burke*, p. 45.

protestants were reluctant even to have the matter discussed in the 1780s. The question was ducked by the Volunteer convention of 1783, and not endorsed by the delegate congress held in Dublin in 1784; while in the Irish parliament only one or two members (including the eccentric earl-bishop of Derry) were its advocates. At that time, too, the protestant nature of the constitution in Ireland was still upheld by the British prime minister, Pitt.[15] Against this background, Irish catholics themselves remained deferential and unspecific in their requests for further relief, and it was not until 1791, when the international catholic church and the British government found themselves on the same counter-revolutionary side, that the government—urged on by Burke—took the momentous decision to extend political rights to Irish catholics (though not to those in England and Scotland).[16]

Such an unexpected policy took even the Irish parliamentary opposition by surprise.[17] The evidence suggests that the new policy was adopted by ministers as part of a counter-revolutionary imperial strategy in which catholics, at home and in British overseas dependencies, were perceived as actual or potential supporters of existing British institutions against the new radical and revolutionary challenge. Such an outlook rested on the conviction that the main support for revolutionary ideas came from radicals in the protestant dissenting tradition who were either near-atheists or dangerously heterodox in religion.[18] Compared with a Dr Price or a Dr Priestley catholics appeared to be

15. For Burke and Lecky, see Edmund Burke to Richard Burke, jun., 26 Jan. 1792, in *The correspondence of Edmund Burke*, ed. P.J. Marshall and John A. Woods, vii (Cambridge & Chicago, 1968), pp. 40-41; W.E.H. Lecky, *A history of Ireland in the eighteenth century*, abridged ed. (Chicago, 1972), pp. 90, 114, 280-82. For a different view, see A.P.W. Malcomson, *John Foster: the politics of the Anglo-Irish ascendancy* (Oxford, 1978), pp. 407-8; Jacqueline Hill, 'The meaning and significance of "protestant ascendancy", 1787-1840' in *Ireland after the union* (Proceedings of second joint meeting of the Royal Irish Academy and the British Academy, London, 1986) (London, 1989), p. 1.

16. For the catholics, see R.D. Edwards, 'The minute book of the Catholic Committee, 1773-92', in *Archiv Hib*, ix (1942), 3-172; for the government's new policy see National Archive (State Paper Office), Westmorland correspondence, Letterbook I.

17. Malcomson, *John Foster*, pp. 352-5.

18. Such figures included the Arian minister, Dr Richard Price, and the Socinian minister, Dr Joseph Priestley: see J.C.D. Clark, *English society, 1688-1832* (Cambridge, 1985), pp. 335-46. See also J.C. Beckett, 'Burke, Ireland and the empire', in Oliver MacDonagh, W.F. Mandle and Pauric Travers (ed.), *Irish culture and nationalism, 1750-1950* (London, 1983), p.1 at pp. 5-6.

models of Trinitarian orthodoxy, and highly conservative in their attitudes to politics and society. In the case of Ireland, the prospect of catholics being wooed by radical protestant dissenters also influenced government in the direction of the new policy; but it should be remembered that Canadian catholics received a similar vote of confidence from government when they gained political rights in the Canada constitution act of 1791.[19]

Since public opinion in Ireland was quite unprepared for such a move, the shocked surprise of Dublin Castle on learning of the government's views in December 1791 was understandable. So convinced was the viceroy that any such policy would be bound to overturn 'protestant ascendancy' (or protestant control) in Ireland, hitherto deemed necessary to preserve the established church, the state, and the link with Britain, that the British ministers temporarily backed down, and another year passed before the Castle was instructed to proceed with the plan. By this time news of government intentions had prompted members of the Irish parliamentary opposition (who only months earlier had shown no support for the question) to embrace the policy of catholic political rights; failure to do so would leave a future catholic electorate wholly in the government's debt.[20] But while such shifts helped ensure that the measure granting catholic political rights (including the vote) passed through the Irish parliament in 1793,[21] other organs of protestant (especially anglican) opinion, notably corporations and grand juries, saw no necessity for abandoning long-held principles. Moreover, by this time the Defenders (a secret society whose members were mostly catholics) were already planning revolution in the expectation of French assistance, and suspicion fell on the United Irishmen and on the Catholic Committee for fraternising with them.[22] In this nervous climate, the protestant response to the new catholic political rights was bound to be a cautious one. In corporate towns, where admission to guild and corporate freedom was in the hands of

19. For the conservative and counter-revolutionary motives behind this measure see John Manning Ward, *Colonial self-government: the British experience 1759-1856* (London, 1976), pp. 13-19.

20. Malcomson, *John Foster*, pp. 352-5.

21. The catholic relief act of 1793 (33 Geo III, c. 21) enabled Irish catholics to obtain the parliamentary franchise, hold certain civil and military offices, take degrees at Dublin university, become members of guilds and corporations, and bear arms. In the previous year they had been admitted to the bar and as attorneys (and hence solicitors too) (32 Geo III, c. 21).

22. Marianne Elliott, *Partners in revolution: the United Irishmen and France* (New Haven and London, 1982), pp.38-43.

existing members, few catholics had the usual qualifications (of birth or service) for admission and few were admitted.[23] Urban catholics were disappointed at this outcome, and some joined the United Irishmen. Meanwhile, despite the exhortation of their priests, the Defenders continued with their agitation, later cooperating with the United Irishmen to produce a combination of considerable revolutionary potential, which (had timely French intervention occurred) might have produced a much more serious rising than that of 1798.

These developments, especially the 1798 rebellion, seemed to point to two diametrically opposed conclusions. On the one hand, it could be argued that for the full loyalty and essential conservatism of the Irish catholics to become manifest, it was necessary to remove their remaining political disabilities and admit them to full equality with protestants. The prime minister, Pitt, took this view at the time of the act of union of 1800, but found the king hostile on the grounds of his coronation oath to uphold the established churches of England and Ireland. (It is worth pointing out here that the Irish lord chancellor, the earl of Clare, played an important part in reminding the king of the obligations contained in the oath).[24] The new whigs in England (who had been supporters of the separation of religion and politics since the 1780s)[25] formed the chief parliamentary support for full equality; Irish whigs also lent support. On the other hand, it could be argued that catholics were not loyal and peaceable, and that the barriers which prevented them acquiring office and entering parliament must be retained.[26] While the war with France lasted, supporters of this last position were in the majority among both Irish and British MPs. Catholic spokesmen themselves were naturally in a difficult position. If they remained passive and deferential, in keeping with their demeanour from the mid-eighteenth century to the early 1790s, they risked confirming the traditional protestant view that 'popery' was incompatible with the exercise of full

---

23. See Jacqueline Hill, 'The politics of privilege: Dublin corporation and the catholic question, 1792-1823' in *Maynooth Review*, vii (1982), 17.

24. Malcomson, *John Foster*, pp. 424-6. But it should also be noted that the coronation oath had been appealed to by English critics of earlier moves by government to admit the catholic church to quasi-establishment status (in the Quebec act of 1774); see Jacqueline Hill, 'Religious toleration and the relaxation of the penal laws: an imperial perspective', in *Archiv Hib*, xliv (1989), 98.

25. Clark, *English society*, p. 349.

26. See Richard Musgrave, *Memoirs of the different rebellions in Ireland*, 2nd ed. (Dublin, 1801), pp. 181-82.

political rights. If, on the other hand, they took a more assertive line, they risked exacerbating protestant fears for the safety of the constitution. The matter was complicated by the fact that at the time of the union negotiations, catholics had been given to understand that emancipation would be facilitated by the union.[27]

By 1805 catholic spokesmen had decided to petition parliament for the repeal of the remaining penal laws. Their petition prompted Fox, the leader of the English whigs in the house of commons, to move for a committee on the question. The motion, which was lost by a large majority, led to a debate which affords an opportunity to consider the arguments used against emancipation; and particularly those of a leading Irish defender of the protestant constitution, Patrick Duigenan, professor of feudal and English law at Trinity College, and MP for Armagh.

Duigenan's speech against emancipation reveals an attitude of guarded hostility towards catholics. Outright animosity would have led him to describe catholics as 'papists', or 'popish subjects', descriptions which catholics disliked and which protestants by the end of the eighteenth century were beginning to drop in favour of 'roman catholics'. Duigenan did not talk of 'papists', and even occasionally used the term 'roman catholics', but he more frequently referred to the 'romish' church, and to its members as 'romanists'. His personal background may be relevant here. He had been born into a catholic family (O'Duibhgeannain) but was educated by the local Church of Ireland clergyman, and subsequently converted to the established church, becoming one of its most outspoken supporters, and serving as the vicar-general for three successive dioceses.[28] However, it is important to look beyond the tone of his speech at the arguments themselves. Duigenan's case rested on two main platforms: the nature of catholic allegiance, and the nature of the British constitution. On the former, his concern was to restate the familiar protestant argument that 'the religious tenets of romanists render them irreconcilable enemies to a protestant state'.[29] Such tenets, affirmed in the past by councils of the church, included 'no faith is to be kept with heretics'; and 'no oaths of allegiance to an heretical prince or government are binding'. Duigenan acknowledged that the catholic petitioners disclaimed holding such views. He admitted, too, that they claimed that their allegiance to the pope extended only to

27. Gearoid O'Tuathaigh, *Ireland before the famine, 1798-1848* (Dublin, 1972), pp. 48-9.
28. See *DNB*.
29. *Hansard's parliamentary debates* (hereafter *Hansard*) 1, iv, 892 (13 May 1805).

spiritual matters.[30] But what of the church authorities? Noting that no catholic ecclesiastic had signed the petition, Duigenan reminded his audience that as recently as 1791 at the time of the English catholic relief act, spokesmen for the church authorities had been critical of attempts by the laity to disclaim tenets which had not been disavowed by the church.[31] Accordingly, he suggested,

. . . let the supporters of the present measure inform the house, at what period, and by what public authority did the romish church or its votaries renounce or disavow these principles . . .[32]

Furthermore, Duigenan challenged the catholics over the matter of the oaths which alone kept them out of parliament. He conceded that the declaration against transubstantiation represented a real stumbling-block for a conscientious catholic, and suggested that if catholics indicated a willingness to take the oath of supremacy, there might be a case for modifying the declaration.[33] But catholics refused to take the oath of supremacy, although it made no claim for sacerdotal powers in the monarch, and was in effect simply an oath of allegiance, designed to affirm the independence of the state from any foreign power:

that is, in other words, they refuse and reject an oath of allegiance to the state, and insist that there is an extraneous power paramount to that of the state, to which their allegiance is due in all spiritual matters, or in all matters which that power shall deem spiritual; and in all temporal matters which are inseparably connected with such spiritual supremacy, which amount to nearly one half of the whole temporal power of a state; and may indeed swallow up the whole, which it has attempted in many countries: because the determination of what portion of dominion, in temporal matters, is within the vortex of spiritual supremacy, is left to a foreign ecclesiastic, and his vassals the romish priests, within this empire.[34]

Thus, for Duigenan, it was not enough for individual catholics to disavow traditional church teachings on relations with heretics, or to insist that their allegiance to the pope was confined to purely spiritual matters; their own church authorities had not only failed

30. Ibid.
31. Ibid., iv, 867-9.
32. Ibid., iv, 879. Confusion over the church's position on such matters continued to worry protestants and embarrass catholics for many years. See O'C. *Corr.*, v, letter 2263b.
33. *Hansard*, iv, 870.
34. Ibid.

to endorse such assertions, but claimed the right to decide exactly what were the dimensions of spiritual jurisdiction.

Duigenan's case against emancipation, however, did not rest simply on the question of catholic allegiance. The nature of the British constitution also concerned him, and his argument here fell into two parts. First, he contended that the protestant nature of the constitution was not incidental but fundamental. The revolution of 1688 represented the culmination of a process, beginning in the reign of Elizabeth, by which more and more legal safeguards for this protestant character had been written into the constitution. James II had provoked the revolution by dispensing with such laws (the test and corporation acts) and appointing catholics to local and national office, thereby endangering the protestant constitution. As a result, James had lost his throne, and had been replaced by protestant monarchs who, from 1689 onwards, had been obliged to promise in the coronation oath that they would uphold the protestant reformed church as established by law. Moreover, the act of settlement of 1701 had settled the crown on the Hanoverians on conditions which obliged them to be 'in communion with the Church of England, as by law established', and subsequently the Scottish act of union obliged the monarch to preserve unaltered the Church of England in England, Wales and Ireland. Duigenan argued that if James II had been right to dispense with the law, in favour of appointing catholics to office, then he had been unjustly dethroned, and George III's title was an unjust one. Since this conclusion was an unthinkable one for his audience, it could then be argued that the king was bound by his oath to resist the present measure, for it would jeopardise his own title just as it had done in James II's case.[35]

The British constitution, however, was not only unalterably protestant, it was also unalterably 'popular' ('populist' comes closer to what Duigenan meant) in a way that for him placed yet more obstacles in the path of admitting catholics to parliament and to high public office. He conceded that prior to the French revolution catholics were admitted to positions of power in all 'popish' and even some protestant states, without jeopardising the temporal power of the state. But in all these cases, Duigenan alleged, the states concerned

were either despotic monarchies, or equally despotic oligarchies, and . . . the people at large had no political power in them. . . . The great mass of

35. Ibid., iv, 869, 898-902.

the people, being excluded from all manner of power or influence in the state, were, what Englishmen term, slaves: and every question which could arise from the claim of papal supremacy in such states, was decided by the despots and the court of Rome. . . . In protestant despotic states, it is not of great moment to the despot, what religious opinions are held by a part of his subjects: the people have no power in the state, and it is of little consequence to the despot whether the men he employs as his servants are of one religious persuasion or the other, they being merely his creatures. . . . But in protestant states, in which the people, or their elective representatives, have some share in the government, romanists were excluded, before the baneful progress of the French revolution, from all share of political power. . . . If therefore the British empire [i.e., the United Kingdom] is to be influenced by the practice of every popular protestant state in Europe, romanists should not only be excluded from all places of trust and power, but from all situations which would invest them with any share of political power; and above all from seats in the supreme legislative assemblies, the houses of lords and commons. . . . In these two assemblies, but particularly in the house of commons, vastly the most powerful of the two, is vested the greatest and most efficient part of the sovereign power of the state: and to admit the avowed enemies of the constitution in church and state, to form a part of the sovereignty of the state, is so manifestly an absurdity in politics, that it is surprising such a measure should be supported by men of ability professing themselves to be friends of the constitution.[36]

Duigenan's final point was a familiar one in protestant discourse on the catholic question. Catholics, he argued, had nothing to complain of in their present situation under the British constitution. For it was one of the glories of that constitution that even catholics, whose tenets made them a danger to it, enjoyed religious toleration and liberty of conscience. Quoting Pitt in a debate on the repeal of the test and corporation acts in 1790, Duigenan claimed:

Toleration consists in a free exercise of religion according to the tenets of the professors of that religion, and in the enjoyment of the protection of the laws; not in a communication of an equality of political power.[37]

Until they renounced the 'anarchical and degrading' tenet that 'the state is subject to a foreign jurisdiction and is not independent' catholics remained enemies to the constitution, and should therefore rest content with liberty of conscience, security of property, and the parliamentary franchise.[38]

36. Ibid., iv, 880-82.
37. Ibid., iv, 916.
38. Ibid., iv, 915-6.

There are three points to note about Duigenan's case. One is the importance to it of legal arguments, in which he displayed an extensive knowledge, ranging from the decrees of medieval church councils to English constitutional law and the writings of eighteenth-century English jurists such as Blackstone, whose views he was able to cite in support of his contentions.[39] For Duigenan's case for the protestant nature of the constitution was not new, but had been around in essentially the same Whig or Patriot form since the Williamite revolution.[40] It was a case which (within its own terms) his opponents did not find easy to refute. For instance, on the question of the official teachings of the catholic church, Henry Grattan (the chief Irish parliamentary spokesman for the catholics) could only indicate that several catholic universities had given their view that doctrines such as 'no faith to be kept with heretics', and the deposing power of the pope, were effectively obsolete.[41] That did not meet Duigenan's objection, which was that the church authorities themselves had not disclaimed such teachings, and showed no signs of doing so.

Secondly, it is evident that Duigenan's case did not rest on the purely spiritual aspects of catholic theology. If anything, when he did touch on such matters, as in his reference to the declaration against transubstantiation, he showed some sympathy for the view that a catholic could not conscientiously make such a declaration, and indicated a willingness to be flexible in this area. His case against admitting catholics to parliament and to public office rested rather on what he took the political tendencies of catholic beliefs to be, and the implications for the security of the temporal power and authority of the monarch and parliament. In taking such a stand, Duigenan was restating what had been (and from the vote at the end of the debate apparently still was) the general protestant view: and the very fact that it did not rest on an indictment of catholic spiritual beliefs meant that its supporters believed themselves to be free of 'bigotry'. It is instructive to note the similarities between Duigenan's argument, and that of the leading Irish Patriot of the mid-eighteenth century, Charles Lucas:

39. Ibid., iv, 904-5.

40. See Clark, *English society*, pp. 349-59. The main development in the case since the Williamite era was the formal granting of freedom of worship ('toleration' in eighteenth-century terms) to catholics, and the repeal of the greater part of the penal laws against catholics and protestant dissenters.

41. *Hansard*, iv, 919-920.

It is one of the distinguishing marks of true protestants to quarrel with no man for barely differing in opinion or in religious matters. And it is well known, to the honour of our constitution, that all religious sects among us are tollerated (sic) or winked at, unless they profess or propagate a doctrine dangerous to the state ... With men of this per-suasion [catholics] I daily converse; I enjoy their friendship and love ... But if any man can be so weak, as to carry this enthusiasm into temporalities, I must think it my duty, not only to differ from him, but, in just defence of my property, my life, and what I hold more dear, the PUBLIC LIBERTY, to oppose him. If any, among us, can be so mad, as to assert, that any power in the universe can authorise *tyranny*, *persecution of consciences*, *rebellion*, *murder*, *oppression*, *treachery*, or the like, this, and this only, is the man whom I call a *papist*; that is, not a follower of the bishop of *Rome*, for that does not concern me, but a *subject* of the *pope* of *Rome*, who claims a *temporal* power inconsistent with the liberties to which man is heir. . . . From this you may see it is *foreign*, *papal*, *temporal tyranny*, not *religion*, I oppose.[42]

Thirdly, Duigenan's argument rested on an *ancien régime* understanding of the state, in which church and state were in effect two aspects of the same thing.[43] Moreover, even though he contended for the 'popular' nature of the constitution, this did not mean that he understood 'the people' to be represented as individuals, but as groups (such as the landed gentry, and corporate bodies) whose political rights constituted an 'inheritance'. Indeed, one of his objections to the extension of catholic political rights in Ireland was that it would put effective political power in the hands of 'the mob, and the indigent part of the population . . . [who] ought not to be gratified at the expense of the ruin of the loyal, opulent, and respectable part of the state'.[44] It was quite consistent with such an understanding of the constitution that Duigenan should reject the view that the king was bound to give his assent to an emancipation bill, should one pass the two houses of parliament: the monarch must retain the freedom of action necessary to secure the fundamental laws of the state.[45]

Not surprisingly, Duigenan was not an admirer of Burke, whom he regarded as one of a number of 'active and able romish agents', who in the early 1790s had influenced the government to

42. A.F. Barber and Citizen [Charles Lucas], *A third letter to the free-citizens of Dublin* (Dublin, 1747), pp. 18-19 (italics as in original).

43. *Hansard*, iv, 904. On the *ancien régime*, see Pierre Goubert, *The ancien régime: French society 1600-1750* (London, 1973); Clark, *English society*.

44. *Hansard*, iv, 916.

45. Ibid., iv, 906.

embark on its policy of political rights for Irish catholics.[46] But their differences over the catholic question should not blind us to the fact that in other respects their understanding of the constitution was very much the same; both believed in prescriptive laws, in the representation of groups rather than of numbers, and in the constitution as an 'inheritance' which should be approached with veneration, to be altered only with care in particular cases of demonstrable necessity, not according to broad principles such as 'the rights of man'.

Nearly a quarter of a century later in 1828, the challenge to the protestant constitution, so long resisted, was on the brink of success. The remarkable achievements of the Catholic Association in Ireland since 1823, and especially O'Connell's election for Co. Clare in July 1828, had brought the political system under great strain. It was evident that what could be done in Clare could be done elsewhere, rendering the political system unworkable. From the government's point of view, it was not easy to see how the emancipation movement could be curbed without unacceptable repression, and the only alternative seemed to be to yield. After all, bills for emancipation had passed the house of commons more than once during the 1820s;[47] it was chiefly the lords and the king who were standing out. Accordingly, during 1828 the duke of Wellington began to put pressure on opponents of emancipation in the house of lords to modify their hitherto unfavourable attitude.[48] Outside parliament, however, public opinion in protestant circles remained largely hostile. In these circumstances, a populist movement sprang up in 1828, which saw the formation of 'Brunswick clubs' (named after the royal family) in England and Ireland, with the purpose of defending the protestant constitution.[49] Two of O'Connell's leading opponents in the legal profession took an active part in these clubs; the father of the bar, William Saurin, who had been attorney general from 1807 to 1822, and had subsequently returned to practice at the bar, and Thomas Lefroy, first serjeant. In February 1829, as a government bill for emancipation was going through parliament, both men spoke at the second general meeting of the Brunswick Constitutional Club of Ireland, held in Dublin. Their speeches afford an

---

46. Ibid., iv, 886.
47. Clark, *English society*, pp. 387-91.
48. Ibid., p. 397; Anthony Bird, *The damnable duke of Cumberland* (London, 1966), pp. 168-94.
49. Clark, *English society*, p. 371.

opportunity of examining the case, through lawyers' eyes, for the protestant constitution on the eve of its demise.[50]

The historian of the protestant constitution has drawn attention to the difficulty experienced by English supporters of the constitution in finding something new to say on a topic which had been so thoroughly and so frequently rehearsed during the debates on emancipation since the early years of the century.[51] As might be expected, several of the arguments used by Saurin and Lefroy were the same as those used by Duigenan in 1805. Political office did not exist in the original state of nature (a point that Burke, too, had made) and accordingly there could be no 'natural' right of eligibility for it; this was a civil matter to be decided by the state. The exclusion of catholics from the throne and from public office was a necessary and fundamental part of the constitution, designed to secure its protestant character; the king should refuse his assent to an emancipation measure even if it passed the two houses of parliament. The existing constitution was not intolerant: catholics already enjoyed extensive rights (including the vote) under it, and should remain content with them.[52] Certain new themes appeared, or were given new emphasis. Lefroy argued that if catholics were to enter parliament or obtain office they would acquire the power to interfere with matters of ecclesiastical patronage and other issues relating to the established church—yet they absolutely refused to recognise any right on the part of the state to interfere with their own religion.[53] Here Lefroy was reacting to the refusal, since 1808, on the part of Irish catholic spokesmen to entertain the possibility of a government veto over episcopal appointments, along the lines of that accepted (in effect) by the catholic church in Quebec.[54]

Perhaps the most significant aspect of the case presented by Saurin and Lefroy, however, was that for them, even more

50. William Saurin, *Speech . . . delivered at the Rotunda in the city of Dublin, on . . . the 19th February, 1829: being the second general meeting of the Brunswick constitutional club of Ireland* (Dublin, 1829); Thomas Lefroy, *Report of the speech delivered . . . at the second general meeting of the Brunswick constitutional club of Ireland* (Dublin, 1829).

51. Best, 'The protestant constitution' (note 11, above), 107-9.

52. Saurin, *Speech*, pp. 10-11, 13-16; Lefroy, *Report*, pp. 4-9.

53. Lefroy, *Report*, pp. 10-11.

54. See Hill, 'Religious toleration and the relaxation of the penal laws'; C.D.A. Leighton, 'Gallicanism and the veto controversy: church, state and catholic community in early nineteenth-century Ireland', in R.V. Comerford, Mary Cullen, Jacqueline Hill and Colm Lennon (ed.), *Religion, conflict and coexistence in Ireland: essays presented to Monsignor Patrick J. Corish* (Dublin, 1990).

decisively than for Duigenan, emancipation constituted 'a revolution in the government'. Thus Saurin:

I oppose this measure as a revolutionary measure—a measure flowing out of the spirit and principles of democracy. There is, and has been, a party in this country, having for their object the utter subversion of the British constitution, and to establish in its place, a constitution of government on the basis of the equality of political rights, on the model of the government of the United States of America—a government founded in diametrical opposition and contrast to that of Great Britain. ... The principle of that [American] constitution is equality of political rights to all people; every office in the state is open alike to every citizen; representation is there founded on universal suffrage; under that constitution of government there is not, nor could there be a national religion, nor an established church. Such an institution would violate the principle of equality of political rights, the basis of that constitution, under which all power flows from the people. Look, my lord, to the British constitution; by that constitution the executive authority of the state, is vested by right hereditary, in one individual of one family, and from that office every other individual is interdicted. No rank, no services, no talents, entitle any person, to aspire to that office. The next branch of the British constitution is the house of peers, legislators and judges, by hereditary right, and in total independence of the people. The only branch of the legislature in which the people appear to have any share, is the house of commons; but according to the principles of our constitution, that assembly never was a representation of the people, but a representation of the property and intelligence of the country.[55]

Having set out the differences between the British and American constitutions, Saurin went on to examine the history of the demand for catholic emancipation. He traced it back to the 1790s:

It is now forty years since a conspiracy was formed in this country, under the name of the United Irishmen, for the purpose of subverting the British constitution, and establishing on its ruins, a government, having for its foundation, the principle of equality of political rights on which that of America is based, and which is utterly incompatible with the principles of our constitution. To forward the ends of that conspiracy, the two measures which have so long agitated the country, under the specious name of parliamentary reform, and the still more preposterous denomination of catholic emancipation were first adopted. Such were the engines made use of to engage the people, and the roman catholics, (the principal objects of the enterprize,) in the revolutionary measures then contemplated. Accordingly, you will trace the arguments used by the United Irishmen in the address to the roman catholics by Theobald

55. Saurin, *Speech*, pp. 5-6.

Wolfe Tone. . . . I have been looking on for many years, and have observed the uses made of these instruments of delusion, for the purpose of exciting disaffection and discontent among the people of this country; and they have to a great degree succeeded. The roman catholics were told, that while living under a constitution, the freest, and mildest in the world, . . . they were slaves and outlaws. I solemnly declare . . . if I did not know that they enjoyed the same protection by Magna Charta, the bill of rights, the habeas corpus act, and trial by jury, as I myself . . . I, myself, would be the foremost to place my hand on that guilty constitution which had done [them] wrong. But this is the jargon of democracy . . . [56]

For Saurin, then, a measure which in the early 1790s had been supported by Burke and intended by government to reinforce the existing constitution, had itself given rise to a revolutionary challenge to that very constitution. Since this perception was shared by many protestants well into the second half of the century, it is worth remembering what aspects of catholic conduct in the emancipation campaign during the 1820s tended to reinforce such a view: the organisation of the masses in support of a political goal, on similar lines to developments in Jackson's United States; the widespread abandoning of 'deference' in voting behaviour (Duigenan had forecast this development in 1805: twenty years later it was taking place); [57] O'Connell's own implicit support for the separation of church and state, and his rejoicing at the progress of 'democracy'; the resistance to the veto, which implied a refusal to acknowledge the full extent of the royal prerogative.[58]

That figures like Duigenan, Saurin and Lefroy had a vested interest in the existing constitution, which would be jeopardised by the admission of catholics to full political rights, is not in question. But it should be borne in mind that the cause they were defending was being championed with equal passion and intensity in Britain, where catholic numbers were too small to make much of a dent on the protestant monopoly of office. It seems worth at least entertaining the possibility (which O'Connell himself, on occasion, was prepared to concede) that the passion and intensity

56. Ibid., pp. 6–8.
57. Hansard, iv, 894–5 (13 May 1805); see also Fergus O'Ferrall, *Catholic emancipation: Daniel O'Connell and the birth of Irish democracy, 1820–30* (Dublin, 1985), pp. 30–31, 117–52.
58. The catholic bishops repudiated a veto in September 1808. For O'Connell's views, see O'C. *Corr.*, iii, letters 1404, n. 1, 1485. O'Connell became a more open supporter of the separation of church and state after emancipation had been won. Ibid., iv, letter 1709.

arose from real convictions about the rectitude of the constitution. In this respect, it is worth mentioning that every defender
of the constitution considered above, including the chairman of
the Co. Dublin grand jury, made a connection between what they
saw as the excellence of the constitution and the unprecedented
prosperity which had come to Britain and Ireland during the
eighteenth century.[59]

III

On 13 April 1829 George IV (having bowed to ministerial
pressure) gave his assent to the government bill that admitted
catholics to parliament and high public office. This action demolished the view that the constitution in its entire civil as well as its
ecclesiastical capacity was fundamentally and unalterably protestant. Only the monarchy itself and a few key offices remained
subject to the old restrictions. Compromised, too, was the view
that the royal prerogative gave the monarch the power (indeed,
the duty) to overrule the other two houses of the legislature in
order to safeguard a 'fundamental' law of the constitution. From
the point of view of the supposed beneficiaries, however, a change
in the law (as historians have often pointed out) did not necessarily guarantee a change in catholic experience. Emancipation
enabled a small number of catholics to obtain parliamentary seats;
a few were appointed to public office; but, given the nature of the
existing political system and the relatively small catholic landed
class, in other respects catholics gained little from the measure.
For instance, as long as corporate bodies, rather than individuals,
were recognised for the purpose of parliamentary representation,
as long as recruitment to the public service depended on patronage rather than competitive examination, the growing catholic
middle classes faced serious obstacles to advancement. And this
at a time when the protestant middle classes in southern Ireland
were being seriously depleted through emigration.[60]

Accordingly, there was a strong incentive for catholics to rally
behind O'Connell as he joined the whigs and radicals in the next

59. O'C. *Corr.*, iii, letter 1438; Kramnick, *Edmund Burke*, p. 35; Duigenan, in
    Hansard, iv, 898 (13 May 1805); Saurin, *Speech*, p. 8; Lefroy, *Report*, pp.
    11-12.
60. See Kerby A. Miller, 'No middle ground: the erosion of the protestant
    middle class in southern Ireland during the pre-famine era', in *Huntingdon
    Library Quarterly*, xlix (1986), 295.

assault on the *ancien régime*, the campaign for parliamentary reform. To modern eyes, the 1832 reform act appears a limited and moderate measure, which effectively safeguarded aristocratic and landed dominance in the political system for decades to come. Yet in certain respects, notably in the abolition of the chaotic variety of borough franchises in favour of a uniform ten pound household franchise, the act contained precisely that systematic reforming principle which Burke had regarded as being incompatible with the British constitution ('A prescriptive government, such as ours, never was the work of any legislator, never was made upon any foregone theory').[61]

While emancipation paved the way for catholics to be elected for Irish counties, the 1832 reform act opened up the borough representation, a development which was exemplified by O'Connell's election for Dublin city in 1832. But even these reforms did not loosen protestant control in urban local government, and catholics continued to be denied the civic status they sought. It is not surprising, then, that municipal reform for Ireland was one of O'Connell's chief objectives during the 1830s. The setting up of a commission to investigate the working of the Irish corporations (1833), and the passage of a municipal reform act for England (1835), heralded the introduction of a whig/O'Connellite measure for Ireland; and the champions of what was left of the protestant constitution prepared to defend the Irish corporations. The campaign was to last for seven years, during which period some of the most able protestant members of the bar, including Thomas Lefroy, Joseph Jackson and Isaac Butt, opposed the reform measures proposed by the government and its O'Connellite allies.

The case for reform took on new dimensions after the report of the commissioners on the Irish corporations (1835).[62] The commissioners, who were mostly whigs or O'Connellites, had no sympathy for the Irish corporations, which were in most cases under the control of their political opponents, the ultra-protestants. The result was a report which presented the corporations in the worst possible light—as inefficient, backward-looking bodies, with little sense of public responsibility, apt to squander public money without providing adequate civic services, and, to cap it all, incorrigibly exclusive and sectarian. The defenders of the corporations contended, with some justice, that the commissioners had adopted a partial view, and that many of the charges laid

---

61. Clark, *English society*, pp. 405-12; Kramnick, *Edmund Burke*, p. 35.
62. *First report of the commissioners appointed to inquire into the municipal corporations in Ireland* (hereafter *Report, M.C. (I)*), H.C. 1835, xxvii, xxviii.

against the corporations could be satisfactorily answered.[63] But in fact the underlying issue was not how the corporations had handled their civic responsibilities; rather, it was their exclusive nature, which appeared to be anomalous in the aftermath of the repeal of the test and corporation acts (1828), catholic emancipation, and parliamentary reform. By 1835 the government had introduced the first of what were to be six bills for Irish municipal reform (only the last became law), all of which made provision for the abolition of the existing variety of civic franchises in favour of a uniform franchise related to property, and without regard to religious distinctions.

How did the lawyers who opposed the government measures make out their case? They all began from the prediction that the introduction of a new, uniform civic franchise would have the effect of placing most of the Irish corporations in catholic hands. This would be the effect, it was argued, whether the new franchise was set at a low rate (five pound rent-payers) or a high one (ten pound householders).[64] In the early years of the debate, members of the government (who lacked systematic information on the matter) were inclined to be sceptical of such forecasts, but it was their opponents who were vindicated by events.[65]

The implications of placing control of the corporations in catholic hands were explored from a number of perspectives. Three of these in particular are worth examining. One concerned the future of Anglo-Irish relations. Speaking before the house of lords, Butt directed the lords' attention to the case of Dublin:

My lords, I have shewn you the enormous influence, and patronage, and power, which will be conferred upon the new corporation of Dublin: it is wisdom, at least, to pause and weigh well the uses to which they will be likely to turn the powers which you bestow on this body . . . You make them the accredited, the constitutional representatives of the metropolis of Ireland, the second city in the British dominions. . . . You are digni-

63. For instance, the commissioners alleged that many of the duties outlined in corporate charters were not being performed (*Report, M.C. (I)*, H.C. 1835, xxvii, 36). But to take the case of Dublin corporation, during the eighteenth century many of its responsibilities had been taken over by statutory bodies, including paving, cleaning and lighting. See R.B. McDowell, 'Dublin and Belfast—a comparison' in R.B. McDowell (ed.), *Social life in Ireland 1800-45* (Cork, 1957), p. 11 at p. 17.

64. *Hansard 3*, xxxi, 1323 (7 Mar. 1836); ibid., lii, 256-7 (14 Feb. 1840); Isaac Butt, *Irish municipal reform. The substance of a speech delivered at a meeting of protestants and freemen . . . on the 13th February, 1840* (Dublin, 1840), pp. 7-9.

65. *Hansard 3*, lii, 257 (14 Feb. 1840); Oliver MacDonagh, *Ireland: the union and its aftermath*, revised ed. (London, 1977), p. 21.

fying them with ancient authority, investing them with constitutional influence; you give them the power to legislate and to tax; you enact for them their sittings; you give them their meetings, which no law can suppress without a violation of all constitutional principle, which may defy the government and agitate the public mind, without the power of parliament to interfere. No coercion act will ever be tolerated to suppress the legalised meetings of a corporation. Suppose this corporation is directed by some active and unscrupulous popular leader, under whose control they direct all their energies to the repeal of the union, or the destruction of the Irish church. You have established this body in the metropolis, where all the discontented and ambitious spirits of the country naturally congregate—where the profession of the bar will be at hand to supply its candidates for popular patronage and fame. If such should be the character of a metropolitan corporation, with such power of rewarding its adherents, is it possible to over-estimate the extent of the mischief it will do?[66]

Although not all Butt's forebodings about the implications of municipal reform for Ireland were borne out by events (he admitted as much in the 1840s, having become a member of the reformed Dublin corporation),[67] his prediction concerning the contribution which the Irish corporations, and especially Dublin, would make to the repeal movement proved quite correct.[68]

Secondly, there was the question of the past conduct of the existing corporations and their members. The commissioners had found various shortcomings in the way in which the corporations had carried out the responsibilities placed upon them (although spokesmen for the corporations complained that they had not the opportunity to put their own case). The opposition lawyers set out to rebut some of these alleged deficiencies; and although these counter-claims cannot be considered in detail, one general theme, which was stressed repeatedly, is worth examining. Lefroy conceded that the corporations were for the most part exclusively protestant bodies. But this, he argued, was an obligation that had been laid on them by their charters.[69] Butt took the argument further. The early seventeenth century, he pointed out (correctly), had witnessed the setting up of a number of corporations for the

66. Isaac Butt, *Irish corporation bill. A speech delivered at the bar of the house of lords, on . . . the 15th of May 1840 in defence of the city of Dublin* (London, 1840), pp. 89-90.
67. See Butt's speech on the occasion of the inauguration of Alderman Roe as lord mayor of Dublin, *Nation*, 5 Nov. 1842.
68. Jacqueline R. Hill, 'The role of Dublin in the Irish national movement 1840-48' (unpublished Ph. D. thesis, University of Leeds, 1973), pp. 170-88.
69. Butt, *Irish corporation bill*, pp. 24-38; *Hansard 3*, xxxi, 1322 (7 Mar. 1836).

express purpose of fostering protestantism and British authority in Ireland. The point was not, Butt suggested, whether that purpose had been correct in the context of the seventeenth century; the point was that such corporations

were bound by their charters, and bound by their trusts, to promote British authority by the influence of intelligence, of civilisation, and of privilege, in opposition to numbers. For this, and the advancement of the protestant religion, was the very end and object of their existence.

Following the Williamite revolution, and until 1793, catholics had been excluded by law from the corporations. The 1793 relief act made it possible (but not compulsory) to admit catholics; but the measure had been passed at a time of widespread disturbances, culminating in the rebellion of 1798. Only after 1829 could it be said that parliament had given a lead in the matter of abandoning the principle of exclusivity; but the granting of emancipation had been followed almost at once by O'Connell calling on his supporters to join him in a campaign to repeal the act of union. In such circumstances, Butt contended, the corporations could be forgiven for failing to admit catholics.[70]

However, a third aspect of municipal reform which the opposition lawyers took up was perhaps the most significant in its implications for future developments in Ireland. It concerned what might be called community relations. The government, with its O'Connellite allies, contended that the existing system was in need of reform because it was exclusive; because it placed urban government in Ireland in the hands of 'a party'.[71] Critics of the government proposals acknowledged that the existing system was exclusive. They even acknowledged that it was in need of reform. But they argued that by introducing the democratic principle, the effect of the proposed reforms would be to replace one kind of exclusivity by another; the corporations would pass out of the hands of one party into those of another. For, although protestants would of course be eligible to vote on the same basis as catholics, given catholic numbers and the operation of the

---

70. Butt, *Irish corporation bill*, pp. 15–16, 44–49. On the establishment of protestant corporations, see T.W. Moody, 'Early modern Ireland', in T.W. Moody, F.X. Martin and F.J. Byrne (ed.), *A new history of Ireland, iii* (Oxford, 1976), pp. xlv-xlvi. O'Connell called for repeal of the union in a public letter 'to the people of Ireland' on 7 Jan. 1830 (*Dublin Evening Mail*, 11 Jan. 1830), and repeal was among the aims of the society of friends of Ireland of all religious persuasions, founded by O'Connell on 6 Apr. 1830 (*O'C. Corr.*, iv, letter 1672, n.6).

71. *Hansard 3*, xx, 264–5 (1 Aug. 1833).

democratic principle, protestants would be in a permanent
minority on the new bodies. In countries where there was general
agreement about fundamental national values (as in England) the
existence of permanent minorities did not matter very much. But
where parties were deeply divided, as in Ireland, over such matters
as the existence of the union, the existence of the established
church, the fundamental question of whether Ireland was a 'protestant' or a 'catholic' country, to place one party in a permanent
minority was to jeopardise its very existence. How were protestants to safeguard their property, and their institutions? The effect
of such a reform would simply be to replace one 'tyranny' by
another. Thus Lefroy, making the case in a debate on the 1836 bill:

He was quite ready at the same time to admit, that they [the corpo-
rations] could no longer be maintained under the present exclusive
principle. His objection to the proposed new system was, that it must
necessarily, though in a different way, become as exclusive as the old . . .
The old corporations were gradually decaying, their vigour was in a
great measure gone; but by this bill there would be brought into existence no less than fifty-four new corporations, in which the principles of
exclusiveness must be immediately put into vigorous operation. The 5£
rent-payers must form the great majority in all these corporations, and
this great majority must necessarily, from the circumstances of the population, be of one religion. Was it to be expected, with all the feelings of
soreness, arising from their late exclusion, still rankling in their minds—
with all their recollections of recent contests and differences, both as
regarded religion and politics—was it to be expected—was it in the
nature of things, that they would not act upon exclusive principles? . . .
No doubt, under this bill, protestants would be eligible to corporate
offices but would they be elected? and were they more likely to be
satisfied with mere eligibility than the roman catholics were?[72]

By no means all the protestant fears about the impact of municipal reform were borne out in practice; but nevertheless Lefroy
was here grappling with a real problem. One of his colleagues,
Serjeant Jackson, proposed a remedy. Speaking in parliament in
February 1840, when the final and ultimately successful bill was
under consideration, Jackson made the following announcement:

It was his intention when the bill got into committee to propose some
amendments, with the view of counteracting the exclusion of protestants. For instance, one amendment which he should propose would be
to this effect—suppose that in a town there were two roman catholic
voters for one protestant voter; to prevent the overwhelming effect of

72. Ibid., xxxi, 1322-23 (7 Mar. 1836).

such a majority he should propose that each elector should only have the power of voting for a number equal to one moiety of the town-council. This was by no means a new principle, but had been acted upon under the English municipal act in the election of assessors and auditors in a borough. The application of this principle also in connexion with Irish municipal boroughs had been recommended by a distinguished states-man in another place, of whom he wished to speak in terms of utmost respect—he meant Earl Grey. That noble earl, in a speech which he made the 27th of June, 1836, said on this subject,

'. . . Suppose, for instance, that every voter was restricted to voting for only half the number of town-councillors. The consequence would be, that there could be no exclusive party established, but that a minority in any corporation, of whatever persuasion they might be, could retain their due share of influence. . . .'

This was the suggestion of the noble earl, and these were the reasons on which it was supported—and nothing could be more just or reasonable than the ground which he took.[73]

But the English tory leader, Peel, showed no interest in the pro-posal. For the government, Lord John Russell was hostile, arguing that Ireland must be governed in the same way as England, and that the proposal would perpetuate division. The amendment was lost at the committee stage by 102 votes to 35.[74]

IV

To Burke and the British statesmen who took up the policy of political rights for Irish catholics in the early 1790s, the measure seemed to be a prudent and far-sighted contribution to the preservation of order and stability. In their eyes, catholics repre-sented a counter-revolutionary force, on account of their social and political conservatism, their orthodox theology, and their deferential conduct.[75] In Ireland, however, even to statesmen

73. Ibid., lii, 258-9 (14 Feb. 1840).
74. Ibid., lii, 265-73 (14 Feb. 1840); O'C. *Corr.*, vi, letter 2689, n. 1. It is worth noting that when the two parts of Canada (Upper Canada, with a predomi-nantly British and protestant population; Lower Canada, predominantly French and catholic) were reunited in 1840, it was stipulated that each part should vote for half the representatives in the united legislature. See Ward, *Colonial self-government*, p. 254.
75. No systematic study has been made of the ideology of those who cham-pioned catholic emancipation, although a useful start has been made by O'Ferrall, 'The growth of political consciousness' (note 5, above), pp. 102-4. It has been taken for granted that catholic arguments, at least by the 1820s, were 'liberal' in nature. But as late as 1824, O'Connell's wife could write to her husband in a spirit which was straight out of Burke:

appointed by the British ministers, the matter appeared in a very different light. The combination of catholic numbers, long proscription from power, and the almost sealed nature of catholic culture made their exercise of political power highly unpredictable. This would have produced a cautious response from protestants in any case; but it was Ireland's misfortune that just as catholics were being made eligible for admission to the existing system of privilege, the system itself was being challenged by radical reformers and agrarian activists, both encouraged by events in revolutionary France. Against this background catholic political rights were to remain, in certain respects, mere paper entitlements; and this in turn fostered sympathy among catholics for those who aimed to overturn the existing system of privilege.

The Irish catholics, then, came to be perceived, not by all but by many protestants, as part of the radical assault on the constitution; and the defenders of that constitution naturally emphasised its 'protestant' character, though not to the exclusion of its other features. Indeed, while it is evident that the constitution they defended was a confessional one, as was characteristic of the *ancien régime*, it is clear that its champions did not perceive it as *merely* confessional, but as a coherent system which had stood the test of time, and which had been compatible with economic prosperity and with the extension of 'toleration' (in its limited eighteenth-century sense) to catholics and other dissenters from the established church.

In the defence of that constitution Irish lawyers, as well as English lawyers, played a central role, not least because before the reforms of 1828–32, law and religion were two aspects of the same thing. As might be expected, they appealed to charters, to custom, to the idea of 'fundamental law' as embodied in the coronation oath: laws which were (or ought to be) impervious to reform. These were not new ideas: at a period in which people still commonly sought authority in the past, much of their force arose from the fact that they had undergone little change since the Williamite revolution. And while it can be tempting to dismiss, as slightly comic, figures like Duigenan, who saw 'romish agents' behind every bush, it is worth bearing in mind that, as long as the debate over emancipation was conducted upon *ancien régime*

'Their assistance [i.e., of catholics], believe *me*, before many years will be wanting to the government. The different sects that are starting up every day will at length endeavour to destroy both church and state, and what is to prevent them if the catholics of Ireland do not come forward which I trust they will not do without getting more than promises . . . '(O'C. *Corr.*, iii, letter 1091).

terms, their arguments had the edge over those of the reformers. It is not surprising that O'Connell and his followers increasingly took up ideas of liberalism and democracy, grounds which were more favourable to them.[76]

By 1832 the old constitution had been substantially modified, and the struggle shifted to the working out of reform at the local level. Urban local government represented one area where the law required to be changed to reflect national changes. In opposing whig/O'Connellite proposals for reform, the lawyers examined here displayed a degree of flexibility, and a willingness to explore alternatives, which is significantly at variance with the traditional, negative picture. Above all, they can be seen to have confronted the problem, which still faces those who live in democratic but deeply divided societies, of how to protect the rights of permanent minorities.[+]

---

76. See Leighton, 'Gallicanism and the veto controversy' (note 54, above).

+ I am grateful to Professor K.B. Nowlan for comments on this essay; remaining errors, of course, are my own.

'Vacancies for their friends' : judicial appointments in Ireland, 1866-1867

DAIRE HOGAN

IN APRIL 1866 the marquess of Clanricarde (a Liberal) asked in the house of lords whether the chief justice of queen's bench in Ireland, Thomas Lefroy, should continue to hold office in view of his advanced age (he was 90) and of certain reports of infirmity and feebleness that had been brought up. A similar question was raised in the house of commons on 3 May and 11 May, the chief secretary for Ireland being asked whether the constitution of the Irish bench, considering the advanced age of some of the judges, 'was satisfactory and conducive to the due administration of justice in Ireland'.[1]

The particular incident which grounded the questions had taken place some months before, when a sentence of death in a murder trial at Tullamore had been mispronounced by Lefroy, and he had been obliged to repeat the correct sentence, it being first dictated to him by the attorney general.

The Conservative member of parliament for Dublin University, James Whiteside QC, remarked that he could not but think it strange that the matter, having occurred in August, should be brought up only in May the following year.[2] He was referred to a week later in the remarks of the member raising the question for the second time, who 'had no doubt that in the course of the evening the member for the University of Dublin would rise and attempt to cast the veil of his eloquence over the receding shadows of a past generation'.[3] Whiteside, then aged 60, was one of the leading advocates, orators and parliamentary debaters of

1. *Hansard's parliamentary debates, 3rd series* (hereafter '*Hansard*'), clxxxii, 1628–36 (19 Apr. 1866), and *Hansard*, clxxxiii, 778 (11 May 1866).
2. *Hansard*, clxxxiii, 358 (3 May 1866).
3. Ibid., 781 (11 May 1866).

his time, and was the man who would have the first claim for appointment to a judicial office from a Conservative prime minister. A friend wrote that 'when there was battle expected in the house [of commons] Lord Derby [the Conservative leader] would say to him "Now Whiteside, where's your shillelagh?"'[4] His politics were 'authentically reactionary', in the words of the most recent study of Irish parties in the mid-nineteenth century.[5] On this occasion he said briefly that, as an appeal had been made 'pointedly' to him, he felt obliged to say that the confusion over the pronouncing of the sentence by Lefroy had arisen only because the courtroom was dark.[6]

Liberal and Tory members and peers exchanged stories in these debates of Lefroy's capability to act as a judge. Depending upon one's point of view he showed a 'notorious incompetence', 'imbecility', 'a hopeless confusion of intellect' and 'the utter breakdown of his mental powers' or was 'the best judge we have, although he is very old and not very vigorous for complicated cases'.[7] The official response on the matter was given by the chief secretary for Ireland, Chichester Fortescue, who said that unless a miscarriage of justice was established the government 'deem it their duty to abstain from expressing any such general opinion as they are invited to do'.[8] One peer quoted the leader of the home circuit as saying that 'when parliament meets I should think [hope] that they will have something else to do besides trying to make vacancies for their friends here'.[9]

As that remark suggests, the controversy was rather more about how and when and by whom a successor to Lefroy would be appointed, and whether he could be brought to retire by public criticism, than a disinterested inquiry into the administration of justice. One person however who seems to have taken it in the latter sense was Joseph Napier, lord chancellor of Ireland 1858–1859, who wrote a letter to the former lord chancellor of England, Lord Chelmsford, containing the phrase about Lefroy being 'the best judge' which was quoted by Chelmsford in the house of lords. A week later he was obliged to say in the house that he understood that the terms of the letter had 'given great offence' to

---

4. Percy FitzGerald, *Memories of an author* (London, 1895), p. 82.
5. K. Theodore Hoppen, *Elections, politics and society in Ireland 1832–1885* (Oxford, 1984), p. 279.
6. *Hansard*, clxxxiii, 794 (11 May 1866).
7. *Hansard*, clxxxiii, 780–90 (11 May 1866); *Hansard*, clxxxii, 1634 (19 Apr. 1866).
8. *Hansard*, clxxxiii, 782 (11 May 1866).
9. *Hansard*, clxxxii, 1636 (19 Apr. 1866).

the presiding judges of the other two courts of common law in Ireland, the chief justice of common pleas and the chief baron of the exchequer, 'as it was supposed that the letter conveyed a disparaging comparison with respect to those learned judges'. This was not the intention, and at their request this explanation would be given in the same place as the original remarks had been made.[10]

Lefroy had been born in January 1776, and had reputedly known Jane Austen at Bath in the last decade of the eighteenth century.[11] He was appointed a judge in the exchequer in 1841 and in 1852, when Lord Derby became prime minister for the first time, Lefroy was appointed chief justice of queen's bench.[12] This was in succession to Francis Blackburne who, having been appointed by Peel in 1846, had now been appointed lord chancellor of Ireland by Derby. It was generally assumed in 1866 that Lefroy was not willing to retire voluntarily until the government had changed, after which the appointment of his successor would be in the hands of Lord Derby. If he had left office at any time since the summer of 1859 (when Lord Derby's second short-lived government retired after losing a general election) his successor would have been appointed either by Lord Palmerston (prime minister 1859–1865) or by Lord John Russell, who became prime minister on Palmerston's death in 1865 and was in office at the time of the April and May debates.

In the middle of June, a few weeks after the May debates, Russell's government was defeated in the house of commons over an amendment to the Second Reform Bill, as a result of skilful parliamentary manoeuvres by the Tories, and shortly afterwards resigned. On 27 June Lord Derby was invited by the queen to form a government (without an election being held).[13]

On 2 July Lefroy's son (Anthony Lefroy, who was the second MP for Dublin University) contacted Derby to indicate that his father was prepared to resign as chief justice. In thanking him Derby said that he would be 'happy to see you for the purpose of receiving the communication you have to make to me, the purpose of which I can conjecture … it will be more advisable to postpone the interview till the government shall be actually formed, which I hope it will be in 2 or 3 days'.[14]

10. Ibid., 744.
11. *Letters of Jane Austen*, ed. by Lord Brabourne (2 vols., London, 1884), pp. 126, 132 and 163.
12. F.E. Ball, *The judges in Ireland 1221–1921* (2 vols., London, 1926), ii, 354.
13. Robert Blake, *Disraeli* (London, 1966), pp. 444–5.
14. Derby to A. Lefroy MP, 2 July 1866, Papers of the 14th earl of Derby (Liverpool Record Office) (Derby papers) 191/1.

Lefroy's willingness to resign meant that not only the office of lord chancellor but also the office of chief justice of queen's bench, the two leading judicial positions in the country, would be vacant. The lord chancellor of Ireland was not only the head of the judiciary but also a member of the Irish administration, advising the lord lieutenant and the chief secretary on issues of the day and not necessarily on their legal aspects alone. Unlike other judges he ceased to hold office when the government changed, indicating the mixed political and legal nature of his position. Despite the title of the office it was frequently held by persons who were not peers. It carried a large salary and a large pension. What might have been regarded as straightforward patronage or personal claims to promotion to these positions were complicated by the wish on the part of Derby and his principal adviser on Irish affairs, Lord Naas, to appoint Abraham Brewster QC, a man who had no claim to preferment from the Conservative party, as lord chancellor.

Naas, the leading Irish Conservative politician and party manager at this time, served as chief secretary for Ireland in each of Derby's three governments (1852, 1858–59 and 1866–68) and was a member of the Cabinet in the last period of office. He was an 'efficient, loyal and dedicated politician of the second rank',[15] and was on the more liberal wing of the party, unconnected with the sectarianism frequently associated with 'ultra' or traditional Toryism. Disraeli considered him to be 'a most able, sensible and enlightened man'.[16] He was assassinated in India in 1872, where he had gone as viceroy in 1868 (having succeeded to the title of earl of Mayo) and this, by a familiar process, cast a favourable posthumous light on his political career. His biographer writing in 1875 said that he was a 'large minded politician, who felt the necessity of belonging to one party or another if he were to effect anything practical'.[17] His period of party management in the 1850s and 1860s, before reforms in the electoral system and the revival of nationalist sentiment changed the rules of the game, was the time of the greatest Conservative electoral success in Victorian Ireland[18]—40 seats in the 1852 election, 46 in 1857, 55 in 1859 and 47 in 1865 out of a total Irish membership of the house of commons of 105.

15. Hoppen, *Elections . . . in Ireland*, p. 293. See also p. 296.
16. G.E. Buckle, *The life of Benjamin Disraeli, earl of Beaconsfield: vol. iv 1855–1868* (London, 1916), p. 482.
17. W.W. Hunter, *A life of the earl of Mayo* (2 vols., London, 1875), i, 78.
18. Hoppen, *Elections . . . in Ireland*, p. 284.

Along with the lord lieutenant (viceroy) of Ireland (the marquess of Abercorn in 1866 and 1867) the chief secretary controlled the distribution of appointments to offices within the gift of the government, an important element—perhaps, indeed, the object in many cases—of party and political management.

The issues of mixed legal and political claims to judicial office are well set out in a letter from Francis Macdonagh QC (MP for Sligo, 1860–1865) to Abercorn written in March 1867 when, as will be seen, the appointment to the office of lord chancellor had become a matter of controversy for the second time within a year.

Macdonagh began by requesting the lord lieutenant's 'favourable consideration of my position at the bar and my services to the Conservative party'. He had not pressed his claims before [at least with Abercorn] 'as I felt assured that your excellency's high sense of honour and recognition of party obligation would ultimately redress the injustice of which I had too much reason to complain'. Lord Derby, he said, had told him in August 1866 that he was sure that Naas or Abercorn would be well disposed to give full weight to his [my] professional and political claims. (In writing to Abercorn about Macdonagh at that time Derby had said that he was 'very hungry and very indignant about being overlooked'.[19])

These claims may be summarised in a single sentence, that is, that I have had a greater experience of the administration of the civil and criminal law than any other man at present at the bar of Ireland whilst at the same time I have fought two contested elections at my own expense and sat in parliament for 5 years in the shade and gloom of opposition, remaining faithful to our party—and have now the intolerable pain of seeing the highest prizes in the law pass into the hands of gentlemen who have been either foes of the Conservative party or who never, for one moment, made a sacrifice for the cause.[20]

While this was written to press his own claims to appointment in the circumstances at the time it is also indicative of the very strong reaction which had been provoked in July 1866, at the time of formation of Derby's government, by the suggestion that Brewster should become lord chancellor.

Abraham Brewster, the man who in July 1866 Naas wished should be appointed as lord chancellor, was born in 1796.[21] He was law adviser in Dublin Castle and subsequently solicitor

19. Derby to Abercorn, 10 Aug. 1866 (Derby papers, 191/2).
20. Macdonagh to Abercorn, 22 March 1867 (Abercorn papers (PRONI) D 623/A/308/35 pt. 1).
21. Ball, *Judges*, ii, 365.

general in the government of Sir Robert Peel in the 1840s, an appointment which had initially been opposed but which Blackburne had insisted should be made[22] and had remained a follower of Peel when the Conservative party had split in 1846. Lord Aberdeen, who succeeded Lord Derby as prime minister at the end of 1852, appointed him as attorney general in Ireland, a position which he held until Aberdeen left office in 1855. He voted in the general election that year for the Liberal candidate for the City of Dublin, not the Conservative candidate[23]—this was a matter of public record, since the secret ballot was not introduced until 1872. This continuing association and support in the 1850s of the remnants of the Peel party was noted by Conservative politicians and lawyers.

In 1859 Napier (who at the time was the lord chancellor of Ireland in Derby's second government) had proposed to the lord lieutenant, Lord Eglinton, that Brewster be appointed a judge but 'he told me he could not venture to do so without giving so much offence to our friends as would be intolerable'.[24]

While Napier may have been prepared, perhaps on a legal rather than a political basis, to recommend Brewster for appointment as a judge in 1859 he was among the leaders of the opposition to him in the summer of 1866. He told Derby early in July that Brewster 'has been our most insidious and consistent opponent from 1852 to the present time. His money, his influence and his votes have been freely given to our inveterate opponents'. That he should be promoted to lord chancellor 'over the heads of others who had been fighting the Conservative battle with untiring zeal and indomitable perseverance, when the cause was a losing one and was thought hopeless, while he was enlisted in the ranks of the enemy'[25] would be outrageous.

Napier, who had been born in 1804, was an articulate and intelligent man, closely connected with Dublin University, for which he was successively one of its members of parliament (before his brief period of office as lord chancellor) and vice-chancellor.[26] Like Whiteside (who was his brother-in-law) he was associated with the more sectarian side of the Conservative party. He had a rather unctuous manner, exemplified by the letter in May to Lord Chelmsford which had led to private and ultimately

22. E. Blackburne, *Life of Francis Blackburne* (London, 1874), pp. 208–16.

23. *Daily Express*, 27 July 1874.

24. Napier to Derby, undated (early July 1866) (Derby papers, 112).

25. Ibid.

26. Ball, *Judges*, ii, 361.

public apologies and embarrassment. He was a prominent member of the Church of Ireland, with a reputation for piety, and a couple of years later was to be prominent in the opposition to the disestablishment of the church.[27] A hostile memoirist said that he was generally regarded as having a 'profession of religion which was altogether false'.[28] A more neutral one said that he had 'a voice slow and solemn, as of one preaching'.[29]

Whiteside told Derby, more directly than Napier, that the 'rumoured arrangements ... would be fatal to the Conservative party in Ireland'[30] and informed the chief whip of the party in Ireland that he would not serve under Brewster in any capacity,[31] that the possibility of his appointment seemed entirely inconsistent with Brewster's record over the years 'and because I think his nomination [contrary to] judicial tone and purity in Ireland. May I disclaim any personal objection'.[32] He was backed in this stand by a large number of his parliamentary colleagues.[33]

Napier wrote again to Derby to say that he did not 'think it possible to make a selection more likely to cool our friends and heat our enemies ... he would be subject to such suspicion of indirect influence to the prejudice of our most trusty supporters and would undermine the confidence without which political union cannot exist'.[34]

While Napier, as a former lord chancellor, might have been regarded as suitable for appointment again it is less likely that Whiteside as a great common law advocate and orator, would have been seriously considered in that context, at least insofar as some familiarity with equity and the court of chancery would have been thought appropriate for the position. Nevertheless on his death in 1876 the obituary in *The Times* said that he had felt slighted by the fact that he was appointed to be the chief justice of queen's bench, not lord chancellor. 'The office which he filled and which if it had fallen fairly to him, in the lottery of party and had no disparagement in the claim, might have been accepted

27. A.C. Ewald, *Life and letters of the rt hon Sir Joseph Napier, Bt.* (London, 1892), pp. 276–84.
28. J.G. Swift MacNeill, *What I have seen and heard* (London, 1925), p. 47.
29. R. Denny Urlin, *Journal and reminiscences* (Letchworth, 1909), p. 134.
30. Whiteside to Derby, 4 July 1866 (Derby papers, 122/8).
31. Sir Thomas Bateson to Naas, 11 July 1866 (Mayo papers (NLI) MS 11,143(4)).
32. Whiteside to Col. T.E. Taylor, undated (early July 1866), Mayo papers, MS 11,143(3).
33. Ball, *Judges*, ii, 300.
34. Napier to Derby, undated (early July 1866) (Derby papers, 112).

with gratitude as one of the highest distinction. The slight which this proceeding seemed to convey weighed upon his sensitive pride and he never appeared to be quite at ease in his position as chief justice.'[35]

The suggestion that Brewster might be appointed as lord chancellor thus caused a very strong reaction, and it is indicative of the importance that Derby and Naas attached to having Brewster's advice available to the government, apart from his judicial services, that they were prepared to run risks with the support of many Irish Conservatives by proposing his appointment.

On 8 July Naas wrote to Derby, from his constituency in Cumberland, expressing surprise at 'the stories that the rumour of Brewster's appointment has raised among our Irish political friends' and reporting that Whiteside had written to say that if Napier was not to be re-appointed as lord chancellor he considered that he would have the first claim to the position. Naas now thought that if Brewster would alienate their supporters his appointment could not be proceeded with: 'Abercorn will want a sage adviser constantly present. I would, I know, work well with Brewster but political ties must be respected and an appointment distasteful to the majority of our supporters would be a bad thing to start with.'[36]

Derby and Disraeli, the Conservative leader in the commons, were quite convinced that Whiteside would not accept any office if Brewster was appointed chancellor,[37] and to proceed without him would not have been feasible. Abercorn and Naas met on 12 July with Derby, who wrote to Disraeli later in the day that

we have a way out of the difficulty. We propose to ask old Blackburne, now the lord justice of appeal, to oblige us by taking the chancellorship pro tem. This will allow us to put Napier in his place, which is what he wants and which he is fit for (indeed the whole arrangement is of his concoction). His appointment would gratify Whiteside and Napier on his part would strongly urge on Whiteside the acceptance of the chief justiceship pur et simple.[38]

Napier believed that Blackburne was willing to participate in the scheme.[39]

35. *The Times*, 27 Nov. 1876.

36. Naas to Derby, 8 July 1866 (Derby papers, 155/2).

37. Derby to Disraeli, 12 July 1866 (Disraeli papers (Bodleian Library, Oxford), B/XX/5/396).

38. Derby to Disraeli, 12 July 1866 (Disraeli papers, B/XX/5/395).

39. Ibid.

Hugh Cairns, one of the leading Conservatives (an Irishman, from Belfast, who had been called to the English bar and was now to be appointed attorney general, and subsequently lord chancellor of England by Disraeli in both of his governments[40]) was at the time in Dublin and Derby asked him to stay over for a day to 'negotiate personally' with all concerned on Derby's behalf. 'A delay of a few months would serve to cool down the present excitement . . . and a day spent in Dublin would be well spent if you can carry it into effect.'[41]

The scheme was put in more formal terms to the queen by Derby, who told her by another letter that day that 'mutual personal jealousies' among the candidates for office had delayed his proposals for Irish judicial appointments, but that the scheme now proposed seemed likely to command the assent of all parties. He acknowledged that he was 'very desirous of introducing Mr Brewster, but the tide of political feeling was so strongly against him that [I] dare not attempt it at present. The temporary possession of the great seal by Lord Justice Blackburne may give time for these feelings to subside and facilitate a future fusion of parties'.[42]

A fourth letter that day from Derby then contained a strong appeal to Blackburne to join in the arrangements:

I write to you with the frankness of an old friend, who ventures to think that you will be willing to do something to aid his government which from various causes which I need not specify is in considerable difficulty about the Irish legal appointments. But if you would consent again to take (if only for a short time) the duties of lord chancellor I think the ground is cleared of the chief difficulties . . . In short the whole of our arrangements depend upon your acceptance, and will be in utter confusion if you fail to aid us.[43]

Blackburne (who was not significantly younger than Lefroy, having been born in 1782) had first known and worked with Derby in the 1830s when he was attorney general in the reform government of Lord Grey (prime minister between 1830 and 1834) and Derby (Stanley) held office as chief secretary for Ireland. When Derby became prime minister in 1852 for the first time he had appointed Blackburne as lord chancellor.

40. R.F.V. Heuston, 'Hugh McCalmont Cairns', in *NILQ*, xxvi (1975), 269.
41. Derby to Cairns, 12 July 1866 (Derby papers, 191/1, p. 85).
42. Derby to the queen, 12 July 1866 (Derby papers, 191/1, p. 82).
43. Derby to Blackburne, 12 July 1866, in Blackburne, *Life*, p. 301.

The proposal satisfied all those who were to receive appointments. Blackburne accepted promptly (by telegraph, in the light of the urgency of the situation, giving rise to some confusion later as to whether he had formally accepted the offer and had received a sufficient acknowledgement from Derby[44]), although Derby believed that the acceptance was based upon Napier being his successor.[45] Whiteside told Derby on 14 July that 'the arrangements are satisfactory and expedient...I regret your lordship should have had so much trouble about this appointment of mine. I feel relieved that all your trouble respecting my position has now ended'.[46]

The arrangement, however, attracted immediate criticism from those outside the circle in which the appointments had been made. Questions were raised in parliament about both the age of Blackburne and the deafness of Napier.

The objection to Blackburne was based both on the general ground of his advanced age and on the more specific suggestion that eight years earlier he had declined Derby's invitation to resume office as lord chancellor (after his brief tenure in 1852) on the grounds of what was then his age. It was true that he had received an offer from Derby in 1858, but the letter conveying the offer was not couched in anything like the urgent terms of the more recent one: 'it is fair to tell you that the prospects of my continuance in office are very precarious, and I shall neither be surprised nor offended if, under such circumstances, you prefer to retain your present high and permanent office',[47] namely that of lord justice of appeal, to which he had been appointed in 1856.[48]

On 19 July in the house of commons Disraeli said that it was difficult to remember all the offers of office that had been made in 1858, but that Blackburne's refusal at the time was not based on his age.[49] This was not correct. In explaining to the queen in 1858 why Napier and not Blackburne was to be appointed chancellor Derby had said that Blackburne's age and his state of health would incapacitate him from the discharge of the duties of the office.[50] Blackburne's son, writing his biography in 1874, confirmed that his age and the state of his health had made him reluctant to

44. Blackburne to Derby, 23 Aug. 1866 (Derby papers, 122/7B); Derby to Naas, 30 Aug. 1866 (Derby papers, 190/2, p. 241).

45. Derby to Naas, 13 July 1866 (Mayo papers, MS 11,144).

46. Whiteside to Derby, 14 July 1866 (Derby papers, 154/6A).

47. Derby to Blackburne, 24 Feb. 1858, in Blackburne, *Life*, p. 296.

48. Blackburne, *Life*, p. 293.

49. *Hansard*, clxxxiv, 1072 (19 July 1866).

50. Derby to the queen, 26 Feb. 1858 (Royal Archives (RA) C29/37).

take on the office again then.[51] Early in August Naas fended off a similar line of questioning in the house of lords,[52] to Blackburne's great satisfaction.[53]

Napier's appointment raised a greater storm, however. He had long suffered from a degree of deafness, which instantly and, as he believed, at the instigation of Brewster and his associates, became a ground of objection to his appointment. In writing subsequently to the queen's secretary Derby said that the 'expression of feeling [was] partly personal, partly political'.[54] The public comment on this was such that on 16 July, within a week of the scheme of appointments being conceived and implemented, Derby wrote to him asking him to consider 'carefully and conscientiously' whether he would be fit to carry out the duties of lord justice of appeal, and to consult his friends, 'who may be more fully acquainted than you can be with the real state of public opinion in the profession'.[55]

Napier replied the following day saying that he was satisfied that he could discharge the duties, remarking that while his hearing might not always have picked up all that was said in court this would not be of significance in the court of chancery appeal.[56] This was received with dismay by Derby, who told Naas that 'we must now stand by the appointment, unpopular as it may be',[57] and by Naas who replied that he had written again to Napier 'but I fear it will be of little use'.[58] While the letters which Napier received from Naas have not survived, he told Derby that they 'have given me great pain, as much from the sense of injustice to myself as from the trouble which I have most unexpectedly caused to you'. He added that he knew that Derby would not 'allow me to be trampled upon'.[59]

Derby and Naas, working through Napier's friend and political associate, Lord George Hamilton (who was Abercorn's third son), persuaded Napier to travel to London to meet Derby ('in his hands all that I value is safe'[60]). Naas had suggested that if

51. Blackburne, *Life*, p. 298.
52. *Hansard*, clxxxiv, 2032 (3 Aug. 1866).
53. Blackburne to Naas, 5 Aug. 1866 (Mayo papers, MS 11,143(8)).
54. Derby to General Sir Charles Grey, 29 July 1866 (RA, A77/6).
55. Derby to Napier, 16 July 1866 (Derby papers, 191/2).
56. Napier to Derby, 17 July 1866 (Derby papers, 112).
57. Derby to Naas, 18 July 1866 (Derby papers, 155/2).
58. Naas to Derby, 18 July 1866 (Derby papers, 155/2).
59. Napier to Derby, 20 July 1866 (Derby papers, 112).
60. Napier to Hamilton, 25 July 1866 (Derby papers, 155/2).

Napier still declined to resign he should be asked to discuss the matter with Lord Chelmsford and Cairns,[61] and Derby arranged this meeting, adding Hamilton to the group—'they meet you as friends, giving you, in that capacity, and on your invitation, the best advice which they can give for your own credit, for the character of the government and for the public opinion of the administration of justice in Ireland'.[62]

The group at their meeting succeeded in inducing Napier to withdraw from his position, but as Derby told Disraeli, 'the chancellor [Chelmsford] has undertaken that he shall have a baronetcy, which he was hardly entitled to promise'.[63] In his letter of resignation to Derby, which was read to the house of commons, he said that while there was no justification for the impression which had been created that his partial defect of hearing might interfere with the discharge of his duties 'the nomination to so high an office should not be open to a moment's cavil'.[64]

The vacancy caused by Napier's resignation was filled a few days later, after Naas and Abercorn had conferred with Derby,[65] by the appointment of Brewster, despite continued opposition from those who had blocked his appointment as lord chancellor less than a month earlier.[66] Blackburne approved, and Naas forwarded to Derby a letter from him, commenting that he believed it to express 'the general opinion of the thinking public'; a month earlier, before any appointments had been made and it was becoming clear that Brewster would not be acceptable as chancellor he had suggested to Derby just this outcome, with Brewster instead of Napier as the first choice to be lord justice of appeal.[67]

Additional contentious political and legal choices on other appointments presented themselves a few days later in August, through the death of the master of the rolls (Thomas Barry Cusack Smith, who had been appointed in 1846) and the illness and resignation of Edmund Hayes, a puisne judge of the queen's bench, who had been appointed by Derby in 1859.

61. Naas to Derby, 26 July 1866 (Derby papers, 155/2).

62. Derby to Napier, 27 July 1866 (Derby papers, 190/2, p. 202).

63. Derby to Disraeli, 28 July 1866 (Disraeli papers, B/XX/5/358).

64. Napier to Derby, 28 July 1866 (Derby papers, 155/2); *Hansard*, clxxxiv, 1658 (30 July 1866).

65. Naas to Derby, 4 Aug. 1866 (Derby papers, 155/2).

66. Sir Thomas Bateson to Naas, 5 Aug. 1866 (Mayo papers, MS 11,143(8)).

67. Naas to Derby, 8 Aug. 1866 (Derby papers, 155/2), Naas to Derby (undated, early July 1866) (Derby papers, 155/2).

The first thought of Derby and Naas was that Francis Fitzgerald, a baron of the exchequer, who had been appointed by Derby in 1858, should be offered the position of master of the rolls, which would in turn create a vacancy for Henry George QC, Tory MP for Co. Wexford.[68] Naas told Disraeli that he was 'anxious to get George out of Wexford', for the better party management of 'the Wexford Tories, who are stiff prots'.[69] Fitzgerald declined the offer, however, and Derby turned down a casual proposal by Naas that Cairns might be suitable and in due course take the position of lord chancellor of Ireland in succession to Blackburne[70] ('we cannot let you have Cairns nor do I think he would accept it'[71]). He responded more sharply to a suggestion from Naas that Brewster should be offered the position, saying 'it would have a bad effect if we were to fall back upon him for every legal or judicial appointment we may have to dispose of'.[72]

The attorney general, John Edward Walsh, then pressed his claim to the Rolls, and wrote directly to Derby on the subject,[73] leading Derby in turn to tell Naas that the Irish ministers should protect him from direct appeals of this nature on matters with which they were dealing.[74] Since Walsh had been in office (and in parliament, having been elected to the seat vacated by Whiteside) only for the few weeks since the formation of the government Derby told Naas that 'he ought to do us at least some service in his present office before he seeks promotion'.[75] He ultimately accepted however that there was no alternative to Walsh.[76]

The unwillingness of Derby and Naas to let Walsh exercise the traditional prerogative of an attorney general to be appointed to any judicial vacancy that arose stemmed primarily from their wish to retain his services for the government—'the AG will be a great loss to us', Naas told Derby, 'he is shrewd and determined and would be just the man if we have any further trouble with the Fenians'.[77] They also anticipated difficulty in making appointments

68. Naas to Derby, 15 Aug. 1866 and 17 Aug. 1866 (Derby papers 155/2); Derby to Naas, 21 Aug. 1866 (Mayo papers, MS 11,144).
69. Naas to Disraeli, 17 Aug. 1866 (Disraeli papers, B/XX/BO/21).
70. Naas to Derby, 25 Aug. and 26 Aug. 1866 (Derby papers, 155/2).
71. Derby to Naas, 30 Aug. 1866 (Derby papers, 191/2, p. 241).
72. Derby to Naas, 6 Sept. 1866 (Derby papers, 192/1).
73. Walsh to Derby, 4 Sept. 1866 (Mayo papers, MS 11,144).
74. Derby to Naas, 6 Sept. 1866 (Derby papers, 192/1).
75. Derby to Naas, 16 Aug. 1866 (Mayo papers, MS 11,144).
76. Derby to Abercorn, 14 Sept. 1866 (Derby papers, 191/2, p. 107).
77. Naas to Derby, 11 Sept. 1866 (Derby papers, 155/2).

consequential upon his promotion, since Michael Morris, MP for Galway and a protégé of Lord Clanricarde,[78] who had been appointed to the position of solicitor general in July, would in turn expect the usual promotion to be attorney general.

They had little confidence in Morris, having had misgivings about his initial appointment,[79] and foresaw renewed objections to him from Conservative MPs, who had not been pleased at his appointment in July. However the other candidates, such as Francis Macdonagh QC or Stearne Ball Miller QC, MP for Armagh, seemed even less suitable. Naas reported on the subject to Derby, who was 'sorry that you cannot give a more favourable report of the Conservative bar in Ireland'.[80] Derby also wrote to Naas that 'I observe that in connection with legal appointments you never mention the name of Francis Macdonagh. I do not know him personally... and he considers himself to be very ill-used'.[81]

Naas told Derby that 'the immediate elevation of Morris to be attorney general will not be relished by a large number of our political friends—Miller is a great difficulty. He is really quite unfit for a law officer, and we really could not depend only on such assistance as he and Morris together could give in parliament'.[82] While the claims of Miller 'have been very strongly pressed by a great many of our northern friends',[83] Naas was able eventually to report to Derby that 'with great difficulty he has consented to forego his claim to the solicitor generalship'.[84]

In the end Derby accepted Naas' recommendation that the appointment of solicitor general be given to Hedges Eyre Chatterton QC, although he was not a member of parliament at the time and there was a doubt whether the electors of Dublin University would return him,[85] and George filled the vacancy on the bench.[86]

The new year 1867 opened quietly, save for a letter from Napier to Derby, referring to himself as a 'dead man out of mind'

78. Blake, *Disraeli*, p. 446.
79. Derby to Naas, and Naas to Derby, 18 July 1866 (Derby papers, 155/2).
80. Derby to Naas, 6 Oct. 1866 (Mayo papers, MS 11,144).
81. Derby to Naas, 6 Oct.1866 (Mayo papers, MS 11,144).
82. Naas to Derby, 11 Sept. 1866 (Derby papers, 155/2).
83. Naas to Derby, 2 Oct. 1866 (Derby papers, 155/2).
84. Naas to Derby, 19 Oct. 1866 (Derby papers, 155/2).
85. Naas to Derby, 6 Sept. 1866 (Derby papers, 192/1); Naas to Derby, 19 Oct. 1866 (Derby papers, 155/2).
86. Naas to Derby, 2 Oct. 1866 (Derby papers, 155/2).

and complaining that the promise of a baronetcy had not been honoured. Derby told him frankly that, while not repudiating what Chelmsford had said in July, 'in the expectation which the chancellor held out to you he somewhat exceeded any authority I had given him'. Napier would have to be patient: 'if I were now to submit your name to the queen it would bring down upon me a host of disappointed applicants, who would not leave me an hour's peace.' He could offer 'in lieu of a baronetcy the immediate honour of an English privy councillorship',[87] but Napier, having consulted his relatives and friends, did not accept that.[88]

Blackburne wrote to Derby in the middle of January to thank him for a pheasant, 'proof that you hold us in kind recollection and regard' and to tell him that he had got through 'a vast deal of business in the last term without injury to my health and strength'.[89] Blackburne's health soon deteriorated, however, and he was suffering from a severe attack of gout when the Fenian rising took place on the night of 5 March. He was confined to his home (Rathfarnham Castle), and unable to join in advising the government in the crisis. Pressure grew for him to step down, and on 12 March he wrote to Derby stating that he would be willing to resign the office that he had accepted 'under very peculiar circumstances' if Derby considered 'that my resignation would be conducive to the interests of the party of which you are the leader and calculated to promote the peace and prosperity of the country'.[90] He sent his eldest son, William, and his secretary to London with this offer, but they also brought a report from Blackburne's medical adviser to the effect that he would be 'as well able in a few days to perform all the functions of his office as he was when he accepted the appointment'.[91] The doctor said that he had made this report in consequence of erroneous remarks or reports he read daily in some of the influential papers.

The offer of resignation had been arranged by Naas ('a very difficult and delicate matter'[92]), who was intent on securing the appointment of Brewster now, eight months after the first attempt. He told Derby on the same day that 'Brewster is really the only man we could have on the woolsack. His experience and sagacity will be of the greatest use to us on all matters of

87. Derby to Napier, 11 Feb. 1867 (Derby papers, 192/2, p. 19).
88. Napier to Derby, undated (late Mar. 1867) (Derby papers, 112).
89. Blackburne to Derby, 15 Jan. 1867 (Derby papers, 122/7B).
90. Blackburne to Derby, 12 Mar. 1867 (Derby papers, 122/8).
91. Robert Adams MD to Blackburne, 12 Mar. 1867 (Derby papers, 122/8).
92. Naas to Derby, 12 Mar. 1867 (Derby papers, 155/3).

administration, especially with reference to the forthcoming [Fenian] trials ... Brewster's appointment will be cavilled at by some of our ultra friends, but I feel certain that we have no choice'.[93] Derby wrote back that he had told Blackburne's son and private secretary during their interview (which Naas had not known about when writing), that he would not accept the resignation (in the light of the medical attendant's letter 'certifying his perfect ability to perform all the duties of his office') without further advice from Abercorn and Naas. 'I am sorry to interpose any delay in your arrangement but it is quite clear that if Blackburne be removed he will consider himself, and his friends will consider him, as "turned out" to make way for Brewster . . . it will certainly add to the dissatisfaction of the ultra party if it should appear to be forced upon the chancellor.'[94]

Naas replied that it would 'stand over for a few days'. His emissary, Judge Keatinge, who was Blackburne's oldest friend, had told him that Blackburne had appeared to accept that 'in the present state of the country the absence of the principal legal member of the government from all its counsels was a very great evil'. Naas would be sorry to offend Blackburne in any way, but thought that his messengers in London had been speaking more their own sentiments than his.[95]

On 20 March Naas returned to Derby Blackburne's letter of resignation and said that it was now essential to accept it,[96] which Derby did later that day,[97] and steps were taken immediately to appoint Brewster. The appointment, Derby said, 'will be an immense relief to your attorney general, who has been in a great state of alarm',[98] some evidence of the reservations which had attended Morris' appointment the previous autumn. At this stage Macdonagh wrote the letter to Abercorn cited earlier about the promotion of judges not known to be Tories—a reference not only to Brewster but also to Jonathan Christian, who replaced him as lord justice of appeal.

The replacement of Blackburne by Brewster was the culmination of a series of controversial appointments. In the same week Blackburne's health declined again and for a time he was not

---

93. Ibid.
94. Derby to Naas, 13 Mar. 1867 (Mayo papers, MS 11,150).
95. Naas to Derby, 14 Mar. 1867 (Derby papers, 155/3).
96. Naas to Derby, 20 Mar. 1867 (Derby papers, 155/3).
97. Derby to Blackburne, 20 Mar. 1867 (Derby papers, 192/2, p. 56); Blackburne to Derby, 21 Mar. 1867 (Mayo papers, MS 11,150).
98. Derby to Naas, 22 Mar. 1867 (Derby papers, 192/2, p. 63).

expected to survive from day to day,[99] giving rise to the thought that those responsible for removing him from office might also be responsible for his death.

Whiteside was reported as falling into a 'tempestuous state of rage' at Brewster's elevation.[100] Naas was initially sanguine about his reaction, writing to Abercorn that 'Whiteside will be in a fury. I hope that it will not dispose him to let off the Fenian prisoners'.[101] He had to be encouraged by Derby a few days later, however, after some particularly unpleasant criticism, who told him that 'neither you nor I have anything to reproach ourselves with. My conscience entirely acquits me of having done anything in any way injurious to a very old friend, and I feel satisfied that if we had delayed accepting his resignation when we did we should have failed in a public duty at a very serious crisis'.[102]

Derby alleviated the party discontent with Brewster's appointment by honouring the promise to Napier to arrange with the queen for the honour of a baronetcy to be conferred. When advising Naas of this he expressed the hope that 'this may be a sop to the protestants, which may neutralise the Brewster pill'.[103] At the same time Mr Benjamin Guinness, MP for Dublin, was given a similar honour on the basis of his restoration of St Patrick's cathedral—'this act of munificence is well worthy of recognition on the part of the crown'.[104]

Debate over Blackburne's resignation being called in by the government focussed on whether the admittedly temporary appointment was to be terminated at a time of his choosing or of the government's. The expression 'if only for a short time' had been used in Derby's letter of appeal on 12 July to Blackburne to accept the office of lord chancellor. Blackburne's son Edward, writing his father's biography in 1874 and reflecting the Tory view in March 1867, said that 'the true and natural meaning of the words is plainly this: "The government are in a difficulty; your acceptance of the great seal will relieve them from it. You are not, however, to be in any way fettered, but are to be a free agent to resign it when you please." '[105]

99. Brewster to Naas, 24 Mar. 1867 (Mayo papers, Ms 11,147(13)).

100. FitzGerald, *Memories of an author*, p. 82.

101. Naas to Abercorn, 24 Mar. 1867 (Abercorn papers, D623/A/304/11).

102. Derby to Naas, 29 Mar. 1867 (Mayo papers, MS 11,150); see also Naas to Abercorn, 23 Mar. 1867 (Abercorn papers, D623/A/304/10 pt. 3).

103. Derby to Naas, 25 Mar. 1867 (Derby papers, 192/2, p. 67).

104. Derby to Grey, 25 Mar. 1867 (RA, A35/52).

105. Blackburne, *Life*, p. 303

Derby explained it in a different way to the queen when seeking her consent on 22 March to Brewster's appointment. This was 'in accordance with the wish of the lord lieutenant [Abercorn] and indeed in pursuance of an understanding arrived at from the first... It is important that this office should in the present state of Ireland be filled up with the least possible delay'.[106] Three days later, in apologising to the queen's secretary that the appointment had become known before the formal consent had been given, he expanded on this: 'it is fair to say that the appointment of Mr Brewster was contemplated from the first formation of the government and was only delayed in consequence of the great hostility of the strong protestant party, Mr Blackburne's appointment, at the age of 83, being avowedly only provisional'.[107]

A final curious episode connected with Blackburne's resignation took place over a request from his eldest son, William, in April 1867 to Derby that Blackburne should receive 'some recognition from her majesty',[108] a suggestion shortly afterwards made in more specific terms, that 'the offer of a baronetcy or a peerage would be highly gratifying to him and the family'.[109] Blackburne's health was failing completely and unless something was done at once 'the whole thing might lie over until too late for him to feel his last days had been well spent in earning some honourable distinction from his sovereign for his family'.[110]

Early in May Derby offered Blackburne a baronetcy. In his reply (written by his son Edward) Blackburne said that the offer was unexpected and unsought and would not be accepted.[111] Derby told Naas that he thought that this was because they had hoped for a peerage 'a la Lefroy', an indication of a similar (and likewise unsuccessful) approach by Lefroy and his family for the conferring of a higher honour upon his retirement.[112]

The refusal horrified William Blackburne, whose wife wrote to Naas to say that her husband had not been consulted about the offer and, as Naas put it to Derby, 'the counsels of the second brother prevailed who, as he is to be equal in fortune, was unwilling that the elder brother should be superior in rank'.[113]

106. Derby to the queen, 22 Mar. 1867 (RA, A35/51).
107. Derby to Grey, 25 Mar. 1867 (RA, A35/52).
108. William Blackburne to Derby, 11 Apr. 1867 (Mayo papers, MS 11,147 (14)).
109. William Blackburne to Naas, 30 Apr. 1867 (Mayo papers, MS 11,147 (14)).
110. Mrs William Blackburne to Naas, 25 Apr. 1867 (Mayo papers, MS 11,147 (14)).
111. Blackburne to Derby, 6 May 1867 (Derby papers, 53/2).
112. Derby to Naas, 7 May 1867 (Mayo papers, MS 11,150).
113. Naas to Derby, 11 May 1867 (Derby papers, 53/2).

My husband is very ill from over-fatigue in his attendance on his father, also from annoyance at the baronetcy being refused for him by his younger brother, Mr Blackburne himself being quite incapable of making any decision. Two months ago when my husband went over to tender his father's resignation to Lord Derby his last words were 'I shall apply for a baronetcy or peerage for you' and his father entirely acquiesced.

Mr Blackburne's mental powers were now so far gone it seemed scarcely fair to take his refusal as final.[114]

On 22 May Edward Blackburne wrote to Naas to say that misrepresentations had been made about his father's position. 'The act of refusal was altogether his own, and the letter which conveyed it was dictated by himself, the result of deliberate consideration and judgment—his mind and understanding being as capable as they ever were.'[115]

Blackburne died in September 1867. In his biography his son Edward wrote that 'the shock of the events of his last days in office had hastened his death—all could see that mental depression was preying upon him and that this, acting upon his bodily health, would ere long bring him to the grave'.[116] The demand for his resignation 'was a harsh and a cruel return for his abnegation of self and for the sacrifices which he had so cheerfully made'; he was, it was said, a victim of intrigue and had received unworthy and ungrateful treatment after years of service to his party.[117]

I acknowledge with thanks the gracious permission of Her Majesty Queen Elizabeth II to make use of correspondence of the 14th earl of Derby in the Royal Archives, and of the following persons and institutions to make use of manuscript material in their possession or in which they hold the copyright, namely the National Library of Ireland (Mayo papers), the Deputy Keeper of the Records, Public Record Office of Northern Ireland (Abercorn papers), the earl of Derby (papers of the 14th earl of Derby) and the National Trust (Disraeli papers).

114. Mrs William Blackburne to Naas, 11 May 1867 (Mayo papers, MS 11,147 (14)).
115. Edward Blackburne to Naas, 22 May 1867 (Mayo papers, MS 11,147 (14)).
116. Blackburne, *Life*, p. 312.
117. Ibid.

The records of King's Inns, Dublin

COLUM KENNY

KING'S INNS, DUBLIN, came into existence sometime between the years 1539 and 1541.[1] The surviving records of that society constitute a potentially useful source of reference for both general and legal historians. But they have not been widely consulted. This fact has reflected a lack of information about their contents as well as certain practical difficulties which have been involved in inspecting them. It was only during 1988 and 1989 that the first descriptive list of many of the records was compiled. The society retained for this purpose the services of an archivist, Ms Julitta Clancy. Her guide is available for inspection at the King's Inns and has been circulated to a number of libraries. Hitherto, one had to conduct random searches of archives which were kept in physically unpleasant and undesirable conditions in the society's records room. Were it not for the willing assistance of the librarian and his staff, even that much would not have been possible.

Ms Clancy has attempted to arrange the papers and records of the King's Inns in a way which will allow researchers easier access and a better appreciation of their contents. Her list is an accurate and useful outline of the contents of the records room at King's Inns, but certain statements about the history and constitution of the society, apparently drawn from secondary sources, need to be treated with caution.

An effort is also being made by the society to improve the physical environment in which its records are stored. In recent years portion of the society's archives have been kept in a safe, including the particularly valuable Black Book. Some twentieth-century records have been kept in the under-treasurer's office. But

---

1. W.F. Littledale, *The society of King's Inns, Dublin, its origin and progress* (Dublin, 1859), pp. 6–10.

most material, spanning three centuries, has lain in the official record room, partly on tables and partly in damp tea-chests or other boxes and in a most disordered state. In the course of my research into the history of the society, I felt obliged to don rubber gloves and a surgical mask on occasions in order to conduct searches through the partly foul mass of papers to which I was given access and which constituted a substantial portion of the manuscripts of King's Inns. In retaining the services of an archivist, the benchers recognised that such circumstances were neither conducive to legal research nor indicative of a professional body which respects its origins. By recently improving the physical conditions in which the books and papers are kept in the records room, the society has further shown itself to be interested in its past.

In describing the wealth of material which the society has in its possession, one may divide it into two sections chronologically. The first comprises that which survives from before the reforms of the late eighteenth century and the second that which came into existence afterwards. There is much less of the former than of the latter. It is not my intention in either case to give an exhaustive list of volumes or documents but rather to indicate generally areas which may be of interest to the researcher and to discuss these from the perspective of one who has been a student of the society's history for many years. For additional detail the reader is referred to Ms Clancy's list. There is little prospect of a full catalogue of manuscripts being published, as was done in 1972 for the Inner Temple.[2]

Before turning to the records themselves, it is worth remembering that the present library building was only completed and opened in the 1830s.[3] Records were subsequently transferred to the new library from the building which still houses the dining-hall and which then served also as a temporary library. While these records included the most important manuscripts, there were certain volumes which were not moved and which only came to light by chance in 1988, while the archivist was preparing her list. A member of the staff who had worked for a period in the library found some old volumes and recognised their possible significance. While generally not as important as the manuscripts which were already stored in the library and mostly referring to

2. J.Conway Davies (ed.), *Catalogue of manuscripts in the Inner Temple library* (3 vols., Oxford, 1972).

3. Minutes of benchers, 1819–30 (King's Inns MSS, pp. 33, 97, 100, 146, 158, 171, 174, 253, 268); Minutes of benchers, 1830–35 (King's Inns MSS, pp.45, 115); Daire Hogan, *The legal profession in Ireland 1789–1922* (Dublin, 1986), pp.26, 93.

housekeeping matters after 1789, these items do include some gems such as a receipt book for money paid to the architects Cooley and Gandon. They have now been transferred to the library.

Among modern writers who have inspected some of the records of King's Inns, in particular, sections of the Black Book, have been Denis Johnston, T.C. Barnard, Hans Pawlisch and Wilfrid Prest. More recently, Daire Hogan relied on the minutes of meetings of the benchers of the society and certain admission records when writing his history of the legal profession in Ireland from 1789 to 1922.[4] There was also extensive use made of various admission papers when Keane, Phair and Sadleir compiled their published list of King's Inns admissions. In the process of their research they re-arranged some papers alphabetically instead of replacing them in chronological order. Their decision to do so has been severely criticised by one of the librarians at King's Inns.[5] Recently, Tom Power published an introduction to the Black Book with an abstract of its contents. The records have been my main source of information in writing a history of the society to 1800.[6]

RECORDS BEFORE 1789

In his account of King's Inns, Bartholomew Duhigg suggested in general terms that the records of the society were not complete.[7] But, while some books and papers have been damaged or lost over the years, Duhigg's statements can be misleading and need to be treated with caution at all times and no more so than when dealing with the records; for it appears that Counsellor Duhigg himself defaced the books of the society. Duhigg was a political

---

4. Denis Johnston, *In search of Swift* (Dublin, 1959); T.C.Barnard, *Cromwellian Ireland* (Oxford, 1975); Hans Pawlisch, *Sir John Davies and the conquest of Ireland* (Cambridge, 1985); Wilfrid Prest, *The inns of court under Elizabeth I and the early Stuarts 1590–1641* (London, 1972); Wilfrid Prest, *The rise of the barristers: A social history of the English bar 1590–1640* (Oxford, 1986) (Prest has informed this writer in personal correspondence that he consulted a microfilm of the Black Book); Hogan (note 3, above).

5. *King's Inns admission papers, 1607–1867*, ed. E.Keane, P.B.Phair and T.U. Sadleir (Dublin, 1982); Nigel Cochrane, 'The archives and manuscripts of the King's Inns library' in *Irish Archives*, i (1989), 27–8.

6. Tom Power, 'The Black Book of King's Inns: an introduction with an abstract of contents' in *Ir Jur*, xx (1985), 135–212; Colum Kenny, 'The history of the King's Inns, Dublin, to 1800' (unpublished Ph.D. thesis, University of Dublin, 1989).

7. Bartholomew Duhigg, *History of the King's Inns* (Dublin, 1806), pp.172, 271–2.

activist who wished to construct a version of the society's past which suited his view of the world.[8]

Early in the nineteenth century both Duhigg, who was the society's junior librarian, and Fox, who was its treasurer, made returns to queries which had been sent to them by order of the Irish record commissioners.[9] Duhigg admitted that he had already formed an opinion that some records were missing even before he undertook a search for the commission. He mentioned that he had reviewed a manuscript list of King's Inns members by John Lodge, being convinced that several books and documents had disappeared, 'both from accident and design'. He claimed that 'books underwent that gentleman's review which no longer grace our treasurer's office or King's Inns library'.[10] However, in error or in earnest, Duhigg was laying a false trail. Lodge himself had written of his manuscript list that it was 'extracted from the books of the society, being five in number'. He expressly mentioned the Black Book and the 'Green Book' and there are three other books extant today to which he appears to have been referring and which were actually listed by Fox in his return to the record commissioners.[11] Thus, the books which Lodge himself used still survive and there is no reason to accept Duhigg's suggestion that Lodge viewed other volumes which subsequently disappeared.

Two further references by Lodge tend to confirm his having relied only upon the five books of the society mentioned above and identified by Fox. Firstly, in his alphabetical list of King's Inns members Lodge referred to the fact that no record of admissions of attorneys from 1679 until 1752 appears in the extant books of the society. Lodge seems to have compiled his list of King's Inns members about 1769–70 and the small number of attorneys whom he does show as being admitted in the first half of the eighteenth century were probably known to him personally.

8. Colum Kenny, 'Counsellor Duhigg—antiquarian and activist' in *Ir Jur*, xxi (1986), 300 at 318–20.

9. *Rec.comm.Ire.rep., 1811–15*, pp.321, 444.

10. Ibid.; An alphabetical list of King's Inns members (PROI, Lodge MSS 1a. 53.72). There are later transcriptions of the greater part of this manuscript at the College of Arms, London, and at the Genealogical Office, Dublin (GO 288), the former giving more of the original than the latter. For more on these transcriptions see *Anal Hib*, no. 27 (1972), 66.

11. An alphabetical list (PROI, Lodge MSS, title-page); Admission of benchers, 1712–42 (King's Inns MSS) is the 'Green Book' (MS B 1/3–1). The other King's Inns manuscript volumes which Lodge appears to have read are: (i), Admission of benchers, 1741–92; (ii), Admission of barristers, 1732–91; and (iii) Admission of attornies, 1752–92 (MS B 1/3–2; MS I 1/1; MS I 1/2).

Secondly, Lodge wrote that he had also made use of 'the books of the society of King's Inns' in compiling his manuscript list of king's counsel up to 1768. In neither the list of members nor that of king's counsel is there any information which suggests that Lodge relied upon records of King's Inns which have been lost since his day.[12]

Thus, it is not evident why Duhigg stated that Lodge had reviewed books which no longer graced the society's premises. In giving his list of the records in his office, Fox, as treasurer, also suggested to the record commissioners that 'many of the old documents have, it is presumed, been lost'. But he may simply have relied upon the assistant librarian for his information and neither he nor Duhigg attempted to identify what was lost.[13]

However, to dismiss the claims of Duhigg and Fox as unsubstantiated is not to deny the possibility that some records did disappear over the years and the extent of such possible loss is considered below. Unfortunately, Sir John Gilbert did not live to complete a report on the records of King's Inns which he started to prepare about 1890. This would have allowed us at least to discover if anything had been removed from the library in the past century but there do not appear to have survived even notes for his report.[14]

The following is what I have found in the custody of the librarian for the years before 1789.

(i) 1539–1607

Although King's Inns was founded between 1539 and 1541, there do not exist any records at all for the period from the society's foundation until its revival in 1607. This was also the conclusion of a committee of junior barristers which investigated the matter at the end of the eighteenth century, and nothing has emerged since then to suggest that they were wrong.[15] By contrast, the inns of court in London all possess records which date from the sixteenth century or earlier.

(ii) The Black Book, 1607–1730 (MS B 1/1)

The decision to keep a Black Book was taken in June 1607 at the very first meeting of the council of the revived society of

---

12. List of patentee officers (PROI, Lodge MSS 1a.53.75, i, 149); *Liber mun.pub.Hib.*, pt.2, pp.76–7; Alphabetical list (PROI, Lodge MSS, ff.53v, 134 and latest dates on list); see also Lodge, *Peerage Ire.*, v, 141 n., for use of the Black Book in the context of information about Richard Bolton.

13. *Rec.comm.Ire.rep., 1811–15*, pp. 322–3.

14. *H.M.C. rep.12*, p.52; *H.M.C. rep.13*, p.57.

15. Minutes of benchers, 1792–1803 (King's Inns MSS, f.13v).

King's Inns.[16] As bound today, the volume known as the Black Book consists of 360 folios. These contain records of admissions, accounts and minutes of the society which relate, among other things, to chambers, property, payments and regulations. The entries are written in various styles which can be difficult to decipher and some are in Latin. The volume contains no records for some years and few records for others. There was money 'paid for binding the Black Book' in Easter term, 1667.[17] The front and back covers are embossed with the royal arms as used by the Stuarts. These decorations are now almost totally worn away.

Cross-referencing between entries which were made in the Black Book in the 1650s and 1670s suggests that by then folios had come to be marked with a series of numbers which are still visible but which were subsequently crossed out.[18] Lodge used the old foliation in 1769 when including some extracts from the Black Book at the end of his alphabetical list of King's Inns members.[19] So too did the author of the somewhat later transcription of the Black Book (below).

Duhigg informed the record commissioners that 'the Black Book fell into my hands with the cover completely broken, and the leaves perfectly loose . . . The book has been carefully bound, the mouldering or broken leaves strengthened, and even its original cover preserved'.[20] He does not state whether or not it was he himself who also re-arranged the order of folios.

According to a note on the inside front cover of the Black Book, that volume was 'carefully refolioed' in ' '63' (1863). The note is signed 'E. Hayes'. This was probably Edmund Hayes, the bencher and judge of the queen's bench from 1859 to 1866 who also wrote two law books.[21] According to a loose note inserted at the back of another of the society's manuscript volumes entitled, 'Entrys of the benchers', Hayes was sent in October 1863 this book of entries together with the six record books containing the minutes of benchers' council meetings between 1804 and 1856. The phrase 'carefully refolioed' is ambiguous. Did Hayes see that the Black Book had been bound in such a way that the old folio

---

16. Black Book, f.170.

17. Ibid., f.219v.

18. Ibid., f.179 and f.230.

19. These extracts are present in the original volume which contains his list at the PROI and in the transcription of it at the College of Arms, London, but they are absent from the transcription in the Genealogical Office, Dublin.

20. *Rec.comm.Ire.rep.,1811–15*, p.322.

21. Ball, *Judges*, ii, 361.

numbers no longer corresponded to the sequence in which he found the folios and did he, therefore, decide to renumber them? Or did he himself reorder the actual pages? Certainly at some time the folios were both renumbered and reordered, the old numbers being crossed out. The sequence of new folio numbers suggests that the book survives intact since whenever it was marked with them. But the sequence also gives grounds for believing that some pages were lost between the unknown dates of the two main sets of numberings. Thus, the new ff. 88–108 are blank. These pages display the old crossed-out folio numbers 91–8 and 117–43. One might jump to the conclusion that old ff. 98–117 were also blank and that the binder simply decided to omit them. However, it is the case that at least one missing folio, old f.114, had information on it relating to the treasurership. Duhigg gives an unreliable list of treasurers in his history of the society, and such evidence as that contained on the missing folio may have contradicted his version.[22]

In July 1811, in his second general report to the record commissioners, the commission's secretary wrote that,

as a curious illustration of the customs and introduction to the members of the legal body, on the revival of the King's Inns Society, 'the Black Book', which is so fully described in the return by the librarian of that society, or selections from it, may possibly be deemed not unworthy of publication.[23]

But it was incorrect to say that Duhigg had 'fully described' the Black Book. He merely referred to it briefly in his return to the commissioners. Moreover, he totally omitted to mention that it had suffered erasions or mutilations of any kind, although he had already disclosed this fact in general terms in his history of the society published in 1806. Nor did he refer either to the transcription or to Lodge's 'alphabetical list', both of which manuscripts are of considerable use in deciphering some entries defaced on the original.

The commissioners suggested in their report that an edition of the Black Book ought to be published but their suggestion was not taken up then or later. A 'photozincograph' of a folio of the Black Book for 15 November 1687 was printed in 1884, and

22. Entries of benchers, 1794–1864 (King's Inns MS B 1/3–3); for old folio 114 see Transcription of the Black Book (King's Inns MS B 1/2, f.43); Alphabetical list (PROI, Lodge MSS, f.128); Duhigg, *History of King's Inns*, pp. 359–61.

23. *Rec.comm.Ire.rep.*, *1811–15*, p.415.

some other facsimiles were included by Denis Johnston in his book on Swift.[24] More recently, the whole volume has been microfilmed by the Irish Manuscripts Commission, so that it is less likely than otherwise to be completely lost to future generations. But neither the existence of this microfilm nor the publication by Tom Power in the 1985 *Irish Jurist* of his introduction to the Black Book, together with an abstract of its contents, obviates the need for a discrete edition of the manuscript itself so that more people than hitherto may come to appreciate the value of it.

Those who have studied the Black Book will have some sympathy with Duhigg's description of it as 'an obscure, irregular, and almost illegible book, which seemed equally calculated to baffle lettered sagacity or laborious research'.[25] Denis Johnston turned his attention to it in the context of his research into Jonathan Swift, whose father was a servant of the society of King's Inns from 1663 to 1666.[26] He considered the mode and chronology of particular entries, and remarked that some entries appear to have been made later than the date to which they refer. A dozen pages of the Black Book are reproduced by Johnston and his lively book is recommended to anyone interested in the records of the society or in research generally.

Any discrete edition of the Black Book would benefit from a considerable footnote apparatus, through which could be addressed some of the many questions of interpretation and understanding to which its pages give rise. There are certainly folios missing, as noted above and as considered further in some particular cases in my forthcoming history of the society. But what has survived is itself very curious at times. Again and again, one returns to the volume only to discover some new nuance or to be struck by the significance of an entry which may have been overlooked at an earlier reading. Interpreting and unravelling the Black Book is like opening a succession of Chinese black boxes. At first, it can be a slow and frustrating task but, ultimately, it brings with it a sense of satisfaction and discovery.

24. Ibid.; *Facs.nat.MSS Ire.*, iv, pt.2, lxxxiii and intro., cvi; Johnston, *In search of Swift*, passim.

25. Duhigg, *History of King's Inns*, pp. 172–3. DeBrún suggested that this reference by Duhigg might be to some other manuscript but it seems clear from the context that Duhigg was referring to the Black Book (Padraig DeBrún, *Catalogue of Irish manuscripts in King's Inns library, Dublin* (Dublin, 1972), pp.vii–ix).

26. Johnston, *In search of Swift*, pp. 32–3, 47–58, 66–72.

(iii) Transcription of part of the Black Book (MS B 1/2)

This volume is undated and consists of copies of many of the entries in the Black Book for the period 1607 to 1636. These are re-arranged here in chronological order, whereas they are scattered throughout the original in quite a disorderly fashion. The transcription is in a hand which is easy to read and is useful in interpreting parts of the original. The author of the copy was conscious of the fact that the style of dating particular calendar months had changed in the mid-eighteenth century, and took account of this when ordering his entries.[27] The transcription seems to have been compiled in the last decade of the eighteenth century, for the book into which entries from the Black Book are copied is of the same distinctive type as that then being used for contemporary minutes of the benchers, and is embossed on its cover with the seal and motto newly adopted by the society following its reform in 1792. The handwriting appears to be that of William Caldbeck, an official of the society, who began keeping regular council minutes in February 1791.[28] There seems to have been some interference with the transcription subsequent to its compilation and certain pages have disappeared while others have been reordered or re-numbered, particularly some containing entries made in or about the year 1635.

The transcription is remarkable for the many glosses which litter its pages and which constitute a running commentary on those who were members of the society. Most of the glosses appear to be in Duhigg's hand, as may be seen by comparing them to the Duhigg manuscripts which are held by King's Inns library. The glosses are not always reliable, although sometimes they can be helpful. Between folios 148 and 149 of the transcription is bound a printed copy of the memorial of 23 January 1793 from the 'Utter Bar' to the benchers.

(iv) The 'Brown Book', 1635–1715 (MS G 1/2)

Bound in brown calf, this is a large book with many blank pages and a few original records which more properly belong in the Black Book. There are also nearly sixty pages of transcribed petitions and legal documents which relate to a dispute between the Usher family and the judges over title to the old site of King's Inns on the north bank of the Liffey. The petitions and legal

27. Black Book, f.171v; Transcription, ff.17v, 22v; *Sweet & Maxwell's guide to law reports and statutes* (London, 1962), p.29.
28. Admission of benchers, 1741–92 (King's Inns MS, p.192); Treasurers' accounts from 1789 (King's Inns MS).

documents which were copied into the Brown Book in the mid-eighteenth century dated from 1635 to 1677 and no longer appear to survive in their original form. This transcription of them has been of considerable use in piecing together the history of the society and the value of this volume generally should not be underestimated. Neither Duhigg nor Fox mentioned it in their returns to the record commissioners, and even Tom Power appears to have had little regard for it when stating that, 'apart from the Black Book itself no other records of the society from the seventeenth century have survived'. But even if the copied legal documents are not, strictly speaking, records of the society, they do contain much useful information about the King's Inns. Bound with them in the volume are some entries for the periods 1677–80 and 1704–15 which appear to be original. These are scattered over thirty-four pages. Most relate to disbursements. But there is also a lone and unfinished memorandum of admission to the society of Charles, duke of Grafton and lord lieutenant. It has been said that Henrietta Street was so named in honour of his wife.[29]

The name 'Maths. Reily' is signed or written into the Brown Book on the front page where an index of certain of the entries is also given: 'The contents 1635 to 1677 by Maths. Reily . . . signed M. Reily clk. society'. Reilly officiated as steward to the society for a period and was also clerk from 1745 to 1752.[30] He probably transcribed documents into the Brown Book when helping the benchers to prepare a private act of parliament for the appointment of trustees. Such an act was passed in1752. There survives no copy of it among the manuscripts of King's Inns but a scroll copy of an earlier draft, not identical in every detail to the final version, may be inspected. In a letter of 1752 Reilly referred to financial charges made by him 'in relation to the act of parliament'. From this letter it seems that he was a practising attorney who had been retained by the benchers for various purposes including the collection of fees due to the society.[31]

29. Power, 'Introduction to Black Book' (note 6, above), 137; *Georgian Society records of domestic architecture* (reissued Shannon, 1969), ii, 11.

30. Admission of benchers, 1712–41 (King's Inns MS, p.293); Admission of benchers, 1741–92 (King's Inns MS, p.40); Duhigg, *History of King's Inns*, p.377.

31. Scroll draft of act, 1743 (King's Inns MS G 1/1–1) (incorrectly described by Ms Clancy as 'draft of 1751 Act'); *Commons' jn.Ire.* (ed.1613–1800), v, 152, 155; letter from M.Reily (to C.Robinson), 1752 (Gilbert Library, Robinson MS 35, p.89). I am grateful to Tom Power for having drawn this manuscript to my attention.

(v) Admission of benchers 1712–42 (MS B1/3–1)

This volume is also known as the 'Green Book', by virtue of the colour of its cover. It consists mainly of a record of the admission of persons to the society as either benchers or honorary members. But it contains some other information too. For example, we read of the appointments of stewards, treasurers and chaplains, and of rents due and money allegedly owed by members, among other matters. Outstanding fees which were owed by members became something of a preoccupation for the benchers as the society almost disintegrated towards the middle of the century. Lodge says that his 'list of king's counsel is copied from Mr Justice Robinson's manuscripts, but afterwards corrected from the books of the society of King's Inns', and it is clear from a comparison that those books to which he refers are this volume and its companion for 1741–92.[32]

(vi) Admission of benchers 1741–92 (MS B1/3–2)

Similar to the preceding volume in style and content, this consists of over two hundred pages of information relating to both the admission of benchers and honorary members and to the general business of the society.

(vii) Leases, etc., from 1638 (MS G 1/3; MS G 2/4)

Copies of a number of leases or other instruments of conveyance survive from the 1630s onward. So too do some rental books of the mid-eighteenth century which were among those volumes discovered in 1988 near the dining-hall in King's Inns.

This collection of material has been of great assistance in allowing me to chart the lay-out and development of the society's property in the seventeenth and eighteenth centuries. It provides the basis for both a chapter and an appendix in my history of King's Inns. Some later maps of the society's ground also helped in this context, as they were formerly of assistance to Edward McParland in his studies of Gandon and the early history of the present Four Courts building, which was erected on part of the society's old ground.[33]

Among the books which were recently found near the dining-hall of the society and transferred to the library is also one

32. List of patentee officers (PROI, Lodge MSS, i, 149); *Liber mun.pub.Hib.*, pt.2, pp.76–7.

33. Maps and surveys (King's Inns MSS G5); Edward McParland, 'The early history of James Gandon's Four Courts' in *The Burlington Magazine*, cxxii, no.932 (Nov.1980), 727–31; idem, *James Gandon: Vitruvius Hibernicus* (London, 1985), p.152, plate 161.

consisting of some receipts which were signed by the architects Cooley and Gandon in connection with their work at the Four Courts. Before Cooley and Gandon were finally employed to build there, others had turned their attention to the same site. In the record room at King's Inns is a volume of bound notes from 1758 which explain the nature and intent of some accompanying plans for public offices and Four Courts at the society's ground on Inns Quay. Apparently prepared by George Semple, but unsigned, the whole is bound and consists of forty-four pages. It contains a reference to the same author's three-volume work on King's Inns, but no such volumes appear to have survived.[34]

(viii) Records of admission from 1607 (various mss)

Some of these records are included in the Black Book, as now bound, or in the other books of the society; some are bound separately and some are loose. Information extracted largely from these papers and organised as an alphabetical list of admissions of members to the society from 1607 to 1867 has recently been published by the Irish Manuscripts Commission. The editors of the latter volume failed to impart a true sense of the wealth of material with which they dealt.[35] As a rich source of biographical and social information, the admission papers deserve further attention. This author would have preferred to have seen them published in chronological order, with an alphabetical index, and with specific sources more clearly identified in individual cases. Thus, some entries in *King's Inns admission papers* are based only upon a line in the Black Book while others can be backed up by admission papers which include a detailed memorial or a sacramental certificate, which may give further useful particulars. Still other entries in the book contain biographical information which is not to be gleaned from any of the society's archives and which clearly comes from Ball's *Judges*, or elsewhere.

The editors of *King's Inns admission papers* did not include in their list some individuals who may be seen from a close reading of the records to have been members of the society, but for whom no specific record of admission survives. Among these were Henry Cromwell and many of the judges. The names of such people were

34. Receipts for public money, Cooley and Gandon, 1776–88 (King's Inns MS H 1/1–2); Publick offices, etc., 1758 (King's Inns MS H 1/1–1); Admission of benchers, 1741–92 (King's Inns MS, pp. 71–3).

35. *King's Inns admission papers*, pp. xii–xiv for information on the editors' sources. For critical reviews of this work see P.A.Brand in *Ir Jur*, xix (1984), Daire Hogan in *IHS*, xxiv (1985) and A.P.W.Malcomson in *EHR*, cii, no.402 (Jan.1987).

probably entered in the seventeenth century in that book of admittances, to which reference is made in the Black Book on a number of occasions, but which no longer appears to exist.[36] Was this one and the same manuscript as that 'great gilt rowle' to which reference is found in 1628 but of which no distinct trace remains?[37]

Duhigg noted that a book recording some admissions in the seventeenth century had been lost, and remarked on this basis alone that 'these circumstances induce me to think that many and the most valuable documents have been destroyed, either by negligence or design'. This statement is echoed in a gloss in Duhigg's hand on the first page of the transcription of the Black Book, and in the returns of Duhigg and Fox to the record commissioners, but it remains unproven.[38]

There seems to be insufficient evidence for suggesting that 'many and the most valuable' manuscripts of the society have been lost. What does appear to be missing are: (i) the book of certain seventeenth-century admissions, perhaps similar in style and content to those two admission of benchers books which survive for 1712–42 and 1741–92, (ii) some seventeenth-century pension rolls to which reference is made in the Black Book, (iii) an unknown but limited number of pages of the Black Book itself, (iv) the opening six pages of the 'Green Book' and some loose admission papers, including those for Duhigg. A suggestion was made by the editors of *King's Inns admission papers* that the admission papers were kept in the Tholsel until 1804 and that many were lost in the course of their transfer on open carts to King's Inns. However, the editors gave no source for their statement. In her guide, Ms Clancy refers to the period immediately *after* 1804 as being one in particular for which papers are known to be missing. With tens of thousands of documents extant among the admission papers, it is impossible to estimate precisely the size of any gaps until further research is conducted.[39]

By comparison with what does survive, losses among the records seem to have been relatively limited. There have been times when this researcher was tempted to suppose that other archives have also been destroyed, especially where just a shred of

36. Black Book, ff. 64, 139, 145v; Duhigg, *History of King's Inns*, pp.188, 383; Power, 'Introduction to Black Book', 138 n. 8, 159.

37. Black Book, f.312.

38. Duhigg, *History of King's Inns*, p.172; Transcription, ff.1–1v, gloss; *Rec.comm.Ire.rep., 1811–15*, pp. 322–3.

39. *King's Inns admission papers*, p.viii; Julitta Clancy, 'Records of the honorable society of King's Inns: guide and descriptive list' (unpublished typescript, King's Inns library, 1989), pp. x, 57.

evidence, gleaned from some entry in the society's books, or information stumbled upon by chance elsewhere revealed a completely new aspect of the history of King's Inns. But such suppositions border on wishful thinking and it should be borne in mind that those records which do survive tend to consist of entries which are formal and brief rather than expansive and informative. It appears that the society simply did not keep very descriptive records.

RECORDS AFTER 1789

Towards the end of the eighteenth century the society of King's Inns underwent a minor renaissance.[40] A new spirit was evident in the conduct of its affairs, and one manifestation of this was the keeping of more extensive records than had been kept previously. Many of these have survived. They include treasurer's accounts after 1789, some of which were printed for the society. But the centrepiece of the collection of records for the period since 1789 is a series of volumes in which were entered consecutively the minutes of council meetings (MSS B 1/5). These constitute a record of formal decisions taken by the benchers in council and of certain related matters, although they contain little or no information about the position taken by individual benchers during particular discussions. Within these volumes some minutes are very brief and whole years are occasionally passed over without any entry. Daire Hogan refers regularly to the council minutes in his history of the modern legal profession but they have certainly not been exhausted as a source of information. There are fourteen volumes of council minutes covering the period from 1792 to 1953 and they are kept in the record room of the library. Minutes for the period from 1953 to date are kept in the treasurer's office.

In addition to the minutes of council, there survives a single book in which is recorded the attendance of benchers at meetings during the period 1792 to 1804 (MS B 1/4). Separate attendance books do not appear to exist for subsequent years but attendances were then noted in the ordinary council minutes.

After 1844, there exist also general committee books (MSS B 2). These overlap chronologically with one another in places and occasionally duplicate material in each other and in the council books. After 1850, there are records too of a special committee which dealt primarily with educational matters.

40. Hogan, *Legal profession in Ireland*, pp. 19–24, 29–31; Colum Kenny, 'The history of the King's Inns, Dublin, to 1800' (note 6, above), ch. 8.

A 'Letters book 1836–69' (MS C 2/1–1) comprises copies of correspondence and contains some information which is not found elsewhere. The 'Law Students' Society, Secretary's Book' (MS K 1/1) gives some insight into the frame of mind and the pre-occupations of students at King's Inns between 1830 and 1833; there also survives later material concerning student activities.

In addition to these volumes, there are what, until 1989, could be described quite literally as tea-chests full of papers relating to the society's affairs. These have now been sorted into different categories by Ms Clancy and are stored in boxes of an appropriate material for preserving manuscripts. The hitherto chaotic loose papers and small bundles of documents contain much information about the business of the society from the late eighteenth to the early twentieth centuries.

A considerable number of these hitherto unknown manuscripts refer to dealings between the society and the solicitors' side of the profession. Others deal with such matters as professional discipline, financial administration and property matters.

I viewed all of these papers at least once when preparing my history of the society and took care to replace them precisely in the order or, more exactly, the same 'disorder' in which I found them. The fact that the circumstances of their storage has now been improved and that some have been identified and numbered does not lessen the desirability of describing every single document in a comprehensive catalogue. The resources required to do this should be made available so that future researchers and librarians may readily avail of the material and not simply be referred to large bundles with general subject titles.

The need for further work may be seen by reference to just three examples of significant documents which I had read at King's Inns but which are not referred to in the present descriptive list of the principal records. There was a short eighteenth-century legal opinion from Barry Yelverton, a copy of the last will and testament of Primate Boulter and a copy of an important fiant of 1541 under which the society was given its first twenty-one year lease of its former property on the site of the present Four Courts. The original fiant was destroyed in 1922 in the fire and explosion at the Public Record Office, but a copy was uncovered at King's Inns by the editors of *King's Inns admission papers*.[41]

It was not Ms Clancy's task to describe every single item among the many which comprise the records of King's Inns. But

41. *King's Inns admission papers*, p.vii; for a recent photocopy of the King's Inns manuscript copy see PROI MS 999/205.

given her useful groundwork, the benchers might now choose to follow the example of the Inner Temple, for the records of which there was published a detailed catalogue in 1972.[42]

Many of the records are fascinating in their own right, apart altogether from their place in any contemporary chain of events relating to King's Inns. Here, for example, is an opinion by Francis Blackburne (MS M 16/2). There are architectural drawings by Gandon, Cooley, Darley, Farrell and Dixon among others (MSS H4), and deeds and other papers relating to the property at Inns Quay, on Constitution Hill and in Henrietta Street (MSS G2, G3). Somewhere among these deeds is a copy of the will of primate and lord justice, Hugh Boulter, to which attention has already been drawn. Boulter disliked Irishmen of any ilk and believed that official positions in Ireland should be filled by English appointees. The library is built on the site of a house which was once his Dublin residence and in which he is said to have been waked in state. That house later became the prerogative office for a period, before being acquired by the society in the early nineteenth century.[43] Those who have spent a winter's evening poring over old manuscripts in the gloomy basement which houses the society's records would not be unduly surprised to see his ghost wafting along one of the dank corridors or loitering in some recess. Another wake, more remarkable than that of Boulter, is known to have taken place in Mountjoy House, which still stands today across Henrietta Street from the King's Inns library and which was once the home of Luke Gardiner.[44]

Gardiner's house later became the residence of Tristram Kennedy who founded the Dublin Law Institute in 1839. The society holds some cuttings and papers relating to that short-lived institution. But in the late 1930s the benchers appear to have failed to reply to Kennedy's son when he wrote to offer them certain documents which had belonged to his father, and these were subsequently lodged in the National Library. The incident possibly reflected a certain indifference on the part of the society to matters of history, an indifference which was also evident from the conditions in which until recently the records were kept.

42. J.Conway Davies (ed.), *Catalogue of manuscripts in the Inner Temple library* (3 vols., Oxford, 1972).

43. Duhigg, *History of King's Inns*, p.323; G.N.Wright, *A historical guide to ancient and modern Dublin* (London, 1821), pp. 293–4; *Georgian Society records of domestic architecture*, ii, 13; Eoin O'Mahony, 'Some Henrietta Street residents' in *Ir Georgian Soc Bull*, ii, no.2 (April-June 1959), 15–16.

44. Frances Gerard, *Picturesque Dublin, old and new* (London, 1898), pp. 187–91; *Georgian Society records of domestic architecture*, ii, 10.

Similarly, in 1972, the society was criticised for its lack of respect for the past when it decided to sell some antiquarian books from its library in order to finance the construction of a new kitchen at King's Inns.[45]

Hopefully, the decision to employ an archivist and to spend some money on improving the record room, as well as certain other measures, such as the cataloguing of the portraits in the dining-hall or the cleaning of that of Curran over the library fireplace in 1989, indicate that the society today is eager to preserve its heritage.

My purpose in this essay has been to refer in general terms to such manuscripts of the society of King's Inns as constitute a record of the affairs of that society. There are many other manuscripts in the library, both in Irish and English, which are concerned with other matters and not all of which have been catalogued.[46] It is likely that these too will someday repay investigation by a legal or general historian.

45. Ibid.; Hogan, *Legal profession in Ireland*, pp. 104–6; Kennedy manuscripts (King's Inns MS G 3/2–2, King's Inns MSS L 3); letter from Major M.E.Kennedy to the National Library, January 1940 (among Kennedy papers at National Library MS 2987); M.J.Tutty, 'Editorial' in *DHR*, xxvi (Dec.1972), 1; William Dillon, 'Arts and studies' in *Irish Times*, 16 Nov. 1972; M.J.Neylon, 'King's Inns library, Dublin' in *Law Librarian*, iv (1973); Austin Clarke composed a sarcastic 'Song of the empty shelves' about the later incident (see *Irish Times*, 25 May 1972 and W.N.Osborough, 'In praise of law books' in *Ir Jur*, xxi (1986), 350).

46. Cochrane, 'Archives and manuscripts of King's Inns' (note 5, above), 28–30 for some examples.

The lawyers of the Irish novels of Anthony Trollope

W.N. OSBOROUGH

I

NO SMALL PART OF THE CLAIM to excellence that can be advanced on behalf of several nineteenth-century writers of fiction lies in the breadth of their canvas and in their attention to detail. For the social historian of the period the implications are important and instructive: provided he is prepared to work overtime, indulge a catholic taste and read exhaustively, the chances are good that within this corpus of literature he will locate the characterisation, the evolution of plot or the philosophical excursus that is calculated at the very least to confirm his findings or, even better, actually to further his understanding. If the reward promises to be substantial, the challenge remains daunting on account of the amount of obligatory preliminary intellectual labour demanded.

Historians have by no means chosen to ignore evidence of this sort. What it is possible to learn from literary sources about three facets to the Ireland of last century—poverty, the landlords and the 'colonial mind'—have all been the subject of investigation, analysis and debate.[1] A start too has been made with the history of the professions. A.V. Dicey found early use for the evidence of literature when putting his thoughts together on the relationship of church and state for the chapter on that subject in his lectures on law and public opinion.[2] The result is an engaging vignette of the clergy based on Goldsmith, Warren, Dickens and Jane Austen. Dicey's focus is unashamedly on anglican and dissenter, however. For Ireland, the obvious lacuna has recently been expertly filled

---

1. Maurice Harmon, 'Aspects of the peasantry in Anglo–Irish literature from 1800 to 1916', *Stud hib*, xv (1975), 105; Oliver MacDonagh, *The nineteenth century novel and Irish social history: some aspects* (Dublin, 1970); Tom Dunne, *Maria Edgeworth and the colonial mind* (Dublin, 1984).

2. See conveniently A. V. Dicey, *Lectures on the relation between law and public opinion in England during the nineteenth century*, 2nd ed. (London, 1914), pp. 328-9.

by D.A. Kerr who has discovered in literary sources much enlightenment on perceptions of the catholic clergy that were current in the earlier half of the nineteenth century.[3] From Gaelic sources there is presented a synthesis of the views of poets such as Seán Ó Braonáin, Diarmuid O'Shea, Anthony Raftery and Art MacBionaid. Literature in English has also been thoroughly sifted: portraits of priests included in the poetry of John Banim and Thomas Moore, the short stories of William Carleton and the novels of William Parnell, Anthony Trollope, the Banim brothers and Charles Lever are all cited as useful contemporary evidence.

Lawyers can equally lay claim to a venerable tradition of being depicted in fiction. They are present both as narrators and as dramatis personae in *The Canterbury tales* of Chaucer. It is notorious that Shakespeare had a particular fondness for introducing justices of the peace; a specimen monopolises the fifth age of man in Jacques' inventory in *As you like it*: [4]

> And then the justice
> In fair round belly with good capon lined,
> With eyes severe and beard of formal cut,
> Full of wise saws and modern instances;
> And so he plays his part.

With the development of the novel, the trickle of representations becomes a torrent. There is an abundance—some might protest, a superfluity—of lawyers in the novels of Henry Fielding, Jane Austen, Sheridan Le Fanu and Charles Dickens—to mention but four writers. These fictional creations together with the legal world they frequented have occasioned a number of studies, two of which can be recommended: that of Sir William Holdsworth devoted to Dickens' lawyers and that of G.H. Treitel to Jane Austen's.[5]

II

To obtain an overview of lawyers in nineteenth-century Ireland the novels of Anthony Trollope are an obvious place to start. The gallery is extensive, and though Trollope never quite manages to

3. Donal A. Kerr, *Peel, priests and politics: Sir Robert Peel's administration and the roman catholic church in Ireland, 1841–1846* (Oxford, 1982), pp. 40–41.
4. Act 2, scene 7.
5. W.S. Holdsworth, *Charles Dickens as a legal historian* (New Haven, 1929); G.H. Treitel, 'Jane Austen and the law', *LQR*, c (1984), 549.

throw off the condescension he displays towards the Irish and their way of life, there is comprehension and, generally too, an absence of rancour. This tentative assessment indicates that his gallery is worth at the very least a fleeting visit. Difficulties—and they are considerable—in putting a historical interpretation on the portraits on display will be faced up to later.[6]

Trollope published five Irish novels. The first two, *The Macdermots of Ballycloran* and *The Kellys and the O'Kellys*, published in 1847 and 1848 respectively, were written whilst he was stationed in Ireland as an employee of the Post Office. Trollope had arrived in the country in 1841 and his job with the Post Office was to lead him to take up residence successively in Banagher, Co. Offaly, Clonmel, Co. Tipperary, Mallow, Co. Cork, and in Belfast and Dublin. Trollope finally left Ireland in 1859. *Castle Richmond*, which appeared the following year, can be treated as a valediction. Two other works with Irish locations were to come later: *An eye for an eye*, written in 1870 but not published until 1879, and the unfinished *The landleaguers*, brought out in 1883, the year after Trollope's death.

In addition, two of the six Palliser novels, *Phineas Finn* (1869) and *Phineas redux* (1874), revolve around the fortunes of an expatriate Irish lawyer and politician. The earlier of the two contains a small number of scenes that take place in Ireland. Though neither work can be regarded in any strict sense as an Irish novel, it would seem churlish in any survey of Irish lawyers in Trollope's fiction to ignore their eponymous hero.

The two Palliser novels stand apart. Of the principal five, *An eye for an eye* and *The landleaguers* are lacklustre, disappointing exercises of the writer's maturity. *Castle Richmond*, a work of Trollope's middle years, is second-rate, but contains some humour and a number of surprises: there is for instance vivid description of the famine and of the schemes of outdoor relief. *The Kellys and the O'Kellys* is excellent, fully deserving the reputation it has long enjoyed as the most successful and the best written of Trollope's Irish novels. Whilst *The Macdermots of Ballycloran* lacks the disciplined structure of *The Kellys and the O'Kellys* and of many of

---

6. On the value generally of Trollope's insights into Ireland see Oliver MacDonagh, *The nineteenth century novel and Irish social history: some aspects*, pp. 8–11.
The same verdict is expressed, if somewhat obliquely, by W.E. Vaughan (*Sin, sheep and Scotsmen: John George Adair and the Derryveagh evictions, 1861* (Belfast, 1983), at p. 31): 'When "fact" in mid-nineteenth-century Ireland resembles the fiction of Carleton and Lever rather than that of Trollope, it should be distrusted.'

Trollope's later novels that have settings in England, it is full of passion, excitement and (certainly to an Irish reader) great interest. For any first novel *The Macdermots of Ballycloran* by any standard is a staggering achievement.[7] All these novels, testifying as they do to the uneven nature of Trollope's genius, are included here, for lawyers dot the landscape of each one.

One feature of *The Kellys and the O'Kellys* merits an additional remark. The early scenes unfold against the background of the Dublin state trials of 1844 when Daniel O'Connell and others were placed on trial for conspiracy; and thereafter occasional allusions are made to the progress of these portentous proceedings. The novel itself was composed soon after the house of lords sitting judicially had on a writ of error thrown out the convictions the crown finally secured.[8] Several of the protagonists in this long-drawn-out real-life drama enliven Trollope's account. The attorneys in charge of the defence of O'Connell and the others, 'the inferior angels of that busy Elysium', all make a brief appearance:[9] Ford, Gartlan and Pierce Mahony. They were 'furiously busy with their huge bags, fidgetted about rapidly, or stood up in their seats, telegraphing others in different parts of the court.' Richard Lalor Shiel, counsel for the accused, seemed 'weak, piping and most unfit for a popular orator,' but Trollope accepted that this was more than counterbalanced by 'the elegance of his language and the energy of his manner'.[10] There are thumb-nail sketches too of the judges of the queen's bench: Lord Chief Justice Pennefather, Mr Justice Burton, Mr Justice Crampton and Mr Justice Perrin. In Trollope's presentation, these latter sketches

---

7. Walpole's criticism of *The Macdermots of Ballycloran* is fair comment. After the murder of Ussher by Thady, he writes (Hugh Walpole, *Anthony Trollope* (London, 1928), at p. 31):

   the story shows certain evidences of Trollope's immaturity. There are fine scenes when Thady is hiding in the hills—the incident between himself and the greedy old man in the cabin is one of the best things in the book—but after Thady's surrender to justice, the story becomes for the first time, prolix. The preparation for the assizes, the long details of Thady's trial, the questions arising around Feemy's evidence, these are external things and tell us nothing about Feemy and Thady themselves. The trial itself fails to be dramatic and vivid in the way in which the earlier wedding and race-course scenes were dramatic.

   For a modern re-assessment of *The Kellys and the O'Kellys*, see Oliver MacDonagh, *op. cit.*, pp. 8–11.
8. *O'Connell* v. *R.* (1844) 11 Cl & Fin 155, 8 Eng Rep 1061.
9. *The Kellys and the O'Kellys*, p. 15. This reference is to the ed. in the 'World's Classics' series brought out by the Oxford University Press (repr. 1978).
10. *The Kellys and the O'Kellys*, p.16.

are supplied by John Kelly, a knowledgeable attorney's clerk and brother of Martin, one of the major characters in the novel. The brothers are ardent Repealers and, unsurprisingly, no good word is found for any of the judges with the exception of Mr Justice Perrin.[11]

The purpose of the present survey is not to deal with such recreations of actual legal and judicial personages. It is to concentrate rather on Trollope's fictional legal characters. As has already been explained, Trollope's Irish novels (together with the two Phineas Finn books) furnish a not inconsiderable number of the latter. The plan is straightforward. These fictional lawyers will be examined category by category—the lower branch (attorneys and solicitors), the upper branch (barristers) and the holders of judicial office (the magistrates and senior judges).

III

In *The Macdermots of Ballycloran* Trollope charts the downfall of the Macdermot family. Their extinction was to be accomplished by a combination of disaster and pathos: it is unadorned Greek tragedy albeit played out against an early nineteenth-century Irish backdrop. Feemy Macdermot is seduced by Myles Ussher, the local sub-inspector of the revenue police, and the night of their planned elopement Feemy's brother, Thady, kills Ussher. For this Thady is eventually brought to trial, found guilty and executed. Feemy meanwhile dies in pregnancy.

The problems of the family went back to the decision of Thady's grandfather, Thady senior, to build a new, grandiose home—the Ballycloran of the title. Thady senior had found himself unable to pay the bill, whereupon the builder, Flannelly, had taken a mortgage on the property. Thady senior and subsequently Larry, Thady's ineffectual father, experienced constant difficulty in collecting enough rent from their tenants to pay the mortgage interest and prevent Flannelly from foreclosing. This thankless task eventually devolved on Thady who worked at it even harder:

of an evening after his punch, he would be totting and calculating, adding and subtracting at his old greasy book, till he would turn into bed, to forget another day's woes, and dream of punctual tenants and unembarrassed properties; alas! it was only in his dreams he was destined to meet such halcyon things.[12]

11. P.15.
12. *The Macdermots of Ballycloran*, i, 108–9. This reference is to the three-vol. 1st ed. brought out by T.C. Newby, London, in 1847, and repr. by Garland Publishing, Inc., New York and London, 1979.

The predicament of father and son worsens once Flannelly the builder makes the acquaintance of Hyacinth Keegan, 'the oily attorney' of Carrick-on-Shannon.[13] Keegan 'usually managed to add certain mysterious costs, and ceremonious expenses'[14] to Flannelly's regular financial demands. News spreads, as the plight of the Macdermots continues to deteriorate, that the demands of Flannelly and Keegan are becoming more imperious. The local tenantry for their part dread a change in their landlord, predicting that Keegan would become agent to Flannelly and already aware of Keegan's reputation for ruthlessness. The possible use of violence against Keegan could not be ruled out. 'The first time', the treacherous Pat Brady confides in Thady, Keegan

goes collectin' on the lands of Drumleesh, it's a warm welcome he'll be gettin'; at any rate, he'd have more recates in his carcass than in his pocket, that day.[15]

Flannelly eventually instructs Keegan to make an offer to the Macdermots to buy Ballycloran. Old Larry would have an annuity settled on him of £50 a year and Feemy and Thady would each receive a lump sum of £100. Thady proceeds to bargain, but Keegan is not prepared to listen. Relishing the prospect of Larry reduced to penury, the attorney informs Larry to his face that he would 'tell them down at Carrick, to keep a warm corner for you in the lane there, where them old hags of beggars sleep at night'.[16] Larry responds by calling Keegan 'a d—d pettifogging schaming blackguard'. In the ensuing fracas, Thady tries to attack Keegan and receives a blow from Keegan's stick for his pains.

As the prospect of Flannelly and Keegan actually taking over the Ballycloran estate looms ever closer, a prospect at which the tenants still stand aghast, the decision is reached by members of the local conspiracy to teach Keegan a lesson. One afternoon he is ambushed, knocked off his horse and horribly mutilated. One of Keegan's three assailants had an axe. The attorney begged for his life:

Before the first sentence he uttered was well out of his mouth, the instrument fell on his leg, just above the ankle, with all the man's force; the first blow only cut his trowsers and his boot, and bruised him sorely for his boots protected him; the second cut the flesh, and grated against

13. *The Macdermots of Ballycloran*, i, 15.
14. i, 22.
15. i, 33.
16. i, 263.

the bone; in vain he struggled violently, and with all the force of a man struggling for his life; a third, and a fourth, and a fifth, descended, crushing the bone, dividing the marrow, and ultimately severing the foot from the leg . . .

In a short time Keegan fainted from loss of blood, but the cold frost soon brought him to his senses, he got up and hobbled to the meanest cabin, dragging after him the mutilated foot, which still attached itself to his body by some cartileges, which had not been secured, and by the fragments of his boot and trowsers, and from thence reached his home on a country car, racked by pain, which the jolting of the car, and the sharp frost did not tend to assuage.[17]

This gruesome incident occurs shortly after Thady has killed Ussher and become a fugitive from justice. The violence directed at Keegan does not aid Thady's cause when the latter is put on trial for his life. Keegan, now crippled and convinced of Thady's involvement in the attack perpetrated on himself, makes it a personal crusade to secure Thady's conviction. His exertions to that end are unnecessary however, since for a variety of reasons, principally the reputation that the locale had now obtained for unprovoked violence and the need to combat it with matching severity, nothing and nobody, not even the distinguished counsel briefed to defend him, are capable of saving Thady. He is doomed to hang, and hang he does. Keegan's days of ascendancy are drawing to a close however. Following Thady's execution, friends of the family apply to have trustees appointed to manage Bally-cloran on behalf of Larry who is now a lunatic. In the end the estate is sold to a stranger and Keegan never gets his hands on it.[18] After these momentous events, Keegan tries to stand out against the hatred of his neighbours and endure the odium of public opinion. He loses his agencies; no one comes to him to seek advice. He perseveres for three years. After his old friend Flannelly dies, the attorney 'is forced to leave the town and he vanished no man knoweth whither'.[19]

Trollope's evocation of this unscrupulous schemer is completely convincing. The portrait is fully rounded since a great deal of detailed information on Keegan is given: his family background for instance and such things as his conversion from catholicism, a step deliberately undertaken to help advance his professional career. He is furnished with a nagging wife and it is very obvious that he is a practised sycophant. On the other hand—and it is a

17. iii, 12–13.
18. iii, 425.
19. iii, 431.

strength of Trollope's characterisation that a few redeeming traits
are identifiable—Hyacinth is endowed with a certain natural
bravery and determination and he is a hard worker.

Trollope's most detailed description of Keegan accompanies
the Carrick attorney's arrival at Ballycloran with Flannelly's offer
to purchase the estate:

His father was a process-server living at a small town called Drumsham-
bo, that is, he obtained his bread by performing the legal acts to which
Irish landlords are so often obliged to have resort, to get their rent from
their poor tenants. This process-server was a poor man and a R.C., but
he had managed to give his son a decent education; he had gotten him a
place as an errand boy, in an attorney's office, from whence he had risen
to the dignity of clerk, and he was now, not only an attorney himself, but
a flourishing one, and a Protestant to boot. His great step in the world
had been his marriage with Sally Flannelly, the rejected of Macdermot;
for from the time of his wedding, he had much prospered in all worldly
things. He was a hardworking man, and in that consisted his only good
quality; he was a plausible man, a good flatterer, not deficient in that
sort of sharpness which made him a successful attorney in a small
provincial town, and could be a jovial companion, when called on to do
so. Principle had never stood much in his way; and he had completely
taught himself to believe that what was legal was right, and he knew how
to stretch legalities to the utmost. As a convert, Mr Keegan was very
enthusiastically attached to the Protestant religion, and the Tory party,
for which he had fought tooth and nail at the last county election, and
with such success that he had convinced that party that he would in
future be their most fitting electioneering agent.

Mr Keegan boasted a useful kind of courage; he cared but little for
the ill-name he had acquired in the country, among the poorer classes,
by his practice: and to do him justice, had shown pluck enough in the
dangerous duties which he sometimes had to perform; for he acted as
agent to the small properties of some absentee landlords, and for a man
of his character such duties in County Leitrim were not at that time without danger. He had been shot at, once knocked off his horse, and had
received various threatening letters; but it always turned out that he
discovered the aggressor, prosecuted and convicted him. One man he had
transported for life; in the last case, the man who had shot at him was
hung, and consequently the people began to be afraid of Mr Keegan.

Our friend was fond of popularity, and was consequently a bit of a
sportsman, as most Connaught attorneys are. He had the shooting of
two or three bogs, kept a good horse or two, and went to all the country
races, and made a small book on the events of the Curragh; these
accomplishments all had their effect, and as I said before, Mr Keegan
was successful. In appearance he was a large, burly man, gradually
growing corpulent, with a soft oily face, on which there was generally a
smile, and well for him that there was; for though his smile was not

prepossessing, and carried the genuine stamp of deceit, it concealed the malice, treachery and selfishness which his face so plainly bore without it. His eyes were light, large and bright, but it was that kind of brightness which belongs to an opaque, and not to a transparent body, they never sparkled; his mouth was very large, and his lip heavy, and he carried a large pair of brick coloured whiskers. His dress was somewhat dandified, but it usually had not a few of the characteristics of a horse jockey, as bright green cutaway coat and brass buttons, or a large cashmere scarlet choker, a broad brimmed felt hat, or similar personal attractions. In age he was about forty-five.[20]

Keegan participated in the revelry and the excesses after the dinner held on the eve of Carrick's social event of the year, the annual horse-races. Here Trollope conveys very well the artificiality and even the nauseous stench of the celebration, a celebration which forms a clear contrast with the episode, not long to be delayed, when a sober Keegan would be waylaid and mutilated in the lane near Drumleesh:

There he was, smiling and chatting, oily and amiable—getting a word in with anyone he could—creeping with intimacy with those who were not sharp enough to see what he was after—jabbering of horses, of which he considered himself a complete judge, and shooting, hunting and racing, as if the sports of a gentleman had been his occupation from his youth upwards.[21]

In relation to the races scheduled for the morrow, an auction is held and Keegan draws Pat Connor's mare from Strokestown, called Diana. The night meanwhile wears on:

Keegan had become very drunk and talkative, had offered to sing two or three songs—to make two or three speeches, and had ultimately fallen backwards, on his chair—being drawn away from which position he was unable to get up, and little Larry's brother was now amiably engaged painting his face with lampblack; Mrs Keegan the while was sitting in her cold, dark, little back parlour, meditating the awful punishment, to be visited on the delinquent when he did return home.[22]

And irreversibly on:

Vain woman, there she sat till four—while Hyacinth lay happy beneath the table, nor did he return home, till brought on a waiter's back, at eight the next morning.[23]

20. i, 238–42.
21. ii, 154.
22. ii, 170.
23. ii, 171.

It will not have been a pleasant or sweet home-coming in Mrs Keegan's book. Indulging a coarse streak, Trollope lets fall a single telling item of intelligence on the condition of the attorney as he is helped in through his own front door at eight o'clock in the morning. A companion in the night's potations, 'conquered by tobacco and whiskey', had earlier been decried 'leaning his unfortunate head on the table, and deluging Keegan's feet with the shower which he was unable to restrain'.[24]

In *The Macdermots of Ballycloran*, with the exception of a brief reference to Messrs Hall and Tomkins, the firm of attorneys who help to prepare for Thady's defence, Hyacinth Keegan ploughs a lonely professional furrow. In his second Irish novel, *The Kellys and the O'Kellys*, Trollope brings on stage a veritable multitude of attorneys. There is the firm of Grey and Forrest in Clare Street in Dublin.[25] Lord Ballindine (The O'Kelly) recommends them to his tenant, Martin Kelly, for advice on the form of marriage settlement that would best protect the interests of Anastasia or Anty Lynch, the heiress with whom, at the start of the novel, Martin is planning to elope. Martin tells Lord Ballindine that he had contemplated as an alternative the firm of Dublin attorneys who employed his brother John as one of their clerks, but had decided against it as they were not suitable: 'it's about robberies, and hanging and such things they're most engaged.'[26] In light of this detail it is hard to fathom how brother John had acquired the knowledge of the rudiments of the law of real property as well as the extent and nature of Anty Lynch's wealth which he was to communicate so freely to Martin[27]—both matters so crucial in their way to the unfolding of the plot.

At the end of the novel two other firms of attorneys surface. Both are involved in the drawing up of the settlements required by virtue of the impending marriage of Lord Ballindine and Fanny Wyndham, Lord Cashel's niece and ward. For Lord Ballindine, there is Mr Cummings 'recommended by Guinness' and, for Lord Cashel, Green and Grogram who knew all about Fanny's property and the existing settlements governing it.[28]

A generation back other lawyers too had played a significant role in the interlocking fortunes of the two families of the Kellys and the O'Kellys. In the life-time of Lord Ballindine's grandfather,

24. ii, 172.
25. *The Kellys and the O'Kellys*, p. 42.
26. P. 41.
27. P. 8.
28. P. 503.

his agent Simeon Lynch had squandered much of the substance of the estate by fixing rents that were too low. When Ballindine's father inherited the property, clever attorneys were brought in to advise on leases that could be broken, ones that might 'have a ghost of a flaw in them'.[29]

Pivotal to an understanding of the sequence of events which the novel itself relates is the breach that opens up between Simeon Lynch and his son, Barry, shortly before the death of the former. To wreak his revenge on Barry, Simeon rewrites his will to divide the inheritance equally between Barry and his sister, the Anty on whom Martin Kelly's interests have fastened. This untoward reversal in Barry's expectations ushers in a succession of attorneys with whom Barry has dealings in a vain endeavour to recapture the total inheritance. Barry consults his friend Molloy, an attorney in Tuam, as to the validity of his father's will: Molloy can find no fault with it.[30] Subsequently, the matter is also brought to the attention of Blake, the family solicitor. Blake consults with McMahon; the latter however refuses to handle the case, reporting that there was nothing that he could properly place before the lord chancellor.[31]

The third attorney whom Barry consults professionally over the set-back in his fortunes is another Tuam attorney, a Mr Daly. Daly is destined to play a central role in the story. Trollope relates at great length Daly's conduct of Barry Lynch's business. In the process, the characterisation of a second fictional Connaught attorney begins to take shape.

Daly's entry on stage needs further elaboration. Barry Lynch had been disappointed at Molloy's advice and dismayed too by Blake's inability to effect any kind of improvement in his prospects. He decides to make a direct approach to his sister. Anty however rebels and, when Barry resorts to force against her, she flees home to seek sanctuary in the inn kept in the local village of Dunmore by Martin Kelly's mother. Matters could not therefore have stood in a worse condition for Barry when he determines to call on fresh legal assistance.

The plan that Barry hatches is to have Anty committed as a lunatic, a plan that would enable him to control her share of the inheritance. The recent accretion to the ranks of attorneys in Tuam would, he believed, have few qualms of conscience over its implementation: 'Young Daly, he knew was a sharp fellow, and

29. P. 21.
30. P. 27.
31. P. 107.

wanted practice, and this would just suit him.'[32] Daly is invited to
his house the following night.

Barry's assessment of Daly was not wide of the mark, for the
latter 'was beginning to be known as a clever, though not over-
scrupulous practitioner'.[33] Questioned earlier over his acceptance
of the job of a second legal adviser to Barry, Daly breezily remarks:
'a man that's just come to his property always wants a lawyer; and
many a one, besides Barry Lynch, aint satisfied without two.'[34]
This braggadocio enables Daly to carry through a large share of
the schemes to ensnare Anty and the Kellys that Barry and he
now proceed to concoct together (though as the affair drags on,
admittedly with increasing reluctance on his part).

Any challenge to old Simeon's will is dropped on Daly's advice:

It's as well to let the will alone. The Chancellor won't put a will aside in
a hurry; it's always a difficult job—would cost an immense sum of
money, which should, any way, come out of the property; and, after all,
the chances are ten to one you'd be beat.[35]

Barry next spins a yarn that his debts are properly his father's
(though standing in his own name) and are, therefore, justly
chargeable against the estate. Daly doubts Barry's veracity but, on
the assumption the yarn could conceivably be true, he again
proffers sound legal advice. Barry finally lays his cards on the
table. He wants Anty committed, and solicits Daly's aid to that
end: 'she's not right in her upper storey. Mind I don't mean she's
a downright lunatic; but she's cracked, poor thing, and quite
unable to judge for herself in money-matters, and such like . . .'. [36]
Daly listens politely, sums up the situation at once and promptly
dissuades Barry from embarking on so rash a course of action. He
brings forward an alternative which, if it succeeded, he assures
Barry, could well achieve all that the latter sought: the return of
Anty to Barry's house, the dropping of any talk of Anty marrying
Martin Kelly and the prospect of Barry being able ultimately to
lay his hands on Anty's property.

The attorney's alternative strategy is to seek to browbeat Anty
into surrendering her interest into her brother's grasp: Barry
should prefer charges of criminal conspiracy against the Kellys
founded on the twin allegations of enticement and of an attempt

32. P. 86.
33. P. 99.
34. P. 99.
35. P. 108.
36. P. 110.

to gain possession of Anty's property. The charges would not be proceeded with if Anty returned voluntarily to her brother's house and into his care.

The strategy does not succeed: both Anty and the Kellys are made of sterner material. As the affair gets nastier—Daly bribes Anty's own agent to join forces with Barry—Anty herself falls ill, from nervous exhaustion and talk of legal proceedings. The continuing stubbornness of the Kellys convinces Daly that his correct course of action is to persuade Barry to come to terms with Anty and the Kellys, to dispose of the ancestral estate and to retire to the continent. At first Barry is prepared to accept this advice, and abide by the solution it guaranteed for his various difficulties but, on receiving news that Anty's illness has worsened and that she is at death's door, he changes his mind. Barry's villainy is finally unmasked and his departure from Dunmore and Ireland suddenly brought forward when, in a last desperate fling, he attempts to bribe the family doctor, Dr Colligan, into ensuring that Anty does not recover from her illness.

Long before this, relations between client and attorney had soured. Barry, consumed by his hatred for the Kellys and his contempt for Anty, had come to have little patience with his more diplomatic and crafty accomplice. 'Obstinate puppy', he remarks of Daly,

if he'd had the least pluck in life he'd have broken the will or at least made the girl out a lunatic. But a Connaught lawyer hasn't half the wit or courage that he used to have.[37]

At a later stage Barry regrets his initial acquiescence in the suggestion that he come to some accommodation with Anty and the Kellys. It was a mistake to have reached that decision in Daly's office in Tuam rather than in his own house in Dunmore:

I should have had him here, and not gone to that confounded cold hole of his. After all, there's no place for a cock to fight on like his own dunghill.[38]

From the start of the relationship, and despite appearances to the contrary, Daly, for his part, had entertained serious qualms about his own line of conduct. On hearing for the first time of Barry's plan to have his own sister committed, Daly's 'heart misgave him, even though he was a sharp attorney at the idea of assisting such a cruel

37. P. 224.
38. P. 262.

brute in his cruelty'.[39] While undressing for bed that night, Daly ruminated further on the events of the evening:

he reflected that during his short professional career, he had been thrown into the society of many unmitigated rogues of every description; but that his new friend, Barry Lynch, though he might not equal them in energy of villainy and courage to do serious evil, beat them all hollow in selfishness and utter brutal want of feeling, conscience and principle. [40]

Though the idea of launching criminal proceedings against the Kellys had originated with Daly, the attorney knew the idea stank—and stank to high heaven. He could nevertheless still find justification for what he was about: 'he was young in business and poor, and he could not afford to give up a client.'[41] The doubts of the young attorney, however, now began to be more frequently sensed and more regularly expressed. This involvement with Lynch, Daly argued with himself, could injure his character; the undertaking of so very low a line of business might ultimately tell against him. [42]

The final break with Barry is postponed for two more chapters. Anty's illness finds Barry determined to jettison Daly, 'the luke-warmness and timidity' of whose advice he had come to despise.[43] He brazenly proposes to Daly that the latter should draw up Anty's will (leaving everything to her brother, naturally) and cause her to sign it; he guarantees Daly £70 per annum in perpetuity should he oblige. Daly is flabbergasted and the professional and ethical instincts of the man at long last burst free. Barry is turned out into the public street in Tuam and is told that he will be unceremoniously kicked out of the attorney's office should he ever set foot there again.[44]

For all his exertions on Barry's behalf, Daly eventually earned not a single farthing. He did, however, receive an invitation to Anty's wedding,[45] a remarkable act of forgiveness considering the devastation wrought on Anty's health by an earlier visit of his to her at Dunmore on professional matters. Anty had collapsed and it was to take many weeks before she began to mend. Like many another innocent caught in the toils of the law, she had not been

39. P. 114.
40. Pp. 116–7.
41. P. 232.
42. Pp. 252–3.
43. P. 296.
44. P. 297.
45. P. 511.

able to penetrate the machinations of lawyers and detect where lay bluster and where lay truth:

The very presence of an attorney was awful to her; and all the jargon which Daly had used, of juries, judges, trials, and notices, had sounded terrible to her ears. The very names of such things were to her terrible realities, and she couldn't bring herself to believe that her brother would threaten to make use of such horrible engines of persecution, without having the power to bring them into action.[46]

Hyacinth Keegan in *The Macdermots* and Mr Daly in *The Kellys* are both major characters. Thaddeus Crowe, the attorney from Ennis who appears in *An eye for an eye*, is a walk-on part. His task is to buy off Captain O'Hara, the drunkard father of Kate, the girl with whom Fred Neville has fallen in love and whom he is about to jilt. 'Honest, intelligent and peculiarly successful',[47] Crowe manifests disbelief when Neville mentions the exact sum he wishes the attorney to offer O'Hara:

'Two hundred a year!', said the Ennis attorney, to whom such an annuity seemed to be exorbitant as the purchase-money for a returned convict.[48]

Crowe, nevertheless, does as he had been bid, interviews O'Hara, and concludes the business satisfactorily:

The Captain endeavoured to hold up his head, and to swagger and to assume an air of pinchbeck respectability. But the attorney would not permit it. He required that the man should own himself to be penniless, a scoundrel, only anxious to be bought.[49]

For Neville, now ennobled as the earl of Scroope, and about to set out for his meeting on the cliffs of Moher with Kate's mother and with destiny, the transaction was effectively the last he would successfully put in train on earth.

Mr Prendergast, the family solicitor, occupies a much more prominent position in the pages of *Castle Richmond*, a novel which is set principally in Co. Cork. Sir Thomas Fitzgerald has been unable to bear the strain of dealing with the blackmailers who have

46. P. 247.
47. *An eye for an eye*, ii, 74. The reference is to the two-vol. 1st ed. published by Chapman & Hall, London, 1879, and repr. by Garland Publishing Inc., New York and London, 1979.
48. ii, 76.
49. ii, 82.

made his life a misery. The claim of the latter is indeed grave—
that his wife committed bigamy when she married him, a claim
which carries the implication that their son Herbert is illegitimate
and thus incapable of inheriting as heir-at-law. In despair, Sir
Thomas turns to Prendergast who comes over from London at his
special request. Prendergast carries out an inquiry, concludes that
the blackmailers (the Mollets) are telling the truth and breaks the
news of the calamity to everyone concerned. Satisfied by the
thoroughness of his inquiries, Prendergast has one last service to
render his client before Sir Thomas, worn-out with grief, breathes
his last—to draw up on his behalf 'a will, leaving what money he
had to his three children by name in trust for their mother's use'.[50]
Faced with financial ruin, Sir Thomas' 'widow' and her children
move to London, and Herbert adjusts to the prospect of an
eventual career at the bar.

   The London solicitor's services to the Fitzgerald connection
are not yet concluded however. Several months later new information becomes available and this leads Prendergast to re-open his
investigations into the Mollets. The outcome is a discovery well
within the comprehension of any first-year law student who has
had to wrestle with the question of mens rea in bigamy and section
57 of the Offences against the Person Act, 1861. At the time Lady
Fitzgerald had indeed gone through a ceremony of marriage with
Mollet, the latter, unknown to her, had another wife living: Lady
Fitzgerald had, therefore, been free to marry Sir Herbert, it was
accordingly a valid marriage, and Herbert could now look forward
to assume his landed inheritance, abandon his new-found career
and return to Ireland.

   In summoning Prendergast to investigate the allegations made
by the Mollets and generally to deal with them, Sir Thomas sensed
he had no alternative. The reputation of the family was at stake and
legal questions arose: recourse to the services of the family solicitor
was plainly indicated. That awesome presence from *Bleak house*,
Mr Tulkinghorn, would have understood only too well.

   Yet it is surely ironical that the London solicitor did not
immediately get to the bottom of the business, with the dire consequences for everyone that that failure was to entail. No one was
more acutely aware of what had been at stake than Prendergast
himself. Though he had scarcely been negligent, the discovery
that he had been wrong was still a very great shock. At the

50. *Castle Richmond*, iii, 44. The reference is to the three-vol. 1st ed. published
    by Chapman & Hall, London, 1860, and repr. by Garland Publishing Inc.,
    New York and London, 1979.

meeting between Prendergast and Herbert when the latter is informed that he is not a pauper after all, Trollope sets out to describe what was then passing through the solicitor's mind:

Mr Prendergast had in his countenance not quite so sweet an aspect. Mr Die [a barrister acquaintance] had repeated to him, perhaps once too often, a very well-known motto of his; one by the aid of which he professed to have steered himself safely through the shoals of life— himself and perhaps some others. It was a motto which he would have loved to see inscribed over the great gates of the noble inn to which he belonged; and which, indeed, a few years since might have been inscribed there with much justice. 'Festinâ lentè', Mr Die would say to all those who came to him in any sort of hurry. And then when men accused him of being dilatory by premeditation, he would say no, he had always recommended despatch. 'Festinâ', he would say; 'festinâ', by all means; but 'festinâ lentè'. The doctrine had at any rate thriven with the teacher, for Mr Die had amassed a large fortune.[51]

Over the Mollet inquiry Prendergast may indeed have hastened too fast. There was another professional characteristic he possessed, however, where deviation from the norm on his part was much less frequent. Prendergast had to an unusual degree the ability to distance himself emotionally from the plight of his client. It was a talent Trollope seems to have admired:

A surgeon to be of use should be ruthless in one sense. He should have the power of cutting and cauterising, of phlebotomy and bone-handling without effect on his own nerves.[52]

But even the most hardened of lawyers could not always contrive to resist the pull at the heart-strings, and Prendergast was no different:

Herbert himself had seen tears in the eyes of that dry time-worn world-used London lawyer, as the full depth of the calamity had forced itself upon his heart.[53]

Trollope's detailed portrait of Prendergast is inserted at a curious moment in the story. Herbert had just made the acquaintance of the gang of labourers recruited for a famine relief scheme that involved the levelling of Ballydahan hill. The contrast between the London lawyer and the Irish manual worker is naturally

51. iii, 223.
52. ii, 85.
53. ii, 249.

suggestive, but the portrait of the former nonetheless remains generally sympathetic:

Mr Prendergast was a man over sixty years of age. . . . He was short of stature, well-made and in good proportion; he was wiry, strong and almost robust. He walked as though in putting his foot to the earth he always wished to proclaim that he was afraid of no man and no thing. His hair was grizzled and his whiskers were grey, and round about his mouth his face was wrinkled; but with him even these base things hardly seemed to be signs of old age. He was said by many who knew him to be a stern man, and there was that in his face which seemed to warrant such a character. But he had also the reputation of being a very just man; and those who knew him best could tell tales of him which proved that his sternness was at any rate compatible with a wide benevolence. He was a man who himself had known but little mental suffering, and who owned no mental weakness; and it might be, therefore, that he was impatient of such weakness in others. To chance acquaintances his manners were not soft, or perhaps palatable; but to his old friends his very brusqueness was pleasing. He was a bachelor, well off in the world, and, to a certain extent, fond of society. He was a solicitor by profession, having his office somewhere in the purlieus of Lincoln's Inn, and living in an old-fashioned house and not far distant from that classic spot. I have said that he owned no mental weakness. When I say further that he was slightly afflicted with personal vanity, and thought a good deal about the set of his hair, the shape of his coat, the fit of his boots, the whiteness of his hands, and the external trim of his umbrella, perhaps I may be considered to have contradicted myself. But such was the case. He was a handsome man too, with clear, bright, gray eyes, a well-defined nose, and expressive mouth—of which the lips, however, were somewhat too thin. No man with thin lips ever seems to me to be genially human at all points.[54]

A single attorney's clerk is depicted in the Irish novels: John Kelly, the older brother of Martin who in *The Kellys and the O'Kellys* finally marries Anty Lynch. John effectively disappears after the first few chapters which are played out in Dublin. John earned a guinea a week.[55] Trollope is most forthcoming about his politics: unlike Martin, John did not admit that repeal of the act of union would automatically ensue should O'Connell be acquitted at his trial, a contingency both brothers were convinced was certain:

John was neither so sanguine nor so enthusiastic; it was the battle rather than the thing battled for, that was dear to him; the strife, rather than the result. He felt that it would be dull times in Dublin, when they

54. ii, 83–5.
55. *The Kellys and the O'Kellys*, p. 10.

should have no usurping Government to abuse, no Saxon Parliament to upbraid, no English laws to ridicule, and no Established Church to curse.[56]

John was not only a violent Repealer and something of a prophet. He was also an accomplished young man about town whom those he might chance to meet would be likely to regard as either charming or insufferable. Marginal to the story, John's character undergoes no development. What meagre information Trollope imparts is not enlightening on Irish attorney's clerks of the period. Details of the kind that it is Trollope's fashion to furnish nevertheless possess their own fascination:

The elder of them was a three-year-old denizen of Dublin, who knew the names of the contributors to the 'Nation', who had constantly listened to the indignation and enthusiasm of O'Connell, Smith O'Brien and O'Neill Daunt, in their addresses from the rostrum of the Conciliation Hall; who had drunk much porter at Jude's, who had eaten many oysters at Burton Bindon's, who had contributed to many rows in the Abbey Street Theatre; who, during his life in Dublin, had done many things which he ought not to have done, and had probably made as many omissions of things which it had behoved him to do. He had that knowledge of the persons of his fellow-citizens, which appears to be so much more general in Dublin than in any other large town; he could tell you the name and trade of every one he met in the streets, and was a judge of the character and talents of all whose employments partook, in any degree, of a public nature.[57]

There is a second fictional representation of an attorney's clerk that may be compared. The representation is that of Mr Bowles who is included among the passengers on board the 'Alcyone' in William Golding's modern novel *Close quarters*, which is however set in the year 1815. Bowles possesses much accurate legal knowledge in the sphere of international law. When a suspect French man o' war is decried on the horizon, he shows no hesitation in advising his fellow passengers on what they should and should not do in order to preserve their status as non-combatants under the laws of war:

I believe we passengers may 'run up a gun', as it is called, which entails hauling on a rope. We could plead compulsion. But seen on deck with sword and pistol in hand and we are legally entitled to have our throats cut.[58]

56. Pp. 17–8.
57. P.4.
58. William Golding, *Close quarters* (London, 1987), ch.3.

It seems unlikely that John Kelly's intellectual attainments, so far as actual knowledge of the rules of law and the ability to apply them were concerned, could have begun to rival those of Mr Bowles.

I V

Three barristers are portrayed in *The Macdermots of Ballycloran*: Counsellor Webb, whose role is confined to that of resident landlord and active magistrate, and the barristers concerned with the prosecution and defence respectively of Thady Macdermot.

Appearing for the crown is Mr Allewinde, an embryo Chaffanbrass of Irish extraction. He was

a most erudite lawyer—he has been for many years employed by the crown in its prosecutions and with great success. He knows well the art of luring on an approver, or crown witness, to give the information he wants without asking absolutely leading questions—he knows well how to bully a witness brought up on the defence, out of his senses, and make him give evidence rather against than for the prisoner—and it is not only witnesses that he bullies, but his very brethren of the gown. The barristers themselves who are opposed to him, at any rate, the juniors, are doomed to bear the withering force of his caustic remarks.[59]

He did his job competently:

how Demosthenic is his language when addressing the jury on the enormity of all agrarian offences—with what frightful, fearful eloquence does he depict the miseries of anarchy, which are to follow nonpayment of tithes, rents and taxes, and with what energy does he point out to a jury that their own hearths, homes and very existence depend on their vindicating justice in the instance before them.[60]

To defend Thady at his trial, his friends resolve to secure the services of Mr O'Malley, 'the most talented' member of the bar on the Connaught Circuit and 'one of the most able . . . in Ireland'.[61] O'Malley's fee would not be insubstantial and Father John, Thady's parish priest, travels to Dublin to raise part of the sum from his brother, who is in business as a butter-merchant in Capel Street. The brother is initially reluctant: 'as long as you were

59. *The Macdermots of Ballycloran*, iii, 229–30.
60. iii, 232.
61. iii, 42, 43.

pleased, I didn't care if you pitched it into the Liffey—but it do seem a pity to be giving so much money to them scoundrelly lawyers.'[62] (The riposte anticipates that of the widow Kelly in *The Kellys and the O'Kellys* when she hears that Martin has had dealings with lawyers and doubtless paid them a huge sum for what she describes as a 'gander's job').[63] But the brother finally relents, Father John meets O'Malley and persuades him to take the brief, whereupon a lengthy passage follows in which the barrister explains the difficulties of Thady's defence and what the choice of tactics should be. O'Malley naturally is a prominent figure at Thady's trial, but the impression that remains fixed is that left on Father John when the latter first meets him:

Mr O'Malley was sitting behind a huge table covered with papers in a back parlour of the house. He was a small, dark, swarthy man, with small bright eyes, large black eye-brows, and a quantity of very black hair. The upper part of his countenance would have given him an austere stern look, had it not been for the good-humoured smile which continually played around the corner of his mouth.[64]

From a later chronological period Trollope supplies a portrait of an altogether different species of Irish barrister, the archetypal defender of those whom Trollope had come to count among the worst villains in Christendom. In *The landleaguers* defence counsel for Pat O'Carroll is a Mr O'Donnell. Little is gleaned of O'Donnell from Trollope's account of the O'Carroll trial in view of the premature termination of the latter when the chief crown witness, O'Carroll's own brother, is murdered in the well of the court. Elsewhere, though, it is related that O'Donnell 'was accustomed to speak of all the Landleague criminals as patriotic lambs—whose lamblike qualities were exceeded only by their patriotism'.[65] Earlier still, whilst Florian Jones was still alive, the family's friend and confidant, Captain Clayton RM, who had prevailed upon Florian to break his oath of secrecy and confess all he knew of the opening of the sluice-gates, had warned Florian's father of the difficulties the boy would face when giving his evidence at the assizes. These difficulties would stem from the antics of the kind of lawyer (of which O'Donnell was presumably a fair specimen)

62. iii, 103.
63. *The Kellys and the O'Kellys*, p. 103.
64. iii, 108–9.
65. *The landleaguers*, iii, 126. The reference is to the three-vol. 1st ed. published by Chatto & Windus, London, 1883, and repr. by Garland Publishing Inc., New York and London, 1979.

who might be expected to be engaged to represent the accused.
Florian, observed Clayton,

will want all his pluck then, and all the simplicity which he can muster.
You must remember that a skilful man will have been turned loose on
him with all the ferocity of a bloodhound; a man who will have all the
cruelty of Lax [the arch-conspirator of the novel], but will have nothing
to fear; a man who will be serving his purpose all round if he can only
dumbfound that poor boy by his words and his looks . . .
    And there will be no mercy shown to him because he is only a boy . . .
A lawyer in defending the worse ruffian that ever committed a crime will
know that he is called upon to spare nothing that is tender. He is
absolved from all the laws common to humanity.[66]

So deadly an advocate assumed, in Trollope's eyes, a yet more
sinister mien. The analysis is again that of Captain Clayton:

A man, when he has taken up the cause of these ruffians, learns to
sympathise with them. If they hate the Queen, hate the laws, hate all the
justice, these men learn to hate them too.[67]

    Trollope was still at work at *The landleaguers* when he died in
1882. The didactic tone of this unfinished novel provides the
principal ammunition to support the assertion, frequently made,
that Trollope's attitude towards Ireland and her problems had
perceptibly hardened, certainly since he himself ceased to live there
in 1859. This is plausible, but in a sense there was little enough to
differentiate between the mutilation of Hyacinth Keegan and the
murder of Florian Jones and Pat O'Carroll's brother. If the Irish
idyll ever corresponded with reality, that idyll could, as Trollope
seems to have been fully aware, be as easily destroyed by events
occurring in the 1840s as in the 1880s. The characterisation of
O'Donnell nevertheless remains a vital clue. In this connection,
however, it is worth noting an early indication of Trollope's
distaste for Irish barristers, a distaste, which in Captain Clayton's
discourse on hate, is seen to have assumed, in the novelist's last
months, the proportions of something close to an infatuation. The
indication occurs in *Phineas Finn*, in an exchange of seemingly
light-hearted banter between Phineas and Madame Max Goesler.
Madame Max had asked Phineas what he proposed to do should
loss of office force him to return to Ireland and start in practice at
the Irish bar:

66. ii, 98–9.
67. ii, 99.

PHINEAS: Anything honest in a barrister's way that may be brought to me. I hope that I may never descend below that.

MADAME MAX: You will stand up for all the blackguards, and try to make out that the thieves did not steal?

PHINEAS: It may be that that sort of work may come in my way.

MADAME MAX: And you will wear a wig and try to look wise?

PHINEAS: The wig is not universal in Ireland, Madame Goesler.[68]

An Irish bar student in London is encountered in the final section of *Castle Richmond*: the Herbert Fitzgerald who, following the reversal in his family's fortunes, was forced to earn his bread. There were various options: the civil service; the church (Aunt Letty pressed this: 'Trinity College Dublin was in her estimation the only place left for good Church of England ecclesiastical teaching')[69]; and, last but by no means least, the law. Herbert chooses the law and with the help of Mr Prendergast, the family solicitor, is settled in legal chambers in London presided over by Mr Die, a renowned chancery barrister. He determines to work hard, so the prospect of long days in a lawyer's chambers and longer evenings 'spent over his law books with closed windows and copious burnings of the midnight oil'[70] did not dismay him.

Doubts, nevertheless, soon begin to assail Herbert. He visits one of the courts in London, but the impression is the reverse of favourable. The comparison with Ireland was undeniably to the advantage of the latter: 'There was no life and amusement such as he had seen at the Assize Court in county Cork, when he was sworn in as one of the Grand Jury'.[71] The contrast was almost too dreadful to behold:

Here, whatever skill there might be, was of a dark subterranean nature, quite unintelligible to any minds but those of experts; and as for fury or fun, there was no spark either of one or the other. The judge sat back in his seat, a tall, handsome speechless man, not asleep, for his eye from time to time moved slowly from the dingy barrister who was on his legs to another dingy barrister who was sitting with his hands in his pockets and with his eyes fixed upon the ceiling.[72]

68. *Phineas Finn*, ii, 391. The reference is to the two-vol. ed. in the 'World's Classics' series brought out by the Oxford University Press in 1937.

69. *Castle Richmond*, iii, 52.

70. iii, 109.

71. iii, 112.

72. iii, 114–5.

Herbert remains there an hour, fancying that he might learn
something that would be of use to him in his career. But at the
end of that time, the identical charade was being performed:

the judge's eye was still open, and the lawyer's drone was still sounding;
and so he came away, having found himself absolutely dozing in the
uncomfortable position in which he was standing.[73]

Yet that very night in conversation over dinner with Mr Prendergast, Herbert puts those doubts aside and reveals his plans
after qualifying. He had decided not to proceed to the Irish bar
but, equally, he was desirous of acquiring a modest fixed income
as soon as he could. Prendergast applauds Herbert's determination:

No doubt a family connection is a great assistance to a barrister, and
there would be reasons which would make attorneys in Ireland throw
business into your hands at an early period of your life. Your history
would give you an eclat there, if you know what I mean . . . It is a kind of
assistance which in my opinion a man should not desire. In the first
place, it does not last. A man so buoyed up is apt to trust to such
support, instead of his own steady exertions; and the firmest of friends
won't stick to a lawyer long if he can get better law for his money
elsewhere . . .

Good, hard, steady and enduring work,—work that does not demand
immediate acknowledgement and reward, but that can afford to look
forward for its results,—it is that, and that only which in my opinion will
insure to a man permanent success.[74]

There was reassurance too over the money side to things. Any
barrister 'of fair parts and sound acquirements', Prendergast tells
Herbert, could count on a moderate fixed income early in life:
there were 'more barristers now filling places than practising in
the courts'.[75] Other changes too had made the bar an extremely
attractive proposition:

Nowadays a man is taken from his boat-racing and his skittle-ground to
be made a judge. A little law and a great fund of physical strength—that
is the extent of the demand.[76]

73. iii, 115.
74. iii, 119–20.
75. iii, 120–121.
76. iii, 121.

Prendergast himself was not enamoured of these developments, observing, wistfully, that 'fifteen years of unpaid labour used not to be thought too great a price to pay for ultimate success'.[77] Where men had been ambitious but patient, he continued, they were now covetous and impatient. Such reservations did not impress Herbert and Prendergast knew at once the seed had fallen on stony ground. It was a depressing discovery for the family solicitor:

It is sad for a man to feel when he knows that he is fast going down the hill of life, that the experience of old age is to be no longer valued nor its wisdom appreciated.[78]

Herbert is convinced. A career at the English bar it is to be. The hours would be long, the work tedious, Amaryllis would have to be left by herself in the shade and Neaera's locks unheeded. It was a sacrifice worth making.[79]

Everyone's expectations of Herbert are confounded sooner than they could have dreamed. There comes the second, sudden reversal of fortune—the discovery that he is no longer a pauper. And another change of plan: Herbert abandons his career at the bar and returns to Ireland. His tutor, the redoubtable Mr Die, had strenuously argued against just such a move. 'What indeed', he reckoned,

could be more conducive to salutary equanimity in the mind of a young man so singularly circumstanced, than the study of Blackstone, of Coke, and of Chitty as long as he remained there at work in those chambers, amusing himself occasionally with the eloquence of the neighbouring courts—there might be reasonable hope that he would be able to keep his mind equally poised, so that neither access nor failure as regarded his Irish inheritance should affect him injuriously.[80]

Herbert proves adamant however, and announces to an astonished Die that he actually preferred to go back to Ireland 'than to remain in London, sipping the delicious honey of Chancery buttercups'.[81] Phineas Finn, Trollope's more celebrated second Irish bar student, continues where Herbert Fitzgerald leaves off. Phineas qualifies as a barrister in London, subsequently enters politics

77. Ibid.
78. iii, 122.
79. iii, 123.
80. iii, 232.
81. iii, 233.

there and stakes out a promising career. *Phineas Finn* and *Phineas redux* relate the vicissitudes in the life of this not unattractive Irish expatriate. Phineas appears, if fleetingly, in other of the Palliser sequence of novels and a good deal is said about him. Perhaps his only conspicuous vice is a predilection for snobbishness, a vice from which his creator suffered in some measure and which the latter transposed on to him.

The son of a medical practitioner in Killaloe, Phineas is despatched first of all to Trinity College in Dublin. The family was catholic, but more from birth and upbringing than by conviction. Friends of the family in Killaloe, Trollope explains, knew that the catholicism of the Finns was not 'of that bitter kind in which we in England are apt to suppose that all the Irish Roman Catholics indulge'[82] and declared that Dr Finn would not have been sorry if his son had turned protestant and gone in for a fellowship. No one need have entertained anxieties on that score. Whilst constantly appreciative of his education at Trinity, Phineas had set his heart on a somewhat different career—as a barrister, not at the Irish bar, as his father would have preferred, but at the English.[83] Phineas accordingly at the age of 22 moves to London to read with an English barrister. His father paid 'the usual fee to a very competent and learned gentleman in the Middle Temple', and allowed Phineas £150 per annum for three years.[84]

In the nature of things Phineas is duly called to the bar. He does not however make an auspicious start: 'The learned pundit at whose feet he had been sitting was not especially loud in praise of his pupil's industry, though he did say a pleasant word or two as to his pupil's intelligence.'[85] Phineas has already progressed much further than Herbert Fitzgerald but, like the latter, he begins to entertain doubts over his choice of career. To the extreme consternation of his legal patrons, Phineas secures an entry to the social world of London and begins to take an interest in politics. The die is cast. There are to be the set-backs of course. Out of politics at the end of *Phineas Finn*, Phineas is obliged to return to the practice of law in Ireland, finally becoming an inspector of poor houses in Co. Cork at a stipend of £1,000 per annum.[86] But already he has met Lady Laura Standish and Madame Max Goesler and he has fought his duel with Lord

82. *Phineas Finn*, i, 2.
83. i, 2; ii, 123.
84. i, 3.
85. Ibid.
86. ii, 432.

Chiltern over Violet Effingham at Blankenberg in Belgium. Phineas' social and political advancement continues in *Phineas redux*, where the fates somehow conspire in his favour: the election petition is decided in his favour and he returns as an MP, and he is acquitted on the charge of murdering Bonteen. Lizzie Eustace has no time for him: 'He was one of those conceited Irish upstarts that are never good for anything.'[87] But so harsh a judgment seems to have been a minority opinion.

Phineas' growing disenchantment with the law and the challenge of a career divided between it and the lure of politics stimulate Trollope into expansive mood. The indecisiveness displayed by his heroes and heroines, an indecisiveness so frequently central to the development of his plots, is here subjected to scrutiny against this particularised background. Phineas horrifies Mr Low, the barrister of the Middle Temple with whom he had been reading for three years, when he announces his intention of seeking a seat in parliament and of temporarily giving up the bar:

You mustn't give it up at all—not for a day . . . Did a period of idleness ever help a man in any profession? And is it not acknowledged by all who know anything about it, that continuous labour is more necessary in our profession than in any other.[88]

The advice is not totally wasted on Phineas, for at this early stage in his progress he, like Herbert Fitzgerald before, could still contrive to remain philosophical and balanced about the law:

He declared to himself very often that things dreary and dingy to the eye might be good in themselves. Lincoln's Inn itself is dingy, and the Law Courts therein are perhaps the meanest in which Equity ever disclosed herself. Mr Low's three rooms in the Old Square, each of them brown with the binding of law books and with the dust collected on law papers, and with furniture that had been brown always, and had become browner with years, were perhaps as unattractive to the eye of a young pupil as any rooms which were ever entered. And the study of the Chancery law itself is not an alluring pursuit till the mind has come to have some insight into the beauty of its ultimate object. Phineas, during his three years' course of reasoning on these things, had taught himself to believe that things ugly on the outside might be very beautiful within.[89]

But this is soon made to appear but a passing phase. When, at a later stage, Phineas contemplates loss of political office and, as a

87. *Phineas redux*, ii, 42. The reference is to the two-vol. ed. in the 'World's Classics' series brought out by the Oxford University Press in 1937.
88. *Phineas Finn*, i, 51.
89. i, 77.

consequence, an involuntary return to practice at the bar, the thought fills him with gloom:

Life to him without [the air of the house of commons] would be no life. To have come within the reach of the good things of political life, to have made his mark so as to have almost answered future success, to have been the petted young official aspirant of the day,—and then to sink down into the miserable platitudes of private life, to undergo daily attendance in law-courts without a brief, to listen to men who had come to be much below him in estimation and social intercourse, to sit in a wretched chamber of three pairs of stairs at Lincoln's Inn, whereas he was now at this moment provided with a gorgeous apartment looking out into the park from the Colonial Office in Downing Street, to be attended by a mongrel between a clerk and an errand boy at 17*s*. 6*d*. a week instead of by a private secretary who was the son of an earl's sister and was petted by countesses' daughters innumerable—all this would surely break his heart.[90]

Other more practical snags were involved in the transition to a more humdrum life which Mr Low, Phineas' old teacher, was not slow to identify and which, unhappily for Phineas, rang only too true. Attorneys did not like barristers who were anything else but barristers. Besides, Mr Low continued,

it is so difficult for a man to go back to the verdure and malleability of pupildom, who has once escaped from the necessary humility of its conditions. You will find it difficult to sit and wait for business in a Vice-Chancellor's Court, after having had Vice-Chancellor, or men as big as Vice-Chancellors, to wait upon you.[91]

As *Phineas Finn* concludes, Phineas is seen to be left with no other obvious option but to return to legal practice in Ireland. Vacillation ends and this becomes his decision. For Phineas some adjustment to the reality of his diminished expectations is still required. Swagger replaces ruefulness as he convinces himself he will be able to make the change:

He, like Icarus, had flown up towards the sun, hoping that his wings of wax would bear him steadily aloft among the gods. Seeing that his wings were wings of wax, we must acknowledge that they were very good. But the celestial lights had been too strong for them, and now, having lived for five years with lords and countesses, with ministers and orators, with beautiful women and men of fashion, he must start again in a little

90. ii, 122–3.
91. ii, 282.

lodging in Dublin, and hope that the attorneys of that litigious city might be good to him. On his journey home he made but one resolution. He would make the change or attempt to make it with manly strength.[92]

In the novels two veterans of the bar are paraded as the conscience of the profession: Mr Die in *Castle Richmond* and Mr Low in *Phineas Finn*. The former occupies a slightly more significant role. In *Castle Richmond* it is on Mr Die's personal credo—to hasten slowly—that Prendergast, the family solicitor, chooses to ruminate after discovering that he had been in error over Lady Fitzgerald's marital entanglements. And it is against his advice that Herbert Fitzgerald eventually decides to abandon the law and return to his inheritance in Ireland. Mr Die is nearly 70, worked very hard and very late. That Mr Die and Mr Low possessed in equal measure that indefinable characteristic of 'presence', Trollope harbours no doubt. Pondering the attainments of the former, Trollope employs a classical allusion to pose a more general conundrum, to which indeed there would seem to be no simple answer:

In what Medea's caldron is it that the great lawyers do cook themselves, that they are able to achieve half an immortality, even while the body still clings to the soul?[93]

V

There is a sprinkling of magistrates and judges in Trollope's Irish novels. First to be surveyed are the justices of the peace.

Irish justices of the peace, like many other institutions of indigenous legal history, still await their historian. In the 1820s petty sessions districts were delineated for the entire country and from that point on regular sessions were held in each such district for the purpose of the administration of justice. There were invariably more JPs listed in each county's commission of the peace than were required to oversee the system of petty sessions. Usually only a minority—often as few as three—were actually present. Trollope arrived in Ireland in the autumn of 1841 and started to write *The Macdermots of Ballycloran* shortly afterwards. The new system had been in force for not much more than a decade, therefore, when he furnishes an early account of it in operation in his portrayal of the three magistrates in regular

92. ii, 432.
93. *Castle Richmond*, iii, 233–4.

attendance at the petty sessions held in Carrick-on-Shannon. [94]
The justification for the digression is the need to discuss the
attitude of the gentry to the committal of Thady Macdermot on
the charge of murdering his sister's seducer, Myles Ussher.

The cameos of all three magistrates are of absorbing interest.
The chairman was Sir Michael Gibson. He was 'by far the richest,
and would, therefore, naturally have had the greatest number of
followers, had it not been that it was usually extremely difficult to
find out what his opinion was'.[95] Jonas Brown was quite different:

In every case he would, if he had the power, visit every fault committed
by [the defendants], with the severest penalty awarded by the law. He
was a stern, hard, cruel man, with no sympathy for any one, and was
actuated by the most superlative contempt for the poor, from whom he
drew his whole income.[96]

The third member of the triumvirate was Counsellor Webb who
was both clear-headed and very much more talented. Yet here too
there was a flaw:

He was, in the first place, by far too fond of popularity, and of being the
favourite among the peasantry, and, in the next, he had become so
habituated to oppose Jonas Brown in all his sayings and doings, that he
now did so whether he was right or wrong.[97]

The outcome was confusion, a state of affairs creditable neither
from the standpoint of the maintenance of law and order nor
from that of ensuring due respect for them. Trollope summarises
the situation with the insouciance of the hardened journalist:

If a lad were brought before the three, for a row at a fair, Jonas would
send him to the treadmill—the Counsellor would send him about his
business—and Sir Michael was thus left in the disagreeable predicament
of not knowing what to do with him. Jonas Brown would have had the
whole country in prison—Counsellor Webb would have thrown open
the prison doors—and Sir Michael would have alternately done both.
Jonas Brown abused the poor—Counsellor Webb flattered them—and
Sir Michael between the two, at last learnt that the only place for him
was to hold his tongue.[98]

94. *The Macdermots of Ballycloran*, iii, 21–5.
95. iii, 21.
96. iii, 22–3.
97. iii, 24.
98. iii, 24–5.

In a later novel, set in a more violent period, to crave the sort of anonymity to which Sir Michael may well have aspired, would not necessarily suffice to secure immunity from something much worse than the contempt of the magistrate's colleagues—the assassin's bullet. *The landleaguers* is peopled with the true victims, as Trollope would have categorised them, of the land war. If the murder of young Florian Jones represents the principal focus of interest in a less than satisfactory plot, that of a justice of the peace for the counties of Galway and Mayo was equally symbolic, in Trollope's mind, of the genuine horror of the epoch. Robert Morris had had difficulties with his tenants but an abatement of rent had been agreed. Neither did the performance by him of his official duties demonstrate clearly or at all why he had been singled out. Mr Morris

> attended sessions both at Cong and at Clonbur. But when there he did little but agree with some more active magistrate; and what else he did with himself no one could tell of him.[99]

The stipendiary magistrates who in time came to be called 'resident magistrate' are also to be counted among the lower magistracy. Before 1920 members of the Irish legal profession sought to establish an exclusive title to appointments as RMs, citing the need for legal proficiency in those who exercised the RM's multifarious functions. The claim however was never conceded and it was to be left to successor Irish administrations to introduce the necessary legal changes in the 1920s and 1930s.

The most celebrated RM of Irish fiction is of course the Major Yeates of Somerville and Ross' reminiscences. In *The Kellys and the O'Kellys*, Mr Brew, 'the stipendiary' at Tuam, surfaces briefly. Two of the principal characters in the story, Lord Ballindine and the Revd Armstrong, wearing their hats as JPs, threaten Barry Lynch that they will take him before Mr Brew for a formal appearance, unless he admits his guilt over the attempt to bribe Dr Colligan to kill Anty. Barry succumbs to this pressure and agrees to leave Dunmore and Ireland at once—to no one's regret. And the visit to Mr Brew is called off.[100]

In *The landleaguers* Trollope anticipates the Somerville and Ross creation of Major Yeates with a portrait of another ex-British army resident magistrate. His Captain Yorke Clayton RM is a man of a different stamp however, the embodiment in fact of 'no-nonsense' law enforcement which Trollope appears to have

99. *The landleaguers*, iii, 216.
100. *The Kellys and the O'Kellys*, p.100.

concluded was the only intelligent option available to the government when faced with the excesses committed during the Irish
land struggle. Clayton was single-minded, proud and brave. To
Edith Jones he talked of his unrelenting pursuit of Lax, the arch-
conspirator: 'A man in my position neglects his duty if he leaves a
stone unturned in pursuit of such a blackguard as this.'[101] To Mr
Jones he expatiated upon the Land League fellow-travellers he
espied within the ranks of Irish defence counsel:

> When they get hold of me, and I look into the eyes of such a one, I see
> there my bitterest enemy. He holds Captain Yorke Clayton up to the
> hatred of the whole court, as though he were a brute unworthy of the
> slightest mercy,—a venomous reptile, against whom the whole country
> should rise to tear him in pieces. And I look round and see the same
> feeling written in the eyes of them all.[102]

'Recklessness of life' and 'devotion to an idea'—the capture of
Lax—were the two attributes Clayton possessed which Trollope
chooses to proclaim, 'if Fortune helps, may serve to make any
man famous'.[103] Predictably, in the circumstances of the Ireland of
Trollope's tale, this stern, unrelenting servant of the law was a
marked man:

> It is not at all probable that this man wished to die. Life seemed to him
> to be pleasant enough: he was no forlorn lover; he had fairly good health
> and strength; people said of him that he had small but comfortable
> private means; he was remarkable among all men for his good looks; and
> he lacked nothing necessary to make life happy. But he appeared to be
> always in a hurry to leave it. A hundred men in Mayo had sworn that he
> should die. This was told to him very freely; but he had only laughed at
> it, and was generally called 'the woodcock', as he rode about among his
> daily employments. The ordinary life of a woodcock calls upon him to
> be shot at; but yet a woodcock is not an easy bird to hit.[104]

Clayton survives unscathed at least for as long as the final page
of the unfinished novel, and the sketch that Trollope left behind
which outlines the novel's conclusion did not indicate that it was
the author's intention to kill him off. Trollope's 'woodcock' is
thus eligible to be elevated into the company of fictional crusaders
and men of action who have been designed by special intercession
to outwit fate and survive against all the odds. The twentieth

101. *The landleaguers*, ii, 93.
102. ii, 99.
103. i, 245.
104. i, 246.

century, with its proliferation of heroes cast in the mould of a Dick Barton, a James Bond or an Indiana Jones, is of course much more adept at recognising the breed, though less aware perhaps of the fragile basis for such preposterous characterisations.

Two senior judges make an appearance in fictional dress: Baron Hamilton in *The Macdermots of Ballycloran* and Judge Parry in *The landleaguers*. In each case the appearance is brief, and neither portrait is as stark or as splendid as Stevenson's masterly evocation of a Scots judge in *Weir of Hermiston*. The explanation is that, in his literary design, Trollope's two Irish judges are little more than remote and unimpressionable figures. A few extra details help to lift them from the category of utter automatons. There is this, for instance, on the man who presided over the abortive trial of Pat O'Carroll in *The landleaguers*:

Judge Parry was a Roman Catholic, who had sat in the House of Commons as a strong Liberal, had been Attorney-General to a Liberal Government, and had been suspected of Home-Rule sentiments. But men, when they become judges, are apt to change their ideas. And Judge Parry was now known to be a firm man, whom nothing would turn from the execution of his duty. There had been many Judge Parrys in Ireland, who have all gone the same gait, and have followed the same course when they have accepted the ermine. A man is at liberty to indulge what vagaries he pleases, as long as he is simply a Member of Parliament. But a judge is not at liberty.[105]

Not much more is disclosed in Trollope's earlier judicial portrait, that of Baron Hamilton, the judge who presided over Thady Macdermot's trial for murder at the Carrick-on-Shannon assizes. The character of the judge is described to Father John by O'Malley, the barrister retained for Thady's defence. He was, O'Malley confides, 'a bad judge for a cause like this—a stern, cold man— there's no reaching his feelings—but as clear-headed as Solon, and as just as Aristides'.[106] The trial of Thady concluded, it only remained for Baron Hamilton to pronounce the death sentence:

No heartless man; but so powerfully had he schooled his emotions, so entirely had he learnt to lay aside the man in assuming the judge, that had he been the stone he looked like, he could not have betrayed less of the heart within him.[107]

105. *The landleaguers*, ii, 270.

106. *The Macdermots of Ballycloran*, iii, 143.

107. iii, 397.

It formed no part of Trollope's mission in either novel to probe into the persona of the judge any further than that. And it may be remarked that he spends much more time in describing assize week at Carrick-on-Shannon (which had culminated in Thady's trial)[108] and in pondering the secrets that might be told by the dusty canopy of red moreen placed over the trial judge 'of the veracity of judges and of the consciences of lawyers'.[109] Such speculation as is essayed does not proceed far.

VI

From the perspective of the literary critic the lawyers of Trollope's Irish gallery compose a motley crew: there are villains and heroes, creations endowed with character and a substantial role to play, creations endowed with a name and little else. From the perspective of the historian, it has to be acknowledged that while a number of Trollope's lawyers are recognisable individuals or persons possessed of individual traits—and in principle therefore much more believable historical witnesses—the stereotypes are featured too, and in considerable profusion.

This last may be a disconcerting discovery, but it is incontrovertible. In *Guy Mannering* Scott employs the gipsy woman Meg Merrilies to draw attention to writer Glossin's low birth and to criticise him for seeking to have ideas above his station:

Glossin!—Gibbie Glossin!—that I have carried in my creels a hundred times, for his mother wasna muckle better than mysell—he to presume to buy the barony of Ellangowan!—Gude be wi' us—it is an awfu' warld!—I wished him ill—but no sic a downfa' as a' that neither—wae's me!—wae's me to think o't![110]

A similar complaint is levelled at Hyacinth Keegan, most tellingly perhaps by means of the details related regarding his change of religion. Within the literary conventions of the period, a complaint rehearsed with equal frequency is the predilection of the would-be upwardly mobile attorney for flattery and hypocrisy. Josiah Larkin,

108. iii, 221 et seq.
109. iii, 268. This particular passage was one with which Isaac Butt chose to taunt Trollope when the latter appeared as a witness in a Post Office prosecution for theft heard in Tralee, Co. Kerry, in 1849 and Butt cross-examined him: R. D. McMaster, *Trollope and the law* (Basingstoke and London, 1986), pp. 56–58.
110. *Guy Mannering*, ch. 22.

the finely drawn evil attorney of Sheridan Le Fanu's novel *Wylder's hand* (who boasted extreme religiosity as well) perhaps comes top of the league.[111] The 'oily attorney' of Carrick-on-Shannon can however probably be counted a close second.

There is an element of stereotyping too in Trollope's depiction of his second Connaught attorney, Mr Daly of Tuam. In the interests of his client Barry Lynch, Daly pontificated to Anty Lynch and the Kellys about the likely preferment of criminal charges; he also resorted to bribery. What is worth noting about this is that clients in George Eliot's fiction invariably expected the lawyers they engaged to display a rough edge. Wakem in *The mill on the floss* furnishes one instance. In 'Janet's repentance' from *Scenes of clerical life* there is another. Here it is asserted that clients of the firm of Pittman and Dempster

were proud of their lawyer's unscrupulousness, as the patrons of the fancy are proud of their champion's 'condition'. It was not, to be sure, the thing for ordinary life, but it was the thing to bet on in a lawyer.[112]

Mr Daly might have found some reassurance here over his own unscrupulous conduct of affairs in regard to Anty Lynch, perhaps even over his role in precipitating her physical and mental breakdown.

In the case of the two senior judges, their portrayal as stern upholders of the primacy of law, at the expense of the political doctrines with which one of them at least at an earlier stage in his career had dallied, is doubtless a stereotype too. The ineffectual English solicitor who comes to Ireland (Mr Prendergast of *Castle Richmond*) and the charming and ambitious Irish barrister in London, Phineas Finn, are equally utilitarian representations, drawing attention, as both do, to the integrated nature of the legal professional career that was possible under the old United Kingdom of Great Britain and Ireland at the time at which Trollope wrote.

What emerges willy-nilly is that considerable caution in the interpretation of the portraits in Trollope's gallery is called for. 'Novels', Dicey wrote, 'never lie; they always reflect the features of the time in which they were written'.[113] But the imagination of

---

111. Le Fanu on this facet of Larkin's personality merits quotation. Larkin, he writes (*Wylder's hand*, ch. 40), 'had found no difficulty hitherto in serving God and Mammon. The joint business prospered'.
112. *Scenes of clerical life* (Penguin ed., Harmondsworth, 1973), p. 257.
113. A.V. Dicey, *Lectures on the relation between law and public opinion in England during the nineteenth century*, 2nd ed. (London, 1914), p. 328.

the literary artist may invest his characters and his stories with too much that is commonplace or—and this, potentially, is as equally misleading—too much that is implausible, so that the resultant product constitutes no sure guide for the social historian. Oliver MacDonagh's admonition to the historian who would make use of the evidence contained in the nineteenth-century novel bears repeating. The novel, he has written,

is not an historical source as the term is ordinarily understood, nor should it ever be regarded as history manqué. It was not concerned with relative quantities and strengths, with wholeness and full complexity, after the manner of history proper. Instead, in obedience to its own nature, the nineteenth century novel was intense, fragmentary, askew and subjective, if considered as historical material.[114]

MacDonagh concludes:

But provided that all this is borne in mind, it can yield insights and possibilities of recovering special portions of the past, for which we shall search in vain in any other matter.[115]

In effect, MacDonagh is here wrestling with the critical point too as regards the present survey—the relevance and the reliability of literary evidence in constructing an account of the Irish legal profession in the nineteenth century. The resolution of the difficulty has been made only fractionally simpler through MacDonagh's intimating that our quest should be directed towards the recovery of special portions of the past for which no other sources happen to be available.

Trollope incontrovertibly touches on a number of matters connected with the Irish legal system of the nineteenth century and with its practitioners for which other evidence is likely to be in short supply or unlikely to be forthcoming at all. An inventory would include such matters as: inter-personal relations on the magisterial bench (*The Macdermots of Ballycloran*); perceptions by an Irish bar student of differences between the practice of law in England and Ireland (*Castle Richmond*); perceptions by the tenantry of the role of an attorney as land agent (*The Macdermots of Ballycloran*); outrage at the presence of Land League fellow-travellers among the ranks of Irish barristers (*The landleaguers*);

114. Oliver MacDonagh, *The nineteenth century novel and Irish social history: some aspects* (Dublin, 1970), p.3.
115. Ibid. On the same broad theme see the perceptive observations of R.J. White in his *Thomas Hardy and history* (London, 1974), p. 59.

rates of pay for, and the style of life, of a Dublin attorney's clerk (*The Kellys and the O'Kellys*); the belief held by an older generation of practitioner that 15 years unpaid labour was a sacrifice worth making as the prelude to ultimate success at the bar (*Castle Richmond*). Even if Trollope's treatment of these questions cannot be accorded the status of proven historical fact, he has surely helped to shape such final answers as one day it may prove possible to announce.

There is one other suggestion to be made, not bereft of peril either, and which for that reason requires to be presented with equal tentativeness. In the instance of a writer like Trollope, wherever the prose is inspired and the combination of that and the particular subject-matter conveys as strong a hint as it is possible to convey of some approximation to reality, it would be prudent on the part of the reader to pause and at least examine the possibility that he might be in the presence of something of enduring historical worth. Though stereotyping, as we have already seen, spoils the total effect, there are stages in Trollope's development of the character of the two Connaught attorneys, Hyacinth Keegan and Mr Daly, where it would be wise for the reader to stop for reflection.

If writing of distinction and the likelihood of verisimilitude are the key, the places that the lawyers of Trollope's gallery chose to frequent as much as, say, the clothes they wore, should on no account be omitted from the final tally. A major service Trollope rendered Irish social history was his preservation in a literary format of so much of the passing scene, things taken for granted at the time, surviving accounts of which are rare but which, for no especial reason, attracted the attention of a gifted author with an observant eye. There is a surfeit of such glimpses of the passing scene in *The Kellys and the O'Kellys*, the most accomplished of Trollope's Irish novels: in chapter 8 there is to be found his renowned description of the journey by canal-boat from Dublin to Ballinasloe and in chapter 4 a no less remarkable account of the widow Kelly's kitchen at the Dunmore Inn.

A special delight that will surely appeal to lawyers is Trollope's depiction in chapter 18 of the same novel of the premises occupied by Mr Daly, the attorney, in Tuam. The account is presented on the occasion of the critical meeting that Daly has arranged should take place between Barry Lynch, his client, and Moylan, agent to Barry's sister Anty, whose allegiance to Barry's cause Daly has been attempting to secure through a process of bribery. Daly has not been able to bring Barry up to date on the progress of his negotiations with Moylan; it is essential therefore that before

Barry meets Moylan, Daly should have a word with him first.
This 'word' actually takes place in Daly's bedroom, situated on
the first floor. Downstairs there is the parlour at the back where
Moylan is suitably ensconced a full hour before Barry arrives and
is intercepted. A quiet word with Barry in Daly's office (the
downstairs front room) would have been a physical impossibility,
as Trollope proceeds to explain:

It would, I think, astonish a London attorney in respectable practice, to
see the manner in which his brethren towards the west of Ireland get
through their work. Daly's office was open to all the world; the front
door of the house, of which he rented the ground floor, was never
closed, except at night; nor was the door of the office, which opened
immediately into the hall.
    During the hour that Moylan was waiting in the parlour, Daly was
sitting, with his hat on, upon a high stool, with his feet resting on a small
counter which ran across the room, smoking a pipe: a boy, about
seventeen years of age, Daly's clerk, was filling up numbers of those
abominable formulas of legal persecution in which attorneys deal, and
was plying his trade as steadily as though no February blasts were
blowing in on him through the open door, no sounds of loud and
boisterous conversation were rattling in his ears. The dashing manager
of one of the branch banks in the town was sitting close to the little
stove, and raking out the turf ashes with the office rule, while describing
a drinking-bout that had taken place on the previous Sunday at Blake's
of Blakemount; he had a cigar in his mouth, and was searching for a
piece of well-kindled turf, wherewith to light it. A little fat oily shopkeeper
in the town, who called himself a woollen merchant, was standing with
the raised leaf of the counter in his hand, roaring with laughter at the
manager's story. Two frieze coated farmers, outside the counter, were
stretching across it, and whispering very audibly to Daly some details of
litigation which did not appear very much to interest him; and a couple
of idle blackguards were leaning against the wall, ready to obey any
behest of the attorney's which might enable them to earn a sixpence
without labour, and listening with all their ears to the different topics of
conversation which might be broached in the inner office.[116]

    Not only is this fine writing, it has the ring of truth: attorneys'
offices in the rural Ireland of the period were in all probability like
Mr Daly's in Tuam. Here, as much as with the equally evocative
itemisation, supplied in *The Macdermots of Ballycloran*, of Hyacinth
Keegan's wardrobe,[117] we are surely introduced to one of those
'special portions of the past' that literature uniquely helps us to

116. *The Kellys and the O'Kellys*, pp. 226–7.
117. *The Macdermots of Ballycloran*, i, 241–42.

recapture and to which MacDonagh has drawn attention. There is an added interest in the excerpt. It certainly bears comparison with Scott's account of Counsellor Pleydell when the latter is finally tracked down to his lair in the tavern in the narrow streets of the old town in Edinburgh.[118] And if a wider comparison is needed, there is the ambience of the office of another professional man, created at much the same time by a writer of at least equal distinction for a novel that remains much more celebrated. Dr Charles Bovary's surgery, Flaubert writes, was

a small room, no more than six paces wide, with a table, three simple chairs and an office armchair. The six shelves of the fir bookcase were filled almost entirely by a set of the *Dictionary of the Medical Sciences* whose pages were uncut, but whose bindings had suffered in the process of being bought and sold by a long succession of different owners. The smell of cooking sauces came through the wall during consultations, and from the kitchen one could hear the patients coughing and giving detailed descriptions of their symptoms.

(petite pièce de six pas de large environ, avec une table, trois chaises et un fauteuil de bureau. Les tomes du *Dictionnaire des sciences médicales*, non coupés, mais dont la brochure avait souffert dans toutes les ventes successives par où ils avaient passé, garnissaient presque à eux seuls les six rayons d'une bibliothèque en bois de sapin. L'odeur des roux pénétrait à travers la muraille, pendant les consultations, de même que l'on entendait de la cuisine les malades tousser dans le cabinet et débiter toute leur histoire.)[119]

118. *Guy Mannering*, ch. 36.
119. *Madame Bovary*, pt. 1, ch. 5: the translation is Lowell Blair's (New York, 1959).

The Irish Legal History Society

Established in 1988 to encourage the study and advance the knowledge of the history of Irish law, especially by the publication of original documents and of works relating to the history of Irish law, including its institutions, doctrines and personalities, and the reprinting or editing of works of sufficient rarity or importance.

PATRONS

The Hon. Mr Justice T.A. Finlay,
Chief Justice of Ireland

Rt Hon. Sir Brian Hutton,
Lord Chief Justice of
Northern Ireland

LIFE MEMBER

Rt Hon. Lord Lowry,
Lord of Appeal in Ordinary

COUNCIL, 1988–89

PRESIDENT

The Hon. Mr Justice Costello,
Judge of the High Court

VICE-PRESIDENTS

Professor G.J. Hand,
University of Birmingham

His Honour Judge Hart, Q.C.,
Recorder of Londonderry

SECRETARY

Professor W.N. Osborough,
Trinity College, Dublin

TREASURER

Daire Hogan, esq.,
Solicitor

ORDINARY MEMBERS

His Honour Judge Carroll,
Judge of the Circuit Court

Professor D.S. Greer,
Queen's University, Belfast

Dr Art Cosgrove,
University College, Dublin

Professor John Larkin,
Trinity College, Dublin

Dr D.V. Craig,
Director, National Archives